THE ROMAN STREET

Every day, Roman urbanites took to the street for myriad tasks, from hawking vegetables and worshipping local deities to simply loitering and socializing. Hartnett takes readers into this thicket of activity as he repopulates Roman streets with a range of sensations, participants, and events that stretches far beyond simple movement. Because everyone from slave to senator met in this communal space, city dwellers found unparalleled opportunities for self-aggrandizing display and the negotiation of social and political tensions. Hartnett charts how Romans preened and paraded in the street and how they exploited the street's collective space to lob insults and respond to personal rebukes. Combining textual evidence, comparative historical material, and contemporary urban theory with architectural and art historical analysis, *The Roman Street* offers a social and cultural history of urban spaces that restores them to their rightful place as primary venues for social performance in the ancient world.

Jeremy Hartnett is Associate Professor and Chair of Classics at Wabash College, where he holds the Anne and Andrew T. Ford Chair in the Liberal Arts. He is the author of numerous articles and chapters on Roman urban history, the history of photography, and collegiate pedagogy, and he has been awarded fellowships and grants from the National Endowment for the Humanities, the Michigan Society of Fellows, and the Archaeological Institute of America.

THE ROMAN STREET

URBAN LIFE AND SOCIETY IN POMPEII, HERCULANEUM, AND ROME

JEREMY HARTNETT

Wabash College

CAMBRIDGE
UNIVERSITY PRESS

CAMBRIDGE
UNIVERSITY PRESS

University Printing House, Cambridge CB2 8BS, United Kingdom

One Liberty Plaza, 20th Floor, New York, NY 10006, USA

477 Williamstown Road, Port Melbourne, VIC 3207, Australia

314-321, 3rd Floor, Plot 3, Splendor Forum, Jasola District Centre, New Delhi - 110025, India

79 Anson Road, #06-04/06, Singapore 079906

Cambridge University Press is part of the University of Cambridge.

It furthers the University's mission by disseminating knowledge in the pursuit of
education, learning and research at the highest international levels of excellence.

www.cambridge.org
Information on this title: www.cambridge.org/9781107513532
10.1017/9781316226438

First published 2017
First paperback edition 2020

A catalogue record for this publication is available from the British Library

ISBN 978-1-107-10570-6 Hardback
ISBN 978-1-107-51353-2 Paperback

This publication has been supported by a grant from the Samuel H. Kress Foundation,
administered by the Archaeological Institute of America.

CONTENTS

Color plates are to be found between pp. xvi and 1

COLOR PLATES

ILLUSTRATIONS

TABLES

ACKNOWLEDGMENTS

When wrapping up a project, it is especially gratifying to reflect and to offer thanks to all those who have generously lent a hand along the way. This book began its life as a hazy outline sketched out around a door-and-filing-cabinet table in a third-floor Ann Arbor apartment. From that moment of inception, Sue Alcock was instrumental in its growth into a four-chapter doctoral dissertation: prodding with questions, showing an uncanny touch for what to put in my hands (and when), offering verbal and liquid encouragement, and plowing through drafts in record time. Cold sweats sometimes recur when former graduate students recall their doctoral defenses, but it is a testament to the intellectual generosity of my committee – Andrew Wallace-Hadrill, Elaine Gazda, and Bruce Frier – that their questions and contributions have joyously resounded in my head throughout the decade of molding the thesis into a nine-chapter book. I wish that John D'Arms, with whom I was only able to take one course, had lived to be a part of that team. Thanks also to John Pedley and John Cherry for their guidance and friendship at Michigan.

As I consider the roots of this book, however, I see tendrils stretching back to people and places further in the past. It is probably no accident that I ended up writing about streets. Geneseo, New York, showcased a meaningful academic life, and, though the village is smaller and distinctly less dense than Herculaneum, its front porch culture, particularly on Oak Street, spurred my interest in communal space. I want to thank my parents, Kathe and Dale Hartnett, for their enduring affection and support as well as for sharing their loves of exploring new places and of puzzling out the past from its physical remains. They probably did not know, when they first allowed me to prowl the streets of Siena as a teenager, that they were kindling interests that would smolder long after. It is only appropriate to thank Bill Cook immediately after my folks, since I have long cherished his friendship, strive to live up to his model of compassionate humanity and crusading generosity, and feel emboldened when I find his words coming out of my mouth at the lectern. Time in Naples taught me the most about life in a premodern city; *mille grazie* to my partner-in-crime Danilo Allegra for keeping an open door and for always being game for an adventure.

I am deeply grateful to other friends and colleagues who have helped to shape this project over the years, sharing their time, ideas, and gift for well-turned phrases. Many thanks to James Andrews, Rebecca Benefiel, Jo Berry, Mitch Brown, Eugene Dwyer, Lauren Hackworth-Petersen, Claire Holleran, Sandra Joshel, Peg Laird, Brenda Longfellow, Kristina Milnor, Nicolas Monteix, David Newsome, Nigel Pollard, and Josh Ward. Pride of place should go to Molly Swetnam-Burland, whose scholarly fingerprints are all over the pages that follow. All of my academic homes – Oberlin College, the Intercollegiate Center for Classical Studies in Rome, and Wabash College – have blessed me with smart and savvy colleagues. Thanks to Joe Day, Leslie Day, John Fischer, David Kubiak, Derek Nelson, Dan Rogers, Matt Sears, Brian Tucker, and Bronwen Wickkiser for their support and friendship. It has also been a special treat to collaborate with Wabash students Ryan Cairns, James Kennedy, and Miguel Muñoz on the book's illustrations and with Patrick Azar, Matt Binder, Luke Doughty, Alex Gillham, and Patrick Stroud on the text and bibliography.

Asya Graf and Beatrice Rehl at Cambridge University Press have been encouraging collaborators throughout the book's editorial process. I appreciate their patient support as well as the helpful suggestions of two anonymous reviewers for Cambridge University Press, whose keen eyes and helpful comments saved me from errors and pointed me in helpful directions. Likewise, I am grateful to Sheila Dillon and the *American Journal of Archaeology* for allowing my article on benches (Hartnett 2008a) to be reprinted here in edited form as Chapter Six and to Naomi Norman and two readers for improving the original text substantially.

This project would have been substantially poorer if not for the financial and intellectual help of several institutions. A National Endowment for the Humanities (NEH) summer seminar at the American Academy in Rome, "Identity and Self-Representation Among the Sub-cultures of Ancient Rome" under the direction of Eve D'Ambra and Eleanor Leach, offered time, resources, and space for creativity as I drafted much of Chapter Eight. A grant from the New Directions Initiative of the Great Lakes Colleges Association funded comparative work on public life in other times and places; the lessons of Renaissance Florence and challenges of modern Mexico City continue to resonate. The Faculty Development Committee at Wabash College has provided steady support for my research, and I thank Dean Gary Phillips for his flexibility with multipurpose overseas trips. An NEH summer stipend and my term as Wabash's McLain-McTurnan-Arnold Research Scholar in 2011–12 permitted me to draft substantial portions of this book. I am grateful to Wabash for my position as Anne and Andrew T. Ford Chair in the Liberal Arts, whose funds have permitted an expanded program of illustrations, as has a Samuel H. Kress Grant for Publication from the Archaeological Institute of America, which has enabled the inclusion of color plates.

Finally, my greatest debt is to my family. My boys, Henry and Silas, have been sources of joy, wonderment, laughter, and perspective throughout this project, and I am so thankful for their grandparents' willingness to take on extra duties during critical moments in preparing this manuscript. I cannot find adequate words to express my thanks to my wife and partner, Jill Lamberton, whose keen mind, huge heart, steadfast love, and gift for celebrations have buoyed me all along. I dedicate the book to her.

Plate I Along the streets of Pompeii, 100 benches stand in front of all manner of different properties.
Drawing: author.

Legend:
- Domestic
- Bar/Tavern
- Bakery
- Misc. Commercial/Industrial
- Semi-Public
- Civic
- Unclear

Scale: 100m 200m 300m

Plate II This fresco from the Praedia of Julia Felix at Pompeii shows scenes of ambulant vendors selling cloth and metal items in the city's forum.
Photo: Erich Lessing/Art Resource, New York.

Plate III A procession of carpenters appears on a façade painting from Pompeii (on pier between VI.7.8, VI.7.9). Equipped with canes, they carry a ferculum bearing representations of their craft and figures of mythological importance.
Photo: Erich Lessing/Art Resource, New York.

Plate IV On the right jamb of IX.7.1, a fresco depicted a staid and organized procession in honor of Cybele, whose statue is visible at right, along with its porters (carrying canes).
Credit: Alberto Sanarica (in Spinazzola 1953, Libreria dello Stato, Rome).

Plate V A watercolor reconstruction of the mural around a neighborhood altar at Pompeii shows
four distinct scenes (counterclockwise from lower right): snakes approaching the altar itself;
a group of officials sacrificing at an altar; the dei consentes; and a genius (likely of Augustus)
flanked by lares.
Credit: Alberto Sanarica (in Spinazzola 1953, Libreria dello Stato, Rome).

Plate VI This watercolor reconstruction makes clear that the Fullery of Ululitremulus in Pompeii (IX.13.4–6) was not to be missed, since it boasted an attention-grabbing façade of a bright checkerboard pattern as well as images of Aeneas and Romulus flanking the central doorway.
Credit: Alberto Sanarica (in Spinazzola 1953, Libreria dello Stato, Rome).

Plate VII The façade of the Casa di Trebio Valente at Pompeii (III.2.1), visible in a watercolor reconstruction, featured panels marked out in paint as well as an extensive array of painted electoral endorsements.

Credit: Alberto Sanarica (in Spinazzola 1953, Libreria dello Stato, Rome).

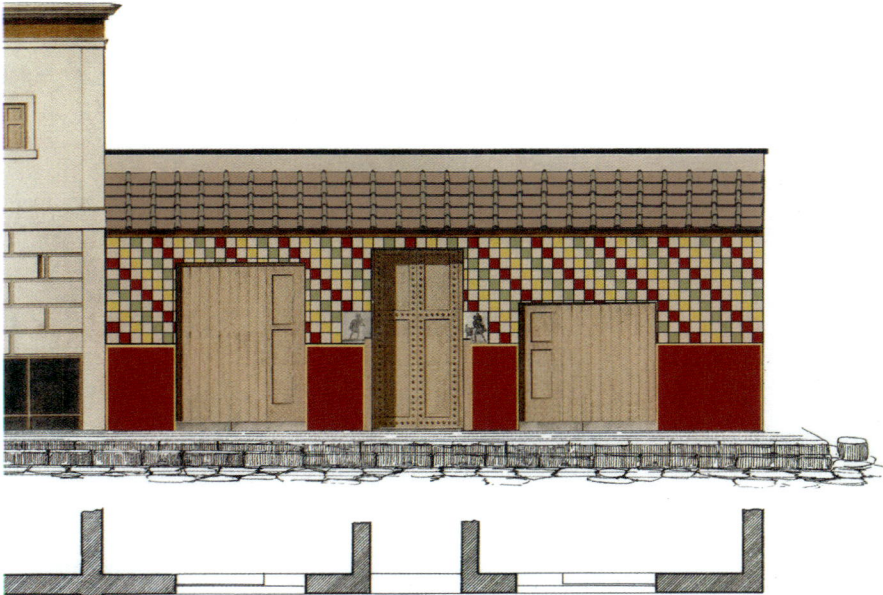

Plate VIII The adjacent Pompeian façades of the Casa di Giulio Polibio (left, IX.13.1–3) and the Fullery of Ululitremulus (right, IX.13.4–6) highlight the potential contrasts between restrained domestic frontages and the more conspicuous façades of industrial or commercial spaces. Drawing: Ryan Cairns (after A. Sanarica in Spinazzola 1953, Libreria dello Stato, Rome, Tav. VII, LXXI).

Plate IX Opposite the figure of Cybele on the left jamb of IX.7.1 (Plate IV) appeared a painting of Venus Pompeiana, the city's patron goddess, accompanied by a cupid, holding a spear and rudder, and wearing all manner of jewelry.
Credit: Alberto Sanarica (in Spinazzola 1953, Libreria dello Stato, Rome).

INTRODUCTION

ROMAN CIVILIZATION WAS DISTINCTLY URBAN. NOT UNTIL THE Industrial Revolution would a comparable percentage of Europeans live in cities.[1] As centers of political, economic, and, therefore, social life, cities offered Romans the greatest opportunities for making their fame and fortunes – or losing them. This book examines how Romans came into contact, interacted, and sought to present themselves in the most used, yet least studied, of urban spaces: the street.

A brief look at three examples illustrates the vividness of the street and its centrality to city life. In his third *Satire*, written around 110 CE, the poet Juvenal imagines his friend, Umbricius, leaving Rome for a new life in Cumae. Amid a litany of complaints about the *caput mundi*, Umbricius targets the street:

> carts thundering by through the narrow twisting streets and the swearing
> of drivers caught in a traffic jam would even snatch away sleep from an
> emperor – or a somnolent seal. When the rich man has an appointment,
> the crowd parts before him as he sails above their heads in his huge galley.
> While he moves along he can conduct correspondence or read or sleep
> inside, for a litter with windows closed is most soporific. But even so he
> will arrive first; though I hurry, I am blocked by a wave of people in front
> of me and the people in a huge rank jab my back. One man digs an elbow
> into me; another strikes me with a hard pole. One man bangs my head

---

[1] Maddison 2007, 40–43; Wilson 2011, esp. 191–193.

with a wood beam, another with a wine jug. My legs are plastered with mud. Then huge feet kick me on all sides, and a soldier plants his boot's nail right on my toe.[2]

For Juvenal, the street was a place of chaotic passage, a space where all manner of goods and people moved through the city in tight quarters and where those possessed of above-average means had ample opportunity to rise above the rank and file.

As a nearly contemporary bilingual inscription from Ephesus shows, streets were also central to communal life and shared identity. The text dating to 103/104 CE commemorates a set of gifts made to the community by a local *eques* named C. Vibius Salutaris. His funds provided, first, for a lottery and cash distributions to many Ephesians, whose flocking together to the famed extramural temple of Artemis would have made for its own spectacle. But that paled in comparison to Salutaris's major benefactions – the creation of about thirty silver statues and their ritual procession through the city's streets. The statues exhibited Ephesus's sacred identity (Artemis appeared at least nine times), displayed personifications of a host of concentric civic bodies from the Ephesian boule to the Roman senate and people, and represented a historical timeline running from the city's origins up through the sitting emperor and empress. The silver participants took to the street about twice per month, accompanied by hundreds of living Ephesians. Highlighted above all were sacred personnel and the body of elite youths known as the *ephebes* who would one day hold the city's chief offices. After it departed from the temple of Artemis, the parade followed a prescribed route, snaking by major urban landmarks before reaching its culmination in the theater, where the text was inscribed; it then circled back to the Artemision.[3] These processions reminded Ephesians of their own history and traditions as well as their place in the empire, all on the street's stage.

Beyond serving as hosts for meaningful movement, streets were also imagined as key venues for many activities, to judge from a singular visual representation found in a Late Antique house in Antioch. Images of life on the city's streets abound in the border ringing the Megalopsychia hunt mosaic, a huge artwork named after the personification in its central medallion and the piece's predominant theme (Fig. 1). The border scenes constitute a topographical tour through

---

[2] Juv. 3.236–248: . . . *raedarum transitus arto / vicorum in flexu et stantis convicia mandrae / eripient somnum Druso vitulisque marinis. / si vocat officium, turba cedente vehetur / dives et ingenti curret super ora Liburna / atque obiter leget aut scribet vel dormiret intus; namque facit somnum clausa lectica fenestra. ante tamen veniet: nobis properantibus opstat / unda prior, magno populus premit agmine lumbos / qui sequitur; ferit hic cubito, ferit assere duro / alter, at hic tignum capiti incutit, ille metretam. / pinguia crura luto, planta mox undique magna / calcor, et in digito clavus mihi militis haeret.* Translations, unless otherwise noted, are my own adaptations of the Loeb Classical Library.

[3] *IvE* 1a, no. 27. For extensive discussion, see Rogers 1991.

1. Sketches of street scenes from the so-called Megalopsychia Hunt Mosaic, discovered in Antioch, showcase the range of activities that unfolded along thoroughfares.
Drawing: Ryan Cairns (modified from Matthews 2006, figs. 4.7, 4.8, 4.12, 4.13).

Antioch, moving from one city gate and continuing through the city proper before reaching springs near Daphne, the suburb where the mosaic was discovered. Along the way, an attendant clears the way for a dignitary entering the city on horseback, men in short tunics scurry along balancing bundles on their heads and backs, another man delivers a refreshment to a reclining figure, a cart lugs timbers, a man drives donkeys, a child led by the hand looks back to wave at someone gazing out a second-story window, a board game occupies figures on folding chairs, two men chop meat atop three-legged butcher blocks, and vendors at tables hawk round bread loaves and other goods. The scenes play out against a long scroll of cityscape: churches, baths, bridges, houses, inns, statues, colonnades, a palace and its racetrack.[4] Overall, the mosaic suggests that, in preindustrial cities, streets were viewed and experienced not only as corridors for passage, but also as places of commerce, leisure, and socializing.

When we take these three sources together, urban thoroughfares emerge as extraordinarily vibrant and compelling spaces. Juvenal's street swarms with activity that besieges all the senses. At night, wagons clang while during the day elbows jab, mud splashes, and toes ache as a variety of individual actors wrangle to accomplish their own business. The resulting scene is chaotic, the sensations staccato. The confusion resulted partly from the people, animals, and vehicles trying to make their way, but the Antioch mosaic points toward the other tasks that competed for the street's space – butchering, eating, selling wares, loitering – as tables, chairs, and the like spilled into the roadway. Indeed, the diverse set of buildings shown on the mosaic emphasizes how many realms of urban life were connected by, and might clash in, the street. In comparison to the other Roman urban environments we could name, such as the forum or amphitheater, the street thus appears less predictable and more inclusive. It comprises a broad cast – from the enslaved to the moneyed, indeed, virtually everyone across society – brought close in a spontaneous and minimally regulated environment.

The effects of that contact were many and important. Amid the din of Juvenal's street, one thing is clear: an awareness of social distinctions ripples through the space. In his litter, the rich man is conspicuous and distinguished from the crowd, literally carried above the rest. All know that he enjoys a profoundly different experience. As he relaxes or dozes, free from the flurry of activity, he even arrives earlier at his destination. If we mentally set the mosaic's action in motion, we can similarly imagine urbanites seeing to their own concerns while also observing what others are wearing or doing; seeing with whom they conducted business or with whom they were on good (or bad) terms; and learning who was leading and who was riding, who hauling and who at leisure, who serving and who relaxing at table. "How do I stack up?" may well have been the question on their lips or in their minds.

Another factor in answering that question were the honorific statues and splendid façades portrayed on the mosaic. They make the point that buildings

---

[4] Levi 1947, 323–345; Downey 1961, 659–664; Dunbabin 1999, 180–183; Matthews 2006, 79–88. Cf. Lib. *Or.* 11.196–245.

and monuments were not faceless containers of the street's space, but were deployed to impress, mark privilege, and differentiate between literal insiders and outsiders. The Ephesus procession makes abundantly clear that the visibility afforded by the street also made it ripe for crafting personal, group, or civic personae – here through ritual movements, elsewhere through deeds, dress, and house decoration. Heritage is celebrated, future magistrates marked out for attention, consumption made conspicuous, and hierarchical relationships defined. Amid the wide-ranging crowd and its diverse activities, in other words, some sought to tame the chaos, mark out distinctions, and underline their own superior position. In front of the broadest audience possible, streets provided unparalleled opportunities for self-aggrandizing display, for scoring off others, and for the creation and resolution of social and political tensions. This is the fascination of watching Roman street behavior: it opens up to our view a vital realm of urban action and interaction.

STREETS PAST AND PRESENT

It is unlikely that this book's subject – the Roman street as a space of social contact and presentation – would have seemed odd to a Roman such as Juvenal. As we have seen, he was careful to draw attention to the street's dynamics, and, as we will see, when he wants to witness the absurdities of Roman life, he simply picks up his notebook and heads to a nearby corner to watch the passing crowd.[5] In a way, many other dwellers did the same when they went to the theater in hopes of some laughs, for the action of Roman comedy took place in front of the façades of two or three houses, in what theatergoers understood to be the street. The impromptu juxtapositions that this setting enabled – between slave and master, lovelorn youth and much-desired courtesan, or long-lost siblings – created the misunderstandings of class, identity, gender, and intentions that underlay Roman comedy. Yet, despite Romans' self-awareness of the street's social roles, the vibrant scenes that authors describe, and decades of studies of Roman streets, roads, and road systems, it is surprising how little has been written about what unfolded along thoroughfares and who used them. Until recently, work dedicated to streets has largely concentrated on how they were built, where they ran, and what sort of traffic they hosted.[6] While virtually every other space in the city – baths, shops, houses, and temples, to name a few – has received extensive attention, this locus of so much daily contact has remained distinctly underobserved.

---

[5] Juv. 1.63–64.
[6] Capelli 1991; Gesemann 1996; Chevallier 1997; Staccioli 2003; Poehler 2006, 2009; Ballet, Dieudonné-Glad, and Saliou 2008; Beard 2008, 53–80; Mertens 2008; Kaiser 2011a; Laurence and Newsome 2011.

We certainly cannot pin a lack of study on a lack of suitable subject matter. Pliny famously reported that Rome in his day had more than 60 miles of streets, just counting those that led from the forum's golden milestone to the edge of the built-up area.[7] The routes of some of these are fossilized in Rome's street plan today, as the same paths have been taken for millennia, simply paved over time and again. Because of Rome's continuous occupation, however, the Eternal City offers very few stretches that preserve their ancient form. Excavation at other sites throughout the empire has revealed well-preserved roadbeds that have survived thanks to their solid construction from humble (not to mention heavy) materials. We can walk some of the self-same streets as Salutaris's procession in Ephesus, for instance. On the Italian peninsula, we can prowl through portions of other cities: Ostia, Paestum, Minturnae, and Saepinum, for example. And, of course, there are the cities buried and thus preserved by the eruption of Mount Vesuvius in 79 CE that offer the primary material evidence for this book. Although only a portion of Herculaneum's urban fabric has been brought to light, Pompeii preserves roughly 7 kilometers of excavated streets, together with much of their bracketing streetfaces.

The issue, then, is not so much one of seeing streets as seeing people on, in, or moving through them. I want to tell the story of the excavation and subsequent presentation of one of Pompeii's chief thoroughfares because it illustrates, from its promising start to its frustrating conclusion, some of the obstacles facing the study of street life. In 1911, when Vittorio Spinazzola began his term as superintendent at Pompeii, he imagined an extremely ambitious course of action.[8] His predecessors, who tended to excavate city-block by city-block, had unearthed much of the western portion of the city but little in the east aside from the amphitheater (Fig. 2). Spinazzola proposed to connect the two areas and to do so by an innovative means – by tracing about a half-kilometer of just one street, the Via dell'Abbondanza, and by unearthing little beyond its bordering façades. That is, his intended locus of inquiry was not the standing remains per se, but also the space between them.

Spinazzola was well aware of the innovative and revisionist approach he brought to the street. In his publication of the excavation, he draws an explicit contrast with earlier attitudes, quoting August Mau and Johannes Overbeck's 1884 publication, which claimed, "Pompeii's streets neither present now nor did they present in antiquity the varied, vivid, and busy scene of medieval and modern cities."[9] Moving forward a generation, Spinazzola also points out how the city's streets were still, in his own time, being imagined as relatively actionless places; he cites the views of Antonio Sogliano, who likens Roman Pompeii to Muslim cities

---

[7] Pliny *NH* 3.67.
[8] Spinazzola's career: Delpino 2001. The following paragraphs draw on Hartnett 2011a.
[9] Spinazzola 1953, 12.

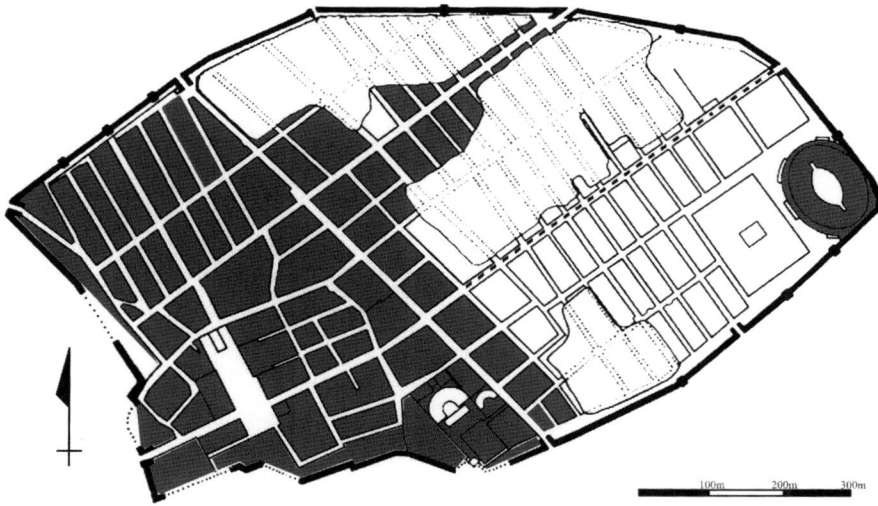

2. Plan of Pompeii, showing state of excavation before Vittorio Spinazzola's campaign to excavate the Via dell'Abbondanza. Shaded portions were excavated by 1911. Spinazzola's target area is indicated with dashes.
Drawing: Ryan Cairns.

of North Africa because its streets, like theirs, are *deserte*, deserted.[10] For his part, Spinazzola was confident, or would at least later claim to be, that much about a city and its inhabitants could be learned by studying the street and its elements – façade paintings, windows, and especially the balconies and overhangs that he recovered but had been missed by previous generations. Over the course of a dozen years, Spinazzola was largely successful in his endeavor, as his crew dug eastward along the Via dell'Abbondanza toward a gate in the city walls.[11]

Just as revolutionary as Spinazzola's excavation strategy was his approach to documenting and reconstructing his discoveries. To record his work, he deployed, to a degree unparalleled in previous excavations, the relatively new technology of photography.[12] And what he chose to show in the photographs of his campaign is revealing. First, he himself appears time and again, often standing next to one of the architectural features that he was proud to have discovered (Fig. 3). Second, the photographs seek to capture the thrill of discovery. At times, they show workmen frantically unearthing an object or architectural feature; at others, the subject of the photograph, such as a statuette, sits alone atop the volcanic debris without any workers, so the viewer is placed in the position of the one making the discovery (Fig. 4). Third, in Spinazzola's publication of his excavation, he regularly

[10] Spinazzola 1953, 13.
[11] It should be said, however, that Spinazzola did not always stick to his plan because, on occasion, he found the façade architecture compelling enough to excavate within buildings.
[12] On the intertwined histories of photography and archaeology: Lyons 2005, esp. 22–28. At Pompeii: Maffioli 1990; Cassanelli 2002; Desrochers 2003; Lyons 2005, 49–59.

3. Vittorio Spinazzola proudly poses next to a roof recovered from the Casa di Paquius Proculus at Pompeii.
Photo: Spinazzola 1953, Libreria dello Stato, Rome, fig. 34.

presents a series of images: one showing the unearthing of a particular architectural feature, a second photo documenting its reconstruction at the hands of workmen, and a third displaying the feature rendered intact once more and now devoid of people (Fig. 5). In other words, the photographs are characteristic of modern archaeological process: they document the intense human work of excavation that results, paradoxically, in a presentation stripped bare of human presence.

This is both important and odd for the study of streets, since Spinazzola's publication is notable for what it does not show: streets populated with workers, authorities, or just about anyone.[13] Populated images of the street were shot and even appeared in preliminary excavation reports, but what made it into the final volumes were typically antiseptic shots of the street scrubbed clean, reconstructed fully (at times, water even gushes in streetside fountains), and left empty (Fig. 6). We encounter the stage-set and none of the action. Spinazzola's images were captured at a time when archaeologists were still working out how to use photography as part of the archaeological process. On that count, it would be wrongheaded to condemn Spinazzola for not populating his street shots, even if

[13] The one notable exception is a splendid photo of the exhausted workforce splayed out in a shady alleyway late in the day, with Spinazzola and a colleague looking on: Spinazzola 1953, 31, fig 30.

4. An archival photograph from Vittorio Spinazzola's excavations in Pompeii captures the excitement of discovery as workmen dig so frenetically in the Casa di Octavius Quartio that their movement is blurred.
Photo: Soprintendenza Speciale per Pompei, Ercolano e Stabia, Archivio Fotografico degli Scavi, B341.

he was deeply cognizant of the power of individuals in photographs and of the history of study of Pompeian streets. If he had chosen shots with many people for final publication, he might well have been criticized as unprofessional. Regardless, we should nevertheless consider the effect his choices may have had on what has or has not been studied.

The resources we use and the definitions we employ inevitably color our approach to any subject. I suspect that one reason street life has been largely ignored, for example, is the ingrained – and understandable – use of architectural plans. As tools for documenting and depicting the layout of a building or a city, ground plans are obviously indispensable in a field such as classical archaeology. Yet their specular perspective, providing essentially a bird's-eye view, separates users from the real, lived experience of urban space, flattening once noisy and bustling spaces into two-dimensional ghost towns. Something similar may be at work with Spinazzola's project. For the past century, the stretch of street that Spinazzola unearthed has been visited by countless archaeologists and historians interested in Roman urbanism, and, for the past sixty years, his publication has taken a prominent place on bibliographies on Pompeii and Roman urban life. (Is there a more well-known street from Roman Italy, aside from the Via Sacra in

5. In Vittorio Spinazzola's publication of the Via dell'Abbondanza, a regular feature is a grouping of three images documenting the discovery and restoration of architectural features. Photo: Spinazzola 1953, Libreria dello Stato, Rome, figs. 37–39.

Rome, than the Via dell'Abbondanza?) Spinazzola's text and images highlight the excavated (and restored) object, thus reducing the attention paid to interaction with and within that built environment. In the end, his project represents an ironic missed opportunity: it was devised in the belief that paying attention to

6. The images of the street in Vittorio Spinazzola's *Pompei alla luce degli scavi nuovi di Via dell'Abbondanza* show reconstructed streetscapes that are notably absent of people.
Photo: Spinazzola 1953, Libreria dello Stato, Rome, fig. 5.

a street could shed light on Roman urban society, but its documentation may have actually delayed scholars' consideration of street life.

In their focus on what was built, Spinazzola's publication and others like it have much in common with other forces that have shaped and continue to shape approaches to Roman urban space and streets. Vitruvius was an architect of the Augustan age whose didactic treatise, *De Architectura*, represents our most extensive document on ancient building and town planning. His proscriptions and categories can be the measuring stick first sought out by those studying cities and individual buildings. The question his work can inspire – "Does this structure adhere to the dictates of Vitruvius?" – channels attention toward those who constructed cities and buildings and away from those who used them. If only building design is valued, then the street becomes a mere architectural void, an empty space between the buildings Vitruvius has instructed us to study. Furthermore, Vitruvius's separation of architecture into genres – civic, religious, and domestic – has left its mark in separate analyses of these individual categories and thus a segmentation of the city along somewhat artificial lines. Likewise, a current method of studying ancient cities – block by block or building by building, as with the *Häuser in Pompeji* series – may be the most feasible but, like the contextless plans it often generates, it divides a once organic city into isolated units. Such approaches deprive the street of the elements that are set, side by side, to form its borders. To study the street and those who pass through it, juxtaposition and context are key.

Finally, in modern cities, the experience of the street contrasts markedly with what any Roman would encounter. Cities are larger and people move across them more quickly via subways, buses, rickshaws, cars, carriages, or bicycles. Streets have been designed with wider dimensions to accommodate vehicular transport. These factors, along with zoning regulations, greatly decrease the amount of face-to-face contact on the street – a key element, as we have begun to see, in recognizing the importance of streets as arenas of social presentation. Visits to the remains of Roman cities run the risk of confirming what architectural plans and our own conurbations have led us to assume. When we do not hear the rumble of carts, smell the stagnant sewage in the roadbed, or see (let alone jostle with) masses of people and animals, the streets can seem empty and lifeless.

WAYS TO SEE THE CITY

How might we envision streets and urban spaces? In *The Practice of Everyday Life*, the cultural theorist Michele De Certeau begins one wide-ranging chapter, "Walking in the City," with a concrete illustration. He imagines looking down at Manhattan from atop the World Trade Center. The view produces "ecstasy," De Certeau admits, yet it does so, he argues, because it represents a sort of "totalizing eye" – synoptic, unified, and ultimately artificial.[14] That is, standing atop a tall building can give us, first, the sense that we are looking at the entire city. And because we think we see all, we expect to know and understand all because everything appears rationally organized and ordered from this perspective. Second, this view is remarkably static, presenting a "gigantic mass ... immobilized before the eyes." Nothing is in flux, limbo, or movement. Finally, De Certeau draws attention to what we are and are not examining from that perspective. He would suggest that "the city," as it appears from the skyscraper's top, is the result of "strategies" of power structures – both the actual institutions and individuals who laid out the city grid, paid for the erection of the buildings, and enacted laws governing behavior as well as the informal relationships that reinforce the social hierarchy. What we miss in a view from the top are individuals and their paths through the city. Because they exist "below the thresholds at which visibility begins," they are distant and remain imperceptible.[15]

[14] De Certeau 1984, 91–110, esp. 91–97.
[15] De Certeau 1984, 91 ("gigantic mass"), 93 ("below the thresholds"), 94–95 ("strategies").

De Certeau prefers "walking in the city" to this elevated vista of the urban expanse because pedestrians are, by his reckoning, the real urban meaning-makers: "The networks of these moving, intersecting writings compose a manifold story that has neither author nor spectator." For De Certeau, a city, as much as the buildings and streets, is the sum total of its inhabitants' movements and actions. When we shift to this perspective, he notes, we see the "tactics" of pedestrians: how they navigate the city in ways that play within, yet also often play off, the plans of organizing bodies. On a literal level, pedestrians might take shortcuts despite the rigid grid plan laid over the landscape, or, more figuratively but just as importantly, streetgoers might assign new meanings to urban elements that are quite different from the ones bestowed by their creators. With pedestrians thus resisting the "strategies" of power structures, the city becomes a more dynamic and contentious entity.[16]

As interest in the spatial component of human interaction has grown in recent decades across the humanities and social sciences, Roman cities have been the focus of intense interest. De Certeau's provocative comparison speaks to the relative strengths and weaknesses of different modes of inquiry into Roman urban space. Scholars have begun to take interest in streets and other "spaces between" – such as porticoes, fora, and temple precincts.[17] In doing so, some adopt approaches that resonate with De Certeau's urbanite-centered outlook by examining phenomenological and subjective perspectives, such as assessing ancient authors' constructions of the street experience and the social meanings of urban movement.[18] Of key assistance in such work have been computerized reconstructions of urban environments, especially in Rome, which permit visualizations from a pedestrian's perspective. To this point, technology has typically been applied to people's experience of grand spaces like the forum rather than more quotidian ones.[19] Moreover, visualizations tend to focus on the perspective of a single viewer of the cityscape rather than imagining swarms looking at buildings *and* one another.

Many more studies of streets and cities align with De Certeau's 110th-floor witness. Like Spinazzola's photos, Vitruvius's text, and architectural ground-plans, they concentrate on the built environment as the immediate object of investigation. A prime and powerful tool has been "space syntax" or "access analysis," which examines architectural units, from rooms to buildings to cities,

[16] De Certeau 1984, 93 ("moving, intersecting writings"), 94–96 ("tactics").
[17] E.g., Gesemann 1996; Bejor 2003; Gering 2004; Lavan 2008; Mertens 2008; Trifilò 2008; Frakes 2009.
[18] E.g., Favro 1996; Larmour 2007; Miller 2007; Betts 2011; Macauley-Lewis 2011; O'Sullivan 2011.
[19] E.g., Favro and Johanson 2010; Favro 2011. More broadly, see the projects produced by the UCLA Experimental Technologies Center (www.etc.ucla.edu) as well as the Rome Reborn initiative (www.romereborn.virginia.edu) and a model produced by the Université de Caen (www.unicaen.fr/services/cireve/rome).

by quantifying their spatial relationship. Investigation along these lines is rigorous, objective, and data-driven and can therefore trace out broad spatial patterns and counteract anecdotal or essentializing approaches.[20] One drawback, however, is that access analysis can feel remarkably abstract and deterministic, leaving little space to consider the agency of individuals as they navigated the built environment. An additional undercurrent in many studies that peer down on the city from on high is their presumption of an inherent order in urban form. They tend to imagine the material remains as a puzzle whose pieces will, if properly and rationally disposed, neatly and sensibly fit together. There is no doubt that Roman cities were systems of sorts, with one action or construction affecting another. But believing that they were efficient and optimized is, as we shall see, problematic.[21]

Finally, in visions of the city that take De Certeau's top-down view, the built environment and its individual elements are studied as artifacts *reflective* of a past reality. This is certainly justified; indeed, studies of urbanism if not archaeology more generally are grounded in this very fact, and a prime goal in the following pages is to use material features of cities as evidence for street life. Yet, as Winston Churchill famously said, "We shape our buildings; and afterwards our buildings shape us."[22] The past was once the present, and thus a closely related task is imagining elements of the urban environment as *affective* agents within their social and physical context, ones that made a difference in how people experienced the city and one another. As De Certeau makes clear, it is critical to bear in mind the adaptive and creative strategies that city dwellers employed as they navigated urban space and society. In sum, the relationship between the urban populace and the city's built environment is bound to have been dialogic (if not still more multivocal). Studying the street means both watching for the impact buildings made on the populace and remaining mindful of the tactics urbanites employed in response.

This book's critical methodological move is the adoption of a close-range, street-level view of Roman urban dynamics. Taking this perspective is not the same as shouldering the mantle of a *flâneur*, the detached nineteenth-century bon vivant who flitted about while enjoying urban drama as an aestheticized object.[23] Rather, it means imagining city life and the street first as a participant did, reanimated with its busy flow of people, animals, obstacles, and sensations. As hinted at by De Certeau but emphasized by Jane Jacobs in her call to arms against the urban planning establishment, *The Death and Life of Great American*

---

[20] E.g., Laurence 2007, ch. 7; Kaiser 2011a; Stöger 2011.

[21] Newsome 2009 offers a balanced and nuanced illustration of both the systemic and inefficient character of street traffic in Pompeii.

[22] Delivered in the House of Commons on October 28, 1943: "The Churchill Centre," www .winstonchurchill.org/learn/speeches/quotations; May 9, 2013.

[23] The *flâneur* and Rome: Larmour and Spencer 2007, 17–18; O'Sullivan 2011, 6–7. Also, Edensor 1998, 212–215.

Cities, the lived experience of the street is emphatically messier than it appears on the drawing board.[24] Jacobs's analysis of her beloved Greenwich Village pushes us to recognize and even revel in the startling juxtapositions that could occur. Just as the street physically connected temples, brothels, shops, governmental offices, and other buildings, so, too, did various realms of urban life – religion, commerce, leisure, and more – overlap in its space. A pedestrian saw these buildings and their denizens cheek-by-jowl with one another and amid an incredibly diverse crowd of streetgoers: child beggars, priestesses, mules, day laborers, dogs, and magistrates. Within this stage-set and among this cast, I seek to envision the street as a space of negotiation – contested and in flux – and to foreground the push and pull among various players in the city. What played out on the street's stage – in exchanges mediated through architecture, images, informal movements, rituals, and dress (among other means) – profoundly affected how individual Romans conceived of the social hierarchy and their place within it. In short, what comes into focus is a space that was critical to generating the realities of Roman urban society and whose study forces us to expand and reconsider our view of the Roman city's social dynamics.

EVIDENCE AND APPROACH I: TIME AND SPACE

Examining street life is challenging because streets are both "built" spaces that required expense to lay paving stones and to erect house façades as well as "negative" spaces, the voids that facilitated movement and served as improvised gathering spots. And, because we are talking about a period 2,000 years in the past, we cannot witness street life directly. Thus, repopulating Roman streets demands addressing a wide range of evidence and employing correspondingly diverse methods. The three vignettes of street activity with which I began this chapter are at our fingertips because of very different types of sources: literary texts, inscriptions, and visual documentation. These sources are, of course, complemented by what Salutaris's inscription mentions, the Megalopsychia mosaic depicts, and Spinazzola and others have unearthed – the remains of streets themselves. Such a multiplicity of evidence makes a point: streets may not have attracted substantial attention as social spaces because no single type of data – on its own – permits an ample reconstruction of activities on them. Material, textual, and epigraphic evidence each independently grant a vision of some aspect of the street, but their combination permits a much richer picture to emerge.

Beyond their genre, our three introductory sources also range widely in time and place: the imperial megalopolis/cosmopolis of Rome, Trajanic Ephesus, and fifth-century Antioch. Streets across the geographical and chronological

[24] Jacobs 1961.

span of Roman dominion certainly shared general characteristics, such as construction technique and transportation technology. But street life was bound to have been locally diverse because climactic patterns and geographical conditions shaped who spent how much time doing what in the public outdoor space that streets offered. Likewise, the political dramas that streets hosted and the tensions to which they gave voice varied extensively. In Alexandria, for instance, the year 38 CE saw long-simmering enmity between Alexandrians and Jews boil over when A. Avilius Flaccus, the Roman prefect of Egypt, allowed statues of Caligula to be erected in the city's synagogues. When the Jews resisted, fighting broke out, with the mob committing what some have called the first pogrom, both assaulting Jews on, and also driving them from, Alexandria's streets. In the account of Philo of Alexandria, streets continued to play a role in these events' aftermath; as Flaccus was exiled, he was paraded in humiliation through several cities before shunning the eyes of all in Andros, his final destination.[25] In Rome itself, there were changes over time, for example, in who could enjoy the singular honor of a triumph – the procession of a victorious general through the streets of the city. What had been open to many aristocrats became the purview almost exclusively of the imperial house in the principate and beyond.[26] Lower down the social ladder, we hear of laments in the wake of Nero's new building laws that followed the fire of 64 CE. Wide and straight streets meant less shade for those lingering in public.[27]

Even as such diversity points up possible future directions for street studies throughout the empire and across time, it also offers warnings about over-generalization. This book thus focuses, to the degree possible, on a rather more narrow time and place: the cities buried, and thus destroyed and also preserved, by the eruption of Mount Vesuvius in 79 CE and the last decades of their ancient life. This is a fascinating period to examine. Rome was learning to live as a thinly veiled monarchy, having recently shaken off the last vestiges of its republican government. The results of such a transition certainly were felt in the street life of the Campanian cities because, for example, Augustus's administrative reorganization of Rome's urban fabric had corollary effects on neighborhood religious life in Pompeii.[28] But politics stand largely in the background, for Roman Italy was also coming to grips with significant social phenomena: not least the emergence of many former slaves (and their off-spring) as a financially powerful and socially striving segment of the population. The street, because it offered somewhat more neutral and common ground, was a prime space for the formulation, negotiation, and contestation of status in this changing world.

---

[25] Philo *In Flacc.* esp. 55, 65, 160. See also Alston 1997; van der Horst 2003; Gambetti 2009.
[26] Beard 2007, 295–305.
[27] Tac. *Ann.* 15.43.
[28] See "The August Lares" in Chapter 8.

An advantage of concentrating on Herculaneum and Pompeii is their abundance of vivid and well-preserved streetscapes that show the street as anything but a "void." In addition to the roadbed, stepping stones, and sidewalks of streets themselves, we have the monuments that dotted them (altars, fountains, and water towers, for instance), the buildings that lined them, and the edifices' own accretions (graffiti, shop signs, plaques, sculpted phalloi, and balconies). As a conglomerate, the many constructions, small and large, provided the "stage-set" for the street's social contact and themselves constituted visible statements forged by individuals and groups. Dating from the same period is a rich array of evidence, most notably historical and literary texts from Rome that directly describe incidents on the street and that reflect attitudes toward the space and its denizens, but also municipal legislation from elsewhere in the Italian peninsula (such as the Tabula Heracleensis) that spells out legal principles related to streets. When testimony runs thin for some topics, however, I cast my net a bit more widely, drawing in sources from the later empire, for example, and setting the fragmentary evidence within a comparative framework derived from better-documented settings.

EVIDENCE AND APPROACH II: SOURCES FOR THE SOFT CITY

In pursuit of Roman street life, then, we must gaze through multiple lenses while maintaining an analytical eye. As we might expect of an environment that many wanted to control, each source about streets approaches the space from its own perspective. The mosaic, for example, presents a vision of urban space curated for a distinct audience – the elite patron of the home whose floor it decorated.[29] And Salutaris's foundation offered an idealized vision of Ephesian history, space, and society, one that we only have because it was recorded prominently and publicly. No data come to us unmediated, of course, but some readers might raise their eyebrows at the extensive use of satire in what follows because the genre and other "realist" texts have frequently been accepted uncritically. Some scholars have even pinpointed Juvenal's third *Satire* as problematic in the creation of "urban dystopias."[30] As a result, I want to return to my opening example – Juvenal's narrator trudging through the streets of Rome – to address why and how I deploy this and related sources.

As a source for social history, satire is both useful and dangerous.[31] For one thing, satire is useful because it is a quintessentially Roman and urban poetic form. No direct parallel tradition grew up in Athens, Pergamum, or Alexandria.

[29] In fact, the mosaic's selection of path and monuments overlaps with a tour of Antioch narrated by the philosopher Libanius (*Or.* 11.196–245).
[30] Laurence 1997.
[31] Satire and social history: Braund 1989a, 1989b; Henderson 1999. Braund 1996, 1–15 on satire and Juvenal's predecessors.

Rather, the value Romans placed on *libertas*, which might be rendered as "free-dom of speech," enabled satire's cutting edge, and a "large cosmopolitan urban environment" offered material galore for that blade.[32] Satire is not just *about* the city, though; it is *of* the city. In Juvenalian satire, as a nonstop flurry of episodes – connected in theme but rarely following a formal structure – catches the narrator's eye, it is as though he were having a street-side conversation with a friend while watching the people streaming by.[33] Additionally, in its tone, satire is, in the words of Luke Roman, "a mode of poetry premised on speed, impromptu wit, and the jagged, surprising texture of urban life."[34]

Second, satire offers a perspective that is distinctly questioning and critical of the perceived social situation, often exposing holes and double standards in the status quo by adopting the vantage point of someone beyond those who make (and benefit from) the rules. In the case of Juvenal 3, for example, one over-arching theme of Umbricius's narrative is the displacement of needy but decent clients by the shameless, foreign, and criminal. "There's no room for any Roman here," he writes, and the chief reason, in his eyes, is the power of money: "Everyone's credit matches the amount of coins he keeps in his coffers."[35] And, by this score, he clearly does not measure up: "There's nothing harder about unfortunate poverty than the way it makes people ridiculous."[36] Streets were full of people like Umbricius, and Juvenal's account sketches an outline of their psychology and worldview. For this reason, I am unwilling to simply disregard Juvenal, his fellow satirists, and also comedic playwrights. To do so would be to disarm ourselves of some of our most powerful and revelatory voices in the street, ones that help outline the perspectives of those outside of litters and grand houses.

Yet, for all the atmosphere it evokes and reflects, satire poses issues because its craft hinges on inverting, exaggerating, and twisting reality. Moreover, any reading of Juvenal 3 must tread carefully on notoriously slippery narratological ground.[37] As a result, I place less emphasis on the details of satirists' portrayals.

---

[32] Miller 2007, 138 (who considers elegy in parallel terms). Roman 2010, 88–89 for a survey of recent approaches to Latin poetry in an urban setting.

[33] Larmour 2007, esp. 171–174. Horace expresses similar sentiments more explicitly: *Sat.* 2.6.17 (*musa pedestris*, "walking muse"); *Epist.* 2.1.251 (*sermones repentes per humum*, "conversations creeping along the ground").

[34] Roman 2010, 89 (writing about Martial).

[35] Juv. 3.119: *Non est Romano cuiquam locus hic . . . .* 3.143–144: *quantum quisque sua nummorum servat in arca, / tantum habet et fidei.*

[36] Juv. 3.152–153: *nil habet infelix paupertas durius in se / quam ridiculos homines facit.*

[37] That is, the laments about street life are not attributed to the poet or his poetic persona, but to Juvenal's "old friend" Umbricius, whose very name is "shady": Motto and Clark 1965; Winkler 1983, 220–223; Braund 1996, 230–236; Staley 2000, 87–89. *Umbra* means shade and thus reflects any area out of the glow of public life, but it also encompasses the shade of the departed, which may reflect Umbricius's destination of Cumae, where Aeneas entered the underworld. And Umbricius longs for an ideal but now lost Rome, a shade of its former self.

At times, it is possible to corroborate those particulars by setting them in conversation with other types of evidence. Juvenal's muddy streets, for example, find distinct parallels in sources of various stripes – not just additional authors, but legal sources that voice concerns about the cleanliness of the street as well as the archaeological evidence from Pompeii, such as the paucity of sewers and abundance of stepping stones that imply a messy situation.[38]

In general, however, we are on safer ground when reading satire for broader sociocultural sensibilities, what has been called the "soft city." This is not the urbanism "one can locate in maps and statistics," but one of "illusion, myth, aspiration, nightmare."[39] Our sources thus enable us to draw out generalized attitudes and social anxieties. And, in particular, they offer a useful corrective to some of our own assumptions. Many commentators on Juvenal's Third *Satire*, for instance, liken Umbricius's experience to the modern traffic jam. True, other sources do describe the substantial congestion on Roman urban streets, similarly bemoaning cities' clogged arteries, and Umbricius's bumps and bruises also find some parallels (though without the same slapstick flurry).[40] But Juvenal/ Umbricius is much less hung up on these physical conditions than on their social meaning; the self-styled pauper repeatedly points out how he endures a much different city from that enjoyed by others. The poor man loses everything in a fire while the rich simply restock with nicer things. The urban racket keeps many awake, but the affluent doze peacefully. And by night a drunken thug hungry for a fight bypasses a wealthy man's entourage and unleashes his anger on Umbricius, who suffers physical and verbal abuse before then getting sued for assault.[41] In sum, the message to take from this passage is not the narrator's being peeved that he is slowed – as we will see, impediments to urban movement were so frequent that Romans could hardly have expected to skate through the street unobstructed – but the social frisson present in the street as some glide along asleep while others suffer indignities. This is the "soft city" that satire exposes.

OUTLINE OF THE BOOK

In Juvenal's portrait of urban life, Umbricius's rant about his street experience is set in a physical context: he links sounds, sleep, traffic, and the tight twisting

---

[38] For a parallel sentiment about the use of ancient sources, see Scheidel 2003. Poor condition of streets: Mart 5.22.5–6, 7.61.6, 10.10.7–8, 12.28(26).8; Sen. *Ira* 3.35.5; Juv. 3.247; Petron. 79; Dio Cass. 59.12; Suet. *Vesp.* 5.3. Legal sources: Tabula Heracleensis, lines 23–49; Robinson 1992, 70–74, 122–124.

[39] Raban 1974, 9.

[40] E.g., Cic. *Planc.* 7; Hor. *Sat.* 2.6.27–31; Sen. *Ira* 3.6.4.

[41] Respectively: Juv. 3.197–222, 232–235, 278–301. Additionally, Umbricius's lament gathers force because he, as a native Roman proud of traditional values (e.g., Juv. 3.21–22, 84–85, 119.), is pummeled, even by a Roman soldier, in the streets of what he calls a *Graeca urbs* (a Greek Rome: Juv. 3.61). Note also the military vocabulary: e.g., *magno . . . agmine; clavus . . . militis*.

streets of Rome in one sentence.[42] As I have been arguing, such a dialogue between urban life and the built environment is fundamental and, in the case of streets, critical for their study, because the street's "frame" and "void" mutually influenced one another. This dialectic also lends structure to what follows. Although no chapter is devoid of either the "negative" space of the street or its physical frame, attention swings between the street's open space (Part I) and its architecture and decoration (Part II), before they are reunited explicitly in the case studies of specific corners (Part III).

Part I focuses primarily on what occurred within the street: the urban population's movements through, activities within, and interactions amid this environment. Chapter 1 is interested in the character of streets and their most obvious use – as facilitators of transportation through the urban fabric. Chapter 2 flips the question and asks how streets functioned as venues unto themselves as arenas for sociability, commerce, housing, and ritual. Chapter 3 picks up on the display evident in this last role and examines the street's social atmosphere to a greater degree: who was present, how they presented themselves to (while simultaneously watching) one another, and what the effects of such interactions were.

As Part II shifts focus to the physical frame of the street, Chapter 4 buffers the transition by discussing a particularly sensitive space – that immediately in front of buildings, especially houses, which was closely tied to a property's owner. The narrow strip formed the fulcrum of a see-saw between individual and public, and it saw battles of many sorts. Chapter 5 focuses on the same space but studies the physical membrane that separated the two realms of interior and exterior: the façade. How did house owners shape the street's walls in answer to its activities, and how did they seek to present themselves to its many users? Chapter 6 also approaches this tension between inside and outside sectors, but does so by investigating one seemingly ephemeral construction: the masonry benches lining the façades of streetside buildings. Built by the structures' owners yet open to use by the public at large, benches offer a fascinating perspective on the dynamics of individual and collective concerns.

Part III explicitly reunites the street's space and framing architecture through two case studies of specific street segments. Chapter 7 zooms in on an intersection near the monumental heart of Herculaneum where we can witness the actions and interactions among a host of different individuals and groups – civic officials and former slaves, for instance – who inhabited this corner, gave it shape, and both met and sought control here. Chapter 8 offers a Pompeian counterpoint on a peripheral, though important, thoroughfare graced by no fancy buildings but where a thorough mix of barmaids, politicians, freedman

---

[42] Juv. 3.236–238.

magistrates, cloth sellers, and worshippers of foreign goddesses vied for the spotlight and shouted down one another's claims.

Paying attention to urbanites' actions with and interactions within the street opens up a new perspective on the "social space" of the Roman city. Roman historians have long recognized and detailed the ways and places in the Roman city where elite members of society constructed, reinforced, and celebrated their status – such as holding priesthoods in temples, orating in the forum, underwriting public amenities, and receiving clients and hosting guests in their homes. The street, meanwhile, has largely escaped notice because it is an ill-defined space that doesn't "belong" to anyone. Yet, ironically, this is where so many people spent much of their time. This book unveils that additional critical venue for self-presentation and social exchange – one that offers a counterpoint and complement to studies of urban society concentrating on fora, theaters, baths, houses, and the like. The street connected these various spheres of urban life and set them in contact both with one another and with the shops, bars, brothels, and hovels in between; it gave urban inhabitants beyond the elite a space of greater agency and impact, and it thus enables a "finer-grained" and more representative image of urban life to emerge.

PART I

REPOPULATING THE STREET

W HEN THE NEAPOLITAN INTELLECTUAL LUCIANO DE CRESCENZO wished to capture the spirit of his birthplace, he picked up his camera. The shots De Crescenzo published in the resulting volume of photographs, *La Napoli di Bellavista* (named after his most famous character, a Socrates-like professor), survey just a few things that unfold daily in modern Naples.[1] We peer into ground floor apartments, called *bassi*, where families squeeze into what were once the stables of grand palazzi, using the main room as kitchen, dining room, and living space. Emotion explodes from the packed stadium of San Paolo, where Naples exalts in a rare moment of victory. At the packed tables of game houses, women and transvestites hunch over cards as they play *tombola*, Neapolitan bingo. In showcasing Naples's remarkable (and even notorious) public life, however, the most numerous and striking photos of De Crescenzo's book represent the street. People converse heatedly, they sell contraband, they carry coffins, and eat pizza (see Figure 7). The images are deeply evocative for anyone who has visited this idiosyncratic place, and, as such, they echo something Jane Jacobs once wrote: "Think of a city and what comes to mind? Its streets."[2]

De Crescenzo's photographic eye tends to focus on individuals or pairs of streetgoers. When we look at specific intersections, the action and cast

[1] De Crescenzo 1979.
[2] Jacobs 1961, 29.

7. Luciano De Crescenzo portrayed the character of his native city, Naples, through photographs of street scenes in *La Napoli di Bellavista*.
Photo: De Crescenzo 1979, pp. 66, 126–127.

8. The busy street scene on Via San Biagio dei Librai in modern Naples.
Photo: author.

broaden and grow richer. Figure 8 shows a segment of Via San Biagio dei Librai, also known as Spaccanapoli since it divides Naples in two, north and south. People stroll, they see one another, they move goods, they catch up with friends, they hawk wares, they pray to the Virgin. This is an undeniably lively scene, and it transpires on a street at least 2,200 years old, for the modern streets in this part of Naples maintain the orientation and dimensions of their

9. Excavations underneath San Lorenzo Maggiore in Naples have revealed a Greco-Roman predecessor of the modern city's streets.
Photo: author.

Greco-Roman predecessors. Via San Biagio was, it seems, the *decumanus maximus* of Roman Naples.

Not far from Via San Biagio, deep below the church of San Lorenzo Maggiore, runs another ancient street. Following the same north–south line as today's Vico Giganti, it measures about 4 meters across. Along the 50 meters excavated stretch of basalt pavers, a dozen doorways open onto bakeries, workshops, a possible treasury, and a market building[3] (Fig. 9). All in all, the thoroughfare bears striking similarities to side streets in Pompeii and Herculaneum. And, like its Campanian colleagues, it is little-visited and thus appears virtually empty; we have a provocative stage-set and little action. Part I of this book seeks to refill the space of streets like that under San Lorenzo, to make them more like Via San Biagio and the images captured by De Crescenzo. Over the course of the next three chapters, goods, people, and

[3] De Simone 1985, 1986.

animals fill the streets, sometimes merely moving from one spot to another, sometimes loitering on sidewalks, and nearly always watching (and preening for) one another, with powerful results. The goal of Part I is therefore to adapt Jane Jacobs' dictum: I want to suggest that when we think of Roman cities and their populations, we should think of their streets.

ONE

STREET FORMS, STREET MOVEMENTS

I N HIS DE LEGE AGRARIA, AMID A DISCUSSION OF HOW GEOGRAPHICAL circumstances influence human character, Cicero seeks to explain the case of Campania, a region whose inhabitants had a reputation among Romans for arrogance. He pins their smugness on their land's fertility, the resultant bounty of crops, and, interestingly, the healthiness, disposition, and beauty of their cities. In a passage that was either sarcastic because of Romans' pride in their seven hills or that needled Romans who were less sardonically inclined, Cicero imagines the perspective of the citizens of Capua, a sizable Campanian city. He writes:

> When they consider Rome – placed on hills and valleys, and with its balconies and overhangs, its streets which aren't the best, its alleys which are really narrow – in comparison with their own Capua – which is laid out perfectly well and sits on a very level plain – they will laugh and disparage us.[1]

In keeping with a theme of the Introduction, we might first note how Cicero imagines both Rome and Capua from a street-level and not bird's-eye view-point. But what is more notable is how, when he considers the cities' urban fabric, he compares their streets and invests meaning in the difference.

[1] Cic. *Leg. agr.* 2.96: *Romam in montibus positam et convallibus, cenaculis sublatam atque suspensam, non optimis viis, angustissimis semitis prae sua Capua planissimo in loco explicata ac praeclarissime sita irridebunt atque contemnent.*

The contrast between Rome's dominance of the Mediterranean and its narrow, curvy streets was not lost on Romans themselves as they sought out an etiology for the phenomenon.[2] And it remains a puzzling irony to some scholars that the two signature cities of classical antiquity, Rome and Athens, did not have straight streets.[3] To put it simply, Cicero recognizes that not all streets are equal, and he implies that Romans, because of their city's form, have a way of urban life that is easily mockable.

This chapter takes some of its cues from Cicero's sentiments. It builds on the comparison Cicero draws to consider what differentiated streets in Roman cities from one another. The variation, as we shall see, can be classed in at least two categories. First, we gain an appreciation for the component features of urban thoroughfares – most obviously, the roadbed itself, the curbstones, and the sidewalks – thus setting the physical stage for many of the dramas that will play out in later chapters. Second, along the way, we gain a sense of the less tangible qualities of streets – their "feel" or "character" – and how factors beyond physical measurements contributed to Roman outlooks on the places they tread.

This chapter also takes up Cicero's collocation of street form and urban life. But beyond examining streets to draw conclusions about urban life, as Cicero's Capuans do, my inquiry reverses the lens and considers what urban life more generally can tell us about what traffic coursed along streets. Embedded in this analysis is frequent comparison between modern and Roman cities. I hope to treat their dissimilarities with a greater sensitivity than Cicero's imagined Capuans. Rather than pushing us to point and laugh, holding these forms of urban life next to one another encourages us to recognize how unlike they were, especially how much more vital the street was in the functioning of Roman cities.

"THE" ROMAN STREET? PHYSICAL FORMS, NAMES, AND TYPICALITY

Throughout this book, I write at some length about "the street." This is admittedly a useful veneer over the immense variety of thoroughfares that coursed through the cities of Roman Italy. Not all streets were identical – far from it. Even within one city, it is obvious enough that there were great distinctions among streets, and raw dimensions provide an immediate index of difference (Fig. 10). At Pompeii, for instance, the main artery that we call the Via dell'Abbondanza

---

[2] Livy 5.55.3–5; Diod. Sic. 14.116.8–9; Plut. *Cam.* 32.3.

[3] E.g., Owens 1991, 11: "Athens and Rome were in many respects unworthy of their reputations as leading cities of Greece and Italy, and as capitals of their respective empires. Both cities were characterized by cramped, overcrowded conditions. The streets were narrow, insinuating themselves between irregular blocks of houses and public buildings."

10. The names of Pompeii's streets and gates were given by archaeologists excavating the city. The plan identifies major thoroughfares and other streets mentioned in this book.
Drawing: Ryan Cairns.

11. The Via dell'Abbondanza in Pompeii swells to form a piazza-like space outside the Stabian Baths.
Photo: author. Courtesy: Soprintendenza Speciale per Pompei, Ercolano e Stabia.

changes width over its length, measuring about 8 meters across in the east and swelling to more than 14 meters in width outside the Stabian Baths (Fig. 11). Yet numerous sidestreets, such as the Vicolo di Tesmo, offer a significant contrast, spanning less than 4 meters from one façade to the other (Fig. 12). Since buildings hugged tight together, leaving no open space between them, and since they also clung to the street and were rarely set back behind fences, yards, external forecourts, or the like, a solid physical boundary penned in the space of the street. On average, at Pompeii, streets measured between 5 and 6 meters façade-to-façade, which is only slightly less than the width of streets in Rome itself.[4]

Of a street's width, a sizable portion could be given over to sidewalks, although here again streets display a diversity of forms. At Herculaneum, the so-called *decumanus maximus* spans over 12 meters in width, about half of which was occupied by sidewalks (see Fig. 69). Its roadbed was largely blocked to wheeled traffic, so it could afford to be atypical. In contrast to most other roadbeds at Pompeii and Herculaneum, which were paved, this street surface

---

[4] I obtained data for street widths by measuring façade-to-façade to the nearest half-meter at both ends of every segment of street at Pompeii and then determining the length of each of those segments. The average was calculated by multiplying the width of each block-length segment of street by the block's length and dividing it by the total length of Pompeii's streets. Measurements in Pompeii: Gesemann 1996; Kaiser 2011a, 71–74. Measurements in Rome (for actual remains and extrapolation from the Forma Urbis Romae): Quilici 1990; Macauley-Lewis 2011, 266–270. Cf. Varro, *Ling.* 5.35.

12. The Vicolo di Tesmo, although among the narrowest streets in Pompeii, appears to have hosted significant traffic.
Photo: author. Courtesy: Soprintendenza Speciale per Pompei, Ercolano e Stabia.

consisted of packed grayish pozzolana earth mixed with small fragments of limestone (into which large wooden supports for awnings appear to have been set). Unique drainage ditches were cut between the roadbed and the sidewalks beyond. Herculaneum's few other exposed streets display an unusual uniformity, all measuring between 5 and 7 meters in width. Yet some were outfitted with sidewalks that took up between 3 and 4 meters, while others lacked sidewalks on one side or altogether.[5] The repeated passage of metal-rimmed cart and wagon wheels wore marks into the roadbed. Such "wheel ruts" show that some streets accommodated two-way traffic while others must have been

[5] Herculaneum: Maiuri 1958, 33–42; Pagano 1993, esp. 597. Pompeii: Saliou 1999.

solely one-way. On still other thoroughfares, wheeled traffic was severely restricted or prevented altogether.[6]

Beyond their physical forms, another difference among streets was the amount of human (or animal) traffic they hosted. By measuring the frequency of doorways and "messages" (both painted signs and graffiti scratched into plaster) along individual streets, Ray Laurence has sought to determine the relative amount of activity on Pompeii's thoroughfares. Some of the results are not surprising: by his calculations, the broadest streets generally tend to be among the busiest. The Via Stabiana, which measures roughly 8 meters across and links city gates to the north and south, scores among the highest densities by both doorways and inscriptions. Yet there are notable exceptions. One stretch of the Vicolo di Tesmo – the narrow alleyway we just encountered – has a very high concentration of messages and an above average number of doorways, perhaps because it offered an attractive alternative to the Via Stabiana, which ran parallel just to the west and hosted much more vehicular traffic.[7] Walking here would have contrasted markedly to the experience of other sidestreets. Similar disparities must have separated the "feel" of a broad street choked with wheeled traffic from one that was entirely given over to pedestrians.

One important point to begin: the remains of individual streets indicate that there was no "typical" street, from a physical standpoint, even in two cities as proximate as Herculaneum and Pompeii. That Romans themselves drew distinctions among streets is evident first in the material remains. At Herculaneum, white limestone paving distinguished Cardo V from its counterparts, which were, in a construction technique typical for this city and much of Roman Italy, carpeted in blocks of basalt, a blackish volcanic stone.[8] The insertion of small limestone chips between the volcanic pavers along Pompeii's Via Marina did much the same, while a few other streets in Pompeii, especially peripheral alleyways, consisted essentially of packed earth.[9] The physical organization of cities into series of long and narrow city blocks – as occurred in some parts of Pompeii as well as in many other cities under Rome's domain – entailed a two-tiered scheme of streets. Such a system, which drew on Greek traditions in urban planning, created tight alleyways along the long sides of a block; the block's short sides formed wider thoroughfares that could accommodate more traffic.[10] The modern urban fabric of Naples preserves just such a Greco-Roman layout, and the effects of this ancient hierarchy are still palpable. The main streets, such as Via San Biagio dei Librai, pulse with activity, while the sidestreets have

---

[6] Tsujimura 1991, 65–68; Wallace-Hadrill 1995, 46–50; Poehler 2006, 2009; van Tilburg 2007, 136–144; Laurence 2008, 89–92; Kaiser 2011a, 94–99; 2011b.
[7] Laurence 2007, Maps 6.1–6.4 (doorways) and 6.5–6.8 (graffiti).
[8] Maiuri 1958, 34.
[9] Alleyways: Gesemann 1996, 57.
[10] Ward-Perkins 1974; Owens 1991.

a semiprivate quality, as residents string laundry between buildings and raise chickens in the roadbed, for example.[11]

Just as Roman urban layouts dovetailed on their predecessors, so too did the Latin terms for streets derive largely from Greek. The words maintain a critical distinction between a narrow alleyway and a more ample street – respectively, a *stenopos* becomes an *angiportus* or a *semita* (the latter of which could also denote a sidewalk) while a broad *plateia* is called a *platea* or a *via*.[12] (Greek had no direct equivalent for *vicus*, which described a sidestreet or an urban neighborhood.) When Romans wanted to emphasize that *all* of the streets of a city were affected, they routinely paired words from each set, such as when Caesar's troops blockaded Alexandria's thoroughfares with a triple barricade: *omnibus viis atque angiportis triplicem vallum obduxerant*.[13]

Another way that streets were distinguished from one another was, naturally enough, the names that city dwellers gave to the thoroughfares they traversed. Inscriptions in Oscan, a language spoken and used administratively in Pompeii prior to its becoming a *municipium*, record place-names for the city.[14] One such inscription found near the so-called Porta Stabia on the city's southern side records the gift of two aediles. They are said to have "marked out this road as far as the Stabian bridge to a width of 50 feet" and "they also marked out the Via Pompeiana to a width of 15 feet as far as the sanctuary of Jupiter Melichius. They also had these roads made up, along with the Via Jovia and the Via Dequaviaris. " The Via Pompeiana can thus be identified with the southernmost portion of the so-called Via Stabiana; the Via Iovis is perhaps what we call the Via del Tempio d'Iside, which branches off to the west, and the Via Dequaviaris may be the Via dei Teatri, which then runs to the north.[15]

Walking through a Roman city and considering the street names could be akin to receiving a lesson in history and sacred spaces. In Rome, revered places, family names, and historical events formed a web of toponyms draped over the city. One might walk up the Clivus Salutis to reach the early republican Temple of Salus (health), amble along the Vicus Dianae, and remember Mercury's preferred offering of milk (rather than wine) on the Vicus Sobrius (Sober Street). African slaves held during the Punic Wars could come to mind as you traversed the Vicus Africus, and the Vicus Tuscus took you back to the

---

[11] De Crescenzo 1979 offers evocative images of such street scenes.
[12] Plaut. *Curc.* 287 for the contrast between *via* and *semita*. For more on terminology, see Kaiser 2011a, 30–34; 2011c. Cf. Harsh 1937; André 1950; Lolos 2003.
[13] Caes. *B Alex.* 2.
[14] *CIL* 4.9159 mentions the "Veru Sarinu," *Porta Salis* in Latin, which likely derives from the saltworks that we know were located near Pompeii (Columella *Rust.* 10.135). It probably corresponds to what we call the Porta Ercolano in the city's northwest.
[15] Inscription: Onorato 1951. Translation: Ling 1990a, 207.

city's Etruscan roots and could conjure up memory of any number of different battles.[16] The Via Cornelia, the Vicus Sulpicius, and the Clivus Scauri kept the names of aristocratic families on Roman tongues well into the empire. Streets named after certain goods or trades – such as the Vicus Unguentarius (Perfume Street), the Vicus Frumentarius (Grain Street), and the Clivus Capsarius (Scroll-tube Incline) – undoubtedly reflect concentrations of certain types of shops and factories. With the normal ebbs and flows of the urban process, however, a street might outgrow its name, as seems to have been the case with the Vicus Sandaliarius (Sandal Street), whose footwear was crowded out by a proliferation of booksellers.[17] Or, some labels might have double meanings. At Pompeii, a graffito near the Casa del Menandro informs streetgoers: "At Nuceria ask for Novellia Primigenia in the Vicus Venerius by the Rome Gate."[18] A temple of Venus may well have stood nearby the Vicus Venerius in the nearby town, but the street's name also apparently refers to a red-light district where one could find a famed prostitute.[19] All of this speaks to the varied meanings Romans invested in different thoroughfares, as well as how those names in turn may have inflected streetgoers' expectations.

In an era before formal postal service, nomenclature would have been a matter of convention and tradition, only on occasion becoming official, such as when streets gave their names to a district, or *vicus*, of a city, as happened in Rome after reforms to city administration under Augustus.[20] In fact, Latin inscriptions from other Italian cities suggest that many streets lacked names. A monument marking a benefaction in Cales, a town in northern Campania, records the paving of "the street from the alley of the Temple of Juno Lucina to the Temple of Matuta and the incline from the gate to the *cisiarios* [a station for a certain type of vehicle] at the Porta Stellatina and the broad street to the Porta Laeva and from the Forum to the Porta Domestica."[21] Similar patterns of circumlocution, even for well-located streets, appear elsewhere on the peninsula, none more surprising than one dating from the reign of Augustus at Ostia: listed first among many donations of temples, dinners, and the like is P. Lucilius Gamala's paving of the street "which is joined to the forum, connecting the

---

[16] Ancient accounts differ on which early military event took place here: Romulus's troops battling against Titus Tatius (Varro *Ling.* 5.46; Serv. *A.* 5.560; Prop. 4.2.49–52), an encampment of Tarquinius Priscus's troops (Tac. *Ann.* 4.65), or the settlement of what remained of Porsinna's army (Livy 2.14.9).

[17] Aul. Gell. 18.4.1.

[18] *CIL* 4.8356: *Nuceriae quaeres ad Portam Romanam, in Vico Venerio, Novelliam Primigeniam.*

[19] The name Primagenia appears multiple times at Pompeii: *CIL* 4.3976, 4.5358, 4.8175, 4.8177, 4.8260, 4.8264, 4.8274, 4.8301.

[20] Lott 2004. History of house-numbering: Tantner 2009.

[21] *CIL* 10.4660: *viam ab Angiporto aed[is] Iunonis Lucinae usque [ad] aedem Matutae et clivom ab ianu ad gisiarios porta[e] Stellatinae et viam patulam ad portam laevam et ab foro ad portam domesticam sua pecunia stravit.*

two arches."[22] One suspects that many streets in Pompeii and Herculaneum likewise lacked names, such as the narrow alleyways in Pompeii's southeast corner. As a result, direction-giving was likely a matter of naming landmarks.[23]

Early archaeologists at Pompeii named thoroughfares as they were unearthed, often drawing inspiration from a distinguishing feature, monument, or potential destination. At the west end of the Via dell'Abbondanza, or Street of Abundance, appeared a fountain boasting a relief of a woman holding a cornucopia, whereas the Via Stabiana was named after the city one eventually reached by following this street out of the city. I employ the conventional nomenclature throughout this book for the sake of clarity but with full awareness that some names are bound to have shaped how we understand these sites and at times to have perpetuated potentially faulty assumptions. Excavators named the *decumanus maximus* at Herculaneum, for example, because they believed that this broad street was the foremost boulevard in the town. Yet archival work has suggested that other streets of the same orientation, dimensions, and grandeur remain buried in the sizable portion of the city's fabric still unexplored via open-air excavations, thus rendering the label and its embedded hypothesis suspect.[24]

For all these dissimilarities across the urban fabric – in street shape, name, sensibility – it is worth noting that the character of a single street varied markedly; it could literally be a matter of night and day. After the sun went down, what light was present filtered out of streetside buildings, such as taverns, which cut visibility and the safety it afforded in cities without a standing police force.[25] Juvenal's narrator Umbricius articulates Roman anxieties about nocturnal passage. He constructs a scene in which a sleepless, drunk thug picks out his prey on the dark streets:

> But however high on wine and burning with young blood the man may be, he steers well clear of the fellow with the scarlet cloak, who is surrounded by a long line of bodyguards plus plenty of torches and bronze lamps. But me, as I return home escorted by only the moon or a sad little candle that demands my constant attention – me he despises. Hear how the pathetic brawl starts – if you can call it a brawl when you do the beating and I just take it.[26]

---

[22] *CIL* 14.375: *[q]uae est iuncta foro ab arcu ad arcum.* Other streets referred to by description rather than names: *CIL* 9.5438 (Falerii), 10.1698 (Puteoli).

[23] E.g., Ter. *Ad.* 572–83. Navigating the city: Ling 1990a; Kaiser 2011a, 7–12. The twenty-four so-called street plaques offered potential reference points in Pompeii's urban fabric: Ling 1990b.

[24] Ruggiero 1885, 154; Pagano 1996, 230. Also: Allrogen-Bedel 1983, 154, n. 87; Scatozza-Höricht 1985, 142; De Kind 1998, 55–58.

[25] *Dig.* 9.2.52.1. Antioch was unique and renowned for having publicly lit streets, though some questioned its cost and impact: Lib. *Or.* 16.41, 22.6, 33.35–37. On policing: Fuhrmann 2012, esp. ch. 3.

[26] Juv. 3.282–289: *sed quamvis improbus annis / atque mero fervens cavet hunc quem coccina laena / vitari iubet et comitum longissimus ordo, / multum praeterea flammarum et aenea lampas. / me, quem luna*

Yelling and insults ensue, and the narrator becomes the thug's punching bag. Roman law appears to have enshrined this diurnal/nocturnal difference, for although it was not legal for objects to be thrown from buildings into the street by day, it was permitted by night.[27] Over the course of daylight hours, the spatiotemporal flow of urban life similarly saw people clustered in different spots.[28] Crowds of customers, for instance, might gather around a neighborhood's bakery in the morning, but the space would be relatively calm by midday. Even more striking contrasts would have been felt on special occasions, as when a street was given over entirely to a public feast or a procession.[29]

These differences – whether across a city or even within a single street – are evident and undeniable. They form part of what lends dynamism, excitement, and unpredictability to urban environments, whether ancient or modern. Moreover, that such diversity plays out on two major registers – a street's physical make-up and the activities it hosted – underlines the interrelated influences of the built environment and the urban population. It was not just "the stage" or "the actors" that determined a street's character, but also the interaction of the two. For this reason, my goal in the remainder of this chapter (and those beyond) is not to ferret out the minutiae of what differentiates this street from that and to categorize such differences. Rather, I aim to refill the space between a street's walls – in this chapter, that means putting wheels, paws, hooves, and feet in motion.

THE STREET AS CORRIDOR FOR MOVEMENT

The most obvious use of streets was to facilitate the movement of goods, supplies, and people across the urban fabric.[30] Refilling the streets of Pompeii and Herculaneum with their coursing traffic is a challenge, however, since we obviously cannot observe the comings and goings directly. In response, I employ three overlapping strategies to help envision the nature and degree of street passage: a close-range examination of the literary and material evidence, a consideration of the needs of the urban populace, and, finally, a macrolevel analysis of Pompeii's urban fabric.

Numerous sources bemoan the carts and wagons that lugged heavy loads to their destination. In the passage that opened this book, Juvenal's Umbricius voices a common complaint about the noise created by such vehicles and their

---

solet deducere vel breve lumen / candelae, cuius dispenso et tempero filum, / contemnit. miserae cognosce prohoemia rixae, / si rixa est, ubi tu pulsas, ego vapulo tantum. Cf. Apul. Met. 2.32; Prop. 2.29a, 3.16.5–6.

[27] Dig. 9.3.6.

[28] Laurence 2007, 154–166; Holleran 2012, 145, 149.

[29] E.g., Cic. Off. 2.58.

[30] Recent surveys of the study of movement and the Roman street: Newsome 2011, 4–20; Kaiser 2011a, 2–7.

drivers; Horace laments the dust they stirred up; the late-republican jurist Alfenus describes their potential dangers in an episode describing a slave-boy being crushed when handlers lose control of a mule-led wagon; and Martial gripes about the inconvenience posed by a long train of mules pulling marble blocks.[31] In a telling reversal, Pliny goes so far in his panegyric of Trajan to praise the emperor for reducing the amount of public construction because fewer people will endure the wagons rumbling through the city.[32] As ever, Juvenal distills popular sentiment into concentrated cinematic form:

> As it approaches, a huge fir log sways on a wagon and another huge cart hauls a whole pine tree. They nod back and forth threateningly way above the people. For if the axle that's lugging a heap of marble snaps and spills the whole overturned mountain on the masses, what would be left of the bodies? Who could identify any limbs or bones? Every poor squashed carcass would vanish, just like its soul.[33]

The dyspeptic poet's remarks about the danger of falling materials were more than an encapsulation of common fears, for they find an echo in legal sources.[34]

Juvenal's words may also reflect legislation passed in Rome. Some of the provisions outlined in the so-called Tabula Heracleensis – a bronze tablet found in Southern Italy and containing a variety of municipal legislation most likely dating to the reign of Caesar – address just such traffic.[35] Heavy wagons called *plostra* were barred from streets in the *caput mundi* until the tenth hour of the day, which would fall in late afternoon. These vehicles (which are elsewhere called *plaustra*) could be behemoths that required eight to ten horses, mules, or even oxen to pull their bulk, which monopolized the roadbed, made for tough turning, and perhaps even required *cursores*, "runners," to shoo away traffic as the vehicles squeezed through streets.[36] The inconvenience they posed for other traffic is presumably the reason for the prohibition, although the tablet made exceptions for certain instances of state religion, civic festivities, demolition, and public or sacred construction. It does not mention smaller vehicles that may have circulated more widely and more frequently than their larger cousins. Nevertheless, in sum, the sources imply the significant demand for and frequent presence of cargo-bearing vehicles on city streets.

---

[31] Juv. 3.236–238; Hor. *Epist.* 1.17.6–8; *Dig.* 9.2.52.2; Mart. 5.22. Cf. Tib. 2.3.43–44.

[32] Pliny *Pan.* 51.1.

[33] Juv. 3.254–261: … *longa coruscat / serraco veniente abies, atque altera pinum / plaustra vehunt; nutant alte populoque minantur. / nam si procubuit qui saxa Ligustica portat / axis et eversum fudit super agmina montem, / quid superest de corporibus? quis membra, quis ossa / invenit? Obtritum vulgo perit omne cadaver / more animae.*

[34] *Dig.* 9.2.27.33.

[35] *CIL* 12.593; *FIRA* 13. Crawford (1996, 355–362) offers text, translation, and commentary. See also: Nicolet 1987; Hartnett 2011b.

[36] *Tabula Heracleensis* ll. 54–69. Various vehicles, including *plaustra/plostra*: van Tilburg 2007, 51–55; Kaiser 2011b. *Cursores*: Sen. *Ep.* 87.9, 123.7; Suet. *Nero* 30.

The granting of concessions to some wheeled traffic does not mean that the passage of carts and wagons on Roman streets was easy. To take the example of Pompeii, numerous impediments both large and small confronted those trying to traverse the city on wheels. First was the challenge of navigating a street network that lacked signage yet contained many thoroughfares that could not accommodate vehicles passing simultaneously in opposite directions. Wear marks on curbstones – themselves an artifact of jostled passages – have allowed scholars to establish probable traffic patterns in the city.[37] What is striking is how indirect those routes could be. For example, because of restrictions to wheeled traffic around the forum and throughout the western portion of the city, a cart carrying goods to the Porta Marina from the eastern half of the city could not take the direct route. Instead, multiple turns, busy intersections, and several hundred more meters were added to the cart's intraurban course.[38] Such inconvenience came on top of numerous smaller obstructions: the stepping stones placed in the roadbed for the convenience of pedestrians passing from one sidewalk to the other, carts stopped to unload merchandise, people or animals walking in the street, and fountains or water towers standing in the roadbed. This evidence, when paired with the restrictions of the Tabula Heracleensis, suggests that optimizing the ease of movement for wheeled vehicles, common though they were, was not a top urban priority.[39]

The mules mentioned in Martial's street snippet were likely a common sight on Roman streets. Along with the pigs and dogs that appear in other scenes, they added free-ranging hooves to the other traffic coursing along.[40] One advantage of animals walking on their own is highlighted by an aside from Pliny the Elder. He writes of a group of pigs that was led to market by their own porcine leader. Even if it is apocryphal, the story underscores how an autonomous passel did not have to be conveyed by other, more unwieldy means.[41] Pack animals certainly passed through narrow streets or around obstacles that slowed carts and wagons even while transporting nearly as much raw weight.[42] Indeed, numerous tethering points for animals were cut through the curbstones in Pompeii. One section of the city, located near the forum and encompassing about 10 percent of the city's excavated sidewalks, had well in excess of 200 sidewalk holes. Although we cannot determine from the holes whether the beasts of burden were freestanding or hitched to a vehicle, such density attests to the frequent use of animals to carry goods into and through the city. Moreover, the holes' presence on some of the busiest and best-connected

---

[37] Tsujimura 1991; Poehler 2006; Newsome 2009; Kaiser 2011b.
[38] Newsome 2009; Hartnett 2011b.
[39] Kaiser 2011b offers a similar sentiment.
[40] Hor. *Epist.* 2.2.75.
[41] Pliny *NH* 8.208.
[42] van Tilburg 2007, 51–52, 72–74.

streets in the city – both wide and narrow – suggests that any animals "parked" in these spots could create a serious impediment to traffic, especially if they were still hitched to a cart or wagon.[43]

When we shift focus to movement along the street by human pedestrians, our sources usually present an image of traffic at its thickest. Typical is Juvenal's narrator: as he tries to make his way along Rome's streets, Umbricius is blocked in front, bumped from the back, and bashed or besplattered by all manner of objects.[44] Seneca, writing of Rome, presents a vision that takes only a small step back:

> Ponder this city, in which the crowd that flows without interruption through the broadest streets is crushed whenever anything stands in the way to hinder its course as it pours like a speedy river.[45]

The necessity of lictors to accompany magistrates and to assist them in making their way through Rome's streets further implies the crowded nature of the city's thoroughfares and the need, at times, for force to make one's way along.[46] Without such helpers, Horace says that he has to start pushing, a tactic resorted to by one of Plautus's characters as well.[47] And some authors discuss pedestrians' ceding parts of the sidewalk to one another.[48]

Of course, we cannot simply take these anecdotes at face value and presume that streets were always so choked with foot traffic; our authors were certainly more likely to complain about the worst conditions than to remark at all about what was normal. Nevertheless, elements of the material remains are suggestive. Stepping stones are set in the roadbed to permit pedestrians to cross from one sidewalk to another, presumably to limit stepping down and then up again, but also probably because the street surface itself was quite messy with waste, mud, and the like. I take up these issues to a greater extent in a future chapter, but for now it is enough to recognize that, if the roadbed offered an undesirable surface, pedestrians were forced onto sidewalks that were quite narrow, on average less than 2 meters in width on each side of the street.[49] Such realizations make our literary sources, with their fairly consistent image of what traffic

---

[43] Weiss 2010, esp. 367–371. The *Digesta* (21.1.40–42) forbids dangerous animals from being tied up along public thoroughfares (*quo vulgo iter fiet*) because they might injure someone or cause other damage. Dogs, hogs, wild boars, wolves, bears, panthers, and lions are mentioned specifically, which implies that others were permitted.

[44] Juv. 3.243–248.

[45] Sen. *Clem.* 1.6.1: *cogitato, in hac civitate, in qua turba per latissima itinera sine intermissione defluens eliditur, quotiens aliquid obstitit, quod cursum eius velut torrentis rapidi moraretur* . . .

[46] E.g., Livy 6.38.6; Juv. 3.128–129. For later depictions of busy streets in smaller cities, see Aus. *Ep.* 6.19–24; Lib. *Ant.* 172.

[47] Hor. *Sat.* 2.6.27–31; Plaut. *Merc.* 111–119.

[48] Hor. *Sat.* 2.5.15–18; Plut. *Rom.* 20.3.

[49] See "Benches as Obstructions" in Chapter 6.

could look (and feel) like at its densest, seem less hyperbolic.[50] Yet these voices also prompt us to consider what conditions led to frequent use of the street as a passageway and whether those circumstances were present in the cities that are the focus of this book. In other words, it is useful to change focus from the streets themselves and to concentrate on urban inhabitants, their fundamental necessities, and the frequency with which they took to the streets to obtain those goods and services.

Urban life in the twenty-first-century West — with cars, semipermanent delivery systems for utilities, and some control over dangers such as fire — makes it easy to forget how venturing through the city for basic provisions was a crucial part of Roman daily life. Although water was channeled into some houses at Herculaneum and Pompeii after those cities were fed by aqueducts, a large portion of the urban population collected water from the dozens of civic fountains scattered throughout the urban fabric.[51] For foodstuffs, a similar structure was in effect. Wilhelmina Jashemski's pioneering excavations of Pompeian gardens have shown that a surprising portion of the city's intramural area was devoted to growing comestibles. The evidence also suggests, however, that heavy horticulture was limited to the city's periphery and that most households bought produce from purveyors outside the house, whether in a shop, along the street, or in a central marketplace.[52] Without electric refrigeration, decomposition and spoilage were concerns, and, as Tacitus comments in an aside of his narration of Vespasian's reign, taking to the street to shop for foodstuffs was a daily activity.[53] Much the same situation held true for bread, a staple of the Roman diet; many city dwellers relied on commercial bakeries, thirty-three of which have been identified at Pompeii. These could offer the final product, bake dough prepared by the customer, or simply furnish ground wheat.[54]

That said, an underappreciated social distinction in Roman urban life was the extent to which one could prepare and eat food in one's dwelling. Fire was a constant foe in cities, and within cramped living quarters cooking or baking with an open flame — even one well-contained in a brazier — was a risky endeavor.[55] The great proliferation of street-side food and drink establishments in Roman cities testifies all the more strongly to how often city dwellers

---

[50] For the scholarly debate concerning the "realism" of satiric portrayals of the Roman city, see Scobie 1986; Laurence 1997; Scheidel 2003.

[51] Laurence 2007, 45–52; Eschebach 1982; Eschebach and Schäfer 1983. Private uses of water: Jones and Robinson 2004 and bibliography therein.

[52] Horticulture and its proliferation in Pompeii: Jashemski 1979, 1993. Urban food production more generally: Purcell 1987.

[53] Tac. *Hist.* 4.38: *vulgus alimenta in dies mercari solitum* . . .

[54] Mayeske 1972; Laurence 2007, 67–71.

[55] Risk of fire: e.g., Juv. 3.6–9, 193–203; Aul. Gell. 15.1.1–3. Legal steps to prevent fire: *Dig.* 1.15.3.4, 19.2.11.1. On fires in general: Robinson 1992, 34–38, 105–110.

procured nourishment on the street. In the excavated portions of Pompeii, there are over 150 fixed bars, which are identifiable by stone counters, at times inset with vessels and outfitted with small ovens.[56] How abundant were these bars? Estimating the city's population is a notoriously fickle proposition, but even a conservative estimate suggests that there was one food and drink establishment for every 55–90 urban residents.[57] To these we likely need to add still more points of sale for comestibles that do not appear in the material record, such as ambulant salespeople or those who prepared food from improvised stands, as happens regularly in many modern settings, such as Mexico City.[58] As a simple point of comparison, there is 1 restaurant for every 340 people in the United States, and 1 in every 213 Italians works as a *barista*.[59] But the situation at Pompeii, at least as evidenced by the archaeological remains, bears closer similarities to the developing world, where there was, in 1983, 1 street food enterprise for every 14 inhabitants of Bogor, Indonesia; 1 enterprise for every 48 inhabitants of Iloilo in the Philippines, and 1 enterprise for every 69 residents of Manikganj, Bangladesh; in Mexico in 2000, 1 of every 70 people in the population worked as a street food vendor.[60] As the hungry set out for a bite to eat, Roman food and drink establishments both helped to generate a significant amount of street traffic and benefitted from passing pedestrians as well.

Just as much food was prepared and consumed outside the household, so, too, did specialized production extend to other realms of urban life, with its own effects on street life. The electoral posters painted along Pompeii's streets – in which candidates for office were endorsed, sometimes by members of specific trades – demonstrate how much manufacturing and how many services were the purview of specific tradespeople. We encounter goldsmiths, cloth makers and dyers, barbers, fullers, chicken sellers, and mat makers among others.[61] Martial's vivid corpus echoes this list and adds others: bankers, cobblers, salt-fishmongers, and undertakers.[62] Whereas we – in an age of mass transit, automotives, modern amenities, and mega-stores selling everything from sushi to car batteries – can obtain many of the most fundamental

---

[56] Ellis 2004.

[57] On the problems of estimating Pompeii's population: Wallace-Hadrill 1994, 95–103. My figure is based on an estimate of 10,000–15,000 intramural inhabitants and on the assumption that the 25 percent of the site not yet excavated, because it featured fewer main thoroughfares, did not maintain the same density of bars.

[58] See "The Street as an Economic Space" in Chapter 2.

[59] United States: *www.restaurant.org/research/facts*. Italian baristas: Settimo 1989, 7.

[60] Tinker 1997, 26 (Indonesia), 47 (Philippines), 76–80 (Bangladesh). Long-Solis 2007, 227–228 (Mexico).

[61] Goldsmiths: *CIL* 4.710. Carpenters: *CIL* 4.960. Cloth workers: *CIL* 4.864. Barbers: *CIL* 4.743. Fullers *CIL* 4.7164. Chicken sellers: *CIL* 4.373. Mat makers: *CIL* 4.7473.

[62] Banker: Mart. 2.57. Cobbler: 3.16, 9.73. Salt-fishmonger: 1.41.8, 4.86. Undertaker: 1.30, 2.61.

provisions of life with a minimum of contact with other people, much that was essential for Romans required transit through the streets to spatially distinct shops for specific services and for much procurement, production/processing, and redistribution of material goods.[63] That is, the pervasiveness of this specialization took many tasks out of the domestic sphere and spread them far and wide through the city, requiring people to head into the street and sending them hither and yon, rather than to one clearinghouse for goods. And traffic grows denser when we consider how the city as a whole was provisioned because many essentials of Roman life – foodstuffs such as wine, oil, produce, livestock, and wheat and other commodities, such as construction materials, wool, wood, and pottery – were not produced in sufficient quantities within cities, but instead were imported from the surrounding area.[64] The limits on wheeled transport in the Tabula Heracleensis suggests how much the traffic of materials into and out of a city was thought to add to streets already busy with pedestrians.

Urban transportation and traffic was more than an interlocking series of isolated starting points and destinations – the homes and shops, fields and fountains – that I have presented to this point. Scholarship on modern cities helps us weigh the spatial relationship between our beginnings and endings since work by city planners and theorists has focused on the neighborhood-level factors contributing to a vibrant street scene. Jane Jacobs, in her jeremiad against contemporary urban design principles, *The Death and Life of Great American Cities*, argued that a thorough mix of industrial, commercial, and residential buildings was imperative for fostering an active street life.[65] Previous planners – both those working on the ground and those, like Le Corbusier or Frank Lloyd Wright, with dreams of utopian cities – had often compartmentalized such activities neatly; they considered the feverish street life romanticized by Jacobs an inefficient slog.[66] A localized blend of uses, Jacobs maintained, helped street life flourish because it gave streetgoers a variety of destinations within a neighborhood, thus bringing together many people engaged in

---

[63] Holleran 2012, esp. 51–60.

[64] A tradition of analysis dating back at least to Max Weber holds the Roman city as a "consumer city," which is not the same as, but is related to, the phenomenon described here: Weber 1958; Finley 1973; Jongmann 1988; Parkins 1997. For an overview of production and consumption at Pompeii, see Laurence 2007, 62–81.

[65] Jacobs 1961, esp. 34–38, 152–177.

[66] Le Corbusier (1929) and Frank Lloyd Wright (1935) represent previous planning principles, although they have distinctly different visions of what a city should or could be. Le Corbusier, in his plan for "A Contemporary City," wished for a high-density urban setting complete with skyscrapers and greenspace, much like the garden city movement. Wright, by contrast, decried such crowding and instead, in his "Broadacre City," made the case for new "cities" to be formed by a wholesale reoccupation of the American rural landscape. What unites these diverse views, however, is a common belief that the segregation of different realms of life was required for proper urban life.

a variety of tasks, rather than relying on the ebb and flow of one particular activity – the rush-hour syndrome.

A movement that Jacobs helped to inspire and incubate – which is called New Urbanism for its departure from previous modes of envisioning and designing urban space – took her precept as one of its central tenets. In 1987, Allan Jacobs and Donald Appleyard sketched city-planning principles in "Towards an Urban Design Manifesto." It was their answer to the Athens Charter of 1943, which outlined planning for a machinelike city, and it sought to create (among other goals) active, lively, and communal spaces. The Manifesto advocates designing cities and neighborhoods with "an integration of activities – living, working, and shopping as well as public, spiritual, and recreational activities."[67] Exactly how this diverse use of streets should be brought about through design has been a matter of debate almost since the concept's original espousal. (Some have even noted the irony of attempting to design an organic cityscape.) But what remains clear and above the fray is the fundamental principle of what makes a busy street according to urban theory: a rich mix of many destinations and activities along a street and in a zone of a city.

The excavated cities of Campania fulfill these requirements. Pompeii has long drawn urban geographers and classical archaeologists interested in Roman urban land use. Hans Eschebach took up the issue by mapping various forms of use throughout the city. His categories are at times more strictly defined and less reflective of spatial realities than we might wish, but his plan shows that no sector of the city lacks commercial, industrial, and residential spaces.[68] Richard Raper both reinforced those conclusions and clarified them statistically by dividing the city into a grid rather than treating it, as Eschebach had, on a block-by-block basis. What emerges, in Raper's words, is "a continuum of indiscrete usage of space," as houses, garden plots, workshops, shops, and craftworks mingle in apparently random order.[69] Specialized studies have sharpened our image of particular segments of the urban economy, but, by and large, as Andrew Wallace-Hadrill has summarized the situation, there was "no real attempt at segregation or concentration beyond the tendency of shops to line the main roads and horticulture to cluster on the margins."[70] Little by

[67] Jacobs and Appleyard 1987. The complete list of goals: livability; identity and control; access to opportunity, imagination, and joy; authenticity and meaning; open communities and public life; self-reliance; and justice. Important texts in the vanguard of New Urbanism: Duany and Plater-Zyberk 1992; Katz 1994; Duany, Plater-Zyberk, and Speck 2001; Calthorpe and Fulton 2001.

[68] Eschebach 1975, 331–338. For a similar approach to Herculaneum, see Guadagno 1993, esp. 87–91 and Tav. 18.

[69] Raper 1977, 208.

[70] Wallace-Hadrill 1994, 136. Closer range studies: Robinson 1997; Schoonhoven 2006; Laurence 2007.

way of what we call zoning was present, as people of very diverse means lived cheek-by-jowl with one another, with spaces dedicated to commerce and industry also in the mix. This situation stands in contrast with what we know of many other ancient societies, such as China around the time of the Han Dynasty, where cosmological or other concerns segregated various activities or created compounds that restricted their residents' broader movement.[71] Pompeii's usage of space, meanwhile, was significantly heterogeneous on a neighborhood scale. Goods, services, and housing were not separated into delimited pockets, but instead spread with some regularity throughout the urban fabric.[72] On the whole, the city thus aligned closely with what urban planning theorists describe as optimal conditions for fostering busy streets. The same could be said for urban features beyond these categories, such as fountains and street shrines. Even if such localized resources made for shorter trips, they still required Pompeians to move about the city as part of their daily business, thus reinforcing the image gained from texts, legal sources, and the organization of the urban economy.

In conclusion, even as applying modern urban theory to the ancient remains offers a reassuring confirmation of what has emerged from texts and the material evidence, it also raises the question of the relationship between our modern experience on streets and what Romans encountered. First, we have to recognize that, in Roman cities, streets were simply much narrower than many to which we are accustomed, and the movement they accommodated took a wider variety of forms: different sorts of vehicles (animal-drawn or human-borne, of course, rather than automotive), pedestrians, and also animals walking on their own. Second, the Roman experience was bound to have been much more herky-jerky and inefficient, not just because of the uneven surface of the roadbed, but also due to the numerous obstacles both large and small. Closed streets, narrow alleyways, a lack of signage, and potential obstructions all suggest that, by contrast with our experiences, movement was slower and more interrupted. Third, our consideration of motion has sent people and animals throughout the city, yet these destinations were frequently not within buildings but stood on or near the street. Once someone was on the street, he or she was not quickly off it. Animals were hitched to sidewalks, and people sacrificed at altars, filled vessels at fountains, picked out produce, waited for friends, and found sustenance at bars. That is, our inquiry has introduced uses of the street beyond a simple artery for movement. Investigating those additional functions is the task of Chapter 2.

---

[71] Wheatley 1971; Skinner 1977; Smith 2007.
[72] La Torre 1988.

TWO

LIFE IN THE STREET

IN A POEM WRITTEN IN EPISTOLARY FORM TO HIS FRIEND FLORUS, Horace launches a litany of excuses for why he is a lousy correspondent. Among his reasons is the difficulty of life in Rome and the strain exacted by its streets:

> And anyhow, how do you think I can write poems in Rome, amidst so many cares and so many responsibilities? One man asks me to be his sponsor, another to leave behind all my duties and to hear what he's written: this one's lying sick on the Quirinal, that one's on the furthest part of the Aventine, and yet I've got to pay a visit to both. The distance is hardly convenient. "True, but the roads are clear, so there's nothing to stop you from thinking en route." Sure. First, a builder in a rage rushes by with mules and workmen; then a huge crane hoists a beam and a boulder; and then comes a funeral procession, jostling its way along with lumbering wagons; a mad dog scampers by this way, a muddy pig that: now go and think carefully on some melodious verse![1]

For our investigation of street life, at least two things are fascinating about Horace's portrait of urban life. First, the skeptical voice he embeds in his poem

[1] Hor. *Epist.* 2.2.65–76: *praeter cetera me Romaene poemata censes / scribere posse inter tot curas totque labores? / hic sponsum vocat, hic auditum scripta, relictis / omnibus officiis; cubat hic in colle Quirini, / hic extremo in Aventino, visendus uterque; / intervalla vides humane commoda. "verum / purae sunt plateae, nihil ut meditantibus obstet." / festinat calidus mulis gerulisque redemptor, / torquet nunc lapidem, nunc ingens machina tignum, / tristia robustis lucantur funera plaustris, / hac rabiosa fugit canis, hac lutulenta ruit sus: / i nunc et versus tecum meditare canoros.*

sees Roman streets in much the same way that plenty of scholarship on Roman cities has: they are relatively empty; they primarily offer a means of movement; and, when they are broad, few impediments or distractions will be present. Second, Horace's response confirms what we know intuitively even as we look at relatively desolate streets on archaeological sites – namely, that there was much and many that got in the way.

But who and what were present, and what pursuits they engaged in, can contrast markedly with what we normally experience in cities of the modern West. There is, of course, construction equipment – a timeless complaint, it seems – but also beasts of burden, people carrying materials, funerals lumbering along and aloud, and even loose animals. The scene depicts very little "normal" traffic: people like the poet trying to get from place to place. Aside from the contractor and his crew, the other participants use the street as a stage for ceremony, a staging ground for construction, or, for the animals, a refuge or home. It offers a reminder: when we try to imagine life on Roman streets, we may be tempted simply to look at narrow streets in Tuscan villages or in modern Rome and to replace cars, scooters, and strollers with carts, wagons, and the like. What we would miss is the presence and, as Horace reminds us, also the clamor and confusion caused by a whole host of other features of life in a preindustrial city.

This chapter examines the street as a venue unto itself. For reasons I set out in the Introduction, our vision of Roman urban life tends to focus on what unfolded within definable spaces – in baths, porticoes, the forum, houses, temple compounds, and the like – that were associated with specific spheres of life. But what about the spaces *between* these? One tendency, as I have already hinted, is to imagine streets being used simply as they were most obviously intended: as paths from one point to another. Yet viewing thoroughfares primarily as passageways is to risk importing the perspective of automobile-dominated cities. The following pages highlight the street's role as gathering spot, improvised economic zone, and parade route, among others. All in all, the distinct lack of regulation of the street, together with its stunning range and volume of activities and sensations, combined to forge a space that defied easy categorization and even inspired trepidation. To pass over the street's many nonmotive functions, in other words, is to miss out on an important slice (or several) of urban life.

SOCIALIZING IN THE STREET

Martial, like Horace, bewails the difficulty of composing poetry amid the activity of the city. He laments in 12.57: "For a poor man there's no place in the city for thinking, none for relaxing."[2] And then, tapping into a common

---

[2] Mart. 12.57.2–3: *Nec cogitandi, Sparse, nec quiescendi / in urbe locus est pauper.* . . .

trope of contrasting urban distractions with rural bliss and productivity, he duly catalogs the noises that distract a potential poet.[3] Although the city's sonic environment will be my topic at the end of this chapter, I want to begin by taking up another question raised by Martial: where did city dwellers pass what downtime they had? We know that a fair portion of each grand house was dedicated to potential leisure spaces – reception or dining spaces that look onto a colonnaded and well-manicured garden – and that this impulse was manifested more humbly in smaller dwellings.[4] In these spots, property holders could find peace, some greenery, and a bit of insulation from the city. But where did others find similar relief: those who lived crammed into apartments, those who had no dedicated space of their own in a grand house, or those who slept on mats spread on a shop floor?

Martial offers conflicting answers. While 12.57 claims there is no place for the poor to rest, another poem describes the places and activities the poet (a self-styled pauper) and his companion (also named Martial) would seek out in the city if they could lead their ideal life:

> If I, dear Martial, could enjoy carefree days with you, and if we could pass time at leisure together, and if we both alike had a chance at true living, we wouldn't know anything about the halls and mansions of the powerful, nor gloomy lawsuits and the miserable forum, nor arrogant death-masks: but instead exercising, swapping stories, books, the field, the portico, the shade, the Virgin, the baths – these would be our daily spots, these our labors.[5]

Several of the places Martial names – the portico and the baths, to be sure – were structures designed to offer repose to city dwellers. And they no doubt did, in substantial numbers, because amenities of this sort were hallmarks of Roman urbanism, and many sources attest to their appeal.[6] Yet such spots dedicated to urban relaxation were not always convenient. They might be open only at certain times of day, custodians might control access, or they might be too far away for a short break, especially for someone charged with keeping watch on a property.[7] At Pompeii, for instance, non-bath green spaces were located primarily near the city's edge.

---

[3] Other poems in Martial's corpus focus on noises as well, particularly in reference to sleep: 1.49.31–36, 9.68.

[4] Wallace-Hadrill 1994, 17–61, 82–87.

[5] Mart. 5.20.1–10: *Si tecum mihi, care Martialis, / securis liceat frui diebus, / si disponere tempus otiosum / et verae pariter vacare vitae, / nec nos atria nec domos potentum / nec litis tetricas forumque triste / nossemus nec imagines superbas; / sed gestatio, fabulae, libelli, / campus, porticus, umbra, Virgo, thermae, / haec essent loca semper, hi labores . . . .* Cf. Mart. 10.47, 12.18; Hor. *Epist.* 2.7.

[6] Porticoes: E.g., Ovid, *Ars Am.* 1.67–88, 3.387–392; *Am.* 2.2.3–4; Prop. 2.31–32. Baths: E.g., Sen. *Ep.* 56.1–2. Cf. Yegül 1992, 30–47; 2010, 1–20; Fagan 1999, 1–84.

[7] Opening times: *CIL* 2.5181. Guards: Macauley-Lewis 2008, 105–106. Cf. Ov. *Tr.* 3.1.67–68; *Her.* 1.14.2–3.

Where else might people catch their breath in the city? The other locations Martial mentions are characterized by their improvised nature – the open space of the *campus*, a bit of shade, or under the arches of an aqueduct (if that is what he meant by the Virgo).[8] Horace concurs in a similarly wistful passage that grants advice to a young man: "Now again seek out the playing field and the public squares and, at the agreed hour, the soft night-time whispers."[9] These sources prompt us, when looking for popular haunts, to search beyond the purpose-built.

Streets offered another popular extempore arena for socializing, for passing time, and for hanging out. Although poets do not grow especially reminiscent about the practice, it is attested by abundant evidence, both more and less direct. Writing about Rome at a later date and from an infamously slanted perspective, Ammianus Marcellinus places the "idle and slothful commons" in public spaces including streets.[10] He pictures them (some shoeless) occupied with wine and dice, frequenting no-good haunts, enjoying games and other pleasures, and being particularly obsessed with the Circus. He continues:

> It's possible to see many groups of them gathered in the forum, the cross-roads, the streets, and their other meeting places, engrossed in feverish quarrels among themselves, some (as you'd expect) defending this, others that.[11]

Earlier sources are less direct in placing loiterers on streets, but what they describe speaks both to the frequency of this phenomenon and to elite attitudes (and indeed anxieties) about what we might call, in homage to the great urbanist William Whyte, "street corner society."[12] Horace, for instance, in a discussion of poetic voices in his *Ars Poetica*, writes of bringing satyrs out of the forest and introducing them to the city. He writes that they:

> should beware of behaving as they were though born at the crossroads and are forum-types, playing the role of the wanton youth with their verses or rattling off their bawdy and shameless jokes. After all, some folks are offended – knights, fathers of the country, and men of substance – and they do not greet warmly or reward with a crown everything that the buyers of roasted beans and nuts like.[13]

---

[8] Virgo: Howell 1995, 101.

[9] Hor. *Carm.* 1.9.18–20: *Nunc et Campus et areae / lenesque sub noctem susurri / composita repetantur hora.* Other potential hang-outs are evident when poets or others go looking for their friends in the city: Plaut. *Epid.* 196–200; *Amph.* 1009–1014; Catull. 55. To judge from graffiti in Pompeii's basilica, which leave a physical record of some friends playing ball, improvised and dedicated spaces overlapped: Benefiel 2008.

[10] Amm. Marc. 28.4.28: *Nunc ad otiosam plebem veniamus et desidem.* See Cracco Ruggini 2003 for discussion and prior bibliography.

[11] Amm. Marc. 28.4.29: *et videre licet per fora et compita et plateas et conventicula, circulos multos collectos in se controversis iurgiis ferri, aliis aliud, ut fit, defendentibus.*

[12] Whyte 1943.

[13] Hor. *Ars P.* 244–250: *silvis deducti caveant me iudice Fauni, / ne velut innati triviis ac paene forenses / aut nimium teneris iuvenentur versibus unquam, / aut immunda crepent ignominiosaque dicta: /*

Horace's picture of crass street language is paralleled by Cicero, who admonishes Cato that men of their stature should not throw around curses picked up from the city corner.[14] Other sources remove the human element and have the crossroads themselves speak. The narrator of Horace's *Satire* 2.3, for instance, gains great wealth in real estate, causing the crowded corners (*frequentia compita*) to give him the nickname of *Mercuriale*, something like "Mercury's pet."[15] And Propertius confides to his lover that "it's been seven full moons since every street corner started talking about you and me."[16]

If some poets embed communal knowledge in the urban fabric itself, others ascribe it to individuals. In his *Amores*, Ovid has the personification of Tragedy address the poet:

> O slow-witted poet, will love ever *not* be your subject? Boozy banquets talk of your worthlessness, so too do the crossroads of every street. Often someone lifts his finger to point out the poet, saying 'That's him, the one wild Love inflames!' You're the common story throughout the whole city, can't you tell? . . .[17]

Populated like this, the crossroads spread word quickly, according to texts like Juvenal's *Satires*. In one episode, a well-connected woman gets rumors from the city gates and shares them with whomever she meets at the street corner.[18] She simply seems a gossipy busybody, but another satire points more clearly to the potentially normative role of street discourse. The narrator discusses rich folk's difficulty in keeping secrets – even if their slaves do not spill the beans, he says, the horse, dog, doorposts, and marble furnishings will. Furthermore, Juvenal's narrator claims that slaves concoct stories in revenge for being lashed, and, "even if you're not interested, there'll always be someone seeking you out at the crossroads, ready to pour his drunken tale into your poor ear."[19] To avoid worrying about your slaves' tongues, the poet finishes, entails living a proper life.[20] In sum, Romans ascribed much to streets, corners, and their denizens. They assumed these spaces had their hangers-on, with a customary manner of speaking and a sort of collective, ever-spreading knowledge.

offenduntur enim, quibus est equus et pater et res, / nec, is quid fricti ciceris probat et nucis emptor, / aequis accipiunt animis donantve corona.
[14] Cic. *Mur.* 13.
[15] Hor. *Sat.* 2.3.25.
[16] Prop. 2.20.21–22: *septima iam plenae deducitur orbita lunae, / cum de me et de te compita nulla tacent.*
[17] Ov. *Am.* 3.1.16–21: *ecquis erit . . . tibi finis amandi, o argumenti lente poeta tui? / nequitiam vinosa tuam convivia narrant, / narrant in multas conpita secta vias. / saepe aliquis digito vatem designat euntem, / atque ait "hic, hic est, quem ferus urit Amor!" / fabula, nec sentis, tota iactaris in urbe . . .*
[18] Juv. 6.408–412. Cf. Hor. *Sat.* 2.6.50.
[19] Juv. 9.102–113 (quotation is 112–113): *nec derit qui te per compita quaeret / nolentem et miseram vinosus inebriet aurem.*
[20] For a development of this theme, see Hopkins 1993.

That such a street culture was present in Roman cities should not be surprising, even as it is little discussed by scholars, since comparative evidence from other cities around the Mediterranean and the globe demonstrates the common use of the street as a zone for socializing and generally passing the time. Scholars of Renaissance Florence, a city whose core maintained the orientation and dimensions of its Roman colony plan, point to the surprising amount of time Florentines spent in their city's public spaces, which functioned, as one scholar has put it, as "social clubs and living rooms for citizens from overlapping spheres of influence." Benches fronting civic buildings and private palazzi hosted, according to contemporary accounts, "patricians, low lifes, learned men, idlers, old men, young men, artists, clerics, and miscellaneous citizens."[21] Streets in modern India offer a wide range of services (e.g., dentists, barbers, letter-writers), play host to domestic tasks (such as collecting dung for fuel, washing clothes, cooking), and on certain occasions can become a "temporary stage where political dramas and religious observances are played out." Amid this, writes geographer Tim Edensor, the street also entails "more mundane social activities such as loitering with friends, sitting and observing, and meeting people."[22] In contemporary Manila, street activity is similarly vast; money-changers proliferate, for instance, and multitudes rent serialized comics and take spots on a wooden bench in what amount to outdoor reading rooms. This unique type of passing time is supplemented by many others, especially of the lower and middle classes, who soak in the street scene, "comfortably seated in lounging chairs, squatting on the pavement, or, often, perched strategically on top of a fire hydrant."[23]

For each case of loitering, the admixture of forces drawing people to the street is bound to be different yet we can recognize some common impetuses, starting with the climate. Around the Mediterranean and elsewhere, hot summer weather and the chance to catch a breeze encourage spending time outdoors. The street also promises an escape from tight living quarters that lack stimuli or that impose stifling pressures (of familial obligations, for instance, or of social expectations). Its general character as "neutral" turf grants the opportunity for communication with others – especially of different ages, sexes, and statuses – without the potential complications of inviting someone into the domestic realm. With such interaction, one might learn or share information, engage in what some scholars have called "interpretative observation," and identify opportunities for support or advancement. In societies with little or no organized communication system, this type of communication can be all the

[21] Elet 2002 (quotations from 445, 452). Cf. Cohen 2008; Laitinen and Cohen 2008.
[22] Edensor 1998, 206–208.
[23] David 1978 (quotation from 38).

more important. Finally, individuals seek out the street for the prospect of a "serendipitous and unscheduled experience."[24]

When we seek to delve more deeply into Roman loitering, we of course cannot generate the raw data and rich texture available from direct observation, nor can we dive into the archival material at our disposal for better documented historical situations. Instead, we are largely at the mercy of two very different types of evidence: *representations* in ancient texts of the "culture of popular sociability," as one scholar has described it, and the *trace physical remains* of such a way of passing time.[25] Yet together these sources help to document both the prevalence of life spent on the street as well as the power Romans ascribed to the people knotted together at corners.

An examination of the word Ammianus Marcellinus uses to describe the small clusters of plebs in the urban fabric, *circuli*, shows that street corner culture was more than a self-contained popular phenomenon. True, not every *circulus* is low-brow or street-bound; we read, for example, of a *circulus* "of learned men" who visit the emperor in his palace.[26] But authors normally use the word to describe a distinctly lower class and spontaneous gathering. To wit, Seneca draws meaningful contrasts in standing and location: "Toil draws out the best men. The senate is often in session the whole day long, though at the same time every useless bloke is either passing his leisure time in the *campus*, lurking in an tavern, or wasting his time in some *circulus*."[27]

Other voices join the chorus. Immediately following Ammianus Marcellinus's initial disparagement of the idle plebs, he probes *circuli* further. With a misguided sense of priorities, they rave hyperbolically about trivia:

> Among them, those who have lived long enough, who are more influential because of their long-standing authority, often shout, swearing by their hair and wrinkles that the state cannot remain if, in the upcoming contest, the charioteer for whom each roots does not jump out of the gates first and, together with his ill-omened horses, round the turning-post while clinging close to it.[28]

---

[24] "Interpretative observation": Suttles 1968, 73. "Serendipitous and unscheduled experience": Levitas 1986, 233.

[25] "Culture of popular sociability": O'Neill 2003, 135 on whom the following pages draw extensively.

[26] Aul. Gell. 4.1.1.

[27] Sen. *Prov.* 1.5.4: *labor optimos citat: senatus per totum diem saepe consulitur, cum illo tempore uilissimus quisque aut in campo otium suum oblectet aut in popina lateat aut tempus in aliquo circulo terat.* Cf. Porphyrio on Hor. *Sat.* 1.6.114: "men higher in *dignitas* would almost blush to stand in these *circuli* of common folk": *porro autem altiores dignitatis homines erubescunt fere in his vulgi circulis stare . . .*

[28] Amm. Marc. 28.4.30: *inter quos hi qui ad satietatem vixerunt, potiores auctoritate longaeva, per canos et rugas clamitant saepe, rem publicam stare non posse, si futura concertatione, quem quisque vindicat, carceribus non exsiluerit princeps, et inominalibus equis, parum cohaerentem circumflexerit metam.*

Peter O'Neill notes how portraying street-side groups as obsessed with unimportant matters made it easier for elites to belittle those people; it was, in O'Neill's words, "well suited to the Roman aristocracy's inclination not to recognize such popular spaces as a legitimate area for political discussion and communication."[29] A more delicate tiptoeing begins, however, when discussion turns to activities the *circuli* shared with elite Romans, such as being at leisure or convincing others of your opinion. For instance, a passage of Cicero's *De Finibus* sees the orator-cum-philosopher attacking men said to frequent *circuli*:

> Consider the most lethargic men: even those endowed with singular idleness always have both mind and body in constant motion; when they are free from all necessary occupations, they demand a gaming-board, go off to some sport, or look for a chat, seeking at some *circuli* or other gathering a substitute for noble and more intellectual delights.[30]

These *inertissimi homines*, so endowed with depravity, cannot win when it comes to Cicero, who famously criticized their manual labor and now gives them the business when they are at leisure.[31] But what was so different between these men and Cicero's circle when they enjoyed *otium* by conversing? Cicero answers by defining the former's topic in the negative – they lack discussion of important and learned matters.[32] Such line-drawing extends to manners of speaking. For Seneca, *circulus* speech is "rapid and overflowing" and not fit for "someone discussing and teaching a great and serious topic."[33] For Quintilian, some speakers address the dingy *circulus* with shouts, bellows, raised hands, running, panting, violent gestures, tossed heads, hand claps, feet stomps, and blows to the thigh, chest, and forehead. But the educated speaker, he continues, varies the tension, style, and material in his speech, keeping within the bounds of decency.[34] As with leisure, then, so with speech.

Perhaps such defensiveness was triggered by the recognition that these groups held potency. In Tacitus's *Agricola*, *circuli* are key arenas for discussion of pressing issues because they help spread the rumor that the title figure's death was hastened by poison administered at Domitian's command. Tacitus's implication

---

[29] O'Neill 2003, 152.

[30] Cic. *de Fin.* 5.56: *quin etiam inertissimos homines, nescioqua singulari nequitia praeditos, videmus tamen et corpore et animo moveri semper et, cum re nulla impediantur necessaria, aut alveolum poscere aut quaerere quempiam ludum aut sermonem aliquem requirere cumque non habeant ingenuas ex doctrina oblectationes circulos aliquos et sessiunculas consectari.* I thank an anonymous reviewer for pointing out that this disquisition actually occurs while Cicero and his interlocutors are in motion.

[31] Cicero's attitude toward labor: *Off.* 1.150–152.

[32] Similar charges could be leveled against rich folk with the wrong type of *otium*: e.g., Tac. *Ann.* 12.49 (*iners otium*); Sen. *Tranq.* 12.2–4; *Brev.* 12.

[33] Sen. *Ep.* 40.3: *sic itaque habe, istam vim dicendi rapidam atque abundantem aptiorem esse circulanti quam agenti rem magnam ac seriam docenti.*

[34] Quint. *Inst.* 2.12.9–11. Cf. Quint. *Inst.* 2.10.74.

is that the speech of *circuli*, although unauthorized, wielded influence.[35] Similarly, at uncertain times in Rome's history, Livy has people huddled in *circuli* to heatedly discuss next steps. Aemilius Paullus, before setting off to wage the Third Macedonian War, complains about the demoralizing talk "in *circuli* and in banquets." There are plenty of urban issues to talk about, Paullus says, and the city should limit itself to them.[36] Second-guessing in *circuli* extended to the army, for Livy describes clusters of soldiers and centurions roaring with discontent in *circuli* before they grow into a mob and congregate before their commander's tent.[37] In other words, as informal venues for passionate resistance, *circuli* were imagined as settings from which a formal movement could spring.

In the end, whatever we make of the ridicule and agency of *circuli*, their frequent mention aids in placing people in the street and marks their interaction as a recognized social phenomenon.[38] As O'Neill puts it, these passages testify to a "widespread popular culture of discussion" that unfolded spontaneously, without official leaders and in improvised spaces.[39] Our earlier focus on poetic voices suggested corner clutches gossiping about love affairs and the like. Examination of *circuli* adds another register. Because such gatherings triggered anxieties from our authors and attendant efforts to define themselves "as distinct from and superior to" the *circulus* and its denizens, we gain a sense of the groups' impact in the city's political and social arenas.[40] Like Juvenal's disquisition on gossip from slaves that leaked into the street, such sources show that street culture mattered a great deal for those both high and low.

SPOTS FOR CONGREGATING

Because loitering on the street appears a common feature of Roman urban life, it prompts a question: where might knots of urbanites have gathered? One answer is simply wherever they bumped into one another. Many such locations of chance encounters are virtually untraceable; even as we suspect that attractions such as fountains drew people outdoors, we can usually only hazard guesses.[41] But evidence from Pompeii and Herculaneum does point to specific spots where people passed the time. One prime location must have been the space around the cities' numerous food and drink stands. These spaces took various shapes and sizes, but many made the most of extremely

---

[35] Tac. *Agr.* 43.1–3.

[36] Livy 44.22.

[37] Livy 7.12.14. Cf. Livy 34.37.1.

[38] Indeed, at several points when *circuli* are mentioned, their existence is treated as customary: e.g., SHA *Prob.* 10.

[39] O'Neill 2003, 162.

[40] O'Neill 2003, 162.

[41] But see Viitanen, Nissinen, and Korhonen 2013.

limited dimensions, cramming service counters, storage, and sometimes also small ovens into narrow spots. One- or two-room establishments, which constitute more than half of the taverns thus far recovered, average approximately 35 square meters of floor space (about the size of an average American hotel room).[42] Few permanent seats were available; if a rear room were present, customers probably sat on wooden stools.[43] As a result, some customers were pushed outdoors to eat and drink around the establishment's door. Martial fingers bars for leaking beyond their thresholds: he claims that jugs are chained to shop columns and that dark *popinae* take over the streets.[44] Although Martial does not identify who or what seeps into the street, a series of paintings from a Pompeian tavern shows a squabbling pair of dice players who get shoved outside by the barkeeper when they come to blows[45] (Fig. 13). And masonry benches were occasionally built outside such shops, presumably to accommodate patrons who wanted to escape the smells, heat, and tight confines inside.[46] It is probably no coincidence that several sources cited earlier collocate bars and loiterers, for the authors likely saw around these establishments' doorways a penumbra of patrons gathered for various sorts of nourishment.

At Pompeii and Herculaneum, the distribution of street-side benches – outside bars and other types of properties – suggests their use as spots for loitering. As I will discuss further in Chapter 6, benches were concentrated disproportionately on the southern side of the street, where they offered a spot to escape the summer Mediterranean sun, which implies that they were built with sitters' comfort in mind[47] (Table 1).

It is likely no coincidence that elite authors sneer at *umbratici* (literal "shady characters") and contrast life in the shade to the public, sun-drenched work of waging war and conducting civic business.[48] Additionally, isolated benches are very rare. The constructions tend to cluster in certain portions of Pompeii, largely avoiding the zone around the forum and instead clumping together in the city's south and east. Of the 100 benches thus far discovered in the city, 76 were located within 10 meters of another bench; only 13 of the rest were further than 30 meters from their closest neighbor (Plate I). In the portion of Herculaneum that has been brought to light, 15 of the 18 street-side benches are within 10 meters of another bench, and the remaining 3 stand

---

[42] Ellis 2008. These data represent his A1, A1H, A2, A2H, B1, B1H, B2, and B2H types.

[43] Representations of bar seating appear in Pompeii: Fröhlich 1991, pls. 18.1, 19.1, 20.1, 62.2, 63.1. Literary sources for bar seating: Mart. 5.70.2–6; Juv. 8.172–178.

[44] Mart. 7.61.5–8.

[45] VI.14.36: Clarke 2003, 161–168.

[46] See below, "Benches and Buildings" in Chapter 6.

[47] Hartnett 2008a, 115–117. See also "Benches as Public Works" in Chapter 6.

[48] *Umbratici*: Plaut. *Curc.* 555–6; *Truc.* 611. Sun and shade contrast: Sen. *De Beat. Vit.* 7.3. Cf. Cic. *Tusc.* 2.27; Quint. 1.2.18; Mart. 10.12.

TABLE 1 *Number and length of street-side benches at Pompeii with respect to cardinal directions*

Side of Street	NNW	ENE	SSE	WSW
Number of Benches	25	19	42	14
Length of Benches	57.9 m	36.7 m	109.4 m	27.1 m

13. Arranged across the interior walls of the Caupona of Salvius in Pompeii (VI.14.36), four scenes display tavern activities, including a pair of dice players being ejected by the barkeep when they start fighting (far right).
Photo: Michael Larvey.

within 30 meters of another. Where there was one bench on which to loiter, in other words, there was almost always another within earshot. Thus positioned, benches certainly fostered a culture of street sociability. Moreover, such spots to congregate, even as they were often shaded, faced onto some of the widest and busiest streets in the city, appearing less frequently on quiet back alleys.[49] Such a trend chimes with comparative evidence from cities such as New York and Manila, where direct observation has shown that, when urbanites looking to sit are presented with the option of facing toward or away from street action, they predominantly choose to look toward it.[50] In Roman cities, the distribution of benches may be testifying to a parallel desire to soak in the street's action, even when a moment of quiet isolation was available.

Now, I am not arguing that each bench hosted loiterers or that benches were the only spot where *circuli* and the like passed the time. In fact, there are a couple of locations that we can pinpoint as loitering spots because of epigraphic evidence, and neither boasts benches. The first we find along a curving alleyway at Pompeii's heart, near the rear entrance to the city's largest public baths. Between the openings of an apparent wine sales point and a so-called *cella meretricia* was a façade fresco depicting a pair of huge snakes approaching a central altar.[51] Above the snakes was painted in white letters: *otiosis locus hic non est discede morator*, "This is no place for idlers; take off, loiterer"[52] (Figs. 14, 15). Whether the

14. Along the Vicolo del Lupanare in Pompeii, a small painted inscription above a fresco of serpents marks a potential spot for loitering nearby several attractive destinations, including an apparent wine shop (center) and *cella meretricia* (beyond painting).
Photo: author. Courtesy: Soprintendenza Speciale per Pompei, Ercolano e Stabia.

[49] Hartnett 2008a, 108–114.
[50] Whyte 1988, 103–131; Kato, Whyte, and David 1978, 2–6, 38, 64–65.
[51] Drink establishment (VII.11.13): *CIL* 4.814, 815. Cella: VII.11.12. The serpents, like their counterparts at domestic and neighborhood shrines, were probably intended to ward off harmful sentiments: Fröhlich 1991, F58.
[52] *CIL* 4.813.

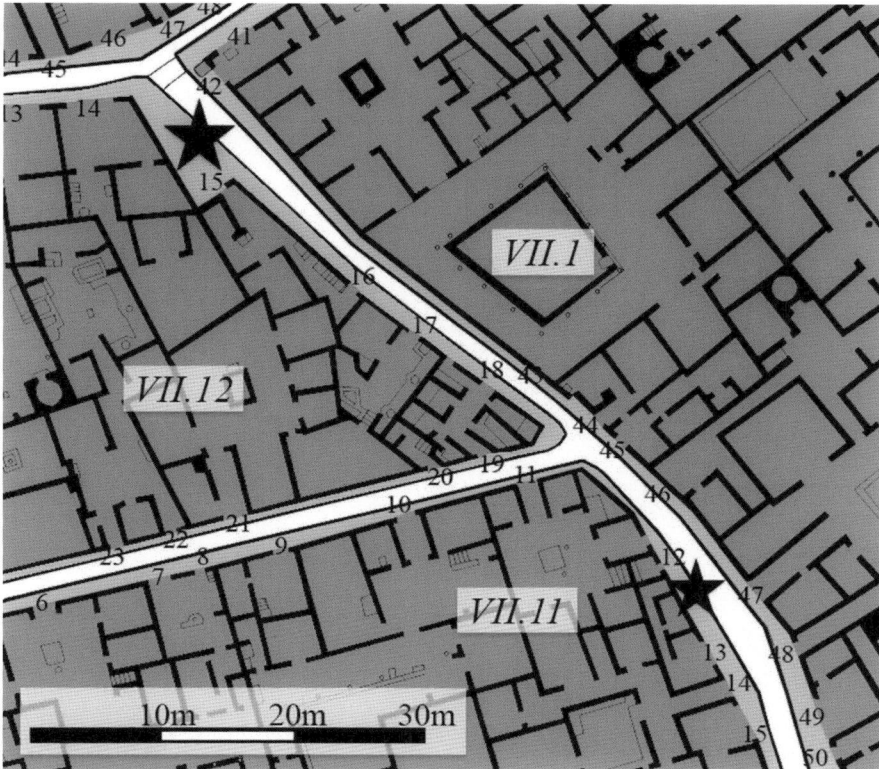

15. Two potential spots for impromptu gatherings stand along the Vicolo del Lupanare in Pompeii. A rich assortment of graffiti highlights a regular cast of characters in the triangular space fronting a bar (VII.12.15), and a small painted inscription locates idlers and loiterers (*otiosi*, *moratores*) outside VII.11.12, a cell for coupling with prostitutes. Both areas are marked by stars. Drawing: author.

moratores/otiosi were drawn by the bar, the bath, the mini-brothel, either of the two possible boarding-houses (*hospitia*) nearby, or the full-fledged brothel/ *lupanar* just up the street, the inscription indicates both that they milled about here and that they provided enough annoyance for someone to encourage them to move along.[53] Interestingly, the admonition nearly scans as hexameter, which could suggest that a degree of thought went into its composition or that the *dipinto* offered a common dictum frequently marshaled against gadabouts but only recorded here.[54]

If *otiosi* continued past the brothel, they passed along an alleyway that widened and then "t-ed" into a cross street to form a small triangular piazzetta. By contrast with the painted reproach down the street, here a host of positive remnants of loitering are documented, as posters painted on the walls and

[53] Potential *hospitia*: VII.11.11, 14; VII.1.44–45 (with *CIL* 4.806–807).
[54] Milnor 2014, 58.

16. Outside a food and drink establishment (VII.11.15), this small eddy in Pompeii's street system once hosted numerous graffiti and painted announcements, which mark it as a potentially popular site for congregating on the street.
Photo: author. Courtesy: Soprintendenza Speciale per Pompei, Ercolano e Stabia.

graffiti carved into the streetface reveal a spot brimming with life and apparently popular with a repeated cast (Figs. 15, 16). Announcements of gladiatorial games and electoral endorsements intermingle with more personal notices: a local cobbler is teased for sleeping when he should be canvassing for his patron, another man is twice called a *fellator*, and a second neighborhood cobbler is named as a bystander while the notice for the games was painted.[55] On the walls of the *lupanar* (whose owner is apparently among those mentioned in the inscriptions) and throughout the neighborhood, some of these figures reemerge. Sometimes they squabble – Salvius accuses Icarus of buggering Ampliatus, who was Icarus's master – and sometimes they hail one another as bosom buddies.[56] All in all, the scratched or painted barbs, jibes, and signs of bonhomie echo interactions that actually unfolded among this band as they hung out within a small eddy in the urban action.

These two examples are not alone. The sheer number of inscriptions found on Pompeian façades testifies indirectly to an active culture of street socializing that their content points toward even more directly. Aside from electoral posters, one of the most common "messages" involves graffiti in which one

[55] The cobbler Vespinus: *CIL* 4.636, 4.1190b. Ismenus *fellator: CIL* 4.2169–2170. Menacrates the sleeping cobbler client: *CIL* 4.822. For the full epigraphic flurry here: Franklin 1986.
[56] Buggering: *CIL* 4.2375. Other squabbles: *CIL* 4.1700, 4.2177. Salvius as buddy: *CIL* 4.2154–2155.

Pompeian greets another. For instance, an especially emotive graffito was written outside the doorway at I.10.7: "Secundus greets his Prima everywhere; I plead, my mistress, that you love me."[57] In the same neighborhood, an apparent response appears: "Prima sends very many greetings to Secundus."[58] These examples, in naming the salutation's greeter and recipient, are more elaborate than many, yet they give a small glimpse of the interactions that unfolded in streets as people took the time to greet one another, to visit, and, on occasion, to scratch a note to a friend.

To sum up, we saw that Martial's own corpus cast doubt on his claim that there was nowhere for a poor man to relax in the city. He names purpose-built spaces that scholars have also imagined as the chief haunts of the urban populace. Our inquiry highlights a different and vital realm of urban sociability that unfolded in improvised spaces. Street socializing is hard to trace because participants did not pass down their reflections and because the practice left few material remnants, yet the various evidence at our disposal does not consign lingerers to dim, hidden corners separate from the world of those who enjoyed leisure spaces within their own residences. In fact, street lingering was imbued with enough agency by our elite authors that it prompted self-justifying remarks and likely factored into their political calculus. In other words, street corner culture both encourages us to rethink what counts as "social space" by joining the devised to the designed, the outdoors to the indoors, and it also pushes us to reconsider the relationship between registers low and high.

Along those lines, our sources' frequent insistence that street lingerers were inert, doing nothing, or wasting their time is certainly wrong on at least two counts. First is a matter of interpretation: what looked like doing nothing to onlookers could have been important multitasking for participants as they ran into someone and began a conversation or as they caught a breath of fresh air or a bite to eat while stepping away momentarily from their shop or workshop. If we believe our elite sources, the Roman day had its rhythms, with time for forensic, salubrious, and convivial activities.[59] But for the lower classes, such a pattern was much less pronounced, and the separations between work and leisure were distinctly less severe than those since the Industrial Revolution. Accordingly, the Roman street offered them an arena that accommodated many needs simultaneously. Second is a matter of mischaracterizing: comparative evidence points to the key communicative role that street sociability plays in the lives of ordinary folk. Passing time on the street is not mere entertainment: it helps people interpret the world, share news, and identify chances to improve their lot. This was not formal work per se, but it certainly was an important tactic for navigating the challenges of urban life.

[57] CIL 4.8364: Secundus / Prim(a)e suae ubi / que isse salute(m) / rogo domina / ut me ames.
[58] CIL 4.8270: Prima Secu(n)do salute(m) plurima(m).
[59] Laurence 2007, 154–166.

THE STREET AS AN ECONOMIC SPACE

For a city's economic life, streets obviously offered the vital arteries through which goods and customers flowed among country, market, workshop, and household. Yet, as Claire Holleran has recently highlighted, the space between buildings also was a critical economic zone in its own right, as those hawking their wares were eager to profit from the street's crowds.[60] The street-as-market began with points of sale anchored in the urban fabric. A hallmark of commercial spaces was a threshold that spanned nearly the full width of a property and was outfitted with shutter-like doors that could be folded back or put away during hours of operation, thus blending interior and exterior space.[61] Such openness lit and ventilated shops while making both goods and workers part of the street scene. In fact, when merchants or craftspeople display themselves at work, typically on funerary monuments, they commonly show a street-side view of their workplace. Placing themselves amid their goods or tools, the proprietors both demonstrate pride in their livelihood and document the blurring of front- and backstage that resulted from the interior's visibility from the exterior (and vice versa).[62]

While eyes were drawn in, it appears that goods and merchandise frequently spilled out. On the one hand, the jurist Papinian requires that nothing be left outside of workshops, allowing only two exceptions, fullers' drying racks and carpenters' wheels, and permitting these only when a vehicle may still pass.[63] On the other hand, Papinian's opinion may have been wishful thinking, for Martial famously praises Domitian's intervention when Rome's thoroughfares were overcome by shops:

> The rash shopkeepers had taken over the whole city; no threshold stayed within its own threshold. You, Germanicus, ordered the narrow streets to expand and what had recently been an alleyway was made a road. No wine jugs are chained up to encircle columns, and the praetor does not have to walk straight through the mud anymore. The random razor is not whipped about in a thick crowd, nor does the grimy cook shop monopolize the whole street. The barber, the barman, the cook, and the butcher all respect their own thresholds. Now it is Rome, just recently it was one big shop.[64]

---

[60] Holleran 2012, 100–157, but esp. 194–231. The following pages draw extensively on Holleran's work.

[61] Ellis 2004, 2011; Holleran 2012, 100–105.

[62] E.g., Kampen 1981, 52–59.

[63] *Dig.* 43.10.1.4.

[64] Mart. 7.61: *Abstulerat totam temerarius institor urbem / inque suo nullum limine limen erat. / Iussisti tenuis, Germanice, crescere vicos, / et modo quae fuerat semita, facta via est. / nulla catenatis pila est praecincta lagonis / nec praetor medio cogitur ire luto, / stringitur in densa nec caeca novacula turba, / occupat aut totas nigra popina vias. / tonsor, copo, cocus, lanius sua limina servant. / nunc Roma est, nuper magna taberna fuit.*

Martial's contrast of alleyway (*semita*) with road (*via*) suggests how much a street's passability and character were at the mercy of commercial endeavors.[65]

Street commerce extended from vendors in buildings to others, like Martial's razor-wielding barber, who set up shop outdoors or peddled their wares while circulating throughout the city.[66] One famous legal hypothetical, for example, entails a street game that sends a kicked ball into a barber's arm, which jerks his razor to kill a slave he is shaving.[67] In another of Martial's poems, a *tonstrix*, a female barber who perhaps doubles as a prostitute, sets up her seat at the entrance to Rome's Subura.[68] Taking a well-known spot on the street, in fact, was a common strategy for those in the sex trade. Martial describes an auction for a girl who was "like those who sit mid-Subura" – code for prostitutes.[69] Catullus rails against his former lover by imagining her as a streetwalker: "that Lesbia, whom alone Catullus loved more than himself and all his own, now in the crossroads and in the alleyways services the grandsons of great Remus."[70] Scattered through Pompeii, but clustered especially toward the middle of the city, were small cell-like rooms separated from the sidewalk by little more than a curtain or wooden door. Called *cellae meretriciae* by scholars (we do not know what Pompeians called them), they contained a masonry "bed," which presumably was padded with pillows or a straw mattress, where prostitutes coupled with clients they met on the street[71] (Fig. 17).

Other forms of improvised labor expand and enliven the street as a prime arena in the urban economy. Because slaves and the recently freed satisfied much of a city's labor demand, argues Holleran, many freeborn poor were left to scratch out livelihoods however they could. Work in the construction industry probably offered day-to-day relief to some, but those with few other options often improvised or hawked goods on the street.[72] Prostitution can be seen in this light; although prostitutes were frequently slaves or ex-slaves, our sources repeatedly describe free women resorting to selling sex because of poverty. A character in Terence, for instance, bemoans a father's lack of

---

[65] Libanius (*Or.* 11.254) brags of the commercial activity in Antioch by noting how full its porticoes are full of wooden stalls.

[66] The work of Holleran (2011a; 2012, 223–230) is fundamental for such itinerant sellers. I draw on it extensively.

[67] *Dig.* 9.2.11.pr. Vitruvius (*De Arch.* 9.8.2.8) describes barbers in *tabernae*.

[68] Mart. 2.17. If she existed, she may well have done both jobs, since, as legal texts acknowledge, only the haziest line separated barmaid or flute girl from prostitute: McGinn 2004, 7–9, 14–30 (esp. 16 n. 6).

[69] Mart. 6.66.1–3: *famae non nimium bonae puellam, / quales in media sedent Subura, / vendebat modo praeco Gellianus.*

[70] Catull. 58.2–5: *illa Lesbia, quam Catullus unam / plus quam se atque suos amavit omnes, / nunc in quadriviis et angiportis / glubit magnanimi Remi nepotes.* See also Hor. *Carm.* 1.25.10; Plaut. *Cist.* 330–331. Cf. Prop. 4.7.15–20.

[71] McGinn 2004, 215–217 and map 2 (for possible locations).

[72] Holleran 2011a, 252–253; 2011b; 2012, 23–38.

17. Small, one-room *cellae meretriciae*, such as this one at Pompeii (VII.11.12), were immediately accessible from the street and separated prostitutes and clients from the street with little more than a curtain.
Photo: Sarah Levin-Richardson

judgment with regard to his son's spending and its effects: "instead of allowing your son to visit a young woman, who was content with very little and took everything as a favor, you frightened him away from home. After that she quite reluctantly began to make a living upon the town."[73] Necessity also drove others to endure the grind of collecting and redistributing cast-off goods: some rounded up scraps of fabric; others dealt in broken glass, presumably for

[73] Ter. *Haut.* 443–447: *primum olim potius quam paterere filium / commetare ad mulierculam, quae paullulo / tum erat contenta quoique erant grata omnia / proterruisti hinc. ea coacta ingratiis / postilla coepit victum volgo quaerere.* Also: Ter. *An.* 70–79; Procop. *Aed.* 1.9.4–5; *Dig.* 23.2.43.5.

remelting; and *scrutarii* scavenged and resold second-hand goods – one person's trash, another's treasure – perhaps after making small repairs. Not surprisingly, when sources describe garbage pickers, it is with a distinct sense of disparagement. Quoting Lucilius, Aulus Gellius writes: "The rascal: to sell his trash, the huckster lauds half a shoe, a split strigil."[74]

But ambulant merchants also sold goods available in shops, a range that encompassed both necessities and odder items alike. Cloth and clothing were commonly available from street vendors, and one passage from the *Digesta* offers what may have been a common arrangement between their production and sale:

> The name of *institor* has been applied to those whom we commonly call peddlers, people to whom tailors and cloth merchants entrust clothes to carry around and to sell piecemeal.[75]

Street retailing of bulk-manufactured goods extended to another major category of goods for sale in public places, namely foodstuffs, for bakeries apparently sent vendors out into the city.[76] Sellers of prepared foods – ranging from sausages and boiled chickpeas to cakes and cheese – set up in crowded areas or made their way through the city's busiest haunts.[77] And we hear of vendors of fish and raw produce bargaining with customers in public places.[78] Yet the goods that peddlers offered for sale were not always cheap essentials; one source describes them as *delicatae merces*, and they extended to wigs as well as unguents extracted from Egyptian palm trees.[79]

While *circitores* and *ambulatores* made their way around a city, *circulatores* spread out a cloth or set up a table in a busy spot from which they would not

---

[74] Aul. Gell. 3.14.10.6 (quoting Lucil. 1282): *et scruta quidem ut vendat scrutarius laudat, praefractam strigilem, soleam improbus dimidiatam.* Broken glass: Mart. 1.41.3–5, 10.3.3–4; Stat. *Silv.* 1.6.73–74. Fabric: Vout 1996, 211–212; Liu 2009, 62–63. See also Hor. *Epist.* 1.7.65; Apul. *Met.* 4.8.27.

[75] *Dig.* 14.3.5.4: *sed etiam eos institores dicendos placuit, quibus vestiarii vel lintearii dant vestem circumferendam et distrahendam, quos vulgo circitores appellamus.* Other cloth and clothing vendors: Pliny *NH* 18.225.3; Juv. 7.221. Plautus (*Aul.* 505–516) comically presents an image of great specialization as one of his characters pictures an urban house under siege from creditors, among them the dealers in flounces, underclothes, and bridal veils; in violet dyes and yellow dyes; in muffs or shoes smelling of balsam; the lingerie dealers; shoemakers; cobblers; slipper and sandal makers; dealers in mallow dyes; belt and girdle makers. It is not clear, however, how many of these merchants were street hawkers.

[76] *Dig.* 14.3.5.9.

[77] Food for sale: Mart. 1.41.5–10; Apul. *Met.* 8.19; Calp. *Ecl.* 5.97; Petron. 7; *CIL* 6.9683; Sen. *Ep.* 56.2 (although in the bath, not on the street).

[78] Haggling: Sen. *Ben.* 3.17.1; *Ep.* 42.8; Apul. *Met.* 1.24–25. Patronizing street hawkers was disparaged as uncouth, to judge from Cicero's portrait of his enemy Piso. The orator (*Pis.* 67) pictures his opponent's house as replete with tacky luxury, such as elderly slaves, couches packed with Greek guests drinking unwatered wine, and bread bought from a vendor.

[79] *Delicatae merces*: Sen. *Ben.* 6.38.3. Wigs: Ovid *Ars Am.* 3.167. Unguents: Pliny *HN* 12.103.6.

soon get booted.[80] At Pompeii, inscriptions mark out temporary points of sale, such as under the arches of the city's amphitheater, which during games were prime locations.[81] Meanwhile, vendors scribbled graffiti to claim spots outside the city's basilica, where many people passed on broad sidewalks near the town's center.[82] Even though it likely romanticizes the space's operations, a painted representation of the city's forum from the Praedia of Julia Felix does offer a picture of street vendors' operations[83] (Plate II). Standing figures hold cloth and display it to customers. A peddler is surrounded by pots and other metal objects; he converses with one customer while a second inspects a vessel's interior. Another vendor sits on a wooden bench before a blanket on which lies a neat array of metal utensils. Such scenes may have unfolded in the forum only on market days yet were more regular occurrences throughout the city's streets.

Competing for attention and money from the street's crowd were those who lacked goods to pawn. Teachers held class.[84] Entertainers juggled, danced, handled snakes, and engaged in philosophical discussion for money.[85] In a dinner discussion in Apuleius's *Metamorphoses*, one participant narrates a lively scene:

> not long ago in front of the Stoa Poikile in Athens, with my very eyes I watched a street performer swallow an extremely sharp cavalry sword with a lethal edge; and soon after I saw the same fellow, for a skimpy price, bury a hunting spear down to the very bottom of his gut, business end first. Then out of the blue, above the metal part of the spear, where the staff of the upside-down weapon rose from his mouth toward the top of his head, a girlishly handsome boy climbed up and unleashed a curvy and boneless dance, twisting and turning, which all we onlookers admired.[86]

Despite some extreme aspects of the story – which was intended to impress fellow guests, after all – the episode nevertheless conjures an image of the spectacles that could unfold in public places in hopes of some small payment. These performers shared space with fortune-tellers, "neighborhood

---

[80] Holleran 2011a, 254.
[81] *CIL* 4.1096, 4.1115, 4.1129–30, 4.2485. In the famed depiction of the riot between Pompeians and Nucerians in 59 CE, wooden stalls also appear near the structure.
[82] *CIL* 4.1768–9. Cf. *CIL* 4.8432–3.
[83] Nappo 1991.
[84] Hor. *Ep.* 1.20.17–18; Dio Chrys. 20.9–10. Cf. Mart. 9.68, 12.57.4–5; Sen. *Ep.* 29.7.1.
[85] Mart. 1.41.7; *Dig.* 47.11.11.pr.1; Sen. *Ben.* 6.11.2; Tert. *Apol.* 23.1; *Priap.* 19.
[86] Apul. *Met.* 1.4: *et tamen Athenis proximo et ante Poecilen porticum isto gemino obtutu circulatorem aspexi equestrem spatham praecutam mucrone infesto devorasse; ac mox eundem invitamento exiguae stipis venatoriam lanceam, qua parte minatur exitium, in ima viscera condidisse. et ecce pone lanceae ferrum, qua bacillum inversi teli ad occipitium per ingluviem subit, puer in mollitiem decorus insurgit inque flexibus tortuosis enervam et exossam saltationem explicat, cum omnium qui aderamus admiratione.*

soothsayers," and interpreters of dreams, who "sell you whatever dreams you want for a tiny coin."[87]

Appealing to the crowd to spare a coin or a scrap of food were those rendered infirm by age, accident, or birth, as well as those lacking goods or services to sell. In a satire about the absurdities of patron–client relationships, Juvenal ridicules a client's lack of shame in fishing for a dinner invitation: "Isn't there an empty sidewalk? Isn't there a bridge or the smaller half of a divided mat somewhere?" A beggar's lot, claims the poet, would be more dignified than what the client undergoes.[88] According to Dio Chrysostom, who traveled widely as a mendicant, begging and comedy could go hand in hand, at least for self-fashioned Cynics, who:

> post themselves at street-corners, in alleyways, and at temple-gates, pass round the hat, and play upon the credulity of lads and sailors and crowds of that sort, stringing together rough jokes and much tittle-tattle and that low badinage that smacks of the marketplace.[89]

But others, bound by poverty and without access to sound medical care, were reduced to pathetic desperation. One lost soul, when rediscovered, is described as "deformed by paleness and gaunt almost to the point of being unrecognizable, like those bad-luck victims who are always begging at street corners."[90] A lost or broken limb was intended to incite generosity, as were children, whom parents might exhibit in the hopes of stirring pity.[91] The elder Seneca proffers a *controversia* in which a man rounds up exposed children, disfigures or maims them, and then sets them begging on the street.[92] The point of debate in this heinous hypothetical is the ringmaster's culpability with regard to the state, but the situation hinges on the vulnerability of children in a society without a formal safety net, under extreme circumstances such as the death of a parent or a downturn in family fortunes. Because of Roman practices of slavery and adoption, exposed or destitute

[87] Cic. *Div.* 1.132; Hor. *Sat.* 1.6.113–114; Plaut. *Mil.* 692–4; Juv. 6.542–7 (quotation from 546–7): *aere minuto qualiacumque voles . . . somnia vendunt.*

[88] Juv. 5.8–9: *nulla crepido vacat? nusquam pons et tegetis pars dimidia brevior?.* Cf. Juv. 9.140. On begging and alms-giving: Parkin 2006.

[89] Dio Chrys. *Or.* 13.1 (experience); 32.9 (quotation): οὗτοι δὲ ἔν τε τριόδοις καὶ στενωποῖς καὶ πυλῶσιν ἱερῶν ἀγείρουσι καὶ ἀπατῶσι παιδάρια καὶ ναύτας καὶ τοιοῦτον ὄχλον, σκώμματα καὶ πολλὴν σπερμολογίαν συνείροντες καὶ τὰς ἀγοραίους ταύτας ἀποκρίσεις (translation: J. Cohoon, H. Crosby). Cf. Luc. *Cyn.* 1.

[90] Apul. *Met.* 1.6: *paene alius lurore ad miseram maciem deformatus, qualia solent fortunae decermina stipes in triviis erogare.* Bridges and sloped thoroughfares – where the flow of people, animals, and vehicles might slow – appear to have been especially popular spots for the indigent, perhaps heaped together with their possessions, to implore those passing by: Juv. 3.15–16, 4.117, 14.134; Mart. 2.19.3, 10.5.3, 12.32.14, 12.32.35.

[91] Injured limbs, actual or feigned: Hor. *Epist.* 1.17.58–62 (with a strong response from neighbors); Mart. 12.57.12. Parkin 2006, 70–74 for additional sources.

[92] Sen. *Controv.* 10.4. Other child beggars: Mart. 12.57.13; *Dig.* 25.3.4.

children may have been absorbed into households more frequently in Roman cities than in others renowned for their street children, such as Mexico City or Bangalore.[93] Nevertheless, Rome had a higher child mortality rate, which meant that a greater percentage of urban inhabitants were children and that poor youth on the street were likely very common.[94] They and other beggars were literally overlooked, suggests Seneca. In his treatise on mercy, he writes that a "wise man" will hand over alms to needy:

> he will not do as the greater part of those who wish to be seen as pitiful do – fling their handouts, loathe the ones they help, and fear being touched by them ... [the wise man] will not cast away his gaze or his sympathy from anyone because of his withered leg or his wrinkled face, and because, in his old age, he is propped up by a staff.[95]

The beggar, shriveled and starving to death, could have been a common sight for anyone who was looking.

This discussion of the urban destitute brings up the street's potential use as housing. "Improvised habitations" – as the United Nations designates the shantytowns of Lagos and other megalopoleis – hosted indigent Romans who similarly assembled discarded materials into makeshift structures of a type described in Vitruvius and others.[96] Outside city walls, some took refuge in tombs or used them as parts of huts or lean-tos.[97] Inside the city, analogous shelters may have been constructed here and there, as happened in Prusa in Bythinia, according to Dio Chrysostom, who characterizes the constructions as "disgraceful, ridiculous ruins, much more lowly than the sheds under which the flocks take shelter ... shanties, moreover, in tumbledown condition, held up by so many props, so that at the stroke of the hammer they quivered and threatened to fall apart."[98] Although dating much later than Dio's speech, the Theodosian Code is nevertheless suggestive. It required lean-tos abutting public or private buildings to be torn down because they posed a risk of fire, narrowed streets, or infringed on porticoes.[99] We lack material evidence for such dwellings as we do also for people who simply slept

---

[93] Mexico City: Magazine 2003; Peralta 2009. Bangalore: Nieuwenhuizen 2006. Poor children in Roman urban settings: Laes 2011, 200–206.

[94] Children, demographics, and urban life: Laes 2011, 22–49.

[95] Sen. *Clem.* 2.6.2–3: *non hanc contumeliosam, quam pars maior horum, qui misericordes videri volunt, abicit et fastidit, quos adiuvat, contingique ab iis timet ... vultum quidem non deiciet nec animum ob crus alicuius aridum aut pannosam maciem et innixam baculo senectutem.*

[96] UN definition: Curriero 2001, 1194. Roman huts, etc.: e.g., Vitr. 2.1.4–5; Apul. 9.32; *Dig.* 50.16.180.

[97] *Dig.* 47.12.3, 47.12.3.11. Cf. Luc. 6.511–512.

[98] Dio Chrys. *Or.* 40.8–9: ἀλλ᾽ οὐκ αἰσχρὰ καὶ καταγέλαστα ἐρείπια, πολὺ ταπεινότερα τῶν κλισίων, οἷς ὑποδύεται τὰ πρόβατα ... καὶ ταῦτα πίπτοντα καὶ ὑπερηρεισμένα, ἃ πρὸς τὴν πληγὴν τοῦ ῥαιστῆρος ἔτρεμε καὶ διίστατο. Cf. Amm. Marc. 14.6.25.

[99] Cod. Theod. 15.1.39. Ulpian (*Dig.* 43.8.2.17) permits constructions in public spaces to stand, provided that they do not obstruct public use, though he does so by claiming that their

in doorways, under bridges, or wherever they found a spot, yet the concerns voiced in legal and other sources about the beauty of the urban fabric presumably viewed makeshift structures as potential threats.[100]

RITUAL AND THE STREET

Although the street lacked the formal trappings of theaters and amphitheaters, its busy space offered a conspicuous performance venue for communal or familial displays. Appropriately enough, neighborhood religion was practiced in communal space as urban dwellers clustered around street-side altars. In Pompeii, the altars consisted of a masonry core covered with plaster, often painted, and sometimes fronting a more elaborate mural. Thirty-eight are known, although some may have fallen out of use by 79 CE.[101] Here, urban dwellers sought to placate the *lares compitales*, the protective deities thought to guard against the danger manifested at crossroads (*compita*).[102] Over time, worship gained an imperial flavor as the *lares Augusti* came to be venerated at the altars as well.[103] Excavators found remains of sacrifices still atop some altars, and we can imagine neighborhood residents regularly offerings of food, drink, or flowers amid the street's hustle-bustle. On the occasion of the *Compitalia*, the annual crossroads festival, crowds gathered as local officials, their heads covered in the traditional manner, propitiated the crossroad deities to the notes of flutes and the smell of garlands.[104]

At the *Compitalia*, the officials may have also ritually traced the perimeter of their city ward, a sacrificial pig in tow, before returning to the altar to strike the death blow.[105] If they did so, they joined numerous processions that used city streets as both corridor and stage. At Herculaneum, during the *Parentalia* in mid-February, a parade honoring the city's patron M. Nonius Balbus departed from the honoree's cenotaph and coursed past Balbus's many donations to the city.[106] A painting adorning a workshop façade (VI.7.8–12) suggests that a guild of carpenters passed through Pompeii's streets while carrying a wooden float

removal would disfigure the city, which implies that he has something else in mind. Cf. *Cod. Iust.* 8.11(12).20; *Cod. Theod.* 14.14.1.

[100] Mart. 12.32 implies that homeless people kept their possessions with them as they moved from place to place. Concerns about disfiguring the city: *Dig.* 43.8.2.17, 43.8.7. The Tabula Heracleensis (ll. 81–82) did permit censors to house slaves temporarily in public porticoes and open spaces.

[101] Van Andringa 2000.

[102] Giacobello 2008, 46–50 for the ancient texts.

[103] Lott 2004, 81–127. Cf. Ov. *Fast.* 5.145–148; Suet. *Aug.* 30; Pliny *NH* 3.66; Dio Cass. 55.8.6–7.

[104] Flowers: Suet. *Aug.* 31.4. Clothing of officials: Dio Cass. 55.8.6–7; Livy 34.7.3–10; Cic. *Pis.* 8; Asc. *Pis.* 6–7C. Other aspects: Dion. Hal. 4.14.3–4; Festus (Paulus) 272–273L; Macrob. *Sat.* 1.7.34–35. Raucous celebrations: Serv. *A.* 8.717. Public feasts may also have occupied the streets: [Verg.] *Catal.* 13.27–30. See "Crossroad Officials" in Chapter 8.

[105] Lott 2004, 36. Cf. *CIL* 6.766. See also Stek 2008.

[106] Maiuri 1942; Schumacher 1976; Hartnett 2008b.

supporting a diorama that, in a characteristic blending of work and religion, honored their patron goddess Minerva and the carpenter-deity Daedalus[107] (Plate III). Another Pompeian shop front represents a procession for Cybele. Although the mural depicts the entourage at rest, as porters lean on canes after setting down the statue of the goddess, it captures the parade's many sensations. The participants, some dressed in colorful garments and carrying instruments, form a potentially noisy crew that drew attention while parading[108] (Plate IV). Spectacles in the forum and amphitheater saw other processions at Pompeii.[109] Overall, amid squeals of sacrificial animals, cymbal crashes, or smells of incense, the street was temporarily given over to groups of revelers.

As families moved in rites of (literal) passage, the street offered a showcase. For funerals of prominent figures, a sizeable mass squeezed its way through the city as the body was processed from its former residence to a city's forum. According to Polybius, who describes a generalized elite funeral of Rome, the *pompa*, or cortège, brought history to life by featuring actors impersonating and wearing masks and clothing of the family's ancestors.[110] Because it shows municipal rather than Roman elites, a famous Late Republican relief from Amiternum lacks the masks and actors but still presents a view of a grand procession. Blasts from three trumpets fill the air and four pipe players join in at the front, but the visual focus is on the bier bearing the deceased behind. Propped up on a double-mattressed couch before rich drapery, the honoree is carried by eight litter-bearers. Female mourners follow behind wailing[111] (Fig. 18). After a speech, the contingent

18. A late Republican relief from Amiternum grants a sense of the sights and sounds of an elite funeral as it passed through the streets of a city.
Photo: Universal Images Group/Art Resource, New York.

[107] Clarke 2003, 85–87.
[108] See below "A Procession of Cybele" in Chapter 8.
[109] *CIL* 10.1074d = *ILS* 5053.4. See also the top frieze of the so-called Pompeii Gladiators' Relief: Maiuri 1947.
[110] Polyb. 6.53–54. The *imagines*: Flower 1996.
[111] Ov. *Met.* 14.748–755 for the effects of hearing a funerary procession.

apparently traversed urban streets again on its way to the deceased's final resting place.[112] Tableaux of families also filled the streets during weddings as the groom arrived at the bride's house, as a wedding feast and its associated entertainment took over the thoroughfare, and certainly at the crowning event as the bride processed to the groom's house, the so-called *domum deductio*.[113] Some jurists, in fact, considered this act the very point at which the bond was forged, which underscores the event's important communal and public nature.[114] For family, neighborhood, craft, cult, and more, street rituals celebrated group identity and reinforced who was within or without a particular group or social class.

THE SENSATIONAL STREET

At this chapter's start, we encountered Martial's claim that there is no place in the city where a poor man could think and rest. To support his assertion, the poet summons a list of sonic distractions that spans many aspects of street life:

> In the morning schoolteachers deny you life, at night the bakers, and all day the hammers of the coppersmiths. Over here the idle moneychanger shakes his filthy counter with Nero's coins; over there the hammerer of Spanish gold dust wallops his worn-out stone with a glistening mallet; and Bellona's frenzied throng doesn't shut up, nor does the talkative castaway with his bundled limb, nor the Jew who learned from his mother how to beg, nor the watery-eyed peddler of sulphured goods.[115]

While his wealthy addressee "does not and cannot know about these things," the poet writes: "the thrusting of the passing crowd awakens me and Rome is at my bedside."[116] The poem thus obviously contrasts the massively different urban experiences of rich and poor, yet it also raises two issues that help us look backward and forward. On the one hand, Martial's sounds reinforce the street's role as a locomotive, social, commercial, performative, and even occasionally domestic zone. On the other hand, Martial shows that city dwellers took in the whole street simultaneously, with its many activities and protagonists adding to

---

[112] Funerary spectacle: Flower 1996, 91–157; Beacham 1999, 15–17, 37–39, 151–153; Bodel 1999; Sumi 2002. Cf. Favro and Johanson 2010.

[113] Feast and entertainment: Plaut. *Cas.* 799, 856.

[114] *Dig.* 23.2.5 (Pomponius), 35.1.15 (Ulpian). In general: Hersch 2010, esp. 140–143. To judge from a painting of the wedding of Hercules in a Pompeian house of the same name (VII.9.47), people outside of legal circles felt the same way. At the center of the scene, the hero-turned-god leads his bride out of her temple, while to the sides the procession is already under way as attendants carry various emblems atop their shoulders on float-like *fercula*.

[115] Mart. 12.57.4–14: *negant vitam / ludi magistri mane, nocte pistores, / aerariorum marculi die toto; / hinc otiosus sordidam quatit mensam / neroniana nummularius massa, / illinc balucis malleator Hispanae / tritum nitenti fuste verberat saxum; / nec turba cessat entheata Bellonae, / nec fasciato naufragus loquax trunco, / a matre doctus nec rogare Iudaeus, / nec sulphuratae lippus institor mercis.*

[116] Mart. 12.57.18: *nescis ista nec potes scire . . . .* Mart. 12.57.26–27: *nos transeuntis nisus excitat turbae et ad cubile est Roma.*

the scene. As a capstone to this chapter, I want to pay closer attention to the street's sensations, which both demonstrate how the street set various ambits of city life in immediate juxtaposition and, in the process, shed light on a variety of urban issues like cleanliness, chaos, and control.

As Martial suggests, sounds of daily life resounded off the stone roadway and echoed along tightly spaced buildings day and night.[117] To the noises already mentioned, we have to add vehicles rumbling over bumpy streets, their drivers' shouting; beasts of burden whinnying or braying; and pigeons cooing and pecking for food scraps in the roadbed. Peddlers' distinctive pitches preceded bargaining with customers. Water splashed into fountains, priests incanted, pots and pans clanged, carpenters sawed and planed, and tintinnabula tinkled in doorways. Extraordinary events interrupted the normal sonic surroundings. Processions passed, like the distinctly foreign sounds of Cybele worshippers; trumpet blasts and roars of the crowd arose from the amphitheater.[118] Yet, for all this racket, we must remember the difference between the modern and ancient city. No automobiles or airplanes roared, no HVAC units buzzed. As noted by Bruce Smith, a pioneering scholar on historic soundscapes, "in the absence of ambient sounds of more than 70 dB (barking dogs excepted), the sound of outdoor conversations would become a major factor in the sonic environment." In Italian cities where automotive traffic is restricted (such as Bologna or Siena), Smith continues, the "highly reflective corridors of these streets" make a conversation audible more than 100 feet away.[119] Numerous texts describe Romans within buildings overhearing sounds from the street. By the same token, streetgoers occasionally perceive noises emanating from houses.[120] Sonically, then, the acoustic environment blurred boundaries both conceptual and architectural.

Smells – because they, too, were only somewhat bound by buildings – intermingled in the street. Although sewers ran underneath thoroughfares in some cities, such as Herculaneum, streets often doubled as dumping grounds for waste, and the urban stench is almost taken for granted.[121] Legal opinions, for example, casually state that creating a foul smell near a public street did not render the offending party liable for prosecution. Animal waste and by-products were partly to blame, as tanners and butchers, among others, had a reputation

---

[117] Garrioch 2003 for a parallel treatment of Early Modern Europe. For a survey of senses in the Roman world and their social meanings, see Toner 2009, 123–161.
[118] Carts and shouting: Hor. *Epist.* 1.17.6; Juv. 3.236–238. Street-sellers: Mart. 10.3; Stat. *Silv.* 1.6.73–74; *Dig.* 14.3.5.4; Sen. *Ep.* 56.1–2. Foreign sounds: Juv. 3.6–8; Stat. *Silv.* 1.6.70–72. Amphitheater: Tomb 14 EN outside the Porta Nocera at Pompeii with *CIL* 4.10237.
[119] Smith 1999, 58.
[120] E.g., Ov. *Met.* 14.748–751; Cic. *Rosc. Am.* 134; Prop. 4.8.51–62.
[121] Camardo 2007. See Poehler 2012 on drainage at Pompeii.

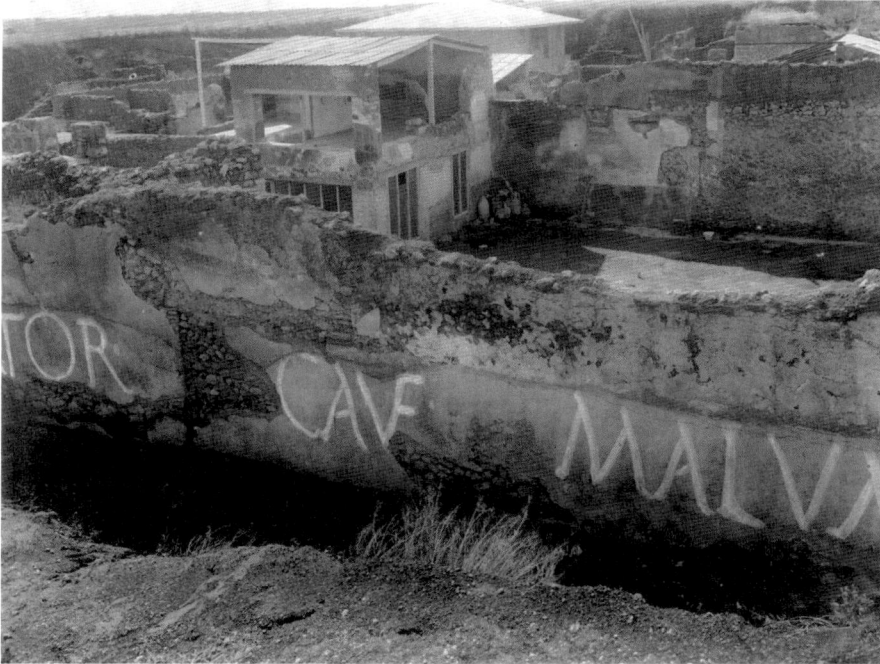

19. This archival photograph captures a painted inscription (*CIL* 4.7715) on the side of insula III.4 in Pompeii that spells out in large letters what is elsewhere written on a more miniscule scale: *cacator cave malum*, "shitter, beware."
Photo: Soprintendenza Speciale per Pompei, Ercolano e Stabia, Archivio Fotografico degli Scavi, C1225.

for causing a stink.[122] Human excrement was present, too. The street-side urinals in which fullers collected their industrial agent were renowned for reeking and had a proclivity toward breaking.[123] Inscriptions along Pompeian streets and near its gates suggest that, if a latrine was not nearby, Roman sensibilities did not rule out public defecation. They admonish *cave cacator*, "shitter beware," and, in service of their goal, they caution the reader to pass by the spot, invoke the name of Jupiter, or even employ a line of hexameter[124] (Fig. 19). The dumping of chamber pots was also a concern; the trouble caused by objects or waste hurled out of multiple-occupant dwellings earned its own chapter in Justinian's *Digesta*, entitled "Concerning those who pour or throw

[122] Animal waste: *Dig.* 43.10.1.5. Butcher: Mart. 6.64.18–21. Tanner: Mart. 6.93.4; Juv. 14.202. Cf. Suet. *Vesp.* 5.4. On health concerns related to smell, see Nutton 2000. On the general issue of the Roman city's cleanliness, see Scobie 1986 (with Laurence 1997); Dupré Raventós and Vallverdù 1999.
[123] Mart. 6.93.1–2; Macrob. *Sat.* 3.16.15; Suet. *Vesp.* 23.3.
[124] *CIL* 4.3782, 4.4586, 4.7714–6, 4.7038, 4.6641. Jupiter's name: *CIL* 4.7716. A line of hexameter: *CIL* 4.7038. Similar sentiments from elsewhere: Milnor 2014, 54–59, 64–66. Cf. Art. 2.26.

things out of buildings," and a painted decree from an aedile at Herculaneum forbids the throwing of excrement into the street.[125] Against this legal backdrop, the hyperbolic remarks of Juvenal's friend Umbricius about the city's nocturnal dangers seem less outrageous:

> At night while you pass by, there are as many causes of death as there are windows that stand open watching you. Therefore you should hope and a make a pathetic vow that they'll be satisfied with pouring out their gaping chamber pots on you.[126]

Such filth may have been purged from the street by overflow from public fountains and wastewater expelled from buildings.[127] Aediles were charged with keeping streets clean – which largely meant ensuring that property owners maintained the street in front of their buildings – but sources regularly bemoan muddy conditions.[128] In an anecdote whose fame probably outweighs its literal historicity, Caligula is said to have dumped mud into Vespasian's toga when the latter was serving, negligently it seems, as aedile.[129] Stepping-stones helped pedestrians cross from one sidewalk to another, and their presence also likely reflects the mess that could lie in the roadbed. Whatever stench permeated streets, it competed with the smoke that poured out of bars, kitchens, and braziers citywide, which likely made pleasant scents stand out all the more.[130] The use of perfume understandably flourished in the early empire; like a fancy article of clothing, it helped distinguish its wearer.[131]

When I considered street traffic in the previous chapter, my assessment weighed urban passage as a whole and focused on its volume. Thinking about movement as a lived experience concentrates our attention on individuals and rounds out the visual and haptic experience that Juvenal described so vividly.[132] Other sources echo the physicality of Umbricius's narrative. Cicero is tossed by the crowd, while Horace is himself the jostler: "it's necessary to battle in the crowd and do damage to the slowpokes." A ruffian replies with enraged curses,

---

[125] *Dig.* 9.3: *De his, qui effuderint vel deiecerint.* Cf. *Dig.* 44.7.5.5. Herculaneum decree: *CIL.* 4.10488. See also "The Water Tower" in Chapter 7.
[126] Juv. 3.274–277: *adeo tot fata, quot illa / nocte patent vigiles te praetereunte fenestrae. / ergo optes votumque feras miserabile tecum, / ut sint contentae patulas defundere pelves.* Umbricius also mentions falling pots and roof tiles. Cf. *Philogelos* 85.
[127] Front. *Aq.* 2.111.
[128] Tabula Heracleensis, ll. 23–49; Robinson 1992, 70–74, 122–124. Cf. Plaut. *Stich.* 352; *Capt.* 791. Poor condition of streets: Mart 5.22.5–6, 7.61.6, 10.10.7–8, 12.28(26).8; Sen. *Ira* 3.35.5; Juv. 3.247; Petron. 79.
[129] Dio Cass. 59.12; Suet. *Vesp.* 5.3.
[130] Smoke: Sen. *Ep.* 104.6; Sid. Apoll. *Epist.* 8.11.3.
[131] Mattingly 1990; Potter 1999, 175–180. Cf. Plaut. *Most.* 38–50, 273–278 on social meanings of smell.
[132] Juv. 3.236–248.

"You would bludgeon everything that stands in your way."[133] When Seneca, in the *De Ira*, ponders the impediments and distractions of life, his mind turns to urban movement:

> Just as one who has to hurry though the busy sections of the city ends up colliding with many people, and in some spot is sure to slip, in another to be kept back, in another to be splattered, so in this scattered and rambling activity of life many obstacles and many chances to complain arise.[134]

Beyond the obstacles already discussed (benches, ambulant salespeople, animals roped to the sidewalk, crowds of loiterers, shops engulfing the sidewalk), the Campanian cities showcase others that might have sprung to mind for Seneca: unexpected dips or rises in the sidewalk, columns or piers supporting upper stories, and façades that jutted out. It is easy to imagine a stubborn donkey or a wagon driver unfamiliar with a city's layout causing traffic jams that had knock-on results for pedestrians.[135] Even when little got in the way, bumpy conditions simply derived from the street's narrowness: the average street width at Pompeii was 5–6 meters. Nothing kept someone from walking in the roadbed, but the presence of wheeled vehicles and animals (not to mention the glop that our sources describe there) likely squeezed most pedestrians onto narrow sidewalks. Even on main streets, four people squeezed shoulder-to-shoulder spanned nearly the whole width of one footpath, which was approximately 2 meters (Fig. 20). This left little spare room for two empty-handed people to pass one another comfortably, even without external interference. Our sources, when they decry street congestion, are bewailing traffic at its thickest, but we nevertheless must recognize that streets in many cities were, in contrast to other urban infrastructure such as aqueducts, surprisingly "under-engineered." There was not much room for people to move about even when few were on the street.

A look at the streets of present-day India is helpful to take stock of the Roman situation. As geographer Tim Edensor notes, the Indian street's many actions and various means of transportation play out at different speeds, resulting in "a host of differently constituted time-space paths," which means that "passage is marked by disruption and distraction, not only by the exigencies of avoidance and the physical collision with others, but also by the distractions and diversions offered by these heterogeneous activities and sights." I will soon say more about these visual effects in the Roman context, but the comparative

[133] Cic. *Planc.* 7. Hor. *Sat.* 2.6.28–31: *luctandum in turba et facienda iniuria tardis. / "quid tibi vis, insane, et quam rem agis?" improbus urget / iratis precibus: "tu pulses omne quod obstat . . ."*
[134] Sen. *Ira* 3.6.4: *quemadmodum per frequentia urbis loca properanti in multos incursitandum est et aliubi labi necesse est, aliubi retineri, aliubi respergi, ita in hoc vitae actu dissipato et vago multa inpedimenta, multae querellae incidunt.* See also earlier, "The Street as Corridor for Movement" in Chapter 1.
[135] For nuisances, see Hartnett 2011a; Kaiser 2011b.

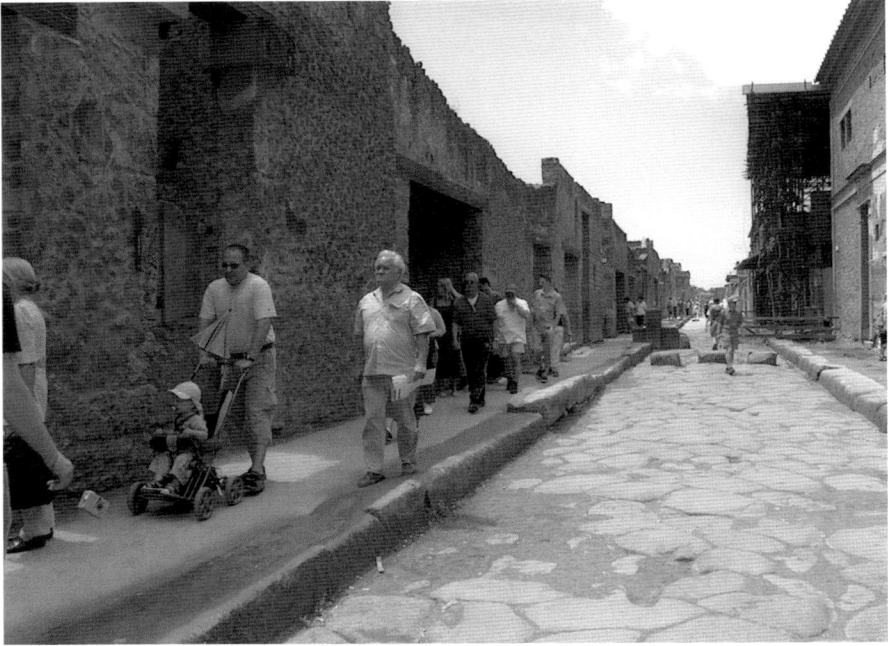

20. The Via dell'Abbondanza in Pompeii was one of the wider streets in the city, measuring approximately 8 meters façade-to-façade in the eastern part of the city, yet its sidewalks still squeezed pedestrians together tightly.
Photo: author. Courtesy: Soprintendenza Speciale per Pompei, Ercolano e Stabia.

evidence is provocative because Indian streets, like their Roman counterparts, host "an ever-changing dance of traffic which contrasts with controlled flow and pace of traffic movement on Western thoroughfares."[136] Modern commentators on urban space often use metaphors of dance to describe movement through streets. Jane Jacobs, for example, refers to the "street ballet."[137] For Roman cities, the choreography of street passage was on occasion closer to a mosh pit.

CONCLUSION

Given the congestion, vivid sensory experience, wide range of activities, and sub-elite flavor that could mark street life, it is no surprise that some marked this space as one of potential chaos and even danger. Beyond the nocturnal threats, our sources describe petty thieves nabbing goods and then escaping into the anonymity of the crowd.[138] We read of fights unfolding in alleys, wild animals

---

[136] Edensor 1998, esp. 209–210.
[137] Jacobs 1961.
[138] *Dig.* 47.11.7, 47.18.1.2. Additional nocturnal threats: Juv. 3.302–308; Tib. 1.2.25–28; Plaut. *Amph.* 153–184. Cf. Prop. 3.16; Juv. 10.19–22; Pliny *NH* 19.59.

on the loose, babies hidden in corners, political strongmen hoarding weapons in advance of a brawl, and even attempted murder.[139] There is no way to confirm or deny these events, but they hint at the mindset Romans brought to the street and remind us of the distinct lack of formal regulation in Roman cities. Aediles were tasked with surveillance of street and sidewalk maintenance and cleaning, but no police force walked a beat to provide uniform protection across the populace.[140] Legal action was rarely prophylactic and official, but typically responsive, arising from the injured party. Little, if any, formal zoning governed what activities could be conducted where. No signs or traffic cops, so far as we know, told people when to go and stop at intersections. Convention, such as driving a wheeled vehicle on the right, might govern, but, in comparison with cities of the modern West, much more negotiation and improvisation was required. Overall, recognizing the lack of public intervention requires a fundamental shift in our thinking. To borrow the phrase of a scholar of Roman law, we see in Roman streets a situation more akin to "old Sicily than modern Zurich."[141]

Our focus on the sensory experience of the street further complicates the story by suggesting how many realms and registers of urban life mixed and mingled in this arena. Just as the street literally connected all physical segments of the city, so its one space also made multiple segments of life part of the same scene. New juxtapositions were continuously revealed as the flow of traffic – complete with different casts of characters and their activities – played out against a shifting background. In other words, for anyone looking, listening, or perhaps smelling carefully, the mixing-pot effect must have been striking and even challenging. Yet perhaps the most profound and meaningful union that the street fostered was that occurring across the full spectrum of society. Almost everyone, regardless of wealth, gender, or degree of freedom, eventually took to the street. And, in moving about, they were brought close with the street's confines. Chapter 3 examines the nature and effects of their contact, interaction, and efforts at presentation in this unique social arena.

---

[139] Fights: Suet. *Aug.* 45.2–3. Animals: Hor. *Epist.* 2.2.75; Auson. *Ep.* 6.21–31; Mart 10.5; Suet. *Vesp.* 5.4. Babies: Plaut. *Cist.* 123–124. Weapons: Cic. *Mil.* 24.64. Attempted murder: Suet. *Galb.* 10.5.

[140] Nippel 1984, 1995; Fuhrmann 2012.

[141] Meyer 2004, 3.

THREE

THE STREET'S SOCIAL ENVIRONMENT

I N JUVENAL'S FIRST SATIRE, HE ENTERTAINS THE QUESTION OF WHY one should write satire. His answer is that it is difficult *not* to do so, given the absurdities he witnesses. Eunuchs get married, upright women hunt boars in the amphitheater, a barber gains unfathomable riches, an Egyptian dons purple and gold – such events fuel Juvenal's determination to join the ranks of poets. Who has the patience and iron-strong will to keep his temper, Juvenal asks, amid a wicked city?[1] A collage of scenes follows. A blubbery lawyer alone weighs down a brand-new litter built for two. Along comes an informer who has made a mint striking fear into (and thus extorting) the aristocracy. You are bumped aside by those who earn bequests by bedding rich old hags. Regular folk get jostled by the sycophants surrounding a guardian who has robbed his ward. Why mess about with typical poet stuff – myth and all its characters – Juvenal asks, when a man prostitutes his wife and pockets the money, or when a young man races down the Via Flaminia like Achilles's charioteer after he has blown his family's fortune on horses and then wants to command a cohort?[2]

For our purposes, what is striking about Juvenal's portrait is not so much its viciousness – fourteen equally spleenful satires still await – as its directness about where one sees the outrages of Roman society. As his examples come to a head in this programmatic overture, Juvenal gets specific about location: "Wouldn't

[1] Juv. 1.22–31 (30: *difficile est saturam non scribere*).
[2] Juv. 1.32–62.

it be possible to fill a whole notebook while you're standing at the street corner?" Two final street scenes follow: six men bear an open litter carrying a fellow who got rich by forging documents, and a distinguished lady who has poisoned her husband walks unabashed behind his bier.[3] Like their predecessors, these examples hinge on a shared pair of characteristics of the street: first, it is a place to observe all of society. Juvenal fills the space with everyone from the humiliated *populus* to the cold-hearted matron. Second, he sees them as they wish to be seen. The outrages to which Juvenal bears witness are products of streetgoers' efforts to posture here — through what they wear, ride, or drive; through their domination of the thoroughfare; or through their ability to keep up appearances despite common knowledge of their transgressions. For them, the street offered an arena for display before the eyes of many. For Juvenal, as for many Romans, the street's broad spectrum and manifold performances triggered reflection about society at large as well as individuals' places, just or unjust, within it.

Over the previous chapters, we have witnessed a remarkable range and volume of movements, activities, and people in the street, yet these actors and actions have largely remained independent of one another. Prompted by Juvenal's opening lines, this chapter now sets those people in contact to consider the consequences of their "human friction." As the street brought the city's whole populace physically close, it fostered interaction that was unique among a city's social arenas, creating many tensions and, at times, also resolving them. Here, everything unfolded before the widest audience possible, who looked on, as they were themselves watched, with a distinctly skeptical eye.

WHO WAS ON THE STREET?

Generating an answer to this section's title is deceptively difficult. On the one hand, individual sources — graffiti, historical or literary texts, or visual representations — grant a piecemeal vision, with each snippet offering its own knothole view into one manifestation of broader practices: regular folk gathering in the street, for instance, or the destitute begging for money. On the other hand, my approach in Chapter 1 — where I considered the necessity of heading into the street for basic provisions — was akin to turning the microscope around to look at the urban population's movements in the aggregate. In the end, since we cannot observe the urban population directly, neither approach will yield a comprehensive vista of who spent how much time in the street and how often. But the evidence we do have points to a general expectation and even an ideology of inclusivity.

---

[3] Juv. 1.63–72 (63–64: *nonne libet medio ceras inplere capaces / quadrivio . . .?*)

Throughout legal opinions on streets, a central thread runs strong: universal access is a foremost value. The jurist Pomponius, in a section of the *Digesta* entitled "Of public ways and places," expresses it most succinctly: "It is open to anyone to claim for public use what belongs to the use of all, such as roads and public ways."[4] The praetor's edict regarding public places and streets approaches the issue from another angle by addressing potential infringements: "You are not allowed to do anything in a public place, or introduce anything into it, which could cause any damage" to someone.[5] Ulpian, the famed legal mind, offers an exegesis on the edict that bridges the gap somewhat, describing public places "as the property of the *civitas* and not of each individual" before adding "we have as much right to enjoy them as anyone of the people has to prevent their misuse."[6] His discussion consistently reflects his vision of the street as a space for universal use without encumbrances, particularly those impinging on anyone else's enjoyment of the space. He writes that "whenever anything is allowed to be done in a public place, it should be permitted on condition that it causes no injury to anyone."[7] And he later adds that legal intervention may be sought "if anyone suffers deterioration or restriction of his view or access."[8] Additional sources confirm that these issues − of universal accessibility and of ensuring everyone's enjoyment of streets − were not insider legal wrangling, but had long been the subject of legislation. The Tabula Heracleensis records a specific parallel to the jurists' formulations in its section on care for streets. Characteristic of other inscribed charters, it entrusts the aediles with preventing anyone from building or constructing anything lying in, blocking, or closing off streets and public spaces if the effect is that those spaces are not open or that the *populus* may not use them (lines 68−72).[9] We do not know to what degree these principles were enforced, but they nevertheless present a consistent ideology of inclusion.

Ancient authors do occasionally offer a more universal image that places the whole urban populace in a city's public spaces. How they paint such a picture is perhaps telling because of what the authors presume. When Suetonius describes Germanicus's victorious *adventus* from Germany, for instance, the biographer

[4] *Dig.* 43.7.1: *cuilibet in publicum petere permittendum est id, quod ad usum omnium pertineat, veluti vias publicas, itinera publica.* On *loca publica* in Roman law, see van Binnebeke 2007.

[5] *Dig.* 43.8.2.pr.: *ne quid in loco publico facias inve eum locum immittas, qua ex re quid illi damni detur. . . .* Exceptions are made in the case of statutes, *senatus consulta*, edicts, or decrees of the emperor.

[6] *Dig.* 43.8.2.2: *loca enim publica utique privatorum usibus deseruiunt, iure scilicet civitas, non quasi propria cuiusque, et tantum iuris habemus ad optinendum, quantum quilibet ex populo ad prohibendum habet.*

[7] *Dig.* 43.8.2.10: *nam quotiensque aliquid in publico fieri permittitur, ita oportet permitti, ut sine iniuria cuiusquam fiat.*

[8] *Dig.* 43.8.2.12: *proinde si cui prospectus, si cui aditus sit deterior aut angustior, interdicto opus est.* A case could be made for *iniuria* if someone was forbidden from, among other things, gaining access to, sitting in, or associating with others in a public place: *Dig.* 47.10.13.7.

[9] Nearly identical phrasing is employed by several early imperial municipal charters: *Lex Tarentina* ll. 39−42; *Lex Coloniae Genetivae Iuliae* 77; *Lex Irnitana* 82. For the first two laws, see Crawford 1996, 301−312, 393−454. For the third, see González 1986.

enumerates the well-wishers: "the whole populace – regardless of sex, age, or rank – poured out of Rome as far as the twentieth milestone."[10] Such emphasis on the presence of every segment of Roman society was something of a trope for *adventus* scenes and their close parallels.[11] Cicero, for example, describes his own return from exile: people of every rank, age, and order happily crowd the city's streets and public spaces.[12] In the hands of Cicero, the picture of popular demonstration is undoubtedly exaggerated, since he is at pains to show that it is rare and noteworthy. But which feature of his account is heightened? That Cicero and Suetonius carefully assure their readers of the population's comprehensiveness – each enumerating multiple axes of difference – reveals where they anticipate being doubted. An unquestioned assumption is that, sooner or later, everyone could and did take to the streets. What was rare was the unanimity of the crowd.[13]

It is notable that few (if any) sources express surprise that a particular individual or class of urban dweller is visible on the street; quite the contrary. The plots of Roman comedies, for instance, often hinged on chance street meetings of people from across the social spectrum. In Plautus's *Menaechmi*, one twin searches for the long-lost brother who shares his name. Wandering through the city, he encounters people of many ranks and eventually bumps into his brother's slave cook – and thus begins a long comedic game of mistaken identity, which ends only when the brothers are reunited in the final scene. Plautus and his fellow comics invert or embellish many features of life for laughs, but they presume the presence of, and contact among, many people in the street as a matter of course. In sum, what is most normal in any society is often least remarked upon. Roman urban life was no exception. Yet even legal sources, whose business was outlining infractions rather than spelling out what was typical, resonate with the broad principles discernable from other sources: that universal access to the street was a prerogative protected by ideology, an aspect of daily life assumed by authors and required by preindustrial conditions, and a reality attested by names and sentiments scratched in plaster.

THE ROMAN STREET'S PHYSICAL ENVIRONMENT
IN COMPARATIVE PERSPECTIVE

When beginning to consider streetgoers' interaction, we should bear in mind the physical details. Since most traffic moved along on foot or at low speeds,

---

[10] Suet. *Cal.* 4: . . . *populi autem Romani sexum, aetatem, ordinem omnem usque ad vicesimum lapidem effudisse se.* Cf. Apul. *Met.* 3.2: *civitas omnis . . . effusa mira densitate.*

[11] On *adventus* scenes: MacCormack 1981; Lehnen 1997.

[12] Cic. *Dom.* 75: *constat enim nullis umquam comitiis campum Martium tanta celebritate, tanto splendore omnis generis hominum, aetatum, ordinum floruisse.* Cf. Cic. *Pis.* 7, 52 (*omnium generum, aetatum, ordinum omnes viri ac mulieres*); *Dom.* 76; *Sest.* 131; *Att.* 73/4.1.4–5.

[13] Cf. Livy 6.25.8–10.

more than a passing glance was possible. On streets in Naples and Siena that preserve the layout and dimensions of their premodern predecessors, individual pedestrians passing in opposite directions amid moderate traffic can see one another for approximately three to four seconds. This period is long enough to inspect others in any close encounter, and it increases with reduced speeds, less traffic, and straighter streets. In fact, the early evening ritual stroll of the *passeggiata* is slower and involves fancier clothing precisely because seeing and being seen are key.[14]

Drawing on analogous circumstances can provide intimations of the Roman situation, but it also risks dulling the differences between our experiences and Romans'. For example, we may not recognize how much automobile traffic and a street's physical dimensions are key factors in urban interaction. In his 1981 book, *Liveable Streets*, Donald Appleyard compared three streets from one San Francisco neighborhood that were virtually identical in all respects (appearance, dimensions, uses of buildings, etc.) but one: the volume of vehicular traffic each supported.[15] He discovered that increased vehicular traffic flow meant significantly fewer social contacts among the street's residents. On the street with the lightest traffic, neighborhood inhabitants counted, on average, three times as many fellow street inhabitants as friends and twice as many as acquaintances than on the street with the highest traffic. The contrast is most powerful in graphic form[16] (Fig. 21). Appleyard's research measures a slightly different phenomenon from the social contact that interests me. Nevertheless, given the principle that motor vehicle traffic and personal exchange are inversely proportional, we might consider how much more contact and connection was possible on the Roman street, where cars' disruptive presence was scarcely replicated.[17] Along similar lines, it is worth emphasizing just how narrow Roman streets were (Fig. 22). The entire width of Fifth Avenue along Central Park in New York is roughly 30 meters, and each sidewalk is the approximate width (7 meters) of an ancient Roman street. Paris' Avenue des Champs-Elysées is twice as wide: 70 meters across, with 11-meter sidewalks. Even famed pedestrian spaces are larger than Roman streets: Bourbon Street in New Orleans squeezes revelers into its 11-meter width, and the

---

[14] Del Negro 2005.
[15] Appleyard 1981, 15–28. The three streets, from heaviest to lightest, are Franklin, Gough, and Octavia, which carried a daily average, respectively, of 15,750, 8,700, and 2,000 vehicles. All part of the same neighborhood, which was originally heavily Italian, these streets were more or less homogenous socially. Data were gathered through interviews and on-site observation.
[16] Other findings included a greater sense of "personal territory" and a greater awareness of particular details of the built environment on lower traffic streets: Appleyard 1981, 23–26 and figs. 4–5.
[17] Appleyard's study of the effects of street-blocking in 1970s Berkeley reached a parallel conclusion (1981: 215–242).

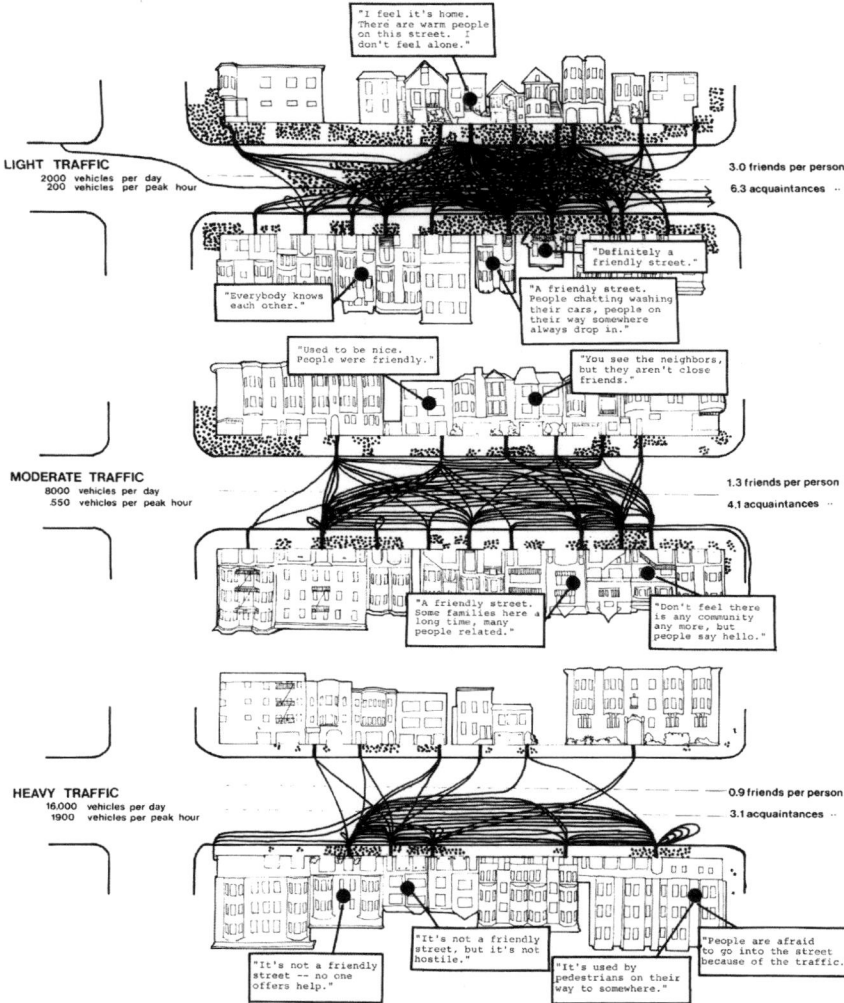

"I feel it's home. There are warm people on this street. I don't feel alone."

LIGHT TRAFFIC
2000 vehicles per day
200 vehicles per peak hour

3.0 friends per person
6.3 acquaintances

"Definitely a friendly street."

"Everybody knows each other."

"A friendly street. People chatting washing their cars, people on their way somewhere always drop in."

"Used to be nice. People were friendly."

"You see the neighbors, but they aren't close friends."

MODERATE TRAFFIC
8000 vehicles per day
550 vehicles per peak hour

1.3 friends per person
4.1 acquaintances

"A friendly street. Some families here a long time, many people related."

"Don't feel there is any community any more, but people say hello."

HEAVY TRAFFIC
16,000 vehicles per day
1900 vehicles per peak hour

0.9 friends per person
3.1 acquaintances

"It's not a friendly street -- no one offers help."

"It's not a friendly street, but it's not hostile."

"It's used by pedestrians on their way to somewhere."

"People are afraid to go into the street because of the traffic."

21. Three San Francisco streets share equal dimensions but different amounts of traffic. From top to bottom: light traffic (2,000 vehicles per day); moderate traffic (8,000 v/d); heavy traffic (16,000 v/d). Lines show where people said they had friends or acquaintances. Dots show where people are said to gather.
Courtesy: Bruce Appleyard (after Appleyard 1981, fig. 3).

central walkway of Las Ramblas in Barcelona concentrates pedestrians in a space 12 to 15 meters wide.[18]

A closer look at a thoroughfare in modern Rome that replicates the dimensions of its precursors sheds light on the effects of such narrowness (Fig. 23). The Via dei Giubbonari, lying southeast of the Campo de' Fiori, looks much like the streets of ancient Rome. Approximately 6 meters in

[18] Jacobs 1995, 97 (Barcelona); 190 (Paris); 199 (New York).

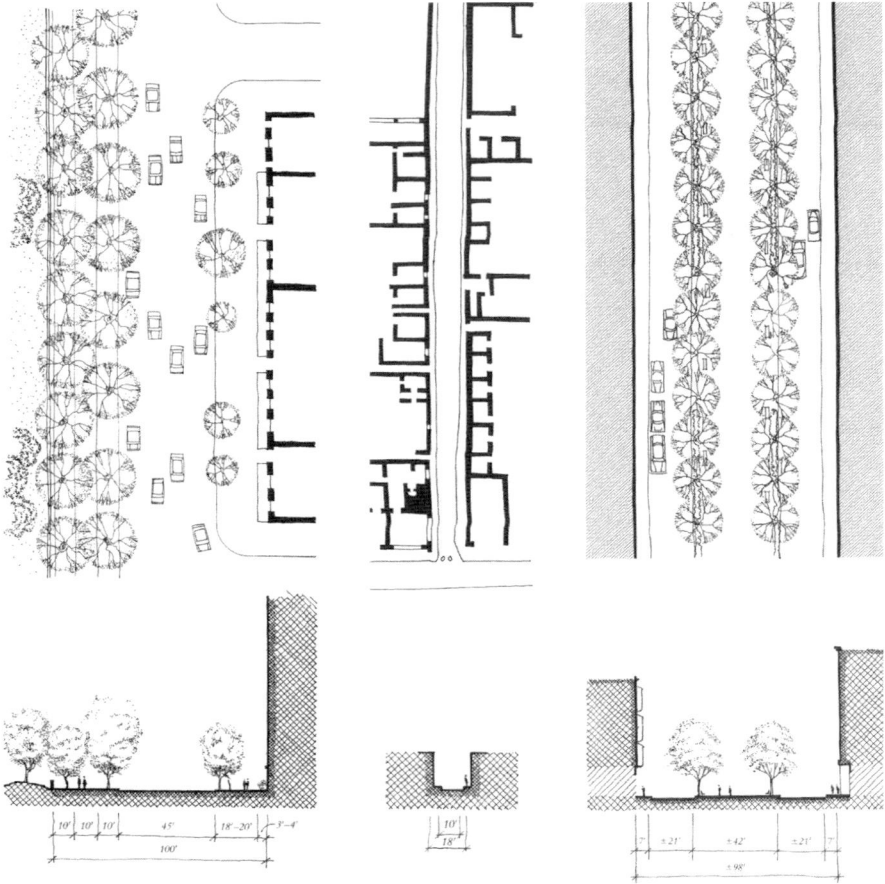

22. Streets in Pompeii were much narrower than their modern counterparts. Plans and elevations of (left to right): Fifth Avenue, New York; Vicolo della Fullonica, Pompeii; Las Ramblas, Barcelona.
Credit: Jacobs, Allan B., *Great Streets*, drawings from pages 137, 147, 199, © 1993 Massachusetts Institute of Technology, by permission of MIT Press.

width, it lacks elevated sidewalks, is lined by buildings three to five stories tall, and has a doorway opening roughly every 5 meters.[19] Carts carry produce to the piazza during the morning, and the rare motorbike or car creeps along, but the space is almost entirely given over to pedestrians. Foot traffic varies throughout the day, sometimes allowing leisurely strolling or brisk pace-making and occasionally becoming so crowded that everyone moves along incrementally. At peak times, foot traffic doubles or triples from six or seven people per minute per meter of walkable width to more than sixteen people

[19] Jacobs 1995, 20–32. Pompeii's Via dell'Abbondanza and Via Stabiana both had doorways opening more frequently than every 3 meters: Laurence 2007, 103–106.

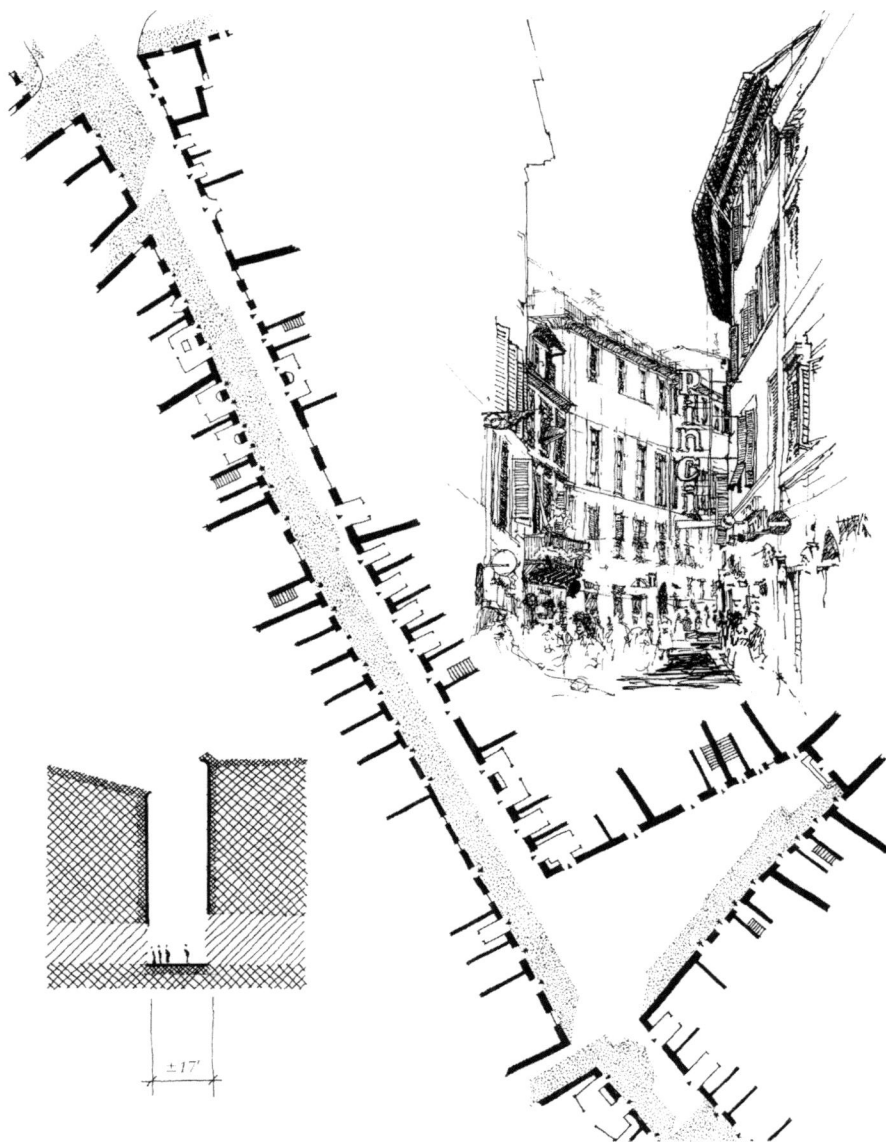

23. The Via dei Giubbonari in Rome replicates some of the characteristics of its ancient predecessors.
Credit: Jacobs, Allan B., *Great Streets*, drawings from pages 22–23, © 1993 Massachusetts Institute of Technology, by permission of MIT Press.

per minute per meter.[20] Allen Jacobs, whose study provides these figures, investigates a number of streets he considers "great." Others have greater

[20] Jacobs 1995, 317. The meters of this measurement are in terms of the street's width, not length. On a Friday evening, there were 6.6 people per minute per meter, whereas during one midday the figure was 7.5 people per minute per meter. In the late afternoon on a Saturday, the traffic was 16.8 people per minute per meter.

volumes – one sidewalk of San Francisco's Market Street had more foot traffic during a ten-minute span (1,110 people versus 840 here) – yet, because of the Roman street's narrowness, none has such a high density.[21]

Attempting to quantify the intensity of traffic for a historical situation would undoubtedly be based on specious assumptions and hindered by a singular lack of pedestrian data. Yet the Via dei Giubbonari – because of its close affinities to its ancient counterparts – offers reminders, first, of how greatly traffic flow can vary over the day's rhythms; second, of how tightly packed people can get when foot traffic is greatest along major yet narrow thoroughfares; and, third, how much that experience of personal contact can differ from many streets we encounter. Whereas roadways full of automobiles and lined with trees, signs, lamp posts, and the like might today screen pedestrians off from one another, Roman streets brought streetgoers physically closer, uniting the street and those who passed along it in one visual arena. Except for certain modes of transportation, such as litters (which, as we shall see, carried their own cultural associations), there was little opportunity to hide or escape notice. Such concentration can leave little doubt that Romans not only saw, but probably bumped into, eavesdropped on, and smelled each other.

SOCIAL CONTACT IN THE STREET AND CITY

Such physical proximity joins a list of the Roman street's characteristics that have come into focus: the variety and intensity of activity; the face-to-face meeting of a broad swath of society; and the spontaneous, somewhat chaotic, and only lightly regulated setting. We can name other urban spaces that also regularly set city dwellers in contact and that were instrumental in shaping how urban society was constituted. However, in some of those social theaters – such as the theater itself and the amphitheater – society was categorized explicitly. Seating arrangements stratified the population, with the highest ranks getting the closest spots and the lowest relegated to upper reaches or excluded altogether. Pompeii's theater, for instance, apparently responded to legislation in Augustan Rome by adding horizontal divisions: all city-dwellers entering this space were able to quickly discern how they and others stacked up.[22] Other locations, such as houses of the elite, also articulated differences spatially. As Wallace-Hadrill writes, "Roman domestic architecture is obsessively concerned with distinctions of social rank."[23] The process began outside, as the task of allowing some entry while barring others fell in grand

---

[21] Market Street (with nearly 12 meters of "effective walk width"): Jacobs 1995, 317.
[22] Edmonson 1996 shows that creating a clear social hierarchy was the goal behind such legislation. See also Rawson 1987; Rose 2005. Pompeii's theater in its local and Augustan contexts: Zanker 1998, 107–114.
[23] Wallace-Hadrill 1994, 10.

houses to a doorkeeper whose interlaced power and arrogance were notorious.[24] For those allowed in, the degree and nature of their access to the owner signaled their relative status. Some parts of the house, such as the atrium, were apparently accessible to many and especially associated with clients, while the owner's intimates were received deeper within.[25]

The street, by contrast, was the most inclusive urban space we can name, apparently hosting all urbanites except chattel slaves. It thus had much in common with baths and fora, both of which included a wide spectrum of society even, in the case of baths, stripped down naked to their common humanity.[26] But what separated the street from these locations was its unpredictability. Its flurry of sensations, mix of activities, minimum of regulation, mélange of users, and, especially, the constant movement of people, goods, and animals made for an ever-shifting, destabilizing scene. One was always in some doubt about who or what might be encountered around the next corner or within the next few moments. Yes, a forum also accommodated a rich range of people and activities. We need look no further than the forum scenes from the Praedia of Julia Felix to see, in addition to ambulatory sellers, a lawsuit being heard, a class in session, people reading political announcements, and a beggar asking for help[27] (Plate II, Figs. 24, 25). But, at the same time, the forum's broad open space, less kinetic environment, and more unified architectural form differentiated it from thoroughfares. In a space encircled by buildings commissioned by their kind, leading men delivered speeches, rendered decisions as magistrates, presided as priests, and sponsored gladiatorial games.[28]

No such atmosphere was predominant in the street. Inclusiveness, unpredictability, and spontaneity rendered it something of an "open field" where, free from immediate "tagging," all came into contact, saw, and were seen without prejudgment or impingement on their ability to forge almost any public image personal resources would allow. Instead, the openness and ubiquity of the interaction that the street fostered was unparalleled, furnishing Romans with unique opportunities for making claims through their appearances and actions. Such freedom had an additional side, however. The same

[24] Doorkeepers' reputation: Juv. 3.184–189; Sen. *Constant.* 15.5; Mart. 5.22.10; Tac. *Ann.* 4.74.

[25] Vitr. 6.5.1–3. On the general question of public and private in the Roman house, see Wallace-Hadrill 1994, Part I, "The Social Structure of the Roman House."

[26] Fagan (1999, 189–219) describes the social make-up of public bathers, from emperor to slave. He concludes (1999, 215–219), contra others (e.g., Toner 1995, 53–64), that communal bathing did not have the effect of social leveling and lists some strategies elites used to distinguish themselves from their fellow bathers. See also Yegül 1992, 32–33. Laurence (2007, 158–165) makes the case for separate bathing times. Add to his arguments *Anth. Pal.* 9.640. Nielsen (1993, 1.146–148) outlines broader arguments for social segregation.

[27] Nappo 1991; Beard 2008, 72–78.

[28] A fitting index of such dominance is the epigraphic record of this space: e.g., Laurence 2007, fig. 2.3. Cf. Mart. 5.20.5–7: . . . *nec nos atria nec domos potentum / nec litis tetricas forumque triste / nossemus nec imagines superbas.*

24. Togate figures read a banner stretched in front of several equestrian statues in the forum scenes painted in the atrium of the Praedia of Julia Felix.
Photo: © Vanni Archive/Art Resource, New York.

characteristics – and especially the relative absence of delimiting social rituals – could challenge social boundaries and make the street an arena where social presentation, the *performance* of status, was key.

The remainder of this chapter entertains several questions about social inter-action and presentation in the street's conspicuous yet chaotic space. How, in this relatively egalitarian zone, did some attempt to tame the chaos and assert a hierarchy? How did potential social climbers take advantage of the street's fluid dynamics? How and on what terms did the urban populace evaluate what they encountered on the street? How could one distinguish a climber from the real article? How did the street's visible stage also offer the less powerful opportunities to attack the public image of their social superiors? More broadly

25. An eighteenth-century engraving replicates painted (but now damaged) scenes of the forum from the Praedia of Julia Felix in Pompeii. On the left, a beggar interacts with an elegantly dressed matron.
Drawing: Ryan Cairns (after *Antichità di Ercolano*, vol. 3, plate 43).

and finally, how did the street function as a political realm, offering a space for the airing of complaints, staging of protests, and celebration of glories? Overall, these different interactions had deep implications for how streetgoers made sense of the social hierarchy, its composition, and their place in it. That is, social contact in the street helped to generate the realities of Roman urban society.

PERFORMANCE AND POSTURING IN THE STREET

One of our best guides for self-presentation through daily street behavior is Horace. In *Satire* 1.6, the poet considers the interrelationship of appearances, lineage, and social climbing: everyone wants to know, he says, the status of everyone's father.[29] Horace seems both thankful for and resentful of his freedman father's efforts at improving the family's standing, not least by shipping Horace off to school in Rome, dressing him up nicely, equipping him with impressive accouterments, and thus disguising a relatively humble background. The poet describes moving through the city and the impression his cultivated appearance made: "Anyone who saw my clothes and attendant slaves – as is the way in a great city – would have thought that such expense was met from ancestral wealth."[30] This episode demonstrates the importance of acting out who you wanted to be in Roman cities and on their streets. Of course, it is impossible to observe similar posturing and viewership directly, and rare is Horace's degree of self-awareness. Nevertheless, with Horace as a prompt, we

---

[29] Hor. *Sat.* 1.6.7–64.
[30] Hor. *Sat.* 1.6.78–80: *vestem servosque sequentis, / in magno ut populo, si qui vidisset, avita / ex re praeberi sumptus mihi crederet illos.* Note the deliberate contrast between Horace's appearance in Rome, surrounded by attendants on his way to school, and the parallel experience of centurions' sons in his hometown as they carry their own supplies and school fees (Hor. *Sat.* 1.6.71–75).

can witness some strategies of self-presentation and draw out common anxieties, concentrating first on personal appearances and then on movement through the city.

An interesting question occupied the cities of first-century CE Italy: to what degree should slaves be differentiated from the free by what they wore? Early in Nero's reign, Seneca described to the young emperor a senatorial proposal to "distinguish slaves from free men in their dress." The measure ended up failing when "it became apparent how great would be the impending danger if our slaves should begin to count their number."[31] Beyond the dynamics of Roman slavery that the episode highlights (such as the free's fear), it illustrates two competing characteristics of Roman society. First, the original impulse to require different clothing shows a desire of some to mark out social or legal distinctions with readily visible signs, chief among them forms of adornment. Yet, second, it also underscores the difficulty – absent the signifying force of clothing, actions, rituals, architecture, and the like – of differentiating among people of diverse statuses and ranks. Because everyone used the street, which was especially prone to such ambiguity, it was a particular locus of concern.

If the proposal had passed, it would have pushed down the social ladder conventions of personal adornment that ran especially strong among elite Romans. Most famously, certain garments were the reserve of citizens: the toga for men and the stola for married women. The toga was more or less required of people appearing in lawcourts and of clients performing the *salutatio*, though not without some complaint from the latter, to judge from satirists who lament its ponderous weight and cumbersome nature.[32] Modifications to the simple white toga identified candidates, those in mourning, and other unique positions. Additional steps in standing (*eques*, senator, censor, *triumphator*) brought special sartorial signs, which underscores the strength of Roman fixation on claims to and markers of status.[33]

Not surprisingly, the connection between adornment and status led some to dress above their station. In Martial's poems, for instance, we frequently read of

---

[31] Sen. *Clem.* 1.24.1: *dicta est aliquando a senatu sententia, ut servos a liberis cultus distingueret; deinde apparuit, quantum periculum immineret, si servi nostri numerare nos coepissent.* It is not exactly clear how this would have been accomplished. Cf. *Dig.* 18.1.5; App. *BC* 2.17; SHA *Sev. Alex.* 27.

[32] Toga and stola: Edmondson 2008, esp. 23–26. *Salutatores'* complaints: George 2008. Additions to the toga were supposed to mark further distinctions in status: both citizen boys and girls wore the toga praetexta, which had a purple border. (Boys also might wear a *bulla* or other small pendant around their necks.) Augustus was especially fervent about the wearing of the toga, apparently excoriating a *contio* crowd for being dressed in dark colors, relegating non-toga wearers to the upper reaches of the theater and asking aediles to keep non-toga wearers out of the forum: Suet. *Aug.* 40.5, 44.2. Yet even Augustus is said to have kept a toga and shoes in his cubiculum should he have to heed the call of official business (Suet. *Aug.* 73), which implies that he went about non-togate at times.

[33] Edmondson 2008, 27–30: *equites* (purple-striped tunic, distinctive shoes, gold ring, and the *trabea*), senators (broader stripe on tunic, own type of shoe), censors (all-purple togas), *triumphatores* (purple tunics with gold vegetal embroidery, gold stars on a purple toga).

imposters, such as the man seated in the theater rows reserved for senators and *equites* whose bejeweled hand, purple tunic, snowy toga, perfumed hair, depilated arms, and senatorial shoes are a ruse: when you remove the patches on his brow, you can see the brand marks from his time as a slave. The theater appears to have attracted special attention from poets because it offered a rare location where appearances could be policed and where crossing a line was most obvious.[34] But the street occasioned griping, as we saw in Juvenal's litany of outrages that pinpoints an Egyptian's donning of a purple cloak and a gold ring as one impetus for writing satire. We also read complaints that bar owners wear gold rings and act like *equites*.[35] The strength of this sensibility occasioned efforts to enact and restate rules about who could wear what. Such repetition was largely a symbolic act designed to showcase an edict's propagator as an upholder of tradition and order, although it likely also reflects people's violation of the code.[36]

Although articulations were marked and defended most fervently among the elite, status symbols were present and valuable lower on the social scale. Indeed, in a broad moralizing current of literature, we read about fakes and knock-offs of fancy jewelry, alchemy that made bronze resemble gold, and gold-plated iron rings.[37] Because most urbanites merely subsisted, wearing a nice article of clothing, a ring, or a gemstone was not about trying to pass as a rich person, but represented a mark of distinction in and of itself. That much is evident in Herculaneum, where excavation along the shorefront has revealed the bodies of more than 300 individuals who took refuge in vaults fronting the beach. In two representative openings, thirty-five Herculaneans were found, and among their skeletons were located twenty-seven total pieces of jewelry: twelve rings, five bracelets, five earrings, at least three necklaces, and two miscellaneous pieces. Of those items that could be linked to a specific individual, ten were associated with three people. This sample may not reflect what people regularly wore around the city's streets because it likely constitutes what victims could grab while fleeing during the eruption. Nevertheless, it suggests

---

[34] Mart. 2.29. Mart. 5.35 has another scarlet-bedecked braggart trace his divine lineage and catalog the sources of his wealth until he is asked to give up his seat; then a huge key falls from his pocket and reveals him to be a doorkeeper. The poem puns on key (*clavis*) and the broad stripe that decorated a garment (*clavus*). Other showy imposters in equestrian seats: Mart. 5.23; Hor. *Ep.* 4.15–16. Cf. Mart. 5.8, 5.25, 5.27, 5.38, 5.41.

[35] Pliny *NH* 33.32. In Mart. 1.103, a figure's countercultural approach underscores the norm: as the man gains riches, his appearance becomes shabbier as he wears dirtier clothes and shoes patched many times. Cf. Mart. 9.49.

[36] E.g., Tiberius (Dio Cass. 57.13.5), Claudius (Dio Cass. 60.7.4), Hadrian (SHA *Hadr.* 22.2). In general, Edmondson 2008, 33–35.

[37] Emphasizing genuine sardonyx: Mart. 4.61, 9.59, 10.87. Imitation gems: Pliny *NH* 37.75–76, 37.197–200; Sen. *Ep.* 90.33. Intimations of fakes: Mart. 8.6, 12.69. Bronze to gold: *PGM* 7.167–186. Gold-plated iron rings: Pliny *NH* 33.23. Cf. Petron. 32.3. See also Mart. 3.29, 5.11, 8.5, 11.37, 14.122.

the proliferation of jewelry (nearly one piece per person) and its concentration in (or on) the hands of a few. A small portion of the population will have had the disposable wealth to afford one decorative item (or the fortune to have inherited it), while for others jewelry was never part of their appearance.[38]

Unlike jewelry, clothing itself rarely survives, but painted representations at Pompeii help to highlight sensibilities and sensitivities. One shop-style door-way, whose interior has not yet been brought to light, is evocative, however, since its façade murals show a range of clothing in production, for sale, and actually being worn[39] (Figs. 88–90). On the bottom right, four bare-torsoed figures roll animal fibers in coagulant to make felt around a furnace.[40] Surrounding them are three figures seated at low tables who wear heavy robes as they card wool. At the far right, a standing individual holds up the finished product: a darker cloth decorated with purple stripes. A sales scene appears in the lower register on the opposite door jamb, where a female in a blue mantle sits amid tables and shelves well-stocked with shoes and skeins of red and yellow cloth. A customer, also dressed in a blue hooded garment, looks on interestedly.

We should not take these images as snapshots. On a shop façade, they are obviously highly interested, and that is the point: gradations in dress mattered and people paid attention to such things. The artist carefully articulates differences in material (felt vs. wool), color, and the role of the wearer. Speaking to that final point are the divine figures in the upper registers on each doorjamb who represent a celestial realm above the terrestrial. On the right, above the workshop scene, appears Venus Pompeiana, the patron goddess of the city, wearing a light blue mantle over a chiton and riding in triumph. On the opposite jamb, Mercury totes his standard caduceus and moneybag while wearing a garment with narrow stripes and shoes that bear distinct similarities to those in the sales scene just below. Not only do the depictions of deities show

---

[38] Bodies: Capasso 2001. Jewelry from *fornici* 7 and 8: De Carolis 2003. Five items were found on skeleton 13 in *fornice* 8, three on skeleton 2 in *fornice* 7, and two on skeleton 8 in *fornice* 7. At least one and possibly two gemstone workshops have been identified in Herculaneum: Guidobaldi 2003. At Pompeii, epigraphical evidence points to gem-cutters and goldsmiths: *CIL* 4.8505, 4.710. For earrings as collateral for a loan: *CIL* 4.8203.

[39] IX.7.7. On these paintings: Spinazzola 1953, 189–194; Angelone 1986; Fröhlich 1991, 172–174, 333–335; Clarke 2003, 105–112. Nearby was an inscription mentioning a linen tunic woven with gold (*CIL* 4.9083: *tunica lintea aur[ata]*), which suggests the range of different materials worn in the city and also likely crowned any sartorial hierarchy in the city, especially if the linen were imported from abroad, as we know occurred: Andreau 1974, 107, 284, 289 n. 3, 292, 323. The sheer number and diversity of enterprises at Pompeii dedicated to the manufacture and cleaning of textiles, especially wool, also suggest a fixation on appearances. By one conservative count, there were at least thirty such establishments, ranging from places where wool was woven to dye-works, fulleries, and felt factories: Moeller 1976, 30–51 (to be read with Jongmann 1988). Cf. Flohr 2007.

[40] An electoral inscription within the painting records an endorsement by the *quactiliarii*, which appears to be local dialect for "felt makers:" *CIL* 4.7838.

how, in the street, various realms mix and mingle – gods push product even as they are revered – but the deities also tellingly match or outclass mortals in their garments.

Representations of Pompeians' garb in public spaces similarly speak to a preoccupation with appearances. The Praedia of Julia Felix frescoes depicting scenes in the forum imagine – in addition to six visible peddlers of cloth, clothing, and footwear – many city inhabitants using the space (Plate II, Figs. 24, 25). Their dress, when we can decipher it, offers several lessons. First is the multiplicity and vibrancy of the colors. Along with white garments, we see men and women alike in yellow, green, red, gray, and brown clothing. Second is the paucity of togas: of the sixty-seven figures whose clothing is reasonably discernible, only five are togate. Even of these, three are red, two white. The other figures wear a mixture of garments; tunics predominate, but a chiton, mantles, dresses of various types, and hooded cloaks also appear. I do not take this to mean that only a handful of the figures are citizens; rather, what is notable is that, of the five togate individuals, four appear to be engaged in distinctly civic-oriented activities. Two read public notices written along a series of statue bases. Two others preside at a legal proceeding. This sense of sartorial appropriateness extends to a bearded beggar who – dressed in rags, carrying a walking stick, and accompanied by a dog – receives a handout[41] (Fig. 25).

Between the poles of beggar and togate figures, little distinguishes people from one another. It is unclear if this was the goal of the artist and commissioner or whether, like the abandoned senatorial proposal to somehow mark out slaves, the paintings reveal a world in which it was difficult – when you could not watch what people did or evaluate other framing devices – to recognize someone's status or role immediately. If the latter was the case, then special adornment was all the more potent a claim about one's status or aspirations for people merely passing in the street. In the end, both this cycle of paintings and our literary sources about adornment point toward a tension between the difficulty of figuring out the status of some and the ease of identifying the rank of others. Such a tension is corollary to the nature of the street more broadly: as the domain of virtually everyone in the city, it could foster an egalitarian aura, yet that very openness and visibility also occasioned efforts to stand out, to perform in this space.

As much as self-presentation on the street centered on what one wore, Horace reminds us that making an impression was also a matter of how and with whom one moved around the city. Most people walked; some drove carts and wagons; a very few rode in carriages; and the richest, if they so chose, could make their way through the city in litters carried on the shoulders of slaves.

---

[41] Nappo 1991. The fifth togate figure appears to be negotiating with a vessel salesman.

Images from Pompeii suggest that the gods made the biggest splash on the streets because they were carried on *fercula*, litter-like floats, in processions.[42] The appeal of transport by litter was at least double: one did not have to walk at all, but could, like the *dives* in Juvenal's *Satire* 3, rest or read; moreover, riding in a litter lifted the traveler above others' heads.[43] There was nothing in and of itself objectionable about litters as modes of conveyance; they were accepted forms of display. Yet, in the hands of someone like Cicero, they could become signs of excessive luxury and moral softness.[44] As we have seen, Juvenal's opening sketch of Roman society absurdly envisions a rich document-forger moving along exposed on all sides. What irks Juvenal's narrator is both the litter's ill fit for an unjustly wealthy person and his lack of modesty: he rides in a reclining chair that is "open and nearly naked."[45] More normal was the situation in *Satire* 3, in which the rider was closed up tight inside.[46] Martial also pictures a would-be braggart turned into a laughingstock when the poet mocks a litter-rider who falls short in wealth, age, and strength. Carried by six Cappadocians, the poet's target is ridiculed "much more than if [he] were to walk naked mid-forum."[47] The litter's appeal and the misgivings many had toward it are neatly summarized by Juvenal: "The man who poisoned three uncles – should we let him ride past on his feathery litter and look down at us?"[48]

Riding in a litter by definition requires accompaniment, and it opens our eyes to an important pair of questions: how often did Romans walk alone through their cities? And what were the meanings of going alone or with a group? Timothy O'Sullivan has recently noted how, when Roman urban walking is described in ancient sources, it is nearly always discussed as a group undertaking. Part of this has to do with whose perspectives we have. O'Sullivan explains, "a class filter ... disguises the true extent of solitary urban walking; we do not hear much from those who had to walk through

---

[42] Although it is presumably fanciful, one depiction of Venus Pompeiana shows the goddess riding a red-prowed boat-cum-quadriga pulled by four elephants. See Fig. 90. For more on *fercula*, see Madigan 2012, esp. 39–42.

[43] Wheeled vehicles: van Tilburg 2007, 51–55; Kaiser 2011b, 188–190. Litters: Brown 1983; McGinn 1997–1998; O'Sullivan 2011, 71–74. The status associated with litter-riding is implied by various restrictions on who could move thusly through the streets: Caesar is said to have promulgated legislation limiting litter use (along with, tellingly, the wearing of scarlet and pearls) to specific groups in Rome: Suet. *Caes.* 43.1. Domitian similarly forbade its use by *feminae probosae*, "disgraced women": Suet. *Dom.* 8.3.

[44] Cic. *Verr.* 2.5.34; *Phil.* 2.58; 2.106.

[45] Juv. 1.65: *patens ac nuda paene cathedra.*

[46] Juv. 3.239–242. Cf. Juv. 4.21; Hor. *Sat.* 1.2.96–100; Brown 1983, 269–270.

[47] Mart. 6.77.1–6 (quotation from 5–6: *rideris multoque magis traduceris, Afer, / quam nudus medio si spatiere foro*). Mart. 6.77.9: *invidiosa tibi quam sit lectica requiris?* Cf. Juv. 7.141–143; Mart. 2.81; Petron. 28; Sen. *Ep.* 17.3.

[48] Juv. 1.158–159: *qui dedit ergo tribus patruis aconita, uehatur / pensilibus plumis atque illinc despiciat nos?*

the city alone."[49] Yet he also notes that the lack of solo walking may result from the relative chaos and danger of Roman urban streets where no police force was present, urbanites hoped for safety in numbers, and they often had slaves with them.[50]

Such retinues were marks of standing as leading men strode to the forum or elsewhere surrounded by clients or dependents. As the practice is described by the *Commentariolum Petitionis*, a handbook on electioneering dating to the Late Republic, a candidate for office should "head down to the Forum at regular times; a sizable crowd of daily escorts (*deductores*) brings forth a strong impression and adds greatly to one's reputation." The *Commentariolum* distinguishes these attendants from callers at a great man's house (*salutatores*) and those who follow him around full-time (*adsectatores*).[51] Some cleared the way for the great man, others followed.[52] Such displays, whether headed to the forum or through the city, are attested in the empire.[53] Juvenal's characteristically exaggerated portrait has someone looking to hire an orator and first considering "whether you have eight slaves, ten clients, and a litter to follow you, and citizens to walk in front."[54] The household tomb of the Statilii Tauri in Rome also suggests the importance of portraying one's wealth through slave attendants. The 116 individual slave and freedman epitaphs with job titles encompass a remarkable diversity and specificity of occupations, such as hairdressers, animal tenders, and gardeners. While the largest class of slaves (nineteen) are room attendants, next come those dedicated to travel in the street or beyond the city: sixteen runners or litter-bearers are listed, and ten bodyguards also appear.[55] A big crowd moving along was supposed to foretell an important person. It elevated the great man's city passage into the realm of formal processions, perhaps even forcing other streetgoers to move aside.

COME AS YOU ARE: EVALUATION ON THE STREET

Broadcasting claims about your social place was one thing; getting others to buy into your presentation was another. Horace's poem about making his way in

---

[49] O'Sullivan 2011, 6–7.
[50] Even in Horace's famous amble through Rome's heart, for example, a slave is along: Hor. *Sat.* 1.9.9–10. Cf. Hor. *Sat.* 1.6.110–115.
[51] *Comment. pet.* 36: . . . *certis temporibus descendito. magnam adfert opinionem, magnam dignitatem cotidiana in deducendo frequentia.* See also Cic. *Mur.* 70–71; *Att.* 1.18.1. On these and related escorts in Rome: O'Sullivan 2011, 54–71 (with prior bibliography).
[52] Mart. 3.46.3–6; Sen. *Ep.* 94.60.
[53] Several sources note how leading men intentionally restricted their escorts to avoid posing a threat to the *princeps*: Tac. *Ann.* 14.56; *Agr.* 40.3–4. Cf. Dio Cass. 59.27.5–6. For a misjudged retinue, see Luc. *Nigr.* 13.
[54] Juv. 7.141–143: . . . *an tibi servi / octo, decem comites, an post te sella, togati / ante pedes.* Cf. Sen. *Controv.* 5.2.
[55] Joshel 1992, table 3.2. Cf. Amm. Marc. 28.4.8.

Rome concludes with a less-favorable counterexample: "No one will call me cheap as he does you, praetor Tillius, when five slaves, carrying a pisspot and a winejug, accompany you on the Via Tiburtina."[56] Both episodes make the obvious point that all performances in the street hinged on observers who made the preening worth its while or who cast aspersions. And they raise questions: how were attempts at posturing received on the street? What kind of eye did Romans bring to these encounters?

In *Epode* 4, Horace and other flabbergasted witnesses soak in the sight of an upstart who dresses above his station:

> You, with your sides scarred by Spanish lashes, with your legs marked by iron fetters. You can certainly strut about, so proud of your money, but fortune can't change your breeding. Don't you see how, as you measure the length of the Via Sacra in a toga that's three yards wide, people going this way and that turn their faces towards you in the most unrestrained indignation?[57]

The populace's reaction chimes with the cutting remarks of Martial and Juvenal. Streetgoers draw poets' attention and scorn for many reasons. It might be their moral shortcomings, like the man who resorts to fraud to gain great wealth. It can be for their shamelessness, such as the widow parading behind her husband's bier after poisoning him. Blatant ostentation is sometimes the cause, as when litter riders throw open the curtains. And deceit also burns, as when Martial has one fellow cut a striking figure with his litter, retinue of attendants, and fancy clothing only to be revealed as resorting to pawning a ring to pay for dinner.[58] This satirical consensus suggests that a key characteristic of Roman streetgoers – in contrast to the *flâneur*, who was characterized by a largely elite and voyeuristic detachment from the city's action[59] – was their deep scrutiny of what they saw, heard, and smelled. Appearances were always open for questioning, and there swirled an embedded desire to pull the mask off pretenders to power, wealth, and status.

Additional evidence from a broader if less direct set of voices testifies to critical viewership that stretched past inspecting the most glaring devices (striped togas, jewelry, litters, etc.) to constant monitoring of more regular actions by more regular folks. Although our modern sensibilities generally hold that someone's outer appearance and inner qualities are largely unrelated, it was widely believed in antiquity that someone's body and its movements revealed

---

[56] Hor. *Sat.* 1.6.107–109: *obiciet nemo sordes mihi, quas tibi, Tilli, / cum Tiburte via praetorem quinque sequuntur / te pueri, lasanum portatntes oenophorumque.*

[57] Hor. *Epod.* 4.3–10: *hibericis peruste funibus latus / et crura dura compede. / licet superbus ambules pecunia, / fortuna non mutat genus. / videsne, sacram metiente te viam / cum bis trium ulnarum toga, / ut ora vertat huc et huc euntium / liberrima indignatio?*

[58] In addition to works cited earlier: Mart. 2.57 (on which see O'Sullivan 2011, 51–52).

[59] Larmour and Spencer 2007, 17–18. Cf. Edensor 1998, 217–218.

something about him or her. In Petronius's *Satyricon*, a woman brags to the narrator and one of his comrades: "I don't know how to predict the future, and I'm not one for astrology; but I can tell people's characters from their faces, and when I've seen someone walking, I know what they're thinking."[60] Whereas Petronius's maid fixated on the face and gait, Pliny the Elder concentrated on someone's eyebrows (pride, he wrote, "is born in the heart, but rises to the eyebrows and is suspended there"), and Cicero expresses a common opinion that the eyes mirrored and thus revealed the soul ("the face is a performance and image of the whole mind, and the eyes its chief indices").[61] All of these attitudes are grounded in what Barbara Kellum has called the "legibility of appearances" in Roman culture.[62] As a general principle, Romans believed that, if you looked carefully enough, you could judge a book by its cover.[63]

Recognizing and exploring this mindset is helpful for our understanding of street life generally because it contextualizes and underscores the critical viewership voiced by poets and also because it opens a point of entry for considering particular features that streetgoers may have looked for as they inspected their fellow pedestrians. As the following paragraphs consider that scrutiny, they focus on one issue that is especially germane to daily life on the street and that has received excellent scholarly attention — how one walked.[64] We need look no further than *Epode* 4 for an example of characterization through gait, as Horace has the former slave strut and walk with a measured step.[65] Indeed, one factor was the speed someone walked. Slaves were reputed to move so quickly as they scurried about on someone else's business, for instance, that the "running slave" was a stock figure in Roman comedy. Performances on stage, O'Sullivan notes, both reflected and contributed to cultural expectations; it made people watch for such behavior on the street.[66] Given such connections, it is not surprising to encounter individuals who monitor their stride. In Plautus's *Poenulus*, one freedman claims, "It's better for free citizens to walk through the city at a moderate pace; I think it up to slaves to run and hurry

---

[60] Petron. 126.3: *nec auguria novi nec mathematicorum caelum curare soleo; ex vultibus tamen hominum mores colligo, et cum spatiantem vidi, quid cogites scio.* There is an irony in her statement because Eumolpus and Encolpius are in disguise as slaves in the scene.

[61] Pliny *NH* 11.138: *haec* [scil. *supercilia*] *maxime indicant fastum, superbiam. aliubi conceptaculum, sed hic sedem habet; in corde nascitur, huc subit, hic pendet.* Cic. *De or.* 3.221: *animi est enim omnis actio, et imago animi vultus, indices oculi.* See also Quint. *Inst.* 11.3.75–76; Wilpert and Zenker 1950, 1.960–961; Corbeill 2004, 146–147.

[62] Kellum 1999, 288.

[63] The work of Gleason (1995, 1999) has been important in articulating this principle, at least in relation to constructions of gender, the body, and sexuality. See, for instance, Gleason 1995, xxi–xxii; Gleason 1999, 75–79.

[64] Corbeill 2002; O'Sullivan 2011, 16–22.

[65] Strut: Hor. *Epod.* 5.71, 8.14; *Sat.* 1.2.25, 1.4.51. Also, *OLD.* s.v. 4. Measure: *TLL* 8.883, 8.887.

[66] O'Sullivan 2011, 18.

about."[67] Part of the joke, of course, rests on the speaker's critique of a way of moving that he presumably had embodied only recently. To add to the gag, he now schleps along with embellished sloth to underscore his new status, which reveals a tension between innate movement and that which was carefully considered. If walking too fast risked being identified as servile, then walking too slow could look feminine, to judge from Cicero's admonishments of his son: "we must beware neither to use an effeminate lingering in our gait (so that we do not seem like floats in parades), nor in hurrying to pick up too much speed."[68] The idea is that such showiness was gendered feminine, while control and restraint were considered masculine.

The widespread contention that character was discernable from someone's style of walking is actually most visible when it is challenged, as when Augustus, according to Suetonius, sought to explain away Tiberius's odd behavior:

> [Tiberius's] gait was a stiff stride, and if he ever broke his usual stern silence to address those walking with him, he spoke with great deliberation and eloquent movement of the fingers. Augustus disliked these mannerisms and put them down to pride, but frequently assured both the Senate and the commons that they were physical, not moral defects.[69]

The *princeps*, while holding the standard belief that Tiberius's smugness was discernible from his walk and gestures, seeks to disavow certain constituencies' worries when they evaluate his adopted son in the same way.

The connection was so ingrained in the Roman mindset that there developed in the imperial period a substantial corpus of literature that systematically outlined how to decipher bodily movements. Maud Gleason describes one of these physiognomic texts as "a highly elaborated operations manual for a technology of suspicion that was indigenous to [the author's] culture."[70] Polemo, one of physiognomy's most famous practitioners, brags, "There are important signs to be found in the voice, the breath, and in the movement of every part of the body."[71] In a world without background checks and Googling, the utility and stakes of "reading" someone accurately are evident:

> If divine men have made any discovery that can be of truly immense benefit to those who study it, it is physiognomy. For nobody would

---

[67] Plaut. *Poen.* 522–523: *liberos homines per urbem modico magis par est gradu / ire, servile esse duco festinantem currere.*

[68] Cic. *Off.* 1.131: *cavendum autem est, ne aut tarditatibus utamur [in] ingressu mollioribus, ut pomparum ferculis similes esse videamur, aut in festinantibus suscipiamus nimias celeritates . . .*

[69] Suet. *Tib.* 68.3: *incedebat cervice rigida et obstipa, adducto fere vultu, plerumque tacitus, nullo aut rarissimo etiam cum proximis sermone eoque tardissimo, nec sine molli quadam digitorum gesticulatione. quae omnia ingrata atque arrogantiae plena et animaduertit Augustus in eo et excusare temptauit saepe apud senatum ac populum professus naturae uitia esse, non animi.*

[70] Gleason 1995, 55.

[71] Polem. *Phgn.* 1,1.168F.

deposit in trust his financial assets, his heirlooms, his wife, or his children – or enter into any sort of social relationship – with a person whose appearance radiates the signs of dishonesty, lechery, or double-dealing. As if by some God-given, inerrant, and prophetic art, the physiognomist understands the character and purposes, so to speak, of all men: how to choose associates only from those who are worthy, and how to guard against the evildoing of unprincipled people without having to experience it first.[72]

A physiognomist, or just about anyone with the right eye for detail, could spot a man walking along with a mincing prance and understand the irrepressible signal: he was a *cinaedus*, someone who operated outside sexual norms by being either oversexed or the passive member of a male–male pairing.[73] Even hidden *cinaedi* could be detected from their affect: "Although they are certainly *cinaedi*, they actually try to remove suspicion from themselves by straining to assume a more virile appearance. They imitate a youthful stride, hold themselves with a peculiar firmness, intensify their gaze and voice, and with their whole body they adopt a rigid bearing."[74] There was little that could escape careful scrutiny, or so many believed.

I will say more in Chapter 5 about the exact characteristics ascribed to "manly walks" and others. For now, what draws my attention from this broader strain of thought are two intertwined issues: first, much more minute signs than the fancy ones we already encountered were visible on the street and were, accordingly, a matter of conscious formulation by a wide swath of society who monitored their gait, expressions, gestures, and general bearing. Horace, it turns out, might have had more in common with Plautus's freedman than he wished: a desire to embody elite forms of movement and to shrug off his family's history of servitude. Second, and perhaps more importantly, physiognomic literature and the wide-ranging cultural trend of deciphering appearances reveal a deep-seated aura of skepticism and questioning of features large and small in Roman visuality. People looked carefully, aiming to spot fissures and signs of imposters. Try as one might to keep negative attributes hidden, exterior signs were understood (for

---

[72] Adam. 1.2, 1.298–299F: θείων δὲ ἀνδρῶν εἴπερ ἄλλο τι καὶ τὸ φυσιογνωμονεῖν εὕρημα πλεῖστα καὶ μέγιστα τοὺς μαθόντας δυνάμενον ὠφελεῖν. οὔτε γὰρ παρακαταθήκην δοίη τις ἂν οὔτε τι κειμήλιον, ἢ γαμετὴν ἢ παῖδας ἢ πιστεύσειεν, ἢ καὶ φιλίας ἁπλῶς ἡστινοσοῦν κοινωνήσειε τοῖς ἀπιστίας ἢ ἀσελγείας ἢ τινος κακουργίας ἐπὶ τῆς μορφῆς σημεῖα προλάμποντα φέρουσι. πάντων γὰρ ὡς ἔπος εἰπεῖν ἀνθρώπων καθάπερ ἀπό τινος θεοπέμπτου καὶ ἀπλανοῦς μαντείας ἦθος καὶ πρόθεσιν βίων ὁ φυσιογνώμων ἐπίσταται, ὡς τὰς μὲν τῶν χρηστῶν φιλίας μόνων αἱρεῖσθαι, τὰς δὲ τῶν πονηρῶν κακίας πρὸ πείρας φυλάττεσθαι (Translation: M. Gleason).

[73] For this example, see Gleason 1995, 64–81. For the broader context of walking and what it revealed about a person, at least in rhetorical invective, see Corbeill 2002.

[74] Anonymous Latin *Physiognomy* 74: . . . *qui cinaedi quidem certa fide sunt, verum suspicionem a se removere conantes virilem sumere speciem sibimet laborant. Nam et incessum pedum iuvenilem imitantur et semet ipsos rigore quodam confirmant et oculos et vocem intendant atque omne corpus erigunt.* . . . (Translation: M. Gleason).

better and for worse) to be both transparent (socially, sexually, etc.) and potent. Such a practice was by no means limited to the street but may well have been most pronounced there because of the space's environment: inclusive and open, yet also interactive and status-conscious. Where more was in play, more was at stake, and, in the street, these efforts at distinguishing oneself and perceiving slight distinctions in others reached critical states.

THE STREET AS AN ARENA OF HONOR AND REVENGE

The visibility and universal access that made the street an arena for showy display and quiet judgment also opened it as a potent platform of rebuke and insult, where the more powerful were susceptible to very public attacks. A large body of Roman law dealt with defamation in public, a fact that, in itself, reveals much about Romans' concerns with their public image and threats to it.[75] At the heart of this issue lies the concept of *iniuria*, which, though it initially encompassed only physical assault, took on progressively broader definitions over time until it included almost any willful slight to a person's dignity or standing.[76] The actionable forms of such insulting conduct – such as trespassing on a man's land or lashing his slaves – were myriad, almost encyclopedic.[77] Interestingly, our sources suggest that the street was a particularly powerful spot for *iniuria* to occur. Seneca, in his exercises for debate, outlines a situation in which a man has been murdered. He is survived by a son who, because the victim was not robbed, suspects a particular rich man of committing the crime. In response, the son takes on an appearance fit for mourning – draped in black, hair disheveled – and stalks the rich man wherever he goes, through the streets and the forum. The rich man sues, demanding that the son bring a charge if he suspects wrongdoing. The son refuses, and when the rich man's subsequent candidacy for office proves unsuccessful, he accuses the son of *iniuria*.[78]

The opinions of jurists speak both to the charge that he could have leveled and to other actions that were thought to carry a similar punch. Ulpian writes:

> The praetor bans generally anything which would be to another's disrepute. And so whatever one may do or say to bring another into disrepute gives rise to the action for insult. Here are instances of conduct to another's disrepute: to lower another's reputation, one wears mourning or filthy garments or lets one's beard grow or lets one's hair down or writes a lampoon or issues or sings something detrimental to another's honor.[79]

[75] For an overview of the Roman law on defamation, see Daube 1953; Manfredini 1979.
[76] On *iniuria*: Crook 1967, 250–255; Pólay 1986.
[77] Trespassing: *Dig.* 47.10.15.31, 23. Slave lashing: Gai. *Inst.* 3.222.
[78] Sen. *Controv.* 10.1.
[79] *Dig.* 47.10.15.27: *generaliter vetuit praetor quid ad infamiam alicuius fieri. proinde quodcumque quis fecerit vel dixerit, ut alium infamet, erit actio iniuriarum. haec autem fere sunt, quae ad infamiam alicuius*

What is done injury is the rich man's *pudor*. That is, being followed by the other man implied that he had done a dastardly act, which didn't threaten his personal self-worth so much as tarnish his reputation and good name. Among the potential retorts that Seneca puts forth for the son, one is particularly telling; the interlocutor implies that meetings between the two men were inevitable since it is not "as if poor men have one street, rich men another."[80] The shared space of the street, the legal right of the destitute and the wealthy to be in the same location, and that spot's visibility before the entire city all offered oppor-tunities for reprisals on the part of those who had suffered wrongs.[81]

Public redress in the street took a host of similar forms. One could weep while following someone around the city, thus similarly implying that he had done something wrong.[82] Another possibility was carrying around a statue of the emperor, as though you were under threat and ready at a moment's notice to seek asylum. That act could produce *invidia* or *iniuria*, according to the *Digesta*.[83] You might claim that someone had not repaid a debt, make a show of asking that person for mercy, or (in a tactic I will entertain in greater detail in the next chapter) raise a ruckus outside someone's house. But, as the legal passage suggests, publishing a poem, singing a song, or confronting someone were, because of their immediate directness, more visible and shameful ways of provoking embarrassment.[84] The heat of street confrontations is palpable in Catullus 42, which portrays an episode that combines various methods and twists them slightly. In place of people, hendecasyllables surround a woman who has taken the poet's notepad and refuses to give it back. They encircle her, make demands, call her a streetwalker, lash out with other insults, resolve into a repeated chant, pile on more insults, and reprise the chant with yet louder shouting. When all fails, they comically try flattery instead.[85] The threat of such an attack motivated good behavior or moderated poor treatment – or at least that is the implication of a declamation ascribed to Quintilian. To a rich man who has left a poor man resourceless, an advocate says: "Don't let a beggar wander through the city arousing hatred for you and, reflecting badly on the source of your misfortune, supply reasons for hating you."[86] A man without

---

    fiunt: ut puta ad invidiam alicuius veste lugubri utitur aut squalida, aut si barbam demittat vel capillos
    submittat, aut si carmen conscribat vel proponat vel cantet aliquod, quod pudorem alicuius laedat.

[80] Sen. *Controv.* 10.1.2: *quasi aliud iter pauperes, aliud divites habeant.*

[81] See also Lintott 1968, 16–18.

[82] [Quint.] 361. Note the emphasis on the public nature of act and the embarrassment it provokes: 361.10–11. See also [Quint.] 260.10 for the potential impact of seeing someone struck down by fortune.

[83] *Dig.* 47.10.38.pr (*invidia*), 48.19.28.7 (*iniuria*). See also Tac. *Ann.* 3.36; Suet. *Tib.* 58.

[84] Most surviving examples of lampoons come from the realm of high politics: e.g., Suet. *Iul.* 49, 51; Mart. 11.20. On the phenomenon, Richlin 1992, 86–96.

[85] On this poem, see Fraenkel 1961.

[86] [Quint.] 9.18: . . . *ne vagaretur per urbem invidiosus mendicus et calamitatis auctori crimin[os]us causas vulgo suggereret odiorum.*

hope, it seems, still held social potency because he could take justice-seeking to the street, where his attempts to convince others of his opinions of the rich man were both more public and potentially more difficult to control.

Plautus mines these situations for comedy when, in the *Pseudolus*, the pimp Ballio, after selling a prostitute he had promised to the love-struck Calidorus, is stopped in the street. Although they are humorously short-handed and therefore cannot encircle the pimp (as Catullus's verses had), Calidorus commands his slave: "Pseudolus, stand on the other side and load this man up with curses!" Then they let him have it, and the pimp admits to each of nearly twenty curses, "Tomb-robber!", they shout. "Certainly," he replies. "Gallows-man!" "Right on!" Ballio's calm responses get laughs because, in reversing normal reactions to such a street confrontation, he accepts with equanimity efforts to shame him.[87] Some authors suggest simply shrugging off insults.[88] The more typical resentment and anxiety engendered by street slander is evident in the reactions of Dio Chrysostom, who voices frustration with the constant threat of being accused of some wrongdoing and thus losing face:

> Is not the trial concerning reputation always in progress wherever there are men – that is, foolish men – not merely once a day but many times, and not before a definite panel of judges but before all men without distinction, and, moreover, men not bound by oath, men without regard for either witnesses or evidence? For they sit in judgment without either having knowledge of the case or listening to testimony or having been chosen by lot, and it makes no difference to them if they cast their vote at a drinking bout or at the bath and, most outrageous of all, he who today is acquitted tomorrow is condemned. Accordingly, whoever is the victim of this malady of courting popularity is bound to be subject to criticism as he walks about, to pay heed to everyone, and to fear lest wittingly or unwittingly he give offence to somebody, but particularly to one of those who are old and of ready wit. For if he should have the misfortune to have offended somebody ever so little, as often happens, straightaway the offended person lets fly a harsh word; and if with that word he perhaps misses the mark, nevertheless he causes dismay, while if he should hit the vital spot he has destroyed his victim forthwith.[89]

---

[87] Plaut. *Psued.* 357–370 for the episode. 357: *Pseudole, adsiste altrim secus atque onera hunc maledictis.* 361: *bustirape. certo. furcifer. factum optume.*

[88] Aul. Gell. 7.14.3; Sen. *Ira* 2.33.2.

[89] Dio Chrys. 66.18–19: ὁ περὶ τῆς δόξης ἀγὼν οὐκ ἀεὶ τοῖς ἀνθρώποις τοῖς ἀνοήτοις ἐνέστηκεν, οὐ μόνον ἅπαξ τῆς ἡμέρας, ἀλλὰ πολλάκις, οὐδὲ ἐφ᾽ ὡρισμένοις δικασταῖς, ἀλλὰ πᾶσιν ἁπλῶς, καὶ τούτοις ἀνωμότοις καὶ μήτε μαρτύρων ἐπιστρεφομένοις μήτε τεκμηρίων; μήτε γὰρ εἰδότες μήτε ἀκούοντες μήτε λαχόντες δικάζουσι, καὶ οὐδὲν αὐτοῖς διαφέρει πίνουσιν ἢ λουομένοις τὴν ψῆφον φέρειν· καὶ τὸ πάντων δεινότατον· ὃν γὰρ ἂν ἀπολύσῃ τήμερον, αὔριον καταδικάζει. οὐκοῦν ἀνάγκη τὸν ὑπὸ τῆς νόσου ταύτης ἐχόμενον ὑπεύθυνον περιέρχεσθαι καὶ προσέχειν ἑκάστῳ καὶ δεδοικέναι μή τινα ἑκὼν ἢ ἄκων λυπήσῃ, μάλιστα τῶν ἑτοίμων τινὰ καὶ τῶν εὐτραπέλων. εἰ γὰρ καὶ σμικρόν, οἷα πολλὰ

Fascinatingly, Dio Chrysostom, in bemoaning the threat to reputation, resorts to an extended judicial metaphor. He denigrates the jurors in this court of public opinion as foolish, uninformed, and fickle, yet still endows them and their "testimony" with persistence and power, and he contends that men of reputation dismiss them at their own risk.[90] The intentional irony of Dio's judicial imagery is that these confrontations were, strictly speaking, extralegal, a fact underscored by a declamation from pseudo-Quintilian. A young cuckold, after discovering the offending couple in the act, contends that he neither took the matter to magistrates nor sought to arouse a public scandal by shouting. (He accepted money instead.)[91] If he had gathered his friends to denounce the wrongdoer, then he would have, like many others, taken advantage of the street's visibility to shame someone more powerful. The street, then, offered the less-powerful an informal "court" that was always in session and that might resolve a perceived wrong when the law could not. Viewed from an elite point of view like Dio's, the street was a danger zone where individuals lived under constant threat of public reproach.

According to legal sources, the street also abounded with hazards for elite women. At the end of a list of potential acts that were prosecutable as *iniuria*, the jurist Gaius appends another one relevant to our arena: persistently following a *materfamilias* (matron) or a *praetextatus* (a prepubescent free-born youth).[92] Ulpian refines the requirements and explains a motivation: "he follows [a woman] who silently and constantly pursues her, for assiduous proximity virtually reveals something disreputable."[93] In other words, the reputation of women was also at stake, but the relevant realm was not politics and business dealings but notions of sexual purity and propriety, as Ulpian makes clear elsewhere when he adds two related activities for which charges could be brought. First was depriving someone of his or her attendant, which would result in a solo walker, with knock-on effects for the public's assessment of someone's moral character. Second was addressing someone, whether the attendant or the escorted person, with "seductive speech" because it represented an assault on someone's virtue.[94] Another jurist adds: "The modesty of a person is said to be attacked when an attempt is made to render a virtuous

---

συμβαίνει, προσκρούσας τινὶ τύχοι, εὐθὺς ἐπαφῆκε ῥῆμα χαλεπόν· καὶ τοῦτο εἰπών, ἐὰν μὲν ἀποτύχῃ πως, οὐδὲν ἧττον ἐτάραξεν· ἐὰν δ᾽ ἐπιτύχῃ τοῦ καιρίου παραχρῆμα ἀνήρηκεν.

[90] For a social inversion involving lower class shouts against the elite and the attendant fear provoked, see Tac. *Ann.* 3.36.

[91] [Quint.] 279.16: *tum iste tamen adiit magistratus, non vociferatione saltem invidiam facere apud populum conatus est. . . .*

[92] Gai. *Inst.* 3.220: *iniuria autem committitur . . . siue quis matrem familias aut praetextatum adsectatus fuerit.*

[93] *Dig.* 47.10.15.22: *adsectatur, qui tacitus frequenter sequitur: adsiduo enim frequentia quasi praebet nonnullam infamiam.* Cf. *Dig.* 47.10.39.

[94] Attendant: *Dig.* 47.10.15.16–18. "Seductive speech": *Dig.* 47.10.15.20: *appellare est blanda oratione alterius pudicitiam adtemptare. . . .* Cf. *Dig.* 47.10.1.2.

person depraved."[95] What an episode of street harassment might entail becomes clearer in Plautus's *Mercator*, when one character ponders sending a beautiful slave girl into the city as an attendant for the *materfamilias*. When asked why he will not allow it, the man of the house replies:

> Because it would be a scandal if a woman of her appearance were to follow the mother of a household; were she to walk through the streets, everybody would stare at her, ogle her, nod to her, wink at her, whistle after her, pinch her, call after her, and be a nuisance.

Even with all the unwanted attention to which the young woman was subjected − the eyes, hands, noises, and gestures − the man's concerns lie with the effects this treatment would have for himself and his wife, not the slave. He worries that his house will be serenaded, elegies will be scrawled on the door, and he and his wife would be ill-spoken because it would appear they are keeping a brothel.[96] Although exaggerated for comic effect (not to mention twisted, with the matron's character impugned and not protected by her companion), the episode outlines the catcalls, groping, and other treatment that may have occurred when the vulnerable were exposed to the eyes, words, and actions of all city dwellers.

This, of course, raises the question of how unattended women, slaves, and the like were treated on the street. Plautus might again offer a hint for, in the *Curculio*, a slave offers advice to his lovelorn master:

> Nobody stops anyone from walking along the public street, provided you don't make inroads on fenced-in properties, and provided you restrain yourself from married ladies, widows, virgins, youths, and free children − otherwise, love whomever you want![97]

Beyond reinforcing the ideology of universal street access, the slave's sentiment pushes in two directions. On the one hand, it points up the extent of protection (legal or social) that many urban dwellers had from sexual aggressors; yet, on the other hand, it also shows how no legal offense occurred if advances were made toward others. Absent attendants, how was one supposed to recognize who was who? In the eyes of the law, appearances were close to reality because the restrictions on addressing someone or abducting an attendant were lessened or dispensed with in cases where someone's status was not immediately identifiable:

---

[95] *Dig.* 47.10.10: *adtemptari pudicitia dicitur, cum id agitur, ut ex pudico impudicus fiat.*
[96] Plaut. *Merc.* 405–411 (quotation from 405–408): *quia illa forma matrem familias / flagitium sit si sequatur; quando incedat per vias, / contemplent, conspiciant omnes, nutent, nictent, sibilent, / vellicent, vocent, molesti sint. . . .*
[97] Plaut. *Curc.* 35–38: *nemo ire quemquam publica prohibet via; / dum ne per fundum saeptum facias semitam, / dum ted abstineas nupta, vidua, virgine, / iuventute et pueris liberis, ama quid lubet.* Cf. Paul. *Sent.* 5.4.21, which includes "flashing" in a list of prosecutable offenses.

> If anyone should speak to maidens who are attired in the garments of
> slaves, he will be considered to be guilty of a minor offence; and still less, if
> they are dressed as prostitutes, and not as matrons. Still, if the woman be
> not in the dress of a matron and someone accost her or abduct her
> attendant, he will be liable to the action for insult.[98]

This opinion highlights the ease with which someone might be misidentified in
the street, the resultant importance of acting out how one wanted to be seen,
and the magnitude of the consequences if one assailed the character or reputation of a person of standing in this most conspicuous urban zone. Here, law
reflects the tenuous nature of the street's stage as a space where impressions
might harden into reputations that were carefully polished and maintained, yet
also where they were vulnerable to speedy erosion and destruction.

MAINTAINING STATUS

In addition to reinforcing the importance of appearances on the Roman street,
physiognomic and other texts underscore Romans' awareness of and attention
to those appearances' legibility. Romans did not just look, in other words, but
knew that they looked and were looked at. Such a dynamic is bound to have
affected what actions were undertaken, moderated, or snuffed out because of
the surveillance one underwent amid this "forest of eyes."[99] If we had more
court speeches like the ones preserved in Attic oratory, we would have a better
grasp of the potentially normative code of the street. As it stands, only occasional snippets offer some sense of popular morality. In Plautus, for instance,
characters chastise one another for what they perceive to be aberrant street
behavior, such as kissing, yelling, wearing too much perfume, and generally
breaking the rules.[100] Cicero cautions against dancing or singing publicly,
saying that these are not the activities of the "good," "righteous," or "wise"
man, which rather leads one to question whether they were frequently practiced by some.[101]

Cicero's connection of actions and reputation offers a reminder, together
with the physiognomists and laws concerning women, that status was a matter
of continual maintenance. Social standing was not simply earned and stored
away forever like a diploma; it required monitoring, negotiation, and performance. To the dialogue between those making claims and those watching
critically or threatening others' reputations, then, we can also spotlight and add

---

[98] *Dig.* 47.10.15.15: *si quis virgines appellasset, si tamen ancillari veste vestitas, minus peccare videtur:
multo minus, si meretricia veste feminae, non matrum familiarum vestitae fuissent. si igitur non
matronali habitu femina fuerit et quis eam appellavit vel ei comitem abduxit, iniuriarum tenetur.*

[99] "Forest of eyes": Gleason 1995, 55.

[100] Kissing: *Poen.* 1301. Yelling loudly: *Truc.* 759. Perfume: *Cas.* 240. Rules: *Poen.* 520–529.

[101] Cic. *Off.* 1.145 (singing), 3.75 (dancing), 3.93 (dancing).

additional responses – moments where someone potentially "lost face" in the street and then sought reprisal in the same venue. These episodes occur in settings grand and humble, in Rome and Campania alike.

The push and pull for status is illustrated by an episode from Rome's Republican past, the events surrounding the passage and repeal of the *Lex Oppia*, which so resonated in Augustan Rome that they earned a lengthy treatment in Livy's history.[102] Originally carried in 215 BCE at the height of the Second Punic War, this sumptuary law cast a broad net over women's activities. It outlawed the wearing of certain parti-colored garments, riding in carriages in Rome, and possessing more than a half-ounce of gold. Theories abound about the law's fundamental purpose – from a measure of financial austerity to a show of common wartime sacrifice – but clearly its terms restricted the appearance of women in public, and, at least for vehicular transportation, they particularly regulated self-presentation in the street. Despite the many questions that the law raises – why parti-colored garments? – the women's reactions twenty years later during debate about the law's possible abrogation have drawn the most ancient and modern interest. In Livy's narrative, the scene is the forum, in 195 BCE; politicians argue about the law's repeal, while supporters of each side pack the city's most prestigious spaces. As men descend into the civic center for the debate, women gather in the streets and block all passageways into the forum, confronting passers-by and imploring them to repeal the law. This strategy, Livy writes, continued for several days as the debate dragged on, with the crowd of demonstrators growing daily as women from nearby towns flocked to lend support. After debate was completed, the number of women on the street swelled still more and, when tribunes threatened to veto the law's retraction, the crowd laid siege to their houses until they backed down.

On one level, the fervent debate over women's adornment and urban movement confirms the categories of display that Horace prompted us to investigate and stresses the power they were thought to wield. And we witness, with each step in this struggle, a different type of street statement. During the war, some segments of society mustered enough strength to promulgate a restriction on female display. After the war, as the women sought to regain their full abilities, their mass display of solidarity and the political leverage they gained from it were manifested in the very space where their actions had previously been restricted. In the end, the women's distinctions were won back when their foray into the streets and the civic arena achieved another piece of legislation. And their proud resumption of once-forbidden garb and mode of conveyance presumably closed the circle. They had fought to claim

---

[102] Livy 34.1–8. Cf. Tac. *Ann.* 3.33–34; Val. Max. 9.1.3. On the episode: Culham 1982; Olson 2008, 99–104. On its place within other demonstrations by women during the Republic: Hemelrijk 1987. On the Augustan sensibility of Livy's narrative: Milnor 2005, 154–179.

back their trappings of standing, scoring political points in the street in the process.

Although the disputes about reputation had a smaller scale, similar instances of give and take are visible on the streets of Campanian cities. Along one bar front at Pompeii (I.10.2–3), for example, two romantic rivals sparred epigraphically:

SEVERUS: Successus the weaver loves the barmaid of the inn, called Iris, who doesn't care for him, but he asks and she feels sorry for him. A rival wrote this. Farewell.

SUCCESSUS: You're jealous, bursting out with that. Don't try to muscle in on someone who's better-looking and is a wicked and charming man.

SEVERUS: I have written and spoken. You love Iris, who doesn't care for you. Severus to Successus.[103]

As each participant in this exchange came along and found the slight that his adversary had scratched into the plaster, he added his own response, thus making visible a contest that was perhaps also evident in other street actions: intimidating or avoiding one another on the sidewalk, parading with Iris, or even resorting to fisticuffs. I will say more about other localized struggles in Chapter 8, but one deserves consideration alongside the *Lex Oppia* episode because of its push-and-pull nature. Near a bar front on the Via dell'Abbondanza in Pompeii, a woman named Zmyrina, who was likely affiliated with the bar, endorsed Gaius Julius Polybius for office[104] (see Figure 86). At some later point, her name was white-washed from the poster, leaving just the candidate's initials. Then, several election cycles later, another poster was painted immediately above the spot where Zmyrina's name had been covered. It read: *C. Lollium Fuscum Asellinas rogant nec sine Zmryina.*[105] Although the apparent accusative of *Asellinas* is hard to understand, the plural of both the noun and verb suggest a collective endorsement, probably by women who worked at the bar. *Nec sine* literally means "not without," but, as an example of litotes, has an intensifying effect, meaning "and especially Zmyrina." In other words, in response to the deletion of their colleague's name, the women likely appended a rejoinder of their own, in effect voicing Zmyrina's agency all the more fervently directly above where it was negated. Taken together, the two bar-front exchanges show the importance of maintaining one's reputation by responding to threats to one's public "face" on

---

[103] *CIL* 4.8258: *Sucessus textor amat coponiaes ancilla,* | *nomine Hiredem, quae quidem illum* | *non curat, sed ille rogat, illa comiseretur.* | *scribit rivalis, vale.* | *invidiose, quia rumperes, sedare noli formonsiorem* | *et qui est homo prevessimus et bellus. CIL* 4.8259: *dixi, scripsi. Amas Hiredem* | *quae te non curat. Sev[erus] Successo ut s . . . . . s . . . . . Severus.* Text and translation of Cooley and Cooley 2004, 77–78.

[104] *CIL* 4.7864.

[105] *CIL* 4.7863.

the street. This impulse is most visible for those who wore gold and rode in carriages in Rome; the counterclaims by lower strata that are recoverable from the material remains, however, demonstrate that the urge to answer back and to fling retorts at catcallers, scrawlers of poems, and those who raised an eyebrow ran strong throughout society's ranks.

POLITICS AND THE STREET

Both the Zmyrina and *Lex Oppia* episodes highlight the street's character as a civic space where political sentiment could be expressed and where corporate urban concerns could be celebrated, mourned, heightened, and occasionally resolved. Most direct are episodes in late republican Rome, when gangs of supporters advanced their leader's cause by strong-arming the opposition in street battles or by blockading streets to the forum.[106] Beyond these rough tactics, we read stories from Rome's earlier days when community sentiment was articulated by granting special rights. A victorious leader like Publicola was awarded honors in the street, such as the unusual ability to arrange his house doors so that they opened not inward, as was normal, but outward into public, where they probably interfered with traffic. This concession, reports Plutarch, allowed Publicola to constantly partake of public honor, which prolonged a fleeting ceremonial moment.[107] Also in the early Republic, when the mother and wife of Coriolanus dissuaded him from attacking Rome alongside the Volscians, Valerius Maximus reports, the senate honored the whole order of matrons by decreeing that men should make way for them on the sidewalk.[108] By contrast, when Rome's political fortunes were lagging, magistrates were attentive to public appearances; after Rome's monstrous defeat at Cannae during the Second Punic War, women were forbidden from the streets because their lamentations brought fear and confusion to the city, according to Livy.[109] The notion of street life mirroring the public mood is also clear in later periods and on more positive occasions. After Pompey recovered from a protracted illness and was traveling from Naples to Rome, each town he passed through feted him in the streets. Feasts, sacrifices, garlands, torches, and flowers, reports Plutarch, were part of the "most beautiful and splendid sight."[110] Of course, cooption of the street, drawing attention, and being celebrated were all part of the ultimate military and political street activity in Rome, the triumphal parade

---

[106] Lintott 1968; Nippel 1995.
[107] Plut. *Publ.* 20; Pliny *NH* 36.112, who calls this the "most notable mark of distinction in the houses of men who had celebrated a triumph."
[108] Val. Max. 5.2.1. They were also honored with fillets and, in a precursor to *Lex Oppia* issues, permission to wear purple and gold clothing. Cf. Val. Max. 1.8.4.
[109] Livy 22.55.
[110] Plut. *Pomp.* 57.1–2: θέαμα κάλλιστον εἶναι καὶ λαμπρότατον.

in celebration of a victorious general, which saw him assume momentary god-like status as he rode through the city.[111]

These episodes capture ways that streets expressed and reflected extraordinary civic honors or disappointments. But politics and the street intersected more frequently, with the street as a venue for voicing or shaping political sentiments. In a letter to his brother, for example, Cicero explains the populace's way of showing their preferences: applause and warm greetings meet one politician in public while another is followed by people hissing and shouting insults.[112] Although similar sounds probably attended leading figures as they made their way, together with their escorts, around streets beyond Rome, our evidence is limited to the physical remains, such as the substantial corpus of electoral posters painted on the streetfronts of Pompeii. More than 2,500 such endorsements have been recorded, and they infuse the city's thoroughfares with a constant awareness of civic affairs. For those running for aedile, electoral posters were expedient because election to that office appears hotly contested. But the practice was largely symbolic for duumvir candidates; it seems that a single slate of two ran. Even a marginally literate visitor to Pompeii could discern the city's political bigwigs while walking to market because their names were splashed big and bold across shop- and house-fronts. Little scholarly consensus has emerged to explain the phenomenon of electoral endorsements, but the frequent naming of specific endorsers — as individuals or groups — suggests that both candidate and endorser stood to gain by linking themselves so visibly.[113]

Popular groundswells took advantage of the street's visibility and connectivity not just to launch someone up the political ladder, but occasionally also to transform the street into a communal space of righting wrongs and airing grievances. Livy tells the story of the appearance, in the year 495 BCE, of a man whom the gathered crowd recognized as a distinguished centurion despite his emaciated, filthy, and overall "savage" appearance. Upon seeing his battle-earned scars and learning of the loss of his family's farm, his subsequent impoverishment, and his eventual enslavement, the throng's outrage crystalized. Soon debtors and others poured into all the city's streets invoking "the protection of the Quirites." Numbers grew, cries pulsed through the streets, and ultimately some protestors confronted senators in the forum. Given the episode's early dramatic date, Livy's account probably treads along a line between myth and history, yet it still suggests how an uprising might gain traction in the streets.[114] Another story, narrated by Aulus Gellius, has more to

[111] Among the lengthy list of works devoted to the triumph, see Beard 2007. Cf. Cic. *Phil.* 2.108 (on which O'Sullivan 2011, 62).
[112] Cic. *Att.* 38.1.
[113] Castrén 1975; Franklin 1980, 2001; Biundo 1996, 2003; Mouritsen 1999; Chiavia 2002.
[114] Livy 2.23.1–7. Cf. Livy 3.38.

do with streets' ability to perpetuate the memory of a nefarious deed. It seems that, after a statue of Horatius Cocles in the Comitium had been struck by lightning, Etruscan diviners were summoned. Because of their persistent hatred of Rome and especially of the general who had defeated their ancestors, one presumes, the Etruscans gave poor advice about the statue's siting. Once discovered, they were put to death, and their comeuppance was immortalized in a song composed and sung by boys throughout the whole city; "Lousy counsel is worst for the counselor."[115] In both cases, then, the corridors of streets stretched an incident from the forum tentacle-like through the city, ensuring that all learned of misdeeds as the noises spread and echoed into windows and shops.

Street scenes even turned public celebrations on their head in an effort to extort or humiliate. In one Italian town, the people blocked a centurion's funerary procession, not letting it out of the forum until the deceased's heirs agreed to fund a gladiatorial performance.[116] In ancient Sena (modern Siena), a mob seized a Roman senator named Manlius Patruitus and beat him at the command of local magistrates, for what reason we do not know. Beyond the physical humiliation, the senator was subjected to wails, laments, and a mock funeral while insults were hurled at the whole senate. The funeral of someone like Patruitus would have trumpeted his deeds through the streets and beyond, but Siena's population, like so many individuals and their public reproachments of the powerful, inverted the normal state of affairs to voice their disapproval.[117] We are accustomed to popular uprisings in the forum and venues for spectacle, but so, too, did the street offer a powerful vehicle for publicizing the opinion of some or many.[118]

CONCLUSION: AWARENESS OF SOCIAL HIERARCHY

One fascinating current in imperial biography involves the emperor "acting-down" and venturing into the city incognito either to revel in low-life haunts or to wreak havoc in disguise. When, at the turning point that typifies many of his biographies, Suetonius wants to show Nero's flaws of character as they bloom, he turns to the street:

> Impudence, lust, extravagance, greed, and cruelty – at first his acts were certainly gradual and hidden and might be chalked up to youthful mis-steps, but even then no one doubted that they were defects of his very nature and not due to his time of life. Immediately after dusk he would grab a cap or a wig and enter the taverns or wander about the streets

---

[115] Aul. Gell. 4.5.
[116] Suet. *Tib.* 37.
[117] Tac. *Hist.* 4.45. Cf. Dio Cass. fr. 39.5–9.
[118] Nippel 1995, esp. 47–60, 70–78; Kelly 2007.

playing pranks, which however were very far from harmless; for he used to beat men as they were returning home from dinner, wounding anyone who fought back and throwing them into the sewers. He would even break into shops and rob them, setting up a market in the Palace, where he divided the booty which he took, sold it at auction, and then squandered the proceeds.[119]

Scenes of emperors entering the street were not particular to Nero but marked a relatively common motif across other imperial lives, both in Suetonius and beyond.[120] Their popularity is probably double: to the biographer, they granted tremendous latitude because he could ascribe all manner of telling but ultimately unverifiable misdeeds to the leader; to readers, they purported to reveal another side of a man whose normal street appearances were choreographed affairs. As he made his way about the city, his clothing, mode of transport, retinue, and so much else screamed that he was unrivaled in prestige and position. The stories' appeal, in other words, rested partly on their twist of the standard assumptions of the street – the most powerful man was voluntarily acting the part of common folk (even if he did not face the same consequences). As such, these episodes offer an odd corollary to what could happen when the mighty were brought low by attacks verbal or physical. Beyond Patruitus, we hear of other leading men who suffered reversals of fortune on the street. In the wake of Caesar's death, for instance, a crowd slew a nobleman they thought had spoken ill of Caesar and then paraded his head, stuck on a spear point, through the city.[121] Amid the street's chaos – full of the collision of various spheres of urban life, rife with all manner of sensations – these were episodes when social leveling prevailed, and, in fact, the masses even inverted the social order to have their way.

Standing in tension with this egalitarian spirit was the daily lived reality that often reinforced the social hierarchy and made urban inhabitants very much aware of their place. We read, for example, of how the crowd was expected to make way for elite men as they moved about the city, even potentially uncovering their heads as a sign of respect.[122] Who greeted whom first signaled the relative position of two people.[123] And, when magistrates met, their

---

[119] Suet. *Nero* 26.1–2: *petulantiam, libidinem, luxuriam, avaritiam, crudelitatem sensim quidem primo et occulte et velut iuvenili errore exercuit, sed ut tunc quoque dubium nemini foret naturae illa vitia, non aetatis esse. post crepusculum statim adrepto pilleo vel galero popinas inibat circumque vicos vagabatur ludibundus nec sine pernicie tamen, siquidem redeuntis a cena verberare ac repugnantes vulnerare cloacisque demergere assuerat, tabernas etiam effringere et expilare; quintana domi constituta, ubi partae et ad licitationem dividendae praedae pretium absumeretur.* For parallel versions of this story, see Tac. *Ann.* 13.25.1–3; Dio Cass. 61.9.2–3.

[120] Suet. *Otho* 2.1; *Calig.* 11.1. SHA *Comm.* 3.7; *Verus* 4.6.

[121] Suet. *Iul.* 85; Val. Max. 9.9.1; App. *BC* 2.147; Dio Cass. 44.50.

[122] Yielding: Cic. *Sen.* 63; Apul. *Flor.* 21; Dio Cass. 45.16.2. Cf. Val. Max. 2.1.9; Cic. *Amic* 12. Uncovering head: Plut. *Quaest. Rom.* 266C, F.

[123] Mart. 3.95.

pecking order was stressed by who ceded the thoroughfare to whom.[124] Juvenal's narrator, Umbricius, certainly expresses a sense of society's order in the street as he lists the ways his experience does not measure up to what the better-off enjoyed. A rich man cruises above the waves of the crowd, reading or dozing in his closed-up litter, while Umbricius is mauled and blocked as he struggles along the noisy street. Similarly, the drunk and sleepless thug bypasses the rich man and his torch-bearing retinue, pulverizing poor Umbricius instead.

Law, too, underscored disparities. While some provisions of the Tabula Heracleensis facilitated a relatively open atmosphere and guaranteed individuals' right to the street, other stipulations spotlighted particular people. Famously, the text forbade *plostra*, cumbersome heavy-wheeled carts, from city streets by day, but with several notable exceptions: they were permitted when carrying construction materials for public works, when parading in public rites and festivals, and when leaving the city empty or while removing *stercus*, likely fecal matter.[125] Amid this social bargain that tolerated infringements on freedom of movement in exchange for the populace's common advantage, specific individuals benefitted. Members of society's highest ranks were prominent as processing priests, riders atop normally outlawed vehicles, or conspicuous *triumphatores*; less directly, they were also highlighted as givers of games, underwriters of public construction, and the like. In other words, the exceptions to the *plostra* prohibition allowed elite individuals to transgress the normal rules and also ritually presented their sanctioned contravention to the public at large. In sum, for as much freedom of movement, access, and ability that everyday Romans felt as they took to the street, loitered, preened for others, and occasionally sought their own brand of justice, plenty showed them, amid this meeting and mixing of high and low, that true privilege lay elsewhere.

It is also telling that in biography – a genre fundamentally engaged with questions about and judgments on character – streets play an important role beyond the emperor-dresses-down motif. A related class of imperial transgressions emerges when the emperor is not in disguise, but his misdeeds – such as trysts played out in moving litters[126] – nevertheless remain hidden. In the nocturnal escapades and the furtive acts alike, Suetonius plays on Romans' sensibilities (and perhaps even hopes) that street presentations were not always what they appeared to be; that, in this potentially topsy-turvy world, the person under that wig might be the emperor, that missteps were tantalizingly close to

[124] Suet. *Tib.* 31; *Ner.* 4; Livy 24.44.10; Plut. *Fab. Max.* 24.2. Cf. Plut. *Pomp.* 23.2; Pliny *Ep.* 1.23.2.
[125] Ll. 56–67. For the provisions and exceptions: Hartnett 2011b, 147–153; Kaiser 2011b, 182–188.
[126] E.g., Suet. *Ner.* 28.2.

detection, and that pretenders were often so very close to being exposed. In some respects, such stories show that the pushes and pulls between chaos and control, between the street as a space for the populace and as a showplace of elite privilege were not fully resolved but instead existed in constant tension as people from across the social spectrum came into close contact or as they imagined what they might learn if they yanked off the wig, pulled back the litter curtain, or rubbed the "gold" ring to see if there was iron underneath.

PART II

THE STREET AND ITS ARCHITECTURAL BORDER

I T SEEMS THAT ONE DAY SOMEONE WALKING ALONG THE VIA DELL' Abbondanza in Pompeii had had enough with a property and its owner (Plate V, Fig. 26). Enough with trudging up or tripping over the extra course of stone on the sidewalk, which elevated the owner's frontage above his neighbors'. Enough with the garish paint job: a checkerboard of green, red, yellow, and white squares that covered the three-doorway façade and contrasted markedly with its staid surroundings. Or enough with the two figures of Romulus and Aeneas painted at eye-level on each side of the central doorway. On the left jamb, Romulus stood triumphant, bedecked with armor and carrying the spoils of his conquered enemy; on the right, Aeneas fled Troy, carrying his father and pulling his son by the hand. Rome's mythical founders, the embodiments of *virtus* and *pietas*, were poor fits, the riled individual could have groused, for a setting related to fulling — the process of purging cloth of impurities by treading upon it in vats of urine.[1]

Whoever was fed up came along and started scratching. Near the figure of Romulus, the painted surface was gouged to reveal the white of the underlying plaster. The graffito read: *fullones ululamque cano, non arma virumq[ue]*, "I sing of

---

[1] Excavation has not proceeded past this structure's façade, yet numerous inscriptions attest to some connection with fullers: *CIL* 4.9125a–c, 9128a–b, 9129, 9131. For instances of the correspondence between fulleries and endorsements from fullers, see I.6.7 and *CIL* 4.7164; I.4.7 and *CIL* 4.998; VI.15.3 and *CIL* 4.3529.

26. The Fullery of Ululitremulus in Pompeii (IX.13.4–6) boasted an eye-catching façade and an elevated sidewalk. (See also Plate V.)
Photo: author. Courtesy: Soprintendenza Speciale per Pompei, Ercolano e Stabia.

fullers and the screech owl, not of arms and the man."[2] By adapting the opening line of Vergil's *Aeneid*, the nay-saying pedestrian deflated the building's puffed-up claims, moving beyond the "façade" of *arma virumque* and unveiling what it sugarcoated, *fullones ululamque*. The screech owl may have lent the graffito a more personal note: not only was this animal associated with fullers, but its name, *ulula*, also puns on the cognomen of the building's likely proprietor, a man named Fabius Ululitremulus, "the owl-fearer," who endorses candidates among the façade's electoral posters. The scrawled retort thus personalized matters, undercutting Ululitremulus's attempted association with the national heroes and lumping him in with the fullers.[3]

Part I sketched the street's physical space, described its activities, and set its dramatis personae in action. This example makes the obvious point that, if the street was a contested arena for personal presentation, then its physical border – the façades, street "furniture," doorways, and paintings – formed part of people's experience. The street's "frame" offered another important way to project a public image and to assert control over the street's topsy-turvy sensory and social environment. A colorful façade drew eyes, figures representing

[2] *CIL* 4.9131. See Milnor 2009, 299–302; 2014, 248–251.
[3] Screech owl and fullers: Varro, *Sat. Men.* 86.4; *CIL* 4.4112, 4118. Ululitremulus's endorsement: *CIL* 4.7963.

Rome's moral touchstones were meant to impress, and a raised footpath required exertion and demanded attention – even the "bad publicity" of inconveniencing others was preferable to being passed by unnoticed. These important tactics marked on the outside of a structure the aspirations of those within. Yet the graffito illustrates that such presentations were open to critical responses that themselves became lasting features of this conspicuous boundary. Outside folk and forces had repercussions for the reputations of those inside.

Part II of this book examines the interface between the exterior space of the street and the interior worlds of structures lining it, especially houses. In studying this border, I consider buildings not as discrete and isolated units but as permeable entities set within their urban context. Germane are both the physical structures and the skeins of meaning within which owners and beholders enveloped houses, their occupants, and their furnishings. Chapter 4 focuses on Romans' conceptions of the structure–street boundary and builds a picture of the manifold exchanges that crisscrossed the threshold. Chapter 5 moves on to examine the specific architectural and decorative forms given to façades, while Chapter 6 revisits the balance between inside and outside in citywide terms.

FOUR

SIDEWALKS UNDER SIEGE

Houses, Owners, and Urban Context

W HEN HIS DE ARCHITECTURA TURNS TO DOMESTIC ARCHITEC-
ture, Vitruvius first tackles the pragmatics of a house: its parts, their
proportions, and their optimal orientation (6.3–4). Next, after generally categorizing the rooms of a house into public and private (the distinction lying in
whether a visitor may enter uninvited), the architect concentrates on the
particular rooms needed by different classes:

> [T]hose who are of ordinary fortune do not need magnificent vestibules,
> tablina, and atria, because they perform their duties by making the rounds
> visiting others and are not visited by others.[1]

Vitruvius then lists several occupations and their corresponding architectural
needs. Those who resell country produce, for example, should have areas for
livestock. Bankers need houses that are rather showy and safe, while advocates
require elegant and spacious rooms. Ultimately, as though being an elite
member of society were itself an occupation, the discussion returns to questions
of status:

> For the most prominent men, who ought to carry out their duties to
> their fellow citizens by holding offices and magistracies, vestibules
> should be constructed that are lofty and lordly, atria and peristyles that
> are very spacious, gardens and walkways that are rather broad and

[1] Vitr. 6.5.1: . . . iis, qui communi sunt fortuna, non necessaria magnifica vestibula nec tablina neque atria,
quod in aliis officia praestant ambiundo neque ab aliis ambiuntur.

117

appropriate for their dignity; moreover, there should be libraries and basilicas outfitted in a similar style to great public structures, because, in such men's houses, public councils and private lawsuits and hearings are quite often carried out.[2]

Vitruvius ostensibly writes about how to fulfill the house owner's needs, but this passage has much to suggest about how domestic architecture was viewed as a status symbol. Vitruvius is careful to draw an explicit connection between the public role of his *nobiles* – they hold positions in the political sphere – and their needs for architectural features reflecting their place in public life. Indeed, their houses are anything but refuges from the public sphere; if we believe Vitruvius (and there is little reason in this case not to), houses of the Roman elite could host civic events and were thus stages on which the master could perform his public roles. Others who do not have this status to uphold, to Vitruvius's mind, are defined by what they *lack* from the *nobiles'* position and, correspondingly, what rooms their lifestyles do not require. Throughout these passages, the fundamental assumption underlying Vitruvius's argument is that your house should match you and your status.[3]

This much has long been appreciated, and, over the course of the past two decades, our understanding of Roman houses has grown increasingly refined as new datasets and novel questions have been brought to bear on domestic dynamics. We now understand much more about how houses were repositories of (and agents in creating) family lineage, memories, and even identity. Examinations of houses' architecture and art (especially wall painting) have shed light on how these features shaped the experience of visitors and house dwellers alike. Facile assumptions about status and decoration – such as freedmen's supposedly poor taste – have been undercut, while domestic environments have proved fertile indices for the diffusion of taste across the economic spectrum. Finally, studies of artifacts and their distribution within houses have tempered with hard data the idealized view presented by Vitruvius and other authors.[4]

Yet, given how much Vitruvius emphasizes domestic architecture's importance for public image, something is odd in his account and in how the house

---

[2] Vitr. 6.5.2: ... *nobilibus vero, qui honores magistratusque gerundo praestare debent officia civibus, faciunda sunt vestibula regalia alta, atria et peristylia amplissima, silvae ambulationesque laxiores ad decorem maiestatis perfectae; praeterea bybliothecas, basilicas non dissimili modo quam publicorum operum magnificentia comparatas, quod in domibus eorum saepius et publica consilia et privata iudicia arbitriaque conficiuntur.*

[3] At 6.5.3, the architect rounds out his discussion by addressing how to avoid unhappy clients. It is possible to escape from censure, he writes, if buildings are planned with a view to owners of different types – (*personae*) *singulorum generum* – a distinct reference to status. E.g., Livy 4.28; Ov. *Tr.* 4.4.2; Hor. *Epod.* 4.6 (setting *genus* in opposition to recently accumulated wealth).

[4] Among recent scholarship on Roman houses, especially in Campania: Thébert 1987; Watts 1987; Gazda 1991; Clarke 1991; Wallace-Hadrill 1994; Berry 1997; Laurence and Wallace-Hadrill 1997; Dickmann 1999; Pirson 1999; Grahame 2000; Hales 2003; Allison 2004; Leach 2004; Hackworth Petersen 2006; Anguissola 2010; Joshel and Hackworth Petersen 2014.

has been studied. When Vitruvius gets specific about house forms, he launches his project by categorizing various types of forecourts – what we normally call *atria* and he termed *cava aedium*. He thus forgoes the façade, which was the house's most public face, the first feature that a visitor would have encountered and the only aspect that many others would have been able to see. Although scholars, by considering how a domestic space was experienced, have counterbalanced Vitruvius's builder-centric viewpoint, their locus of study has largely mirrored the architect's focus on what was *inside* a house. We have been missing how the owner–house connection extended beyond interior rooms and their type, number, size, and decoration. This chapter shifts the inquiry outward and examines this bond from an exterior perspective, where the house, embedded in the urban fabric, met the street. To underscore the manifold discourse and pressures across the house–street boundary, I alternate in the following pages between the outlooks and actions of house dwellers and of streetgoers.

HOUSE EXTERIORS: DISPLAY AND ASSESSMENT

Ample evidence activates the area around a house's doorway as a space where the achievements and characteristics of those who lived inside could be trumpeted by householders and questioned by passersby. In Rome, those who won enemy booty through military valor stuck it up outside their houses for all to see. After Fulvius Nobilior's triumph over Ambracia in 187 BCE, for example, Livy reports what his colleagues were awaiting: "he will carry before his chariot and affix to his doorposts the captured Ambracia [a statue personifying the city], the statues which they accuse him of taking away, and other spoils of that city."[5] The practice was not restricted to triumphant generals or magistrates, for Livy reports that during the Second Punic War, when a depleted Senate needed speedy restocking, among those chosen were men who had spoils on their houses but had not held office.[6] Polybius pushes the practice further down the social ladder to everyday soldiers who accomplished tremendous deeds. Explaining Roman military success to a Greek audience, he enumerates various rewards before ending domestically:

> And in their houses they hang up the spoils they won in the most conspicuous places, looking upon them as tokens and evidences of their valor. Considering all this attention given to the matter of punishments and rewards in the army and the importance attached to both, no wonder

[5] Livy 38.43.9–10: *Ambraciam captam signaque quae ablata criminantur, et cetera spolia eius Urbis ante curram laturus et fixurus in postibus suis.* Fulvius's supporters would later arm themselves with those same weapons: Plut. *C. Gracch.* 15.1. In general on the practice, see Rawson 1990.

[6] Livy 23.23.6.

that the wars in which the Romans engage end so successfully and brilliantly.[7]

While they motivated current soldiers, such displays also had power for future audiences, according to Pliny. Amid a discussion of how family lineages were visible in funerals, in portraits kept in houses, and in family archives and inscriptions, he writes that other presentations of those "mighty spirits" were present "outside the houses and round the doorways" in the form of spoils taken from enemies. He adds that:

> even the buyer was not allowed to unfasten (them), and the houses perpetually celebrated a triumph even though their masters had changed. This acted as a powerful stimulus, since every day the walls themselves upbraid an unwarlike owner with encroaching on the triumph of another.[8]

Indeed, spoils survived into the Empire, according to Suetonius, who records that the great fire of 64 CE consumed "the houses of leaders of old ... still adorned with enemy spoils." He lumps together these sights with long-standing temples and "whatever else had survived from antiquity that must be seen (*visendum*) and was memorable," which recalls other authors' emphasis on these emblems' impact on an onlooker.[9] Augustus's *Res Gestae* suggests the importance of such displays by reserving discussion of the *princeps'* doorway decorations for the inscription's final climax.[10]

Beyond the martial realm, other adornments on or around a house's doorway marked out moments in a family's life cycle: flowers or laurels for a baby's birth,[11] greenery for a wedding,[12] and a cypress branch when a corpse was lying in state within a house.[13] Appearances by individuals attached to a household, on occasions grand and quotidian, also visually linked household and street. Our sources routinely mention the sight of well-wishers or clients grouped

---

[7] Polyb. 6.39.10–11: ἔν τε ταῖς οἰκίαις κατὰ τοὺς ἐπιφανεστάτους τόπους τιθέασι τὰ σκῦλα, σημεῖα ποιούμενοι καὶ μαρτύρια τῆς ἑαυτῶν ἀρετῆς. τοιαύτης δ᾽ ἐπιμελείας οὔσης καὶ σπουδῆς περί τε τὰς τιμὰς καὶ τιμωρίας τὰς ἐν τοῖς στρατοπέδοις, εἰκότως καὶ τὰ τέλη τῶν πολεμικῶν πράξεων ἐπιτυχῆ καὶ λαμπρὰ γίνεται δι᾽ αὐτῶν. This right may have been earned by killing an enemy in one-on-one fighting, thus earning what Aulus Gellius (2.11.3) calls the *spolia provocatoria*. See also Livy 10.7.9 for a speech during the Struggle of the Orders that also implies this practice on the part of nonmagistrates.

[8] Pliny *NH* 35.7: *aliae foris et circa limina animorum ingentium imagines erant adfixis hostium spoliis, quae nec emptori refigere liceret, triumphabantque etiam dominis mutatis aeternae domus. erat haec stimulatio ingens, exprobrantibus tectis cotidie inbellem dominum intrare in alienum triumphum.*

[9] Suet. *Ner.* 38.2: *... domus priscorum ducum arserunt hostilibus adhuc spoliis adornatae ... quidquid visendum et memorabile ex antiquitate duraverat.* Cf. Tib. 1.1.53–58; Prop. 3.9.26.

[10] *RG* 34–35. Coins also depicted the doorway: Zanker 1988, 92–94.

[11] Stat. *Silv.* 4.8.37–41; Juv. 6.77–81. Cf. Macrob. *Sat.* 1.16.36.

[12] Stat. *Silv.* 1.2.231; Catull. 64.293; Juv. 6.227–228; Lucr. 2.354; Ov. *Met.* 4.760.

[13] Serv. *A.* 2.714, 3.64, 4.507. Decoration could also mark gratitude and joy for someone's safety: Tac. *Hist.* 3.84.

around the doorway as part of the *salutatio*. Their number offered an index of the householder's support. By contrast, Cicero insinuates that Clodius's nearly empty threshold signaled the scoundrel's loss of favor. And the link between inside and outside was clearer still when someone spotted the master of the house exiting his structure to lead his supporters to the forum.[14] These actions all speak to the expectation of an external audience whose attention was focused on the doorway.

Strong attitudes toward housing – that a house reflected one's social standing, a splendid one particularly positively – fueled construction of progressively larger and more elegant houses despite an ethos of modesty.[15] As the zeal for magnificence spread down the social hierarchy, one tactic of elites involved simply outbuilding their imitators.[16] Lucius Lucullus, for instance, whose country estate was sandwiched between the luxurious villas of an *eques* and a freedman, thought that he should have the same privilege as his neighbors and defended the extravagance of his own mansion on those very grounds.[17] Yet his example raises the question, in the face of escalating claims, of who deserved what. Cicero, as a new arrival on the political scene, dwelled at length on such outward signs of standing. In the *De Officiis*, he broadly echoes Vitruvius's sentiments about the correspondence between a man's house and standing yet also hints at the skeptical attitude Romans might bring to the assessment: "a man's dignity ought to be enhanced by the house he lives in, but not entirely owed to it; the owner should bring honor to his house, not the house to its owner."[18] Cicero's *sententia* recognizes architectural posturing and also implies that one could overdo it: that to have a house too grand revealed a man too pretentious and something of an imposter. Appropriateness was not, as in Vitruvius, a matter of accommodating an owner's needs but was grounded in the *realia* of Roman social practice. In other words, the critical eye that Romans brought to other street presentations, as I discussed in the previous chapter, was equally active in questioning architectural claims.

Certain circumstances, such as when a property changed hands but not appearances, especially precipitated scrutiny of occupants and their status.

---

[14] Visible supporters: Aul. Gell. 16.5.8–9; Sen. *Marc.* 10.1; Cic. *De or.* 1.200; Sen. *Ep.* 84.11–12. Cf. Cic. *Att.* 1.18.1; *Brut.* 2.4.1; Sen. *Ep.* 19.11, 22.9. Clodius' threshold: Cic. *Att.* 4.3.5. Processing to forum: O'Sullivan 2011, 54–59.

[15] Pliny (*NH* 36.110) narrates the story, perhaps apocryphal but even if so quite telling, of Lepidus's house. In the year of Lepidus's consulship, 78 BCE, his was the most splendid house in Rome. Thirty-five years later, though, it was said not to be among the first one hundred.

[16] Tacitus (*Ann.* 3.55.2) believed this strategy had negative effects. He conceded that such *studium magnificentiae* increased the public image and clientele of aristocratic families, but also contended that it led to their downfall.

[17] To judge from our sources, many recriminated Lucullus and other *principes* for feeding this pattern of competitive construction: Cic. *Leg.* 3.30; *Off.* 140; Varro *Rust.* 1.13.7.

[18] Cic. *Off.* 1.139: *Ornanda enim est dignitas domo, non ex domo tota quaerenda, nec domo dominus, sed domino domus honestanda est . . .* Cf. Cic. *Att.* 18.1.

Cicero gains rhetorical leverage in the *Philippics* from such a situation, since Antony confiscated and occupied Pompey's former home.[19] Moral points are scored in diatribes about Antony's squandering of Pompey's assets, but more interesting is how Cicero depicts the general public's view of the house: "For some time no man could bear to look at the house, none could pass it without crying."[20] Partaking in a diachronic inventory of owners was quite widespread, if an anonymous snippet of poetry that Cicero quotes elsewhere is any indication:

> For it is unpleasant, when passers-by exclaim:
> "O good old house, goodness how different is
> your old owner from your current one!"
> And these days that can be said about many houses![21]

When Cicero's own house was destroyed at Clodius's hands, he appealed to similar logic. Prior to its demolition, Cicero had confessed to his brother that he bought the house to achieve a degree of public standing.[22] Now, he asks, how can good men gaze at its empty site without continuous crying?[23] In the case of Pompey's former house, however, Cicero pushes this questioning still further by addressing Antony directly: "Do you, when you spot those ships' beaks and spoils in the vestibule, think you are entering your own house?"[24] The implication is that Antony himself would admit that he does not.

It is especially noteworthy that Cicero draws Antony's attention to specific features of the house, almost all of which would be visible from the exterior: among them the threshold and the ship prows displayed in the vestibule.[25] Such positioning, on the one hand, underlines the degree to which Pompey, like other victors in war, shaped his public image through emblems visible from the street.[26] On the other hand, a form of *praeterire* ("to go past") is employed both

---

[19] Pompey's house on the Carinae: *LTUR* 2.159–160 ("Domus Pompeiorum," Jolivet).

[20] Cic. *Phil.* 2.68: *quam domum aliquamdiu nemo adspicere poterat, nemo sine lacrimis praeterire.* For a parallel situation, see Cic. *Off.* 1.138, where he contrasts two owners of the same plot: Cn. Octavius (a *novus homo* was thought to have won votes for the consulship in part because of the attractive and imposing house he built on the spot) and M. Aemilius Scaurus (who razed Octavius's structure a century later and built a new wing for his nearby residence there; yet, even though he was the son of a great man, he was met with disgrace and ruin).

[21] Cic. *Off.* 1.139: *odiosum est enim, cum a praetereuntibus dicitur: "o domus antiqua, heu quam dispari / dominare domino!" quod quidem his temporibus in multis licet dicere.* Cf. *Phil.* 2.104.

[22] Cic. *Att.* 1.13.6: *ad dignitatem aliquam pervenire.* Cf. *Dom.* 146, where Cicero describes the house as his *ornamenta dignitatis.*

[23] Cic. *Dom.* 101. See also Cic. *Dom.* 100: *... sin mea domus non modo mihi non redditur, sed etiam monumentum praebet inimico doloris mei, sceleris sui, publicae calamitatis, quis erit qui hunc reditum potius quam poenam sempiternam putet?*

[24] Cic. *Phil.* 2.68: *an tu, illa in vestibulo rostra [et spolia] cum adspexisti, domum tuam te introire putas?*

[25] Cic. *Phil.* 2.67–68. Also listed are the household's *penates.*

[26] The *rostra*, or ship beaks, must have held especial meaning, since they were emblems of public standing particular to Pompey, won apparently during the special command he was granted by the *Lex Gabinia* in the mid-60s to quash piracy in the Mediterranean.

in Cicero's speech and the poetic fragment, which shifts focus to onlookers in a kinetic street-based context, where viewing a house façade summoned appraisals of the owner's status and stirred strong emotions and memories. Such a reliance on a house's exterior is also apparent in the other discussions of housing and status cited earlier. Rarely are particular features of any house described, and those aspects that authors do mention would be discernible from the outside: location and size.[27] For the lived experience of the Roman city, Vitruvius was right in the sense that houses could be a measure of status, but a house's *outside*, in addition to its specific interior rooms, could forge claims and prompt those in the street to gauge, question, and react. These were no boring walls to contain an interior, but conspicuous elements of a public persona.

PAVING THE WAY (AND THE SIDEWALK)

Legal evidence about the seam between private property and the street's communal space further blurs this boundary by pushing owners' obligations and impact out into the street. Our best source for the property–street junction is the Tabula Heracleensis.[28] At the beginning of a section outlining regulations about public spaces, the text assigns responsibility over the roadbed to individual owners. All are to maintain the thoroughfare in front of their properties, ensuring that no water stand in the street (ll. 20–23). The arbiters for this work are the aediles, each of whom is responsible for the street's repair and paving in a different city sector (ll. 20–28). Similar language is later applied to sidewalks: owners are responsible for their paving, with the aediles again determining the work's satisfactory completion (ll. 53–55). Research at Pompeii appears to confirm that the city was subject to this text's principle, if not its direct application. In her intensive study of sidewalk construction, Catherine Saliou has shown that changes in curbstone material and quality often mesh closely with junctures between properties. She deduces that, although some degree of public control governed what was built, the responsibility for the space between the façade and the roadbed fell primarily to property owners.[29]

Further archaeological evidence demonstrates that the sidewalk, more than a zone of individual legal duty, also afforded frontagers the opportunity to draw

[27] Cicero's comment (*Off.* 1.139) about the house of Cn. Octavius – that it was seen by all (*vulgo viseretur*) – advances the connection between exteriority and status still further. The punchline is that the sight of the house helped Octavius secure enough popular support for victory in the consular elections. Could Cicero have us believe that the interior was viewed by enough voters to swing the election? His description of Octavius's house as *praeclara*, an adjective useful in describing the physical beauty of the face and thus a likely reference to the house's façade (*OLD*, *s.v.* 1b; *TLL*, s.v. II.A.1.a; Lucr. 4.1033; Sall. *Iug.* 2.2), suggests that the answer is no.

[28] See "The Street as Corridor for Movement" in Chapter 1.

[29] Saliou 1999, 174–200. Flat stones set into sidewalks at apparent property joins reinforce this point: Saliou 1999, 169–171.

27. The sidewalk in front of the Casa del Fauno in Pompeii (VI.12.1–6) consisted of a grid of white marble chips set in a black matrix, along with a polychrome greeting, "HAVE," spelled in front of the house's main entry.
Photo: author. Courtesy: Soprintendenza Speciale per Pompei, Ercolano e Stabia.

attention to and mark the space as their own. Across the entire front of the Casa del Fauno at Pompeii (VI.12.1–6), for instance, a grid-like pattern of white stones stood out from the sidewalk's black background (Fig. 27). Colored stones in front of the main doorway aided in spelling the tessellated greeting "HAVE."[30] The salutation makes explicit what was normally implicit; namely, that the house's owner was communicating to streetgoers the extension of the house's realm into the sidewalk. Other attempts to decorate and thus lay claim to the sidewalk give a taste of the diversity of sidewalk decoration. Along the main frontage of the Casa del Cinghiale (VIII.3.7–9), white chips form a lattice pattern of elongated diamonds against a *cocciopesto* background. Nearly next door, the Casa del Gallo (VIII.5.1–7) packed polychrome marble chips into a thick matrix along its lengthy frontage, while the Casa dell'Atrio Corinzio at Herculaneum (V.30) saw palm-sized slabs of imported polychrome marbles set into the red pavement at regular intervals.[31] The use of such stones should not be overlooked: first, because of the rarity and expense of such materials even in a secondary market; second, because many properties lacked individualized

[30] Pesando 1996, 199–200; Zevi 1998, 24–26; Saliou 1999, 171.
[31] Saliou 1999, 171, ns. 23–24 for more examples.

sidewalk decoration altogether; and, third, because of marble's strong associations with the civic sphere.[32]

Indeed, the special charge of decorated sidewalks shines through most clearly
in front of public buildings. Large marble pavers carpeted the area between the
entrance to Pompeii's Stabian Baths and the roadbed, thus distinguishing it
from its surroundings (VII.1.8; Fig. 11). Closer to the town's forum, the
sidewalk flanking the Temple of Augustan Fortune boasted tightly packed fist-
sized gray stones. That the sidewalk decoration here, as in front of houses,
terminates at a clear property boundary makes obvious that sidewalk decoration, like curbstone construction, was closely tied to each parcel of land.[33]
Those walking along sensed that the space immediately in front of a structure
was not neutral turf; rather, they could have felt its connection to the building
and, by extension, to its chief proponent. I will return to this issue and its
connection to façade architecture in the next chapter.

Although sidewalk frontage offered opportunities to craft a showpiece, it
potentially exposed owners to shame when their sidewalk or roadbed care was
found lacking. If somone's efforts did not satisfy the aedile, the Tabula
Heracleensis set in motion a conspicuous remedy (ll. 32–45). At the problem's
discovery, the aedile was authorized to let a contract for maintenance.
In a public poster erected in the forum or on his tribunal, the aedile served
notice that he was contracting the work, and he named the street, the default-
ing proprietor, and the date on which work would begin. Notice was also
served to the negligent frontager at the address in question, and the contract was
then let in the forum. In other words, the tablet's provisions outline a process
that took one person's civic (ir)responsibility and opened it up repeatedly to
public visibility, twice in the city's most visible spot and once at the property
itself. For negligent frontagers, such publication of what was ideally an individual matter likely brought undesired notoriety, not to mention substantial fines
for late payment (ll. 42–45). All in all, the tablet's remedy transformed the street
and sidewalk's common space from a sphere of individual duty and display into
a zone of civic intervention that highlighted the magistrate's clout.

SPEECH, SONG, AND ACTION AT THE HOUSE DOOR

Protecting the populace's passage was the nominal reason for a magistrate's
intervention. Such a justification helps reverse our lens of inquiry and allows us
to reconsider the house–street boundary from a streetgoer's perspective. Since

---

[32] The secondary marble market: Fant and Attanasio 2009. Sidewalk decoration has only
survived in about two dozen locations: Saliou 1999, 171, ns. 23–24. Curbstones frequently
were homogeneous for longer stretches, which suggests a corporate effort of construction:
Saliou 1999, esp. fig. 28.
[33] Sidewalks and property lines: Saliou 1999, 169–182.

the space in front of a building was linked to its owner yet also open to the urban populace, owners were exposed to the actions, whims, and (as we shall learn) voices of those in the street.

A graffito from a Pompeian façade furnishes a rare physical trace of this phenomenon. Along the busy Via dell'Abbondanza opened a towering door-way (I.4.25) leading to an enormous three-peristyle house that was apparently shared by two fellow freedmen, L. Popidius Secundus and L. Popidius Ampliatus.[34] In a message scratched into the plaster, the latter came in for written scorn: "Ampliatus, Icarus buggers you. Salvius wrote this."[35] Graffiti elsewhere in the city suggests that Salvius and Icarus skirmished repeatedly, with Icarus slandering Salvius's daughter and receiving a potential death threat in reply.[36] That the feud played out on the town's walls is interesting because it speaks again to individuals' desire to make public what we might consider "private" relationships. But what draws our attention is the slander of Ampliatus immediately outside his house's doorway, a space closely tied to him and therefore a particularly vulnerable spot for expressing personal acri-mony. The nature of the insult is also fascinating. Because it cast Ampliatus as the passive member in a male–male sexual pair, this was no idle jest, but was a particularly charged kind of defamation. Taken literally, the accusation had teeth, for it accused the wealthy man of being sexually dominated by Icarus. For Romans, one's sexual role was more important than the sex of one's partner. Moreover, during the time when he himself was a slave, Ampliatus had likely been subject to his owner's sexual exploitation. The slur's more figurative sense, that Icarus was screwing Ampliatus over, was hardly rosier because it, too, cast down Ampliatus.[37] Overall, the graffito demonstrates how the edifice–street interface offered the public at large, and particularly those of lesser standing, a conspicuous stage on which to level personal rebuke toward a house and its chief occupant.

In the previous chapter, we encountered individuals seeking justice in the street by attempting to shame someone who had done them wrong. We may now revisit that line of thought in its legal and physical context. Roman law outlined remedies for speech that got out of hand. *Convicium* was the term for verbal abuse of someone in public, and it was classified as a subset of defamation more generally. The Praetor's Edict defined actionable *convicium* as shouting at

---

[34] Franklin 2001, 115–116, 169–71. The former was most likely a member of the *Augustiani*, a troop trained to clap rhythmically at the emperor Nero's artistic performances: *CIL* 4.2380, 4.2381, 4.2383.

[35] *CIL* 4.2375: *Ampliate, Icarus te pedicat. Salvius scripsit.*

[36] *CIL* 4.2173, 2175. Franklin 1986, 326–327.

[37] On the specific meaning of *pedico*: Adams 1982, 123–125. On the figurative readings of sexual language: Adams 1982, 132–134. Pompeians frequently named themselves as authors of graffiti (e.g., *CIL* 4.1842; Benefiel 2008), so Salvius's self-identification is not altogether puzzling if he indeed scratched the message.

someone, either by yourself or with a group, in a way that ran contrary to good morals.[38] When jurists weigh in, more points of interest arise, starting with the first location Ulpian mentions when he offers a possible scenario for *convicium* – the house. He writes: "If a person comes to your house while you are away, there is said to be *convicium*."[39] Thus, if you wanted to vent about someone and if you did not or could not confront or pursue that person directly, another option was going to his or her house or workplace and expressing yourself there. This was apparently an old practice, for the Twelve Tables protected a Roman's right to march up to someone's doorway and to shout every third day if that person failed to appear as a witness in court.[40] But Ulpian's discussion makes clear that solo haranguing was not the normal assumption. He offers an etymology:

> The term *convicium* derives from a mob or crowd, that is, a combination of voices. For when several voices are directed at one person, that is called *convicium*, as it were a gathering of voices (*convocium*).[41]

Redress for *convicium*, to judge from Ulpian's commentary, was meant to curtail a situation where a crowd was summoned at someone's house to shout defamations that were intended to disgrace the person and that ran afoul of community values. The legal evidence, in other words, animates the area before a house as a zone brimming with potential for communication from aggrieved parties.[42]

What motivated individuals who resorted to "house-scorning" (as the practice is called in other times and places) is rarely recorded, for typically the *protested*, not the *protestors*, left written records. The realm of Roman comedy, however, provides rich examples because it gives voice to nonelite characters and because its action took place in front of three façades in what was presumed to be the street. In Plautus's *Menaechmi*, for instance, the narrator easily remembers one character's name because he has seen him get roasted with shouts.[43] Moneylenders either threaten raising a ruckus outside a house – it will be loud and long, says one usurer[44] – or actually do so, repeating important words in a rhythmic chant: "My interest, give me back my interest, give it back,

---

[38] *Dig.* 47.10.15.2: *ait praetor: "qui adversus bonos mores convicium cui fecisse cuiusve opera factum esse dicetur, quo adversus bonos mores convicium fieret: in eum iudicium dabo."* The following pages owe much to Lintott 1968, 8–21; Treggiari 2002, 95–102. See also Graf 2005.

[39] *Dig.* 45.10.15.7: *si quis ad domum tuam venerit te absente, convicium factum esse dicitur.* Cf. *Dig.* 47.2.54.pr.

[40] Tab. 2.3. Cf. Fest. 262L, 514L. Alternatively, it was possible to simply stand at someone's door all day: Plaut. *Mostell.* 766–769. Cf. Plaut. *Merc.* 977.

[41] *Dig.* 47.10.15.4: *convicium autem dicitur vel a concitatione vel a conventu, hoc est a collatione vocum. cum enim in unum complures voces conferuntur, convicium appellatur quasi convocium.*

[42] The practice has parallels elsewhere. Some early modern examples: Cohen 1992; Shoemaker 2000; Dennis 2008–2009; Colleran 2010.

[43] Plaut. *Men.* 45–46.

[44] Plaut. *Pseud.* 556–557: *namque edepol, si non dabis, / clamore magno et multo flagitabere.*

you two!"[45] Similarly, we seldom have accounts of how house owners responded, but revisiting another Plautine episode suggests the anxieties that doorstep episodes might arouse. In the *Mercator*, a householder will not think to let a handsome slave girl venture into the streets as a *materfamilias's* attendant, for he fears the men of a city: "they would serenade the doorway; the leaves of my door would be filled by their love poems scrawled in charcoal."[46] His worries about being accused of running a brothel not surprisingly entail the visual realm – the sights of the sexy slave girl, of the gathered crowd, and of the men's literary detritus – but also extend to the noise created by the incident.[47]

When we follow this episode's cue and consider the sonic dimension of extra-residential uproars, the social dimensions of house-scorning become clearer. As the grammarian Festus discusses *convicium*, he first parallels Ulpian and defines it as the confluence of voices. He then adds a second etymology that emphasizes the range of protestors' sounds, contending that the word could emerge from the convergence of neighbors (*con-vicus*). This chimes with his later connection of *occentare*, "rough singing," to *convicium ferre*: "It happens loudly and with a certain chant so that it can be heard from far away. Because it is thought to happen with good reason, it is considered shameful" to the addressee.[48] Shouting protestors could raise a ruckus that drew the attention of streetgoers, and, because of sound's ability to travel where architecture did not permit sight or access, the uproar also pricked up neighbors' ears.[49] (Houses built around courtyards and the stone-lined corridors of streets helped sounds get heard.) A contemptuous rumpus gained greater attention by night, when the protestors' identities were cloaked, when their inhibitions were eroded by drink, and when they caused maximum annoyance by waking the neighborhood.[50]

---

[45] Plaut. *Mostell*. 603: *cedo faenus, redde faenus, reddite!* Soon after follows the father of the money-ower (Plaut. *Most*. 615–617): *quis illic est? quid … praesenti tibi facit convicium?* Cf. Ov. *Ars am*. 3.449; Catull. 42. For an image of call-and-response, albeit in abusive speech in the forum, see Cic. *Q Fr* 2.3.2; Plut. *Pomp*. 48. Caesar was apparently delayed in leaving for his province because debtors were blocking his house: Plut. *Caes*. 11.1. The sting of such a charge is clear from Petronius (57), who has one freedman reproach the giggling Ascyltos and claim to be an honorable man since, among other boasts, he has never been told publicly, *redde quod debes*, "give back what you owe."

[46] Plaut. *Merc*. 408–409: *occentent ostium; impleantur elegeorum meae fores carbonibus*.

[47] Plaut. *Merc*. 408–411. See also Plaut. *Per*. 569–575, where a slave warns that, should a pimp secure a certain girl, the leading citizens of the town "will serenade the door by night, they'll burn down the doors." Cf. Plaut. *Curc*. 145–157.

[48] Fest. 190–192L: *occentassint antiqui dicebant quod nunc convicium fecerint dicimus, quod id clare et cum quodam canore fit, ut procul exaudiri possit. quod turpe habetur, quia non sine causa fieri putatur*. By contrast, if shouting is done without reference to a specific person, the charge of *convicium* is not considered justified: *Dig*. 47.10.15.9.

[49] Dennis 2008–2009, 15 on Renaissance Italy; "perhaps sound's most potent ability … was that it allowed its creators to project themselves into a space to which their physical access was denied."

[50] This is likely the concern in a situation described by Pseudo-Quintilian (*Decl*. 364) in which a poor man habitually jeered nocturnally outside a rich man's house, until one night when the latter had had enough and ordered his slaves to remove the poor man, claiming he was insane.

It was not just that the sounds were audible; their break from the norm mattered, too. Scholars of urban soundscapes note how acclimated city dwellers become to their neighborhood's particular noises: its daily rhythm of voices, cart rattles, barks, and the like. Against this backdrop, they have adopted anthropologist Mary Douglas's notion of dirt as "matter out of place" to urban sounds, noting how unaccustomed noises easily gain notice.[51] Singing or chanting like Festus and others describe was "sound out of place" and thus especially discordant for overhearers. Festus's second etymology even raises the possibility that neighbors, roused from sleep or distracted from their normal tasks, would join in, especially if they also had grievances with those being protested.

It is worth recalling that *convicium* was only actionable if the good morals of the community were violated. Recognizing the necessity of an exterior audience helps to explain Ulpian's initially odd statement that the object of *convicium* need not be home for an illegal event to occur. The legal provision therefore underscores the strength of the bond between a property and its chief resident — even if you were away from your house, everyone still knew you were the target. Also, you were not a suitable judge of whether something illegal had happened because you could consider any shouts and songs detrimental. Rather, the key audience of a rabble-rousing crowd legally (and socially) was composed of those who overheard the joining of voices and were disturbed by its content.

House-scorning is an example of what Natalie Zemon Davis has called the "social creativity of the so-called inarticulate."[52] Weaker members of society hit the powerful where they were most vulnerable: their good name and personal reputations, which Cicero equated with life itself.[53] This is undoubtedly why Cicero states his abhorrence of rough singing (*occentatio*) and of composing verses about someone. Both, he notes, bring about disgrace for their target. He argues that magistrates and the lawcourts, not clever poets, offer proper channels for judgment, and he applauds the Twelve Tables for instituting capital penalties for slander.[54] His sentiments make internal sense because he was very much part of that official world of dispute settlement. In fact, Cicero's feelings were honed by his experience because, during a grain shortage, a crowd gathered by night, probably at *his* house, to demand a remedy.[55]

That said, Cicero did not hesitate to make great rhetorical use of similar episodes at his enemies' houses. Near the end of his Verrine orations, the orator

---

[51] E.g., Garrioch 2003, 14; Colleran 2010, 369 (both with additional bibliography).

[52] Davis 1975, 74.

[53] Cic. *Quinct.* 49–50, 99.

[54] Cic. *Rep.* 4.12. Cf. Fest. 192L.

[55] Cic. *Dom.* 11–14. Cicero, of course, was careful to avoid characterizing the event as a popular uprising, but insinuates that it was spurred by Clodius. For a related example, see Cic. *Q Fr.* 2.11.

summons a powerful double image of Sicily's then-governor: while Verres engaged in a multiday bender, his equally profligate admiral was bungling a battle against pirates. The result was, in Cicero's words, a night during which the Roman governor burned with the fires of lust, and the Roman fleet burned with fires kindled by pirates. When news reached Syracuse – where Verres had processed home amid music and a female retinue – an initial crowd flowed to his house; when the ships' fires became visible, people rushed from all corners of the city to join in the shouting. Stirred from his drunken sleep, Verres emerged to confront a crowd that pelted him with taunts about his debauchments, with the naming of his lady friends, and with questions about where he had been while the fleet floundered.[56] Apparently to show how the matter could have ended differently, Cicero next describes two other episodes when mobs had also besieged the residence of a Roman provincial commander. When Verres was legate in the Hellespont, an outraged throng attacked his door with stones, iron, and fire. Meanwhile, a crowd in North Africa burnt down the house of a Roman official because of his avarice, Cicero says, and killed the governor inside.[57]

In the end, the Syracusan crowd abandons their siege after remembering the threat at hand. Nevertheless, the episodes together make several points. First, although Cicero's rhetorical imagination is very active, his description grants a sense of how something like *convicium* functioned on a grand scale. Second, these events again document the street's role as an arena where political tensions were raised and at times resolved. Third, because the crowd concentrated attention at one house, it channeled attention toward a particular individual and transformed quotidian public space into an impromptu and intensely personal political forum.[58] Overall, "self-help" – whether political or social, and whatever its form (sung verses, a scrawled graffito, or walking in mourning clothes behind someone) – involved accountability-seeking. It reflects a society in which "the normal processes of law are defective" and "popular moral sensibility fills the gaps left by the law."[59] Whether a verbal uproar simply crackled and smoldered or intensified to a fiery conclusion, the street and its informal "people's court" offered a key democratizing venue.

Romans had one other strong association with the area before someone's door – they connected it with affairs of the heart. Within Latin elegy,

---

[56] Cic. *Verr.* 2.5.92–95. We have few other examples of how victims (and neighbors) of house-scorning responded in the Roman period. The evidence is more ample in the Renaissance: Dennis 2008–2009, 15; Cohen 1992, 613–615.

[57] Cic. *Verr.* 2.1.69–70. Cf. Livy *Per.* 86.

[58] Lintott 1968, e.g., Cic. *Mil.* 13, 38; *Har. Resp.* 15–16; Asc. 33, 43. Conversely, when a politician's reputation was threatened, supporters could rally at his residence, as happened when Caesar was stripped of his praetorship by the senate in 62 BCE: Suet. *Iul.* 16. Further examples: Plut. *Caes.* 30.2; *Pomp.* 58.

[59] Kelly 1966, 22.

a particular motif gained popularity in the early Empire – the *paraclausithyron* – which was literally a poem "before the closed door."[60] Its standard poetic conceits, born of Greek roots, are that the lover is closed out from the house, either by his beloved or by those wishing to protect her virtue, and that he thus pens a song describing his predicament.[61] As such, *paraclausithyra* lob more messages at thresholds and populate sidewalks with additional people making appeals. At Herculaneum, we read "here love thirsts" outside one door, while at Pompeii, a full-blown *paraclausithyron* appears.[62] Because the poems hinge on the inside–outside push and pull that has been this section's focus, they get to that tension's heart. No poem is clearer than the opening of Propertius 1.16, which plays with the genre's tropes by letting the door itself speak:

> Once upon a time I had stood open for grand triumphs, a door vowed to Patrician Chastity, whose threshold was crowded with gilded chariots and wet with the suppliant tears of captives. Now, wounded by the nighttime brawls of drunks, I often lament being beaten by shameful hands; disgraceful garlands are always hanging from me and torches never stop lying before me as symbols of the excluded lover. I can't protect my lady from scandalous allegations, since I'm now given over, though I was once so noble, to obscene songs.[63]

Positioning the poetic voice at the threshold allows Propertius to look forward and backward, Janus-like, in both space and time. A key concern is the household's martial and moral reputation, much as we saw with war spoils and street protests earlier. Yet the poem also bewails the slippage from former august victories to present-day baseness. The stately and immaculate image is undercut by events beyond the house's walls, as nocturnal rabble-rousers, wobbly lovers, and their leftovers now litter the doorway. Propertius's speaking door thus offers a reminder: as much as structures sent forth messages, actions on the street were no less visible (or audible), and the sidewalk could teem with assertions over which the household had little control. Yet they, too, shaped public image.

In sum, my goal in this survey of doorstep activities is not to suggest that we should imagine every sidewalk crowded with lovelorn Romeos, scrawling Salvii, chanting crowds, or petty arsonists. It is enough to recognize that, for Romans, this space swirled with a host of associations across a broad range of contexts: religious, political, martial, and amorous. Despite frontagers' legal obligations and

---

[60] Classic treatments of the genre: Copley 1956; Yardley 1978.

[61] E.g., Prop. 1.16.17–26; Ov. *Am.* 1.6.

[62] *CIL* 10.10562: *hic sitiet amor. Paraclausithyron: CIL* 4.5296, on which see Copley 1939; Milnor 2014, 191–227.

[63] Prop. 1.16.1–10: *quae fueram magnis olim patefacta triumphis, / ianua Patriciae vota Pudicitiae, / cuius inaurati celebrarunt limina currus, / captorum lacrimis umida supplicibus, / nunc ego, nocturnis potorum saucia rixis, / pulsata indignis saepe queror manibus, / et mihi non desunt turpes pendere corollae / semper et exclusi signa iacere faces. / nec possum infamis dominae defendere voces, / nobilis obscenis tradita carminibus . . .*

decorations, this space was neither exclusively within the house's domain nor even neutral turf. Rather, as Propertius suggests, a complicated set of exchanges criss crossed the threshold: the reputation, characteristics, or affections of the occupant could be presented, and these were affirmed or challenged depending on the reactions, imprecations, and remonstrations of those in the street.

REACHING BEYOND THE HOUSE

Because we have concentrated on the area in front of a property – governed by the Tabula Heracleensis, paved by the frontager, and occupied by many – our gaze has been static, fixed on one parcel with little consideration of its contexts: nearby properties and urbanites moving through the street. To borrow a cinematic metaphor, I now set our camera in motion, imagining a tracking shot from a streetgoer's kinetic perspective before zooming out to set the edifice–street boundary in a broader context. Doing so highlights owners' attempts at making their properties conspicuous along the street and amid the city largely by intentionally inconveniencing others.[64]

A property on Pompeii's western edge offers a fitting starting point and will remain a touchstone throughout this chapter. Called the Casa di Diana II by its eighteenth-century excavators, the huge double-atrium structure boasted a façade (VI.17.32–38) that was extensively remade in the last decades of Pompeii's ancient life. I will return to its form shortly; I want to focus now on the property's sidewalk and the unusual elevation it traces[65] (Fig. 28; see also Figs. 33, 34). Pedestrians making their way northward in front of the house ascended a slope before reaching the southern of the house's two principal entrances (VI.17.36), where the sidewalk leveled out at its highest point.[66] They then walked upon the elevated footpath for roughly 20 meters until they reached the house's other main entryway (VI.17.32), where they again descended to a height more consistent with the city's other sidewalks. There was little, if any, practical reason for elevating the sidewalk in this way. In fact, the house's "ground" floor was raised artificially on subterranean rooms.

Such sidewalk ramping was not an isolated phenomenon. On the same street, the Via Consolare, five different structures manipulated their sidewalks over approximately 150 meters.[67] Unlike the Casa di Diana II, these properties did not level out their sidewalks for a sustained distance, but formed a peak immediately before the house's main entrance. Still more profound examples are visible elsewhere. Near the city's southern edge, the sidewalk's original curbstones are visible and consistent in height with their neighbors in front of

---

[64] This section draws on Hartnett 2011a.
[65] Long exposure to the elements has eroded the sidewalk's decoration.
[66] To create the incline, some curbstones were flipped vertically.
[67] VI.17.10, VI.17.13, VI.17.25, VI.17.27, VI.1.10.

28. Across the frontage of the Casa di Diana II in Pompeii (VI.17.32–38) ran an elevated sidewalk that lifted the house and caused an inconvenience for pedestrians.
Photo: author. Courtesy: Soprintendenza Speciale per Pompei, Ercolano e Stabia.

the Casa di L. Caecilius Phoebus (VIII.2.36–37) (Fig. 29). Additional courses of stone were piled atop them to create a sidewalk that loomed 1.20 meters above the street's surface.[68] The apogee of slanted sidewalks occurred before the so-called Caserma dei Gladiatori (V.5.3), an enigmatic structure that apparently served over its lifetime as a residence and a gladiatorial training ground (Fig. 30). Across its façade's entire 28-meter breadth, the sidewalk was sloped, building from the lowest points at the property's edges to a peak of 1.30 meters (approximately chest height) in front of the main doorway.

Owners likely stood to gain from such sidewalk ramping in at least three related respects. First, our sources suggest that lofty entrances by themselves could bear connotations of wealth and power and might even engender awe and apprehension in onlookers. When Martial sends a poem in his stead to a patron's house, for example, he seeks to calm nerves: "Straightaway on your left, you must approach the shining façade and the atrium of a lofty house. Make for it. Do not fear arrogance or a haughty threshold."[69] Elevating the house did not end at the sidewalk. Both thresholds at the Casa di Diana II, for

---

[68] Such was the change in sidewalk height that, at one end of the property, stairs had to be built on the footpath to accommodate pedestrians.

[69] Mart. 1.70, 12–13: *protinus a laeva clari tibi fronte Penates / atriaque excelsae sunt adeunda domus. / hanc pete: ne metuas fastus limenque superbum.* Cf. Sen. *Ep.* 84.11–12; Verg. *G.* 2.461–462.

29. Additional courses of stone were added to the original curbstones in front of the Casa di L. Caecilius Phoebus in Pompeii (VIII.2.36–37), which caused stairs to be introduced into the sidewalk.
Photo: author. Courtesy: Soprintendenza Speciale per Pompei, Ercolano e Stabia.

30. A ramped sidewalk ran across the entire frontage of the Caserma dei Gladiatori at Pompeii (V.5.3), reaching a height of 1.3 meters and causing passing vehicles to scrape their axles on its front.
Photo: author. Courtesy: Soprintendenza Speciale per Pompei, Ercolano e Stabia.

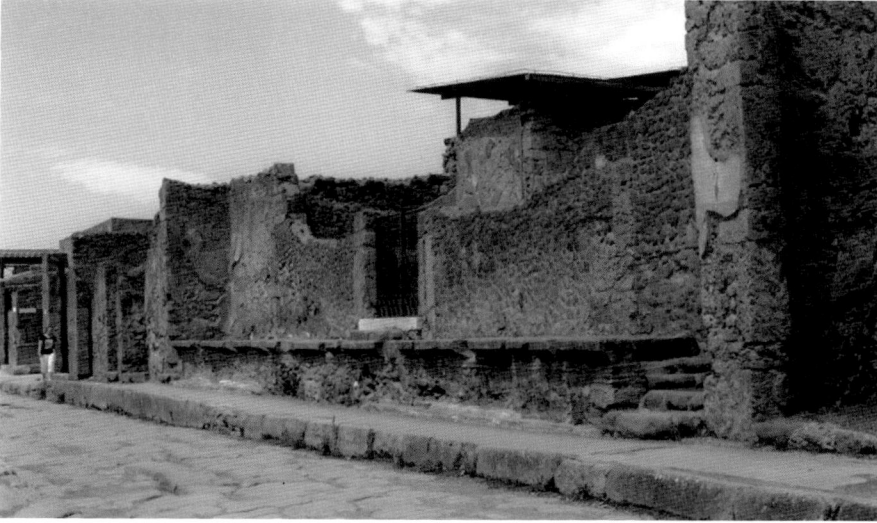

31. The Casa di M. Epidius Rufus at Pompeii (IX.1.20) was lifted above neighboring structures atop a temple-like podium, which supported a secondary sidewalk.
Photo: author. Courtesy: Soprintendenza Speciale per Pompei, Ercolano e Stabia.

instance, were lifted still higher above pedestrians; an elegant travertine stair-case precedes the north entryway, while the revetment on the southern entrance's steps has been lost. Such constructions, visible from the street, were common to properties with ramped sidewalks and further hoisted the house above those walking or riding by.

A threshold that loomed over the street helped to mark out a house from its neighbors. This point is made dramatically by a structure that took a more radical approach to its frontage. Located a block east of the Stabian Baths on the Via dell'Abbondanza, the Casa di M. Epidius Rufus (IX.1.20) had both a conventional sidewalk running along the street and a secondary sidewalk raised on a platform roughly 1 meter higher (Fig. 31). Along the plastered front of this quasi-dais ran moldings, an iron railing stood at its front edge, and staircases gave access at each end. Its lower form thus echoed temple architecture, such as the Temple of Castor in the Forum Romanum, which was also outfitted with an elevated podium, lateral stairs, and railing.[70] Visitors who reached the raised sidewalk faced two more stairs before accessing the house's ornate threshold. Thus, while the ground floors of nearby properties stood at the level of the sidewalk proper, the Casa di M. Epidius Rufus hovered above both action in the street and neighboring buildings.[71] Although not a subtle form of image-crafting, having a higher and larger structure distinguished one's self from others nearby.

[70] Stamper 2005, 56–59, 144–149.
[71] On this façade: Lauter 2009. The façade garnered additional attention by being recessed from the adjacent streetface.

If the structures' height above the roadbed marked out properties for those looking from afar, then a third motivation for ramp building was perhaps attracting the attention of those passing along the street. As we have seen, obstacles to smooth passage were many in Roman cities – from fountains in sidewalks to animals hitched to curbstones. Many nuisances were practical or relatively agentless, but not sidewalk ramps; they filled little discernable need and took shape in a space linked to a house and its owner. In that sense, the exertion that they required from a pedestrian – trudging up and then descending a not insignificant incline – clearly resulted from the whims of the frontager. It added a phenomenological charge to passage and thus extended owners' impact out *past* their façades, into the street's communal world. In brief, by shaping the urban fabric, owners shaped the urban experience.

A subset of the sidewalk ramps presents a clearer picture of efforts at and effects of interference by extending it to wheeled vehicles. Along the front of the Caserma dei Gladiatori, long scrape marks run horizontally across the ramp (Fig. 30). They were left by passing carts, wagons, and the like whose axles extended beyond the wheelbase and typically spun at heights between .45 and .75 meters above the roadbed.[72] Because most curbstones were lower than this height, the axles usually glided above the sidewalk edge without incident. At other spots in Pompeii, however, curbstones were tall enough to scrape axles. Many of these resulted from local circumstances, as where a roadbed descended quickly to exit a city gate. But at the Caserma, and at least eleven other spots in Pompeii, owners did not continue the sidewalk at the same level or slope as adjacent properties, but exacerbated it by building curbstones that stood at least .50 meters above the roadbed.[73] Their intentional constructions thus threatened to scrape the axles of vehicles that passed too closely.[74]

Like their pedestrian counterparts, vehicle drivers were inconvenienced in front of these spots. Just as importantly, the nuisances compelled actions from streetgoers, and, because it was clear who created the obstruction, they symbolically asserted a builder's control over the street. That is, a momentary sense of order was established and a hierarchy of sorts was set up that cast the ramp builders as the dictators of movement and streetgoers as those obliged to respond. Yes, pedestrians and drivers may have taken the initiative and avoided the

[72] Axle heights: Poehler 2009, 72–74.

[73] Locations of intentionally raised curbstones: II.4.2–8, 10–12; V.5.3; VI.1.9–10; VI.11.18; VI.16.15–17; VI.17.10; VI.17.25; VI.17.27–30; VI.17.32–36; VII.7.19; VIII.2.23; VIII.2.36–37.

[74] At some properties, particularly those with high sidewalks, stones were set into the roadbed to create steps up to the footpath. In these circumstances also, a structure's streetward form required action on the part of those moving through the city. As a potential remedy to cart–curb collisions, small lumps of stone, which Saliou (1999, 164–165) calls "bornillons," were occasionally placed at regular intervals along the front side of curbstones (Saliou 1999, table 2 for locations).

nuisances by crossing the street, walking in the roadbed, or steering away. But, in so doing, they nevertheless capitulated by recognizing the nuisance's potential power and reacting to it. However a streetgoer responded, a low-stakes dialogue about control and recognition was initiated when nuisances came into play.

Ramped sidewalks may have been within the letter of the law, which prohibited obstructing thoroughfares or impairing their usefulness, but they were hardly within its spirit.[75] Who would have been behind these efforts at interference and been capable of skirting legal principle and practical enforcement? The properties may hold a clue. Although the twelve locations display heterogeneity by encompassing houses, semipublic complexes (like entertainment complexes for rent), and other types of property, they share some telling features: first, the properties were sizable, averaging 695 square meters of ground area, which was nearly three times the average house size at Pompeii.[76] The properties' large size is a likely proxy for the wealth, if not the status, of their owners. Second, six of the twelve occupy prized Pompeian real estate; namely, those plots on the promontory's western and southern edges that enjoyed views of and breezes from the bay and mountains. The salubrious and comfortable settings place the owners among the city's elite. It is theoretically possible that they received special permission from the municipal authorities to build such obstructions, which would have been quite a statement in itself. Yet if they did not (as I think likely), the effects could have been still greater. Since Roman cities lacked mechanisms to ensure blanket compliance with laws, individuals had to bring suit to prevent nuisances like these. Personal standing and social connections were thus key to individuals' deliberations about whether to sue and to any legal action's success or failure. The ramped and axle-grinding sidewalks, then, with their effects on wheeled and footed traffic alike, may have constituted (or been perceived as) a statement about their owners' ability to marshal the social and political resources to evade the laws' enforcement; that is, to exist above the law. If obstructions were viewed in this way, then people physically experienced messages about position and prestige as they navigated the city on a day-to-day basis.

VISIBILITY AND INTRA-URBAN VIEWS

That architecture sought to impress, intimidate, or shape the experience of streetgoers is not surprising, given what we know about the many claims of

[75] *Tabula Heracleensis* ll. 68–72; *Lex Coloniae Genetivae Iuliae* 104; *Dig.* 43.8.2.32.

[76] See Hartnett 2011a, table 1 for the measurements of each property. Wallace-Hadrill (1994: 72–87, esp. table 4.2) surveys the floor areas of houses in two different samples from Pompeii. His Regio I sample produced an average house size of 266 square meters; that for Regio VI was 289 square meters. Even with the sprawling complexes eliminated, the houses remain squarely in the top quartile of Pompeian houses for ground floor area, averaging 558 square meters.

standing in this ambit, not to mention the house–owner connection. But, as we zoom out, we note, too, how urbanites took special care to shape views of their edifice within the broader urban context.

The power of a building's visibility is widely attested, but Cicero seems particularly obsessed with it, and understandably so, given what he and his house underwent.[77] He refers to his house's location or visual prominence no fewer than six times in the last third of his *De Domo Sua*.[78] At different points, he describes it as standing in full view of nearly the entire city and claims that Rome's busiest and most important sections view its site.[79] Several decades earlier on the same spot, an architect proposed to construct a new house so it would be free from public view. To this his client, Livius Drusus, retorted, "If you have any sort of skill, build my house so that whatever I do can be seen by all."[80] The architect correctly recognized Drusus's concern for the public gaze, but did not understand that his client prized external views and the spotlighting they offered. When visually prominent within the city, a house projected its owner's image far and wide. For Cicero, such visibility had also been a key aspect of the spot because it broadcast his status to the city, but the sword revealed its second edge after Clodius's actions, when the site/sight became a prominent marker of his fall.[81]

When we shift from the hilly cosmopolis of Rome to other cities, we witness the pursuit of visual dominance playing out on the ground. The Casa di Diana II again offers a key example. Whereas the northern half of its façade appears minimally retouched after first-century seismic activity, newer construction techniques, including brickwork, intermingled in the southern half to form a striking array (Figs. 28, 32). A pair of engaged columns on rectangular plinths flanked the main door (VI.17.36). Neither column shaft is preserved to its full height: the 2.5 meters of the northern column soared at least a meter taller. The door-framing ensemble spread laterally, as the columns rested against walls of decorative masonry, and two shorter doorways were placed symmetrically to form an eye-catching pattern of solids and voids, lights and darks. The entryway's particular forms carried further meanings. Its columns resembled the eponymous construction of the Casa del Gran Portale at Herculaneum (V.34–35), whose

---

[77] On the importance of visibility of statues: Stewart 2003, 136–140; Cic. *Pis.* 93; *CIL* 11.1421; *CIL* 5.532. On the *locus celeberrimus* in Roman thought: Newsome 2011, 20–26.

[78] Cic. *Dom.* 100, 101, 103, 116, 132, 146.

[79] Cic. *Dom.* 100: *in conspectu prope totius urbis domus est mea* . . . . 146: *Urbis enim celeberrimae et maximae partes adversum illud non monumentum, sed vulnus patriae contuentur.*

[80] Vell. Pat. 2.14.3: *tu vero . . . si quid in te artis est, ita compone domum meam, ut, quidquid agam, ab omnibus perspici possit.* Cf. Sen. *Ben.* 6.34.1.

[81] Cic. *Dom.* 100: *. . . sin mea domus non modo mihi non redditur, sed etiam monumentum praebet inimico doloris mei, sceleris sui, publicae calamitatis, quis erit qui hunc reditum potius quam poenam sempiternam putet?* Cf. *Dom.* 115, where Cicero paints Clodius as solipsistic by implying that he was primarily interested in the view *from* the property.

engaged columns stood on rectangular bases and were capped with sculpted capitals that carried an architrave (Fig. 34). Only a handful of similar entryways were visible on houses in Pompeii and Herculaneum, and their closest non-domestic cousins were found in public architecture, such as the exterior of Pompeii's Palestra, and grand semipublic complexes, like the Praedia of Julia Felix (II.4.6).[82] Whether the columns at the Casa di Diana II supported an architrave or a pediment, they certainly formed a grand, rare, and visually distinct unit on its façade.

The new doorway's position made an even stronger impression within Pompeii's urban fabric. The owner of the Casa di Diana II, when remaking the façade's southern half, sited the entryway directly in line with one of the city's busiest thoroughfares (Figs. 32, 33). The Via Consolare here cuts diagonally across Pompeii's northwestern section and offered a well-traveled route to a city gate and other Campanian towns beyond. As many travelers moved along, they faced the elegant façade head-on. While the other structures lining the thoroughfare passed by, the Casa di Diana II stood at the street's visual focal point and dominated streetgoers' vision, thus extending the house's impression over a distance of some 70 meters.

A prominent example from Herculaneum suggests how much Romans coveted street-axis views. The first several decades CE saw a major reworking to Cardo V, the city's easternmost thoroughfare. On its east side, a monumental civic palestra was built (Fig. 35). Its colonnaded interior courtyard offered splendid amenities while a large structure — which housed shops, bakeries, and apartments — faced Cardo V.[83] Soaring to at least four stories and measuring some 100 meters in length, the complex's façade dwarfed neighboring buildings. But the structure's visual supremacy was enhanced by its position in Herculaneum's street network because it formed the endpoint of the so-called *decumanus inferior*, the major east–west route for wheeled traffic in the city's south. Directly on the street's axis lay the complex's entrance, which consisted of two large stone Corinthian columns *in antis* before an opulently decorated vestibule (Fig. 36). Tellingly enough, the propylon-style structure

---

[82] E.g., Casa di Loreius (III.5.2). The form's popularity would increase significantly in the following years, as evidenced by its proliferation at Ostia: e.g., Casa del Pozzo (V.3.3: engaged brick columns on stone bases); the Horrea Epagathiana et Epaphroditiana (I.8.3: a similar ensemble crowned by a pediment); and the main entrance to the Case a Giardino (III.9: free-standing columns pushed against a wall).

[83] On this building: Maiuri 1958, 113–143; Yegül 1993; Wallace-Hadrill 2011a, 271–285. The street-facing building was unquestionably conceived as a vital part of the palestra, for the groundplans and the wall-joins of the building's interior and exterior sections are interwoven. Some have suggested that the proceeds from the rental of shops and living units financed the public facilities inside. No explicit proof supports this suggestion, yet it has become a standard feature of the scholarly commentary since it originally appeared in Maiuri (1958, 116–117). See Yegül 1993, 390, n. 2; Pagano 1996, 243.

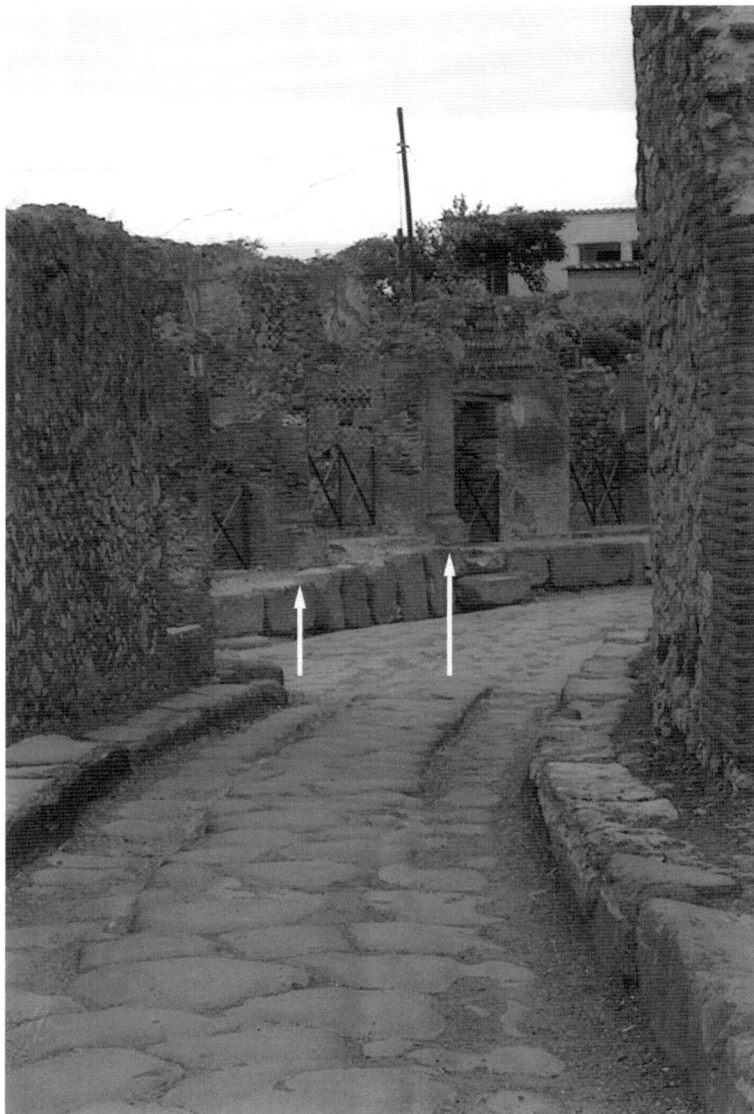

32. A streetgoer looking west along the Via Consolare in Pompeii was confronted head-on with a view of the framed entryway of the Casa di Diana II (VI.17.36). Arrows indicate the location of engaged columns.
Photo: author. Courtesy: Soprintendenza Speciale per Pompei, Ercolano e Stabia.

was originally identified as a temple pronaos because of its size, architectural form, and rich décor.[84] Further excavation discredited the hypothesis, but the

[84] Maiuri (1958, 190, n. 63) quotes Weber's original description of this space as a temple on November 5, 1757. Ruggiero 1885, 233–234, pl. 8, fig. 3 shows the original document. The identification was aided by the discovery in this vicinity of an inscription marking Vespasian's restoration of a temple of *mater deum* after the earthquake of 62 CE (*CIL* 10.1406), now thought to have been carried here by the flow of volcanic material.

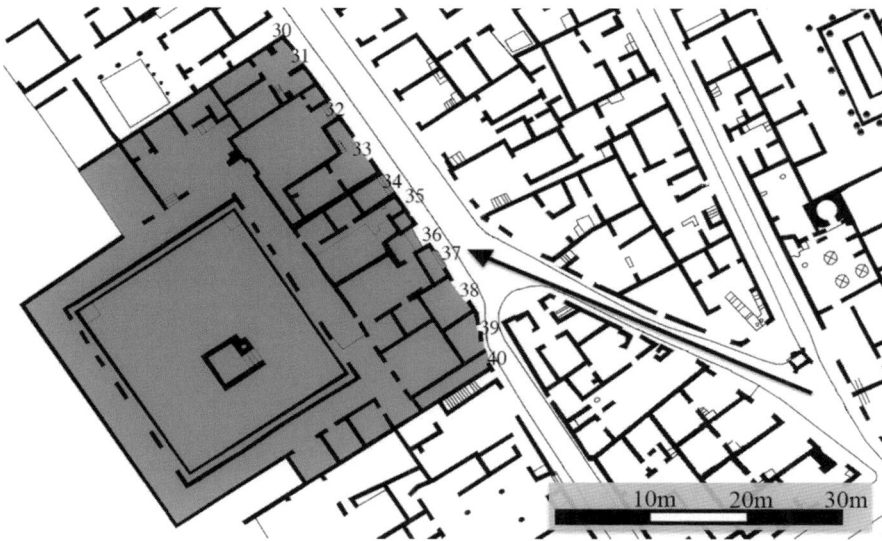

33. A principal entryway to the Casa di Diana II at Pompeii (VI.17.32–38) was constructed directly on the visual axis of the Via Consolare. The arrow represents the view of someone traveling west along the street.
Drawing: Ryan Cairns.

34. When the Casa del Gran Portale in Herculaneum (V.34–35) was carved out of an adjacent house, its presence was marked by a newly created sidewalk and a striking entryway of engaged columns, figural capitals, and a brickwork architrave.
Photo: author. Courtesy: Soprintendenza Speciale per Pompei, Ercolano e Stabia.

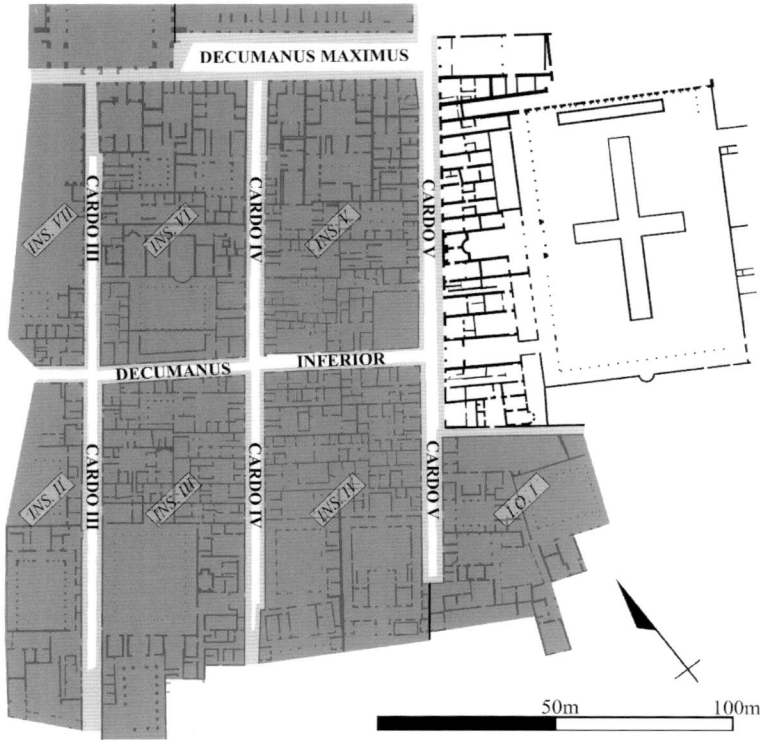

35. The interior walls of Herculaneum's monumental Palestra (at right) were constructed to align with the *decumanus inferior*, rather than being square to Cardo V.
Drawing: author.

entryway is indeed on par with sacred architecture, and it inevitably dominated the view of all those moving eastward on the *decumanus inferior*.

Achieving this street vista was a matter of considerable trouble. Herculaneum's city plan was nearly orthogonal, but the *decumanus inferior* ran slightly out of line with the rest of the streets. The evidence of the palestra itself makes clear that the building's designers, on confronting this unique orientation, prioritized maintaining the street's axis through the palestra's entrance. Rather than set the complex's interior walls perpendicular to its front face, they aligned them with the entranceway and thus with the cock-eyed street. As a result, the entire palestra complex was angled obliquely – a considerable architectural awkwardness to establish the building's commanding position at the street's endpoint.[85]

[85] Near the time of the building's creation, the segment of Cardo V in front of the palestra was repaved in white limestone, which marked the palestra's special status in relationship to the urban fabric. (A narrow sliver of the original volcanic stone remains visible on the street bed's eastern side.) The white paving also extended roughly 20 meters up the *decumanus inferior*, the street along whose length it sought to make a strong visual impression. The physical change

36. The view eastward along Herculaneum's *decumanus inferior* was dominated by the towering columns fronting the vestibule of the Palestra.
Photo: author. Courtesy: Soprintendenza Speciale per Pompei, Ercolano e Stabia.

The Casa di Diana II and Herculaneum's palestra are the most prominent examples of a widespread effort to marshal street-axis views. At Pompeii, the nearly rectilinear street network offered few circumstances for façade vistas along street axes. Nevertheless, of the thirty-six places in the city (as it is excavated thus far) where some version of this view was possible, a full two-thirds (24) have doorways aligned with the approaching street.[86] All manner of

likely marks the minimum streetspace meant to be affected by the axial view of the complex's entrance. On Herculaneum's street paving: Maiuri 1958, 33–43.

[86] Principal entrances to houses located on the axis of a street: 1.10.16; 6.17.36; 7.4.56; 7.4.62; 7.12.26; 7.15.11; 7.16.22; 8.2.21; 9.8.b. Shops appear to take advantage of visibility as well. Across the street from the Casa di Diana II, for example, stands a wine shop that stood directly in the sightline of anyone entering the city from the Porta Ercolano and moving south along the Via Consolare, which could only have aided business. This and other nondomestic examples (1.2.18; 1.7.18/19; 5.2.5; 6.4.1; 6.14.2; 6.16.22; 7.2.46; 7.6.34; 7.16.11; 8.7.10;

buildings sought to take advantage, from food and drink establishments to civic structures like the propylon of the Foro Triangolare, whose six columns were progressively revealed to those moving southward on the Via dei Teatri, thus creating a daunting sight. Yet the greatest portion of the twenty-four examples comes from domestic contexts. Typically, the doorway leading to the house's main interior space – that is, the entrance most closely tied to the house's owner – was featured as the visual focal point.[87] While most structures, because of streets' narrowness, were seen only from an oblique angle and could therefore be easily passed over by the eye, a façade at the endpoint of a street appeared to be its climax, so that other buildings lining the street – inferior in visibility and seemingly less important – were relegated to serving as an approach-way to the now quasi-monumental structure.[88]

The frequency of such street-axis vistas (and the lengths builders went to achieve them) invites further consideration of their appeal and impact. Within the Roman visual and social sphere, face-to-face confrontations in scripted situations held significant power. Nowhere is this dynamic more obvious than the domestic ritual of the *salutatio*. When clients saw their patron framed by a carefully composed architectural ensemble, with everything aligned about an axis, his visual dominance and actual clout were clear.[89] That much has long been clear inside the house. But, in contrast to orchestrated domestic environments, the street was inevitably more spontaneous, contested, and public; many parties deployed diverse statements in an ongoing struggle for status and recognition. A street-axis view, then, influenced the street's dynamics by placing the house and its owner in a position of superiority over others.

CONCLUSION

Throughout this chapter, our attention has ping-ponged between the perspectives of street denizens and house holders. We have seen how buildings were linked to their occupants who used the structures' exteriors to mark achievements and make claims. At the same time, the sentiments of Cicero and others – such as the anonymous author of *fullones ululamque cano, non arma*

9.4.8; 9.7.18) testify more generically to the importance, whether for spreading one's name or selling wine, that Romans attributed to conspicuous locations.

[87] See the Casa di M. Fabius Rufus at Pompeii (VII.16.22) for an example of the considerable architectural awkwardness endured to obtain such a vista.

[88] Augustus's decidedly modest house on the Palatine (Suet. *Aug.* 72.1; Tac. *Ann* 1.5.4; Joseph *AJ* 19.103, 116, 214.), although it boasted a host of decoration around the doorway (*RG* 34–35), also benefitted from a similar relationship to its neighbors: Ov. *Tr.* 3.1.33–34; *Met.* 1.168–176; Wiseman 1987.

[89] On the patron's position in this ritual and his control of sightlines, see Wallace-Hadrill 1989. On the power of viewing within a Roman house as an inherently hierarchical act, see Elsner 1995, 74–87. See also Drerup 1959; Bek 1980; Jung 1984.

virumque – have made clear that passers-by brought a critical eye to such displays and took stock of how owners measured up to their abodes. As our gaze has flashed back and forth, the scope of our discussion has also rippled outward from the edifice–street boundary to encompass a broader domain. Sidewalks, which frontagers were legally required to maintain, offered owners a zone where they could shape the experiences of people passing through communal space. Yet the irony is that the outward blurring of boundaries also opened the space before a house to the population at large – those wishing to scorn or woo a house's residents – with significant effects on reputations near and far. Finally, as we have just seen, owners positioned structures at critical points in the urban fabric to create vistas that had effects well beyond a building's immediate vicinity.

On the one hand, these conclusions strengthen my original contention that buildings made an impact on the street's social dynamics. Such pressure spanned multiple registers (visual, haptic, symbolic) as house owners endeavored to gain streetgoers' notice, compel their movement, or dominate their view. On the other hand, the wide-ranging give and take between house and street, between resident and streetgoers, also highlights a key point – that the junction between these two realms was not a hard and fast line contiguous with a structure's façade. Rather, social space did not map cleanly onto physical space. The sounds of protestors in front of a house poured into neighborhood windows, and a ramped sidewalk drew eyes to a house.

Romans endowed the edifice–street boundary with diverse meanings that were manifest in the charged communication at the threshold and beyond it. This much is supported by assessing houses' *exterior shells*, on which I have intentionally concentrated in this chapter. Yet the actual *façade forms* of several properties we have examined – such as the Casa di M. Epidius Rufus that towered templelike above the street or the Casa di Diana II with its stately engaged columns – hint at a more involved relationship between the street and the specific physical shape given to façades that faced onto it. Chapter 5 takes up this negotiation of inside and outside: how particular architectural details aired additional messages to the street while simultaneously responding to the space's dangers, threats, and social atmosphere.

FIVE

HOUSE FAÇADES AND THE ARCHITECTURAL LANGUAGE OF SELF-PRESENTATION

W HEN, IN HIS PHILOSOPHICAL TREATISE DE RERUM NATURA, Lucretius discusses the optical effects of mirrors and considers why reflected images appear in perspective, he draws an interesting comparison. He writes that looking out a house doorway is akin to looking at a mirror: in both cases, a viewer sees one type of air and light, then an object (the door frame or the mirror), then a new type of air and light (outside the house or the reflection), and, finally, the real objects outside the house or the reflection in the mirror.[1] The technicalities of Lucretius's argument (such as light brushing the eyes) leave something to be desired, but it is notable that, when Lucretius wants an example of two distinct spheres, he turns to the spaces inside and outside a house. The former was prone to spotlighting the chief resident and establishing hierarchies among visitors, while the latter was characterized by the challenging of social boundaries. Yet these two strikingly diverse spaces were immediately adjacent. Only a wall of masonry stood between them. This chapter investigates that architectural interface.

House façades made up much of the street's border and therefore lent much to the space's visual experience. In Chapter 4, as we recognized the close ties binding house to owner and mapped Roman concerns for both exteriority and visibility, street architecture emerged as a means of personal presentation, particularly in the arenas of domination and control, literal or symbolic.

---

[1] Lucr. 4.269–291.

The evidence of sidewalks, ramps, and street-axis views already speaks to a careful consideration of how streetgoers encountered houses and how architecture entered into the street's contestations. Our understanding of houses' power to shape the street deepens when we turn to house façades' specific forms and how they mediated between interior and exterior, individual and communal, protection and display.

If Romans like Lucretius sensed the inside–outside disparity innately, they also experienced it daily. Streetgoers who peered through an open house door might have spotted any number of sumptuous decorations. At Pompeii's famous Casa dei Vettii (VI.15.1), to give an opulent example, their view encompassed a verdant garden, a trickling fountain, finely wrought furniture, and elaborate murals (Fig. 37). Yet the vista was not limited to such lush visual fodder because the house's markedly more staid doorway and façade were also part of the scene (Fig. 38). The exterior of the Casa dei Vettii was divided into broad zones, the socle colored a deep red, the upper section given a whitewash; plaster pilasters surmounted by cubic capitals framed the house's entryway, which an architrave topped. By contrast with what lay within the house, domestic façades like this one were relatively blank and featureless, displaying little ornamental or figural decoration.

Such a dearth of ornament can at first seem surprising. Given what the preceding chapters have shown about the street's importance as a social arena, the key role of domestic architecture in claims of status, the animated communication at the house–street boundary (and beyond), and especially the tactics that house owners employed to draw attention, we might expect that Campanian domestic exteriors would, like their interiors, be more showy. Indeed, such a lack of adornment is one reason that these most visible parts of houses have lagged as the subject of scholarly inquiry.[2] Key texts about houses, as we have seen, do little to help because Vitruvius does not treat house façades at any length. Nor is the situation ameliorated by what is currently visible on site. Authorities have long prioritized the conservation of houses' interiors over their exteriors, which has only exacerbated our perception of the decorative gap between house insides and outsides. While a reconstructed roof protects murals within the Casa del Menandro (I.10.4), for example, the elements have faded and crumbled its once distinct façade presentation (Fig. 39). Excavation photographs prove helpful here and elsewhere in reconstructing façade programs, but they are limited to certain chapters of the city's disinterment and, even then, are hit and miss.[3]

---

[2] Examples of façade studies: Spinazzola 1953, 821–863; Lauter 1972; Thébert 1987; Hoffman 1990; Zaccaria Ruggiu 1994, 1995; Gesemann 1996, 101–156; Bejor 2003; Scagliarini Corlàita 2007; Helg 2009a, 2009b, 2012; Anter 2011.

[3] Casa del Menandro façade: Ling 1997, 12–13, 264, pls. 23 and 27, fig. 28.

37. The view through the doorway of the Casa dei Vettii at Pompeii (VI.15.1) included all manner of luxurious decoration and architecture.
Photo: H. Kaehler/Neg. D-DAI-Rom 59.1615.

When façades have attracted scholars' attention, their appearance is frequently measured by the yardstick of interior decoration. Upon confronting a rare façade decorated with a figural scene, for example, Amedeo Maiuri wrote with apparent surprise that we see "on the outside, a real and true decorative painting, an anticipation of the compositional schemes we find so sumptuously developed on the atrium walls on the interior."[4]

---

[4] Maiuri 1958, 394: "si aveva fare all'esterno una vera e propria pittura decorativa, un'anticipazione degli schemi compositivi che troveremo tanto fastosamente sviluppati all'interno nelle pareti dell'atrio."

38. The exterior aspect of the Casa dei Vettii at Pompeii (VI.15.1) – consisting of a high red socle, pilasters, and cubic capitals – was markedly more reserved than the house's interior. Photo: author. Courtesy: Soprintendenza Speciale per Pompei, Ercolano e Stabia.

Discussing the same surface decades later, another prominent scholar similarly writes of "the tantalizing possibility that decorative motifs *enlivened* the house's façade [emphasis added]."[5] Have we been *expecting* house exteriors to be dead and dull?

A helpful starting point for studying façades anew is the Roman notion of *decorum*, roughly "appropriateness." Ellen Perry's work on the concept in Roman visual culture contends that a concern for *decorum* led Romans to carefully

[5] Clarke 1991, 253.

39. The original façade decoration of the Casa del Menandro at Pompeii (I.10.4), visible in an archival photograph (left), has suffered significantly over the eighty years since the house was excavated, as evident from the difference from its appearance today (right).
Photos: Soprintendenza Speciale per Pompei, Ercolano e Stabia, Archivio Fotografico degli Scavi, C1531; author. Courtesy: Soprintendenza Speciale per Pompei, Ercolano e Stabia.

measure what was suitable for an action or artwork's setting.[6] In this light, the dissimilarity between a house's decoration inside and outside pushes us to consider the façade's context and to reexamine street-facing architecture and ornament as a decorative zone in its own right. That is, shifting our analysis from painting and decoration per se to actions on the street animates the façade, its architectural form, and its decoration as elements that respond to the street's unique ethos while also giving shape to that sphere's physical form and impacting its denizens.

The spotty state of preservation and documentation has an impact on my approach. It precludes an encyclopedic treatment of street-facing architecture and even complicates statistical analyses because the dataset is so perforated by lacunae and question marks. As a result, I necessarily trace patterns in Campanian domestic frontages very broadly, even as they emerge from close examination of a few well-preserved cases drawn largely from the highest echelons of society. Such a selection is partly justified because these structures formed the greatest part of the streetface encountered by streetgoers; moreover, I balance these choices, when preservation allows, by assessing smaller houses. Throughout the analysis, a helpful metaphor is that of language, "with its implicit structures and grammatical rules," as Wallace-Hadrill has described this familiar mode of inquiry.[7] I discuss the general aesthetics of exterior decoration – why did owners employ such a restricted "vocabulary"? – before investigating how owners combined these elements – forming a decorative "syntax" – to make an impact on those

---

[6] Perry 2005, esp. 31–38. Vital passages for this argument: Cic. *Orat.* 70–74; Vitr. 1.2.5; 7.5.4.
[7] Wallace-Hadrill 1994, 14–15. Cf. Bal and Bryson 1991.

passing by. I begin, however, with a still more basic perspective, the question of how houses were accessible from the street.

DOORWAYS, DEFENSE, AND DOMESTIC PRIORITIES

Although Romans seem not to have used any single word to describe a house façade, the material remains make clear that they considered houses, like most buildings, to have one principal side.[8] When a house bordered more than one street, its owner generally privileged the side facing the most impressive or well-traveled thoroughfare, making clear to passers-by that, of the house's external walls, it was preeminent.[9] The Casa dei Dioscuri at Pompeii (VI.9.6–7; Fig. 40), for example, occupied the end of one city block and thus had three sides of frontage; little more than simple plaster adorned the two facing minor streets, while stuccowork evocations of rectangular blocks fronted the broad and prominent Via di Mercurio.

A key feature of any building and its façade is how the contact point between interior and exterior – literally the liminal position – is structured. We can best understand house entryways by first examining doorways to nondomestic spaces. Along busy streets, frontage was valuable; from bars to workshops, small commercial and industrial spaces relied on visibility and ease of accessibility to attract the patronage of passers-by, and they therefore clustered along main streets. To make goods visible and to entice potential customers, shop doorways were broad, often spanning the interior's entire width.[10] Although closures made of tapered planks would shut off these apertures by night, their removal and storage during peak hours of business essentially joined the two spheres of streetspace and shopspace. Breaking down or blurring boundaries was also a matter of actual practice, to judge from descriptions of shops spilling into sidewalks.[11]

House owners' concerns equally, though differently, shaped the architectural relationship between "the out" and "the in." Guarding the domestic realm from threats posed by the street's "outsiders," such as those we met in the

---

[8] *Frons* is the generic term for the face of any building or monument: *TLL*, s.v. II.A.1.b; *OLD*, s.v., 7a; e.g., Petron. 71.6. *Aspectus* seems to convey the broad impression given by a building when viewed from the exterior: e.g., Vitr. 3.3.6, 7.5.5. *Prospectus* is used primarily by Vitruvius (e.g., 5.6.9) to describe temporary stage decorations for different types of productions. Private buildings, their balconies, and windows were visible, the architect writes, for comic productions. See also Spinazzola 1953, 610–611.

[9] Laurence (2007, 73–87) measures the relative frequency of doorways and graffiti to assess the amount of street activity. The depth of wheel ruts provides a direct, but imprecise, means of gauging the degree of wheeled traffic: Tsujimura 1991.

[10] Gassner 1986, 27–30; MacMahon 2003; Ellis 2005, 75–77; Monteix 2010, 56–61.

[11] Mart. 7.61. Cf. Livy 6.25.9; *Dig.* 43.10.1–5. There is also the possibility that shutter-planks, in some cases where a masonry bar was not present, were semipermanently set in place to form partition walls.

40. The Casa dei Dioscuri at Pompeii (VI.9.6–7) presented a façade of plasterwork evocations of ashlar blocks on its western side, which faced the busiest and widest of the three streets on which the house had frontage. The other sides were decorated with a simple red socle below a white upper zone.
Photo: author. Courtesy: Soprintendenza Speciale per Pompei, Ercolano e Stabia.

previous chapter, was a practical concern.[12] Poets mention the tools that they might use on a door that prohibited access to a lover – torches, crowbars, axes, swords.[13] When civil order broke down, houses offered a last spot of refuge: Cicero describes Pompey as shielding himself "by the door and walls of his house, not the right of laws and courts."[14] The weapons cataloged by poets were certainly in the arsenal of brigands and thieves whose repeated appearance in legal texts testifies to the anxieties they aroused. For example, the Twelve Tables justified killing a nocturnal robber in a house, just as they did one discovered in daylight with a weapon.[15] The *Lex Cornelia de iniuriis* of 81 BCE tellingly lumped together having one's house entered by force with being beaten or struck, both marks of the noncitizen. All were prosecutable under a rubric for *iniuria*, insult or "loss of face."[16]

---

[12] The following paragraphs draw on Saller 1984, 353–354; Treggiari 2002, 74–108.

[13] Ov. *Am.* 1.6.57–58; Hor. *Od.* 3.26.6–8.

[14] Cic. *Mil.* 18: *ianua se ac parietibus, non iure legum iudiciorumque texit.* Cf. Cic. *Vat.* 22 (Bibulus is not protected by prestige, the laws' authority, or his *imperium*, but by the defense and security offered by his door and walls); *Fam.* 144 (Cicero orders his wife to ensure that their house is barricaded and guarded).

[15] Cic. *Tul.* 48–50.

[16] *Dig.* 47.10.5.pr.-5.

The symbolic importance as well as the practical necessity of household defense was linked to the sacred aura that enveloped houses. The household gods, *penates*, were frequent metonyms for an entire structure, as when Valerius Maximus tells of a person who broke into a house, expelled the owner's son from his father's *penates*, and claimed that he was the true son.[17] After Clodius built a shrine where Cicero's home was razed, the orator similarly asks whether Libertas wanted to drive out his *penates* and *lares* and to establish herself. He asks, "What is more sacred, what more fortified by every kind of sanctity, than the home of each and every citizen?"[18]

Consequently, the protection of the domestic realm – both structure and contents – was deeply embedded within conceptions of honor for the *paterfamilias*. Discussions of houses frequently employ the vocabulary of sexual purity and pollution. Tacitus and Cicero refer to Rubellius Plautus's and Crassus's houses as *casta* and *castissima*, respectively.[19] Horace praises the moral position of Roman houses under Augustus's reign: each is chaste and unstained by any lewdness.[20] *Dedecus*, literally "disgrace" or "dishonor," on the other hand, mars the households of Verres and Antony.[21] In other examples of sexualized language, Jullus Antonius, the lover of Augustus's daughter Julia, is said to have "violated the house of Augustus," while one of Vitellius's generals sexually "polluted" the houses of his hosts.[22] The gravity of such intrusions was enshrined in both law and mythology. A father had special powers of execution over his daughter and her *adulter* if they were apprehended in his or his son-in-law's house.[23] The fabled Verginius, moreover, to prevent his house from being contaminated by his daughter's rape, is said to have led her to the forum and killed her himself.[24] Sexuality aside, the symbolic dangers of breaking and entering are thrown into high relief by the aftermath of Clodius's funeral. Gangs surrounded the house of the interrex, Marcus Aemilius Lepidus, and eventually forced their way in, throwing down the images of Lepidus's ancestors and smashing his marriage bed, all in front (our source adds) of Lepidus's chastity-modeling wife.[25]

[17] Val. Max. 9.15.5. Other examples of *penates* for the physical structure: Val. Max. 5.6, 9.1.6; Sen. *Clem.* 1.15.3; Tac. *Ann.* 13.4.

[18] Cic. *Dom.* 108: *quid est sanctius, quid omni religione munitius quam domus unius cuiusque civium?* Similarly, When Tacitus (*Hist.* 3.84) wants to paint a picture of Vitellius's troops on their worst behavior, he describes them striving "to defile houses and altars with blood," *domos arasque cruore foedare* . . . . See also Tac. *Hist.* 3.84.

[19] Tac. *Ann.* 14.22; Cic. *Cael.* 9. Cf. Sen. *Clem.* 1.9.10.

[20] Hor. *Od.* 4.5.21: *nullis polluitur casta domus stupris.* Cf. Cic. *Cael.* 49, where Clodia lays open her house and conducts a debauched life.

[21] Cic. *Verr.* 2.4.83; *Phil.* 3.35. Cf. Tac. *Ann.* 5.1.

[22] Tac. *Ann.* 3.18: *domum Augusti violasset* . . . . Tac. *Hist.* 3.41: *rapere inlicitas voluptates adulterisque ac stupris polluere hospitum domus.* Cf. Cic. *Har resp.* 15.

[23] *Dig.* 48.5.23.2, 48.5.25.pr.

[24] Val. Max. 6.1.2. Cf. Livy 29.18.8.

[25] Asc. *Mil.* 33, 36, 43C.

Accordingly, a house's door was cocooned within a host of ritual practices intended to ensure safe-keeping. From the beginning, if you intended to enter a house, you had to be mindful of which foot stepped first.[26] Upon a new bride's arrival at her groom's house, it is said that she anointed the doorposts with pig or wolf fat. One source notes that the wolf fat "keeps out evil potions," while another credits wolves for their fidelity.[27] Romans remarked about the bad luck that attended stepping on or kicking the threshold, especially in nuptial contexts: the bride's feet, upon entering her husband's house, were not to touch the threshold, which was a symbol of Vesta, goddess of chastity and virginity.[28] Any number of totems were hung or displayed at this boundary to ward off evil: a toad at harvest, a phallic tintinnabulum, or a mosaic of a guard dog, any of which may have provoked apotropaic laughter.[29]

Given the concern with maintaining the purity of family members and shielding them from pollution and violation – either moral or corporal – the essentially defensive posture of Campanian houses is surprisingly underappreciated.[30] Physically limiting access started with allowing a minimum of entry points. In larger houses, decoration or dimensions typically demarcated one entrance as the principal locus of admission and departure. Moreover, the few windows that pierced exterior walls on the ground floor were small, covered with grills to prevent intruders, or elevated out of reach.[31] The desire to close off a house from the street, however, was frequently in tension with other pressures, such as taking advantage of frontage along a well-traveled street by opening additional doorways for shops and the like. In such circumstances, some of which we will encounter shortly, owners were especially careful to differentiate the foremost entryway from more quotidian apertures.

The house's protective stance is embodied in the form of the main entrance, which distanced the house from the street through the threshold's width and location. Its opening, often narrower than shops' and secured by double or triple doors, typically was set back slightly from the house's façade and led to the passageway of the *fauces*, whose length further separated the house's interior from the street outside.[32] If a recessed space, often labeled as a *vestibulum*, fronted the doorway, or if a person were posted here to admit or refuse visitors, the inside was buffered still more.[33] Even in their absence, most house layouts

---

[26] Petron. 30; Vitr. 3.4.4; Ogle 1911; Ellis 2011. Cf. Juv. 10.5.

[27] Pliny *NH* 28.135, 28.142, 28.157; Serv. *A.* 4.458. Cf. Donat. *ad Hecyr.* 1.260; Isid. *Orig.* 9.8.

[28] In general: Ov. *Am.* 1.12.2–6. Nuptial: Catull. 61.159–161, 64.292–293; Serv. *Ecl.* 8.29; Juv. 6.51–52; Pliny *HN* 29.30.

[29] Toad: Pliny *NH* 18.303. Tintinnabula: Clarke 2007, 69–73. Dog mosaics: Clarke 1979, 9–12.

[30] Dwyer (1991, 28–29) provides a rare exception to this general trend, noting the massive number of lock parts found in Pompeian houses.

[31] For more on windows, see Spinazzola 1953, 65–80; Gesemann 1996, 145–152.

[32] Means of securing houses: Marquardt 1886, 228–236.

[33] See "Bringing the Inside Outside" in this chapter.

created a single, critical control point that sealed off the domestic realm from the world outside and the incursions it threatened. Deeply embedded in the common architectural form given to house doorways, then, was a fundamental cultural value and a degree of self-presentation. In this sense, we see a fitting introductory example of a façade's architectural and decorative "language." But what confronted those in the street when they looked up from thresholds? What was the precise "vocabulary" of façades? And what meanings did it carry for onlookers?

FAÇADE FORMS

House façades share a general aesthetic more than they exhibit a uniformity of building techniques. Often, a mixture of construction styles was used, such as at the Casa Sannitica in Herculaneum (V.1–2; Fig. 41), where irregularly shaped rocks set in a mortar matrix (*opus incertum*) and netlike diagonals of pyramid-shaped stones (*opus reticulatum*) covered the majority of the façade's surface while small ashlar blocks alone (*opus quadratum*) or mixed with brick (*opus vittatum mixtum*) were used for quoining or door jambs.[34] The masonry was covered by a layer of plaster and then frescoed in broad panels of color, complete with beveled edges similar to those bordering large cut blocks of stone.[35] Elsewhere, the masonry underpinnings were on occasion left unplastered, as at the Casa della Fontana Grande in Pompeii (VI.8.20–22), whose grand rectangular ashlars of Noceran tuff still bear painted notices.[36]

The painted plaster that adorned many house façades usually divided the ground floor frontage into two horizontal bands by distinguishing them in color. Most standard was a red socle topped by a white field, such as spanned a distance of more than 20 meters along the face of Pompeii's Casa di T. Dentatius Panthera (IX.2.16). Spinazzola paid special attention to Pompeii's façade forms and recorded other combinations: white above yellow with red veining, white above black, and red over black, for instance.[37] When façades were elaborated in paint, the socle typically received the lion's share of attention. Horizontal and vertical stripes, varying in thickness from house to house, outlined rectangular zones, typically taller than they were wide. Such a schema, with panels demarcated by double outlines, is evident from archival

---

[34] Ganschow 1989, 221.

[35] As is the case with many façades at Pompeii and Herculaneum, some modern reconstruction has been done on this house's exterior: Ganschow 1989, 221–222.

[36] Other houses with similar street streetward aspects, such as Pompeii's Casa del Fauno (VI.12.1–6) and its towering piers of Noceran stone, show signs of plastering. Cf. the Casa dei Due Atri at Herculaneum (VI.28–29): Maiuri 1958, 276–277.

[37] Yellow with red veining: I.12.3–4; black (all with red outlines in the socle): IX.13.1–3, II.2.4 and III.2.1; red over black (with some green striations): I.12.5.

41. The façade of the Casa Sannitica at Herculaneum (V.1–2) was constructed using a number of different techniques; the masonry was then covered by a layer of frescoed plaster shaped into "blocks" with beveled edges (far right).
Photo: author. Courtesy: Soprintendenza Speciale per Pompei, Ercolano e Stabia.

photographs of Pompeii's Casa di Trebius Valens (III.2.1; Plate VI).[38] As forms of mural painting, façade decoration did not stretch the ability of Roman artists, who were capable of depicting grand architectural perspectives, delicate confections of candelabra, representations of myth, and fantastic evocations of faraway lands. With very few exceptions, however, domestic façades rarely

---

[38] The extensive façade decoration was lost in Allied bombing of Pompeii in 1943: Spinazzola 1953, figs. VI–VIII.

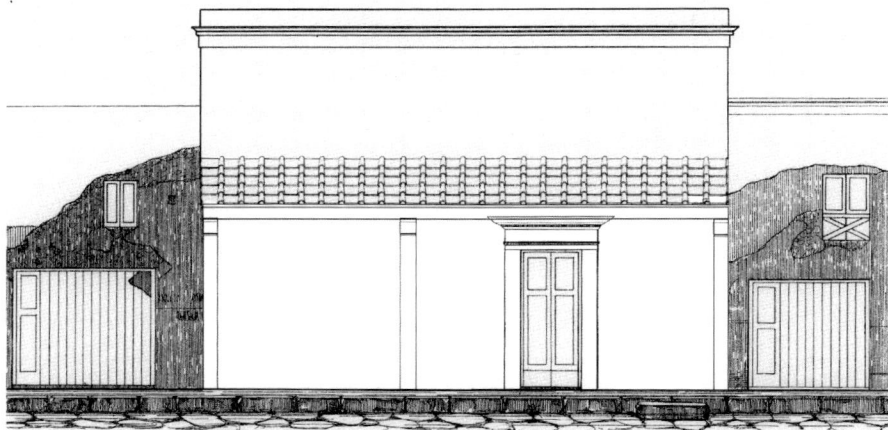

42. The façade of the Casa del Sacello Iliaco at Pompeii (I.6.4), seen here in a reconstruction, featured a plastered wall decorated with simple architectural elements, such as pilasters, a blank frieze, and an architrave highlighting the doorway.
Drawing: Ryan Cairns.

displayed elements that were figural.[39] Modest lines and fields of color were the repertoire.

In addition to broad stretches of simply frescoed wall, the ground floor of façades regularly was adorned with elementary architectural elements, as at Pompeii's Casa del Sacello Iliaco (I.6.4; Fig. 42). Visible at the façade's east end is a plaster pilaster crowned by a capital-like form. A simple blank frieze sat atop this pilaster (and an identical one nearby), passed along the top of a dentiled architrave above the house's lone entryway (which was flanked by pilasters), and ran to the façade's western end, where another pilaster stood. Many of the same elements adorned the façade of the largest house unearthed thus far at Pompeii, the Casa del Fauno (VI.12.1–6; Fig. 43).[40] Pilasters here decorated a series of ashlar piers that separated the façade's many apertures. This example offers a reminder of both the consistency of façade elements as well as the impact of local circumstances on façade forms. Although drawing on the same architectonic palette, this gigantic structure's frontage along a well-trafficked street was devoted largely to shop-style doorways.

The effects of such severe façade presentations on a streetgoer are easily recognizable. Little breakable or readily defaceable ornament was exposed. The street-facing wall, in maintaining the same decoration over several meters, presented an appearance that was consistent, often monolithic, and sometimes even imposing. More than anything, this aesthetic emphasized, as

[39] Of the seventy-two figural façade paintings/ensembles at Pompeii cataloged by Fröhlich (1991), five appear on houses: I.3.24, I.9.1, V.4.12/13, VI.9.6–7, VI.14.43.
[40] Hoffman 1996.

43. The façade of the Casa del Fauno at Pompeii (VI.12.1–6) featured pilasters carved into stone piers that separated broad, shop-style openings.
Photo: author. Courtesy: Soprintendenza Speciale per Pompei, Ercolano e Stabia.

much as local circumstances allowed, the façade's difficulty of penetration; painted decoration did not visually crack open the wall's face through trompe-l'oeil techniques, but drew attention to its surface with two-dimensional schemes. Dividing the wall into segments, particularly on the socle, gave viewers the impression that it was solid and stable – a visual emphasis on impregnability that chimed with householders' interest in appearing to protect the domestic realm within.[41]

THE "AESTHETIC OF AUSTERITY" AND RESTRAINT IN SELF-PRESENTATION

Beyond the immediate physical impact of a severe façade, what emerges across the many types of façade décor is a visual sensibility that stressed starkness and a restricted decorative palette over extensive and elaborate ornament – overall, we might call this an "aesthetic of austerity." I now wish to explore three

---

[41] It is difficult to discern, because of the paucity of evidence, to what degree upper floors maintained such a vision of impregnability. Since second-floor windows were elevated out of reach, they could afford to be larger, as at the Casa dell'Augustale (II.2.4), yet some façades maintain a severe appearance throughout, with small windows (e.g., Casa di Julius Polybius, IX.13.1–3). A rarer example of an elaborate second-story façade is IX.12.1–5, where a long row of engaged columns was displayed to the street. For upper floors, see Andrews 2006.

potential underlying and overlapping reasons why house owners chose this visual mode: the potency of restraint in elite comportment and self-presentation, the paradoxical capacity of decorative severity to help houses stand out, and the cachet of public standing carried by the few architectural elements used on house façades.

If austerity is seen only as a dearth of ornament and not a willful embrace of restraint guided by a sense of appropriateness, then façades are bound to be considered lacking. A leap back into the world of Roman gestures and bodies, their legibility and meanings – physiognomy, in short – helps explain how an intentional paucity of external signs could itself be a strong assertion. As we have seen, Romans from the late Republic through the high empire believed that you could infer a person's true nature from exterior signs – by the way he or she laughed, for example.[42] I wish to pursue further one example of self-presentation and its decoding – namely, walking – since it is frequently discussed by our sources and took place on the street. Dio Chrysostom discusses the simple act: "Walking is a universal and uncomplicated activity, but while one man's gait reveals his composure and the attention he gives to his conduct, another's reveals his inner disorder and lack of self-restraint."[43]

How could you distinguish certain classes of people and their virtues and vices from the way they moved? In the broadest terms, those who were most suspect, such as *cinaedi* (sexual deviants), were identified by their excessive motion. Romans thought that while *cinaedi* strolled, their natural bearing compelled their arms and fingers to move too much, and their necks and sides to rock back and forth.[44] Cicero's directives to his son warn of the results of immoderate walking:

> When these things happen [i.e., when we hurry too fast], it leaves us short of breath, our faces changed, our mouths all twisted; and these are evident signs that steadfastness (*constantia*) is absent.[45]

In other words, Romans were convinced that one's general lack of self-control was manifested directly in the body's excessive movements and vice versa: too much movement was read as a shortcoming in moral steadiness. In a related sphere of public presentation, oratory, Quintilian delves into gesture, and

---

[42] The following paragraphs draw on Gleason 1995; Corbeill 2002; and O'Sullivan 2011. See also "Come as You Are: Evaluation on the Street" in Chapter 3.

[43] Dio Chrys. *Or.* 32.54: ἀλλὰ τὸ βαδίζειν, ὃ κοινόν ἐστι καὶ ἁπλοῦν δήπουθεν, τοῦ μὲν ἐμφαίνει τὴν ἡσυχίαν τοῦ τρόπου καὶ τὸ προσέχειν ἑαυτῷ, τοῦ δὲ ταραχήν καὶ ἀναίδειαν.

[44] *Cinaedi*: [Aristotle], *Phys.* 808a.14–15; Anonymous Latin Physiognomist 74, 98, 115; Polem. *Phgn.* 50; Sen. *Q Nat.* 7.31.2.

[45] Cic. *Off.* 1.131: *quae cum fiunt, anhelitus moventur, vultus mutantur, ora torquentur; ex quibus magna significatio fit non adesse constantiam.* Cf. Quint. *Inst.* 11.3.112.

repeatedly harps on the theme of avoiding immoderate gesticulation.[46] Although he does not write directly about how such unrestraint is received, his descriptions of these motions as *fanaticum*, "frenzied," and *ineptissimum*, "very unsuitable, absurd," leave little doubt about how they could be understood.[47]

Restraint and control, by contrast, were thought to characterize the movements of an elite male. Specialists in physiognomy state that an ambulant man moves in a measured manner and with an ample stride, which "signifies trustworthiness, sincerity, liberality, and a high-minded nature free from anger."[48] Cicero concurs and is more specific, proclaiming that full control of the body is a goal (neck and fingers motionless, body straight) and dictating that "nothing be superfluous."[49] Speed must be deliberately moderate; one's gait should be, in the charged Latin of experts in bodily movement, *gravis*, "heavy, serious."[50] Not surprisingly, Romans were especially wary of a lack of control when manifested as what they considered vulgar showiness. Cicero casts an overabundance of frill in distinctly gendered terms:

> We should consider loveliness as befitting women, and dignity as befitting men. Therefore, let all ornament not fit for a man's dignity be removed from his person, and let him beware of similar faults in gesture and movement.[51]

Criticism for such *ostentatio* also falls to those who tried to draw attention and curry popular favor by gesturing grandly on the rostrum, and we hear Cicero bewailing appearances that are "too exquisite."[52] The orator perpetuates this

---

[46] Quint. *Inst.* 11.3.66 (power and legibility of gesture), 11.3.71 (excessive head motions: *adeo iactare id [scil. caput] et comas excutientem rotare fanaticum est*), 11.3.76 (forbidden appearances of the eyes), 11.3.81 (lips), 11.3.103 (hands), 11.3.118–120, 126, 128 (other excessive gestures or movements).

[47] *Fanaticum*: Quint. *Inst.* 11.3.71; *ineptissimum*: Quint. *Inst.* 11.3.126.

[48] Polem. *Phgn.* 50 (Translation: M. Gleason).

[49] Cic. *Orat.* 59: *idemque motu sic utetur, nihil ut supersit.* Cf. Cic. *De or.* 3.220; Sen. *Ep.* 40.14, 66.5.

[50] Anononymous Latin Physiognomist 100. Quintilian (*Inst.* 11.3.112–3) agrees with the importance of control, even suggesting that an orator's hand should remain between the level of the chest and eye. He adds elsewhere (11.3.137) that another nonverbal aspect of a speaker's presentation – his clothing – should also be toned down: "As with all men of worth, [an orator's dress] should be brilliant and masculine. For a man's toga, shoes, and hair ought to be censured both for too much care and for lack of it"; *quare sit, ut in omnibus honestis debet esse, splendidus et virilis: nam et toga et calceus et capillus tam nimia cura quam neglegentia sunt reprendenda.* Cicero routinely ridicules his enemies for what he describes as their feigned bearing, the movements or habits they affected to disguise their actual nature. For example, if we believe Cicero (*Sest.* 19; *Pis.* 24; *Pis.* 1, fr. 8), Piso sternly paraded in an all too serious manner, while Rullus is accused of trying to conceal his natural mannerisms by adopting a more assertive appearance, voice, and gait (*Leg. agr.* 2.13). Cicero contrasts these actions with *veritas* in movement (*Leg. agr.* 1.23; *Fin.* 2.77). Cf. Anononymous Latin Physiognomist 74.

[51] Cic. *Off.* 1.130: *venustatem muliebrem ducere debemus, dignitatem virilem. ergo et a forma removeatur omnis viro non dignus ornatus, et huic simile vitium in gestu motuque caveatur.*

[52] Cic. *Leg. agr.* 1.23, 2.15; Quint. *Inst.* 2.12.10; Cic. *Off.* 1.130: *adhibenda praeterea munditia est non odiosa neque exquisita nimis, tantum quae fugiat agrestem et inhumanam neglegentiam.*

ideology – that control was a masculine trait – when he claims that *ostentatio* is a poor way to gain *gloria*. Instead, he argues, in both gesture and movement "praise goes to the direct and simple."[53]

All these observations have direct relevance for the type of assessments that regularly happened on the street. Yet they also raise a question: If Romans could see a slower walker or restrained speaker and have images of *gravitas* and *constantia* spring to mind, then what happened when they approached an austere façade? One lesson is that, in the Roman world, aesthetic and moral judgments were virtually one and the same.[54] The example of Augustus's house on the Palatine extends this principle from people to their abodes. Departing from the fashions of the previous century, Augustus occupied a very simple dwelling, which was looked on favorably as a direct reflection of the modesty and restraint of a *princeps*.[55] Against this backdrop and with the notion of *decorum* in mind, we can more fully understand the decided severity of house façades in Pompeii and Herculaneum. Their aesthetic of austerity and lack of frilly adornment held meaning precisely by showing very little. A dearth of decoration did not mean a lack of signifiers, but was a signifier in itself – an architectural and decorative demonstration of, or at least aspiration to, the self-restraint appropriate for elite self-presentation in the public sphere.

AUSTERITY IN ITS PHYSICAL CONTEXT

Beyond this positive definition, austerity in domestic exterior decoration obviously drew potency and meaning from what it was *not*. That is, visual restraint helped differentiate houses from the more ostentatious façades of neighboring buildings. Although ancient cities are often studied on a building-by-building basis, ancient streetgoers' experiences were of course more contextual as they encountered houses, bars, or workshops juxtaposed to one another. The street frontage of commercial properties was generally more extravagant and commonly employed the figural decorations that houses routinely shunned. Adjacent shops on the Via dell'Abbondanza in Pompeii (I.12.3–5), for instance, boasted female faces personifying Roma and Alexandria, while a nearby shopkeeper surrounded his or her entryway with a still more elaborate display (IX.7.1; Fig. 87).[56] A fresco of a resplendent Venus Pompeiana adorned one doorjamb, a procession of worshippers of Cybele was

---

[53] Cic. *Off.* 2.43, 1.130: *quae sunt recta et simplicia laudantur.*
[54] Corbeill 2002, 203.
[55] Suet. *Aug.* 72.1; *RG* 34.2, 35.1; Carretoni 1983. Cf. Tac. *Ann* 1.5.4; Joseph. *AJ* 19.103, 116, 214. Augustus's construction was also a reaction to an elite domestic building craze in the late republic: e.g., Pliny *NH* 36.110.
[56] Spinazzola 1953, 155–159. Fröhlich 1991, 310–311.

painted opposite, and megalographic heads of four deities fronted a saffron field atop the shop's lintel.[57]

The juxtaposition of two façades illustrates the contrasts that could reign along a street. We saw earlier the polychrome checkerboard façade of a possible fullery in Pompeii (IX.13.4–6), complete with paintings of Romulus and Aeneas around the central doorway.[58] Immediately adjacent was the Casa di Julius Polybius (IX.13.1–3) whose two-story façade was a picture of gravity: above a socle of black panels bordered by red lines, a broad expanse of plaster modeled into ashlar-like blocks decorated the first floor, while pilasters stood at the corners, a molding spanned the house's width, and architraves crowned the two main streetside entrances. The tall and severe frontage, seen side by side with its neighbor's busy and aggressively aspirational decor, must have been striking (Plate VII). Many house owners eschewed *ostentatio*, just as their doorways sought to protect, and not to vulgarly divulge, their contents within. In this sense, domestic façades' very severity could literally distinguish them from other constructions along the street.

An imaginary walk down one Herculaneum street grants a sense of the diffusion of such stateliness. People looking at the northeast corner of what we now call Insula III saw the façade of the Casa del Tramezzo di Legno (III.11–12). A strikingly white two-story plane of simple plaster capped by a molding and a third-floor balcony, the restrained composition was interrupted only by a simple shop opening and decoration around the main door.[59] As pedestrians proceeded down Cardo IV, they next came to the Casa a Graticcio (III.13–15), which squeezed at least three separate dwellings and a commercial space into a narrow plot (Fig. 44). Streetgoers saw the results: a balcony and another room spilled over the sidewalk atop three columns.[60] The house's eponymous *opus craticium*, masonry within a wooden framework, was also visible and likely left unpainted.[61] Our pedestrians next encountered the staid façade of the Casa dell'Erma di Bronzo (III.16) and, one door down, the Casa dell'Ara Laterizia (III.17) whose socle's diagonal stripes were a marked departure.[62]

This imagined passage prompts several conclusions. First, even for primarily domestic environments, different degrees of austerity and grandeur were sought along the street. In some circumstances, other priorities or limitations appear to have governed façade presentations, such as a building's use as rental property (as

---

[57] Spinazzola 1953, 213–242; Fröhlich 1991, 182–184, 332–333; Potts 2009. See "Story Three: Shop Façades and Goddesses" in Chapter 8.

[58] Spinazzola 1953, 147–155. Fröhlich 1991, 339–340.

[59] Maiuri 1958, 207–222.

[60] Maiuri 1958, 407–420. But see also Monteix 2010, 26–35 on the potential problems with the reconstruction.

[61] *Opus craticium*: Vitr. 2.8.20, 7.3.11.

[62] Maiuri 1958, 243–247 (Casa dell'Erma di Bronzo), 420–422 (Casa dell'Ara Laterizia).

44. At Herculaneum, the façades of the Casa a Graticcio (left, III.13–15) and the Casa del Tramezzo di Legno (right, III.11–12) suggest the differences that could reign across the frontages of domestic structures.
Photo: author. Courtesy: Soprintendenza Speciale per Pompei, Ercolano e Stabia.

was likely the case with the Casa a Graticcio).[63] The words of Apuleius, who remarks that the important receive more scrutiny for their speech and demeanor, ring true: "Along with ordinariness comes lots of excuses; along with standing lots of difficulties."[64] As in many aspects of Roman society, the elite set the pattern, but not all matched it fully. For those who lacked the financial means or who privileged issues of utility, achieving an impressive façade was either not possible or a lower priority. Second, given the mélange of appearances, especially severe houses likely stood out all the more, and their residents, if they owned multiple plots, may have even sought to create disparities so their seat appeared more prominent. The meaning of our final example's "zebra–stripe" motif is

[63] Pirson 1999, esp. 112–115 for the Casa a Graticcio.
[64] Apul. *Flor.* 9.8: *tantum habet vilitas excusationis, dignitas difficultatis.*

debated, but the decoration clearly departed from what appeared next door, perhaps to the benefit of that house's owner.[65] The terms of that difference, however, bring me to my final point. House façades that displayed apparently aberrant features, such as exposed *opus craticium* or diagonal stripes, differed from the Casa di Julius Polybius or the Casa del Tramezzo di Legno not so much in nature as degree. Forms as unique as the diagonal stripes still demonstrated a concern for emphasizing a house's surface and thus its impenetrability. That is, while some owners of domestic façades appear less concerned with presenting the most severe frontage or employing architectural elements that bore connotations of public standing (a topic I discuss later), they rarely broke from the dominant visual paradigm of austerity.

FAÇADES AND THE FIRST STYLE: FORMS, CHRONOLOGY, AND DEFINITIONS

My final explanation for why house façades were so severe focuses on their specific architectural and decorative vocabulary as much as their general aesthetic. Domestic façades had their greatest overlap with the so-called first Pompeian style. This manner of decoration, through a combination of plasterwork and painting, presented the appearance of regularly cut blocks of ashlar masonry, including details as fine as stone veining and drafted edges.[66] As is visible in the *fauces* of the Casa Sannitica (Fig. 45), the first style routinely featured moldings, cornices, and pilasters — all arrayed in a similar manner to their deployment on the façade of the Casa del Sacello Iliaco (to name a representative house [Fig. 42]). The latter dwelling, that is, also boasts a severe wall treatment framed by pilasters, topped by a frieze, and ornamented by a dentiled entablature. In other words, streetgoers saw domestic façades drawing on the same architectonic palette as the first style; arranging those elements in similar ways; and calling to mind, even if they lacked "blocks," the general aesthetic of consistent stretches of austere decoration. Such extensive intersections must have both reflected and shaped the meanings Romans attached to houses' street-facing architecture and decoration.

Although the first style, appropriately enough, preceded the onset of the other "styles" categorized by August Mau, considering it as a favorite of only a specific period far removed from the fashions current in 79 CE would be

---

[65] Wallace-Hadrill 1994, 39, 222 n. 4; Goulet 2001–2002; Cline 2012. There is a question of whether this decoration's occasional location in service corridors should mark it as very humble or whether it imitates the appearance of stone and thus should be understood in the same light as first-style decoration.

[66] Laidlaw 1985 remains the authoritative treatment of this means of decoration. See also Ling 1991, 12–22.

45. The *fauces* of the Casa Sannitica at Herculaneum showcases canonical first-style forms of plasterwork "blocks" and cornices.
Photo: author. Courtesy: Soprintendenza Speciale per Pompei, Ercolano e Stabia.

a mistake.[67] Doing so would risk regarding its occurrences only as fortuitously preserved antiques. When preservation occurred, it need not have resulted from

---

[67] Mau envisioned an evolution of decoration through a series of discrete, datable stages, and he assigned the first style to the period between 200 and 80 BCE: Mau 1882, esp. 11–123 for the first style. Since Mau, however, the term "first style" has been applied liberally, having on occasion been used to denote this entire chronological period and the construction techniques then employed, such as the actual method of ashlar construction that this style emulated. When one now refers to the "first style," confusion can understandably result – is this a reference to a time period, a type of wall decoration, a method of construction, or all three? As an example of the confusion, scholars at Pompeii have dated actual ashlar façades, such as those of the Casa del Fauno (VI.12.1–6; Fig. 43) and the Casa della Fontana Grande

46. The Casa dei Ceii at Pompeii (I.6.15) presented a façade of plasterwork modeled into evocations of ashlar blocks until 79 CE.
Photo: author. Courtesy: Soprintendenza Speciale per Pompei, Ercolano e Stabia.

neglect or indifference, but rather from owners' conscious and active decisions to retain certain forms on their façades.[68] For example, the Casa dei Ceii at Pompeii (I.6.15; Fig. 46) featured plasterwork "blocks" with drafted edges, pilasters carrying cubic capitals, a dentiled entablature, and a façade-wide

(VI.8.20–22), to the first half of the second century BCE: Hoffman, the principal investigator, writing in Kockel 1986, 493. Meanwhile, Anne Laidlaw's exhaustive study of the first style at Pompeii (1985) has demonstrated that plasterwork emulations of ashlar masonry were still commissioned and employed in the last years of the city's ancient life. E.g., Laidlaw 1985, 45 on room 22 of the Casa di Sallustio at Pompeii.

[68] For a similar sentiment, see Dwyer 1991, 38–39.

reverse cyma molding.[69] The construction date is unclear, but an impressive first-style façade clearly adorned the house in 79 CE, where it was still considered a valid and attractive architectural expression. Similarly, when two adjoining properties were linked in the 40s or 50s CE to form the Casa dei Dioscuri (VI.9.6–7; Fig. 40), the owner unified the two previously differentiated façades – most notably by having blocks run seamlessly over the projecting spur that marked the earlier property line.[70] In a slight departure from the austerity typical of façades, the perimeter of each panel is traced by a thin, molded vegetal border.[71] The flexibility of this decorative language and its continued currency come into focus at a small dwelling attached to the Praedia of Julia Felix (II.4.10–11; Fig. 47), where a plain red socle decorated the lowest part of the wall, while simple red lines, approximately 5 centimeters wide, outlined several courses of "blocks" against a white plaster background above. A patch of this final plaster layer has

47. Near a rear entrance to the Praedia of Julia Felix at Pompeii (II.4.10–11), a patch of plaster with painted evocations of ashlar blocks has fallen away to reveal an electoral endorsement, which dates the painted "blocks" to the final years of Pompeii's ancient life.
Photo: author. Courtesy: Soprintendenza Speciale per Pompei, Ercolano e Stabia.

[69] Laidlaw 1985, 61–64; Michel 1990, 16–18.
[70] The house's groundplan makes clear that two separate dwellings, each with an atrium, were connected when a doorway was cut irregularly into a fourth-style painting in the interior. Most accounts hold that the fourth style emerged in the 40s or 50s CE, thus providing an earliest date for the union: Barbet 1985, table 5.
[71] Spinazzola 1953, 134

fallen away to reveal an electoral poster, whose dating suggests that the façade was decorated in the last few years of Pompeii's life.[72]

These three examples not only show the continued popularity of the first style's sensibility, but also broaden its decorative framework. Such a conclusion aligns closely with Daniela Scagliarini's important contention that Roman wall treatments worked in the realm of allusion, not illusion.[73] With our sensibilities thus attuned to evaluating decoration in terms of its social roles, these houses additionally push us to broaden our notion of what forms carried the cachet of the first style. If simple lines of red paint were part of this general repertoire, then it is likely that other façade forms – those with a similarly austere aesthetic as well as those that marshaled similar architectural elements in similar positions (like the Casa del Sacello Iliaco) – also evoked connections with the broad associations attached to first-style decoration.

THE ARCHITECTURAL LANGUAGE OF PUBLIC STANDING

Plasterwork emulations of ashlar blocks had their origins in Greece but, within the Roman ambit, were most significantly deployed as the architectural idiom of public buildings.[74] In Pompeii, first-style incrustation pervaded virtually all religious and civic structures; it graced the Temples of Isis and Zeus Melichios, and, in the conspicuous area of the forum, the Temples of Jupiter and Apollo.[75] Most famously, the basilica's interior boasted rich polychromatic first-style facing.[76] It is clear that this mode of decoration provided more than fitting adornment for the institutions, actions, and associated moral touchstones that these civic buildings hosted and represented. Pictorial representations, such as on a fresco found in nearby Murecine, thicken this bond.[77] In the painting's foreground, toga-clad figures amass for an animal sacrifice against a backdrop suitable for the ritual's gravity – a wall scored with red lines to emulate the appearance of ashlar masonry. We do not know what building is represented, but that is the point: first-style decoration and its evocations set the proper

---

[72] The circumstances of the programma are a bit odd because it was painted on a rough, preparatory layer of plaster. It was revealed when the overlaying plaster fell off in 1997 and has not yet been published: *L. Ceium. Secundum / Aed. Orphaeus. Facil[...].* I thank Christopher Parslow for his help with this subject. The candidature may date to 76 CE: Franklin 1980, 66–67, tables 6 and 9. Compare, however, Mouritsen 1988, 41.

[73] Scagliarini 1974–1976.

[74] Bruno 1969.

[75] Laidlaw (1985, 307–321) provides a catalog of public buildings at Pompeii adorned with first-style decoration.

[76] Ohr 1991, 17–18, esp. taf. 16–17, 39.

[77] D'Ambrosio et al. 2003, 467; Mastroroberto 2001, 959. As another example, a felt-maker's shop sign in Pompeii shows Mercury standing atop the porch of a temple whose walls are decorated with thin red lines suggesting ashlar blocks: Spinazzola 1953, 207–210; Fröhlich 1991, 172–174, 333–335; Kellum 1999, 289–290.

atmosphere for the rites of public life, regardless of the building type. Tellingly, individuals chose to employ this mode of decoration not just on façades, but on other crucial contact points with society at large (such as tombs), where the evocation of the public realm was of paramount importance for self-presentation.[78]

This series of contexts points up another reason why an architectural language closely linked to the first style proved attractive for house façades – the first style's relative antiquity. This method of decoration preceded others and, as such, could enjoy, even in its later usage, the luster of age. The evocation of the long-standing place of one's family of course constituted an important aspect of self-presentation. Nowhere is that clearer than in the *pompa funebris* of an elite household, which recalled the family's hoary past and referenced its progenitors and their deeds through masks, movements, and speeches.[79] (Interestingly, this procession also passed through the very spaces where first-style decoration is most prominently represented.) Façade decoration that evoked the first-style's aesthetic may have granted houses a patina of antiquity, thereby hinting at a family's deep heritage and distinction.[80]

To further understand the appeal of these forms, it is helpful to revisit the strong visual-ethical connection in the Roman *mentalité* that I articulated earlier. Romans imbued many aspects of their world with a fairly literal moral significance. As Anthony Corbeill has noted, Latin "words denoting ethical and aesthetic concepts derive from concrete and tangible notions in the external world: *rectus* means physically 'straight' as well as morally 'upright.'"[81] In a world of such direct and reciprocal readings, viewers confronted with a façade that had a coherent and monolithic appearance or that seemed to be constructed from ashlar blocks would discern both the wall's two-dimensional impenetrability and also its heft and difficulty of removal. In other words, they could, on both literal and moral levels, perceive its *gravitas* and *constantia*. In sum, drawing on the architectural and decorative language of public stature allowed house owners to claim for themselves a sense of the stability, permanence, reverence, and authority that civic and religious institutions boasted. Their houses, they hoped, would thereby escape the mundane and be elevated to the realm of basilicas and temples.

---

[78] Outside Pompeii's Porta Nocera at least eleven (and likely more) of the thirty-eight tombs thus far uncovered were decorated in the first style, with tombs 10, 12, and 14 standing as particularly well-preserved examples from the first century CE: Laidlaw 1985, 319–321. Compare also Tomb 18 outside the Porta Ercolano: Kockel 1983, 85–90. Tombs, as the architectural legacies of a life, are similar to house façades on many fronts, particularly in their seeking visual prominence before a large audience.

[79] Flower 1996, 91–126; Bodel 1999; Polyb. 6.53; Pliny *NH* 35.6.

[80] We must remember the overlapping usage of *domus*, which encompassed both the physical structure of a house and the houseful within: Saller 1984, 342–349.

[81] Corbeill 2002, 202.

Such alignment with the architectural idiom of public standing could also contribute to our understanding of the writing that appeared on Pompeian façades. The city's more than 2,500 electoral endorsements (often called *programmata*) have long been the object of study, and they were an important feature of streets, arguably the city's most visible form of writing. On the issue of whether posters resulted from top-down organized campaigns or whether they emerged bottom-up and voluntarily from endorsers, a significant gap divides scholarly camps.[82] The proliferation of painted inscriptions, particularly on the busiest streets, has led some scholars to contend that streetfaces were considered communal spaces and that all could paint where they wished. The physical evidence, however, suggests that endorsement painters did not treat all sections of streetface equally because some façades on the same street receive many more endorsements than others. Along the face of one block (I.7) on the Via dell'Abbondanza, for instance, every stretch of street-facing wall except one was inscribed, yet the density of inscriptions varied from 0.5 to 3.4 per available meter of wall space (Fig. 48). The greatest number, in both raw amount and density, was immediately outside the block's largest house, the

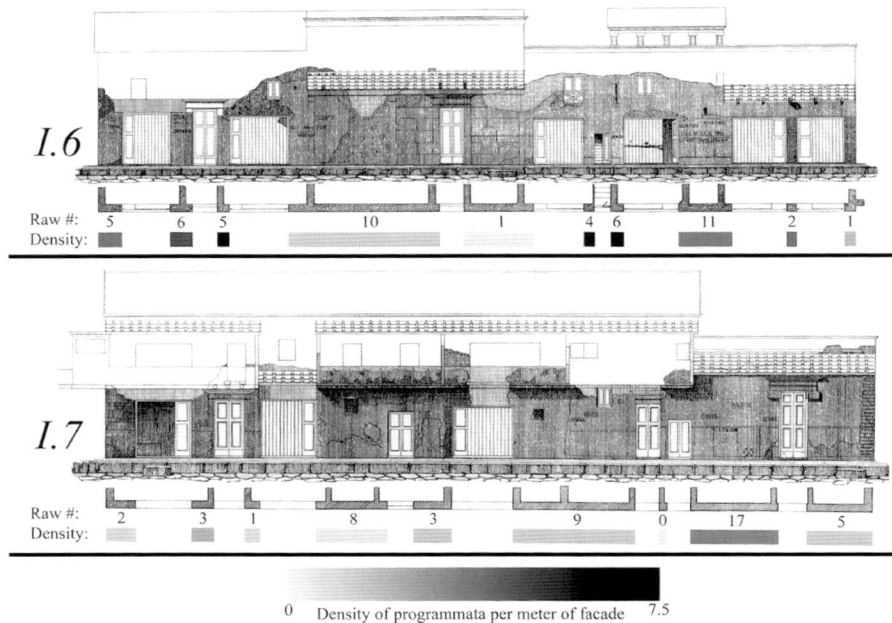

48. Along the busy Via dell'Abbondanza at Pompeii, both the number and the density of electoral endorsements varied considerably from one stretch of wall to another. The northern faces of insulae I.6 and I.7 offer an example.
Drawing: author (after Sanarica in Spinazzola 1953, plates LXI, LXIV).

[82] Castrén 1975; Franklin 1980, 2001; Biundo 1996, 2003; Mouritsen 1999; Chiavia 2002.

Casa di Paquius Proculus (I.7.1). Similarly, on the adjacent block (I.6), inscriptions are packed most densely outside two properties (the Casa del Criptoportico [I.6.1–3] and the Fullery of Stephanus [I.6.5–7]). Such a disparity suggests that the phenomenon is more complicated than has been appreciated. Did endorsers prefer certain structures? Were certain owners more eager to have their façades painted?

More work on the aesthetics of inscriptions is required, but the evidence points to positive connections between political endorsements and house façades. On the heavily inscribed Casa di Paquius Proculus, for instance, a pair of posters endorsing Paquius Proculus flanked the door and were the largest on the façade.[83] It is likely that Paquius Proculus both lived here and splashed his own name and those of his allies on the streetface. And, in an example typical of a broader trend, the *programmata* on the Casa di Trebius Valens largely respect the divisions between the façade's lower "panels," which might reflect input from the house's owner or respect for his façade's decoration (Plate VI). But the façade's upper zone is still more interesting. Here appear much older advertisements – three announcements of gladiatorial games – which were not whitewashed after the event but were retained for decades. (Subsequent inscriptions even appear to "play off" their messages.) Perhaps a fundamental rethinking of our assumptions about these painted messages is required. Where we might see such marks as defacement, Pompeians might have seen an accretion of electoral posters and gladiatorial announcements as representative of an occupant's long-standing engagement with or influence in civic affairs.

An appreciation of house façades' decorative contexts draws us back to the issue of *decorum*, or what was considered fitting for a given setting. In light of contrasts to commercial frontage and affinities with the aesthetic of public structures, austerity was clearly an intentional choice on domestic street frontage, one that shunned forms that were thought prissy or ostentatious.[84] Without attention to *decorum*, we might facilely dismiss the decorative gap between houses' interiors and exteriors. But the model of *decorum* is limited because it privileges context and thereby threatens to mask individual action. Although Roman patrons were bound by notions of what was considered suitable, they also found room within those strictures to forge particular claims. When we turn from façades' architectural language and vocabulary to specific syntactical deployments of those elements, we witness how house owners articulated messages – about their wealth, power, and status – through façade architecture.

---

[83] *CIL* 4.7197, 4.7208. I am grateful to Rebecca Benefiel for her collaboration on a project that considered the aesthetics and placement of electoral endorsements.

[84] These were signs of *indecentia* (the polar opposite of *decorum*), roughly "unsuitability" or "tastelessness." For an example, see Vitr. 7.5.5–7.

FAÇADE FUNCTIONS ON THE OUTSIDE: UNITY AND COHERENCE

Though façades presented rather stark fronts to the street, a streetgoer's visual experience was anything but bland because domestic exteriors took a variety of forms. Some were taller, some more colorful; some consisted of ashlar blocks or extensive plaster ensembles, some left rubble masonry visible; some included shops, some consisted of long stretches of wall. Such diversity of experience is all the more evident when we examine the goals of façade architecture on a house-by-house basis since owners routinely marshaled the few architectural and decorative features on façades to demarcate their own property and to differentiate it from others'.

Designers of street-facing architecture endeavored to make façades cohere visually by granting them a consistent appearance between clearly marked endpoints. The Casa del Fauno in Pompeii (VI.12.1–6) offers a useful starting point for documenting this drive, and it will play a central role as I trace broad façade goals in the following pages. It is true that, as the largest house unearthed in the city, the Casa del Fauno is extraordinary for its size and luxury and that its façade's original construction predates the Roman colony's foundation. Yet the house and its exterior, as I will show, underwent frequent and significant changes over the decades. Moreover, since the façade's features and goals are repeated at many other properties, the house provides appropriate fodder for my qualitative discussion.[85] Along the house's south side, an array of towering ashlar piers originally separated five shop-style apertures and the house's main entrance (Fig. 49). A pilaster adorned each pier; the pilasters around the main door had Corinthian capitals, while the remainder boasted simple moldings. The repetition of identical pilasters unified the façade, and the arrangement drew it together still more. With pilasters at the outside of the end piers, on the inside corners around the doorway, and at the center of every other pier,

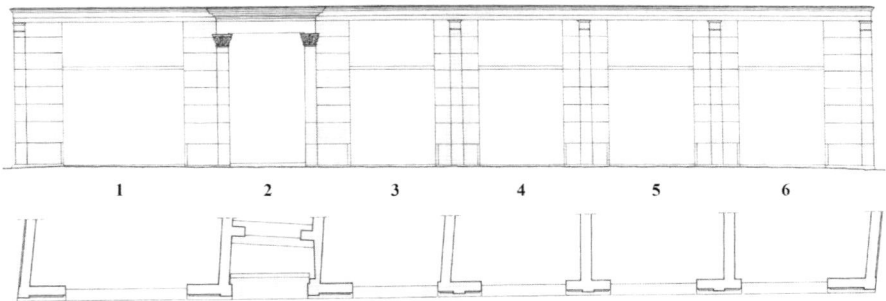

49. The original appearance of the façade of the Casa del Fauno at Pompeii (VI.12.1–6) featured a rhythmic array of pilasters.
Drawing: author (after Hoffmann 1990, Abb. 1).

[85] Casa del Fauno: Hoffman 1990, 1996; Pesando 1996; Zevi 1998; Hoffman and Faber 2009.

a visual unity reigned: the outside pilasters bookended the ensemble and the inner ones rhythmically repeated (except around the main doorway) at regular intervals.

Other strategies of unifying street frontage employed decorative and functional elements of the façade. At Herculaneum's Casa dei Due Atri (VI.28–29), for instance, a terra cotta molding ran the entire width of the house to create a strong horizontal "pull" that drew the façade together visually.[86] On the house's second floor, four identical windows were spaced symmetrically about the line of the main entrance, thus linking the second floor and establishing a strict relationship between the two stories. It would be possible to enumerate further examples of how other components – such as moldings, cantilevered balconies, projecting roofs, benches, and arrays of columns – were consciously organized to achieve a unified appearance.[87] Some of the most telling evidence for the pervasive desire to unify, however, comes from instances in which architectonic elements were, in fact, *not* present. Situated along a bustling Pompeian street, the Casa del Forno di Ferro (VI.13.5–7), for example, had a narrow strip of frontage. Its façade had little standing architecture but was dominated by three openings: a house entryway and two shop doorways of equal width. A strict symmetricality nevertheless governed the layout and linked the façade; the piers and jambs separating the doorways were identical, and even the shop doors opened in different directions to frame the house doorway.

Façades decorated with plaster and paint obviously allowed subtler articulations than did simple voids and solids. The Casa di M. Vesonius Primus (VI.14.21–22) in Pompeii had, aside from two doorways at its southern extreme, a long stretch of unpierced wall. Deep red ribbons of paint, outlined in white, coursed horizontally across the façade, while identical vertical lines framed each doorway, marked the frontage's boundaries, and were placed at regular intervals in between. Such positioning was repeated frequently elsewhere; along the section of the Via dell'Abbondanza excavated by Spinazzola, for instance, no fewer than ten façades employ this pattern of socle-painting, which reproduces the pilaster configurations along the façade of the Casa del Fauno.[88] Such remarkable continuity implies that, despite

---

[86] Maiuri 1958, 275–279.

[87] The Casa dell'Atrio Corinzio (V.30) at Herculaneum shows how carefully free-standing features could be arranged to create a harmonious exterior appearance. Here, a builder found an elegant solution to a difficult dilemma: columns were needed to hold aloft a sidewalk-spanning balcony, but arranging them evenly across the façade would have blocked the house's off-center doorway. In a novel solution, conjoined double columns framed the doorway, and the space between them was widened so the remaining intercolumniations would be equal and would also allow columns to stand at the property's boundaries. This organization served both to mark the doorway and to signal that their wider berth was an intentional break from the rhythm established by the other columns.

[88] I.7.1, I.7.2–3, I.11.2–3, I.12.4–5, II.2.4, III.2.1, III.5.2, IX.7.1, IX.13.1–3, and IX.13.1–3.

a diversity of forms, consistent aesthetic principles governed façades, chief among which was demonstrating visual integrity.

What motivations might underlie these phenomena? Coherence of façade appearance offered a visual counterpoint to the street's realm, in which a jumble of people, animals, and vehicles jerked along while occupied with innumerable tasks. In contrast to that morass of movement, noise, and confusion, a façade adhering to these tenets stood as a serene visual monolith. An organized house façade – as the contact point between an individual or household and the broader society passing through the street – conspicuously signaled that, while frenzied chaos enveloped the street, tranquil order clothed its owner's affairs.[89]

SIZING THE HOUSE: SIDES AND SIDEWALKS

When streetgoers viewed individual decorative schemas side by side, property borders became clearer and comparisons between houses – along multiple indices, but especially size – were inevitable. That a house's size served as a status symbol, albeit a rather unnuanced one, is evident from the material remains yet was rarely stated explicitly in literary sources. In the previous chapter, we saw Vitruvius link certain professions with specific domestic forms; as he moves up the social scale, he tellingly assigns particular rooms, such as atria for *nobiles*, and also describes these spaces' magnitude in relative or superlative terms: *alta vestibula* (lofty vestibules), *laxiores ambulationes* (wider walkways), and *amplissima peristylia* (very spacious peristyles).[90] A late Republican municipal law from Tarentum in Southern Italy, in mandating a minimum house size for the town's senators, also associated larger spaces with higher status.[91] Roughly speaking, bigger was better, and many owners seized the opportunity offered by façade decoration to draw attention to their houses' dimensions.

[89] Strict consistency is one of Vitruvius's crucial yardsticks – and goals – of architecture: 1.2.1–7. Indeed, a widespread sensitivity to aesthetic coherence appears to have infused Roman sensibilities. Scholars of rhetoric emphasize the proper arrangement and organization, or *collocatio*, of speeches (e.g., Cic. *De or.* 1.142; Quint. *Inst.* 3.9, 7.1) and even use the metaphor of façade architecture in making their arguments. Cicero (*Orat.* 50) writes that a good orator "will certainly make fair entryways (*vestibula honesta*) and gorgeous approaches (*aditus illustris*) to his oration." His following sentiments also resonate with the goals of façade architecture: "And when he has gained attention by the introduction, he will establish his case, refute and parry his opponent's argument, *choosing the strongest points for the opening and closing*, and inserting the weaker points in between [my italics]."

[90] Vitr. 6.5.1–2. Cf. Cic. *Off.* 1.138–139.

[91] The so-called *Lex Tarentina*, ll. 26–29: Crawford 1996, 301–312; *FIRA* 18. The law, using the standard measure of floor area in the Roman world, mandated that each decurion own a building roofed by at least 1500 tiles and thus occupying approximately 440 square meters. By way of comparison, the average house size in Wallace-Hadrill's sample of Pompeii and Herculaneum is 271 square meters (1994, 76).

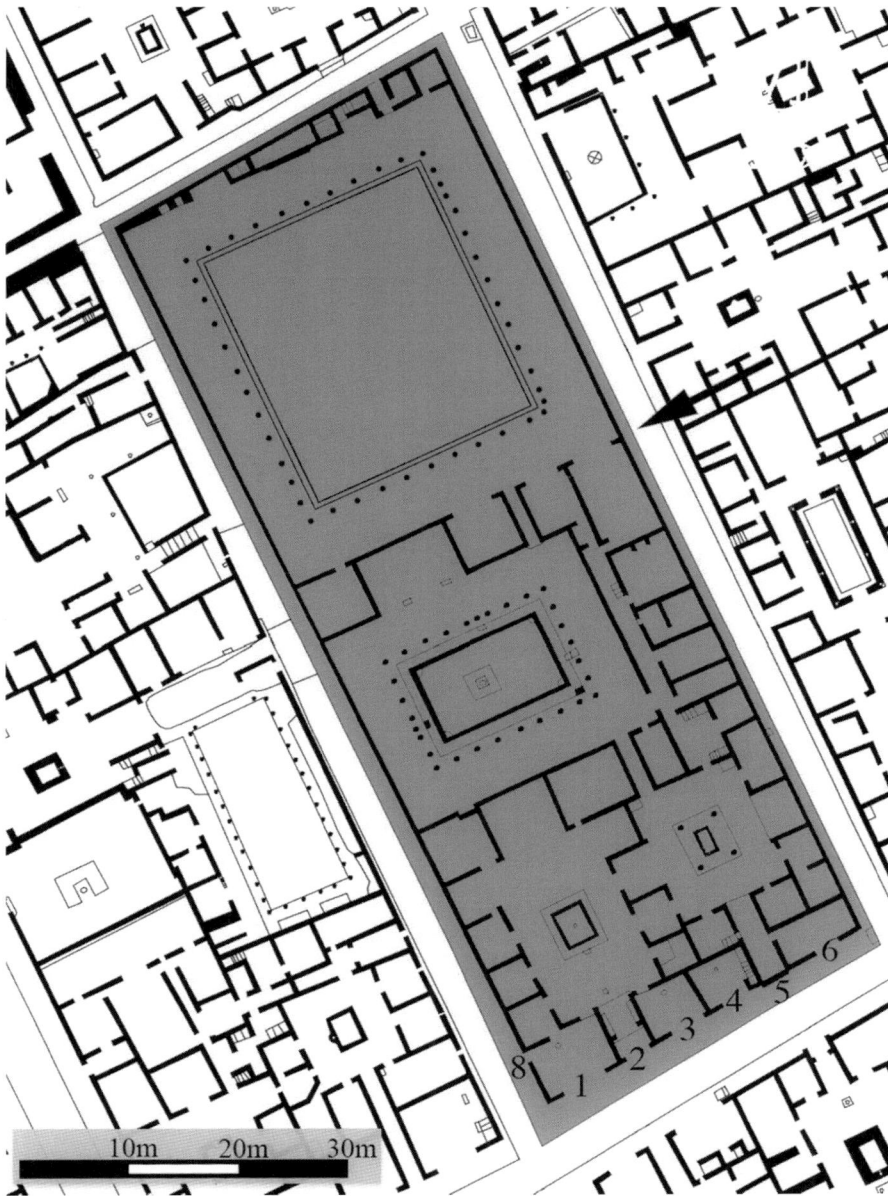

50. The Casa del Fauno at Pompeii (VI.12.1–6) occupied an entire city block. The arrow on the eastern side indicates the location of a plaster pilaster, which marked the southern extent of the house's sizable second peristyle.
Drawing: Ryan Cairns.

The Casa del Fauno (VI.12.1–6) again offers a strong example. In addition to its carefully linked façade, its exterior decoration demonstrated that its owner possessed a rare expanse, an entire city block (Fig. 50). Aside from one doorway at the house's extreme southwest corner, no entrances pierce its

51. The sides of the Casa del Fauno at Pompeii (VI.12.1–6) were marked by ridges that departed from the top of the façade's lowest block and ran the entire depth of the block.
Photo: author. Courtesy: Soprintendenza Speciale per Pompei, Ercolano e Stabia.

sides, a characteristic highlighted by the long ledge that departed from the façade's lowest course and ran uninterrupted along each side of the house (Fig. 51). While the façade demonstrated that the house occupied the insula's *width*, the ledges – a frontal motif that traced the entire lateral length – revealed the house's block-long *depth*. Pompeii's Casa dei Dioscuri (VI.9.6–7; Fig. 40) shows a similar strategy for drawing attention to an owner's power and wealth. We have already seen the house's western façade of plasterwork "blocks" above a high socle. Although the structure's eastern and southern exposures had simple planes of red plaster above a white socle, they had their juncture at the exact height as the main face. This division "turned" the house's corner, spanned the southern face, and continued on the eastern side. Encompassing about 150 meters overall, the ornamental continuity made this house's impressive dimensions clear to anyone in the street. Indeed, such assessments could have been made at many properties, as streetgoers, aided by many visual prompts (coherent painting, ledges, projecting roofs, lines of columns, etc.), discerned the extents of various houses.[92]

---

[92] For example, along the western flank of the relatively small Casa di Minucius at Pompeii (1.10.8–9), an attention-grabbing circular emblem stands next to a 20-meter long horizontal

The subtlety of these architectural cues is one likely reason they have escaped scholarly notice. But the experience of ancient city dwellers was additionally bolstered by features of a house's street presentation that are now less apparent, such as the sidewalk decoration discussed in Chapter 4. Paving in front of the Casa del Cinghiale (VIII.3.7–9) and other properties demarcated a structure's frontage and extended its owner's decorative reach into the street's public space. As we recall, such a situation on the ground aligns closely with the regulations spelled out in the Tabula Heracleensis.[93] It is unclear how many houses presented conspicuous sidewalk decoration similar to that fronting the Casa del Cinghiale. Certain sections of Pompeii and Herculaneum lacked sidewalks altogether, some had them only intermittently, and quite often whatever decoration was originally in place has been lost or removed.[94] In recent years, in fact, campaigns of repaving by Pompeii's archaeological authorities have replaced what survived along several prominent streets, thus erasing evocative evidence for owners' self-fashioning.[95] Nevertheless, examples such as the Casa del Fauno (VI.12.1–6; Fig. 27) – with its gridlike pattern of white stones and special greeting – provide a sense of these displays' potential.

Viewing isolated decorative programs can be illuminating, but juxtaposed pavements give a better sense of how sidewalks signaled property boundaries. A rare section of preserved sidewalk along Cardo V in Herculaneum fronts three consecutive dwellings, each with its own pavement: palm-sized chunks of colorful marbles were set into red *cocciopesto* along the Casa dell'Atrio Corinzio (V.30), fist-sized gray and white stones carpeted the frontage of a three-room structure (V.28–29), and simple gray *cocciopesto* begins at property V.27 and continues northward (Fig. 52). Pedestrians passing along this street, like many others, were made acutely aware of each property's width as well as when they passed from one owner's frontage into another's.

The Tabula Heracleensis raises another issue that helps to draw together my argument. On the basis of the inscription's earlier sections, it has been suggested that a form of registration (*professio*) was required of urban landholders, whereby they declared their financial assets, including the expanse of their property.[96] The law specifies that, from such information, proprietors' eligibility for the grain dole was assessed, and, so the theory goes, their liability for road repair was determined. An urban survey, such as Julius Caesar employed in Rome when reducing the dole's enrollment, likely aided both processes and

---

leveling course of *opus listatum*, which contrasted markedly with the *opus incertum* wall below to mark out the house's depth within the insula. See Ling 1997, 289, pls. 102 and 107, fig. 31.

[93] See "Paving the Way (and the Sidewalk)" in Chapter 4.

[94] Even along streets that lack sidewalks, some owners took the initiative to build isolated stretches of footpath in front of their own properties: e.g., the Casa del Gran Portale at Herculaneum (V.34–35) and the Casa del Granduca Michele at Pompeii (VI.5.5/21).

[95] The Via di Mercurio and the Via dell'Abbondanza are notable examples.

[96] *Professio*: ll. 1–19; Nicolet 1987, esp. 15–25; Cic. *Att.* 13.33; *Fam.* 16.23.

52. At Herculaneum, three distinct forms of sidewalk paving are visible in front of three adjacent properties (V.27–30). From bottom to top: gray *cocciopesto*, white and gray cobbles (some of which are missing), and red *cocciopesto*.
Photo: author. Courtesy: Soprintendenza Speciale per Pompei, Ercolano e Stabia.

could have inspired an early imperial map of Rome, the so-called *Via Anicia* plan.[97] The fragmentary marble slab depicts a portion of Rome's urban fabric, including private architecture, a temple, and, in tiny Roman numerals, the width of streets and lengths of Tiber frontage. By itself, the plan attests to an administrative procedure concerned with property measurements, but the nature of the *professio* indicates a tighter nexus of connections among owners, street frontages, and wealth. Accordingly, such administrative policies cement

---

[97] Caesar's survey: Suet. *Iul.* 41.3. Via Anicia plan: Rodríguez-Almeida 1988 and bibliography therein.

and expand the contention I made in the previous chapter, that streetgoers, as they walked along a sidewalk, did not have the sense that they were passing through simple, communal territory; instead, they perceived that they were moving into a prism of space fundamentally connected to an individual on both cognitive and visible levels. Owners were individually judged along the axes of wealth and civic responsibility in precisely the place where they controlled adornment and sought to impress those traveling through their "decorative domain." As streetgoers bustled along, next to them ran façades seeking to demarcate boundaries through various means: the positioning of pilasters, stripes of paint, or balconies. Between the endpoints, regularized arrangement of doorways or decoration made pedestrians recognize the property's breadth. Up, down, or to the side, almost any direction passersby looked, they saw some element within a house owner's control and were enveloped in that person's sphere of influence at least for a discrete amount of distance, space, and time.

BRINGING THE INSIDE OUTSIDE

A fundamental question that practicing architects and architectural historians ask of the structures they design or encounter involves the relationship between interior space and exterior aspect. At times, the correlation can be literally transparent, as at Philip Johnson's famous Glass House, whose glass walls and minimalist sensibility erase virtually any inside–outside boundary. Near the other extreme is Le Corbusier's Villa Savoye; its simple exterior disguises the interior's complex play of open and closed areas, rectangular and curvilinear spaces, and multiple levels.[98]

The place of Roman domestic façades between these extremes has begun to come into view. From my initial characterization of the façade as an architectural interface, we have seen the façade exert pressure outward, with potent effects on those who passed by it. The membrane has remained fairly impermeable, however, which is not surprising when we recall that fostering an appearance of impenetrability was tied to shielding the house's contents from danger. Yet this protective stance was in fundamental tension with another impulse: the display of a house's status-bearing features to the street. Efforts to delineate houses' impressive dimensions point in this direction, but, as others have shown, *interior* elements of the house – such as specific room types, painting, and other ornament – forged more eloquent social statements than did mammoth size.[99] How did house owners resolve the tension between sheltering their houses from the street and making interior elements outwardly apparent?

---

[98] Glass House: Lewis, Johnson, and Payne 2002. Villa Savoye: Sbriglio 1999.
[99] Among others, Clarke 1991; Wallace-Hadrill 1994.

The doorway allowing passage from the street to a house's interior, what I will call an "access doorway," was clearly a strategic point, as we have seen time and again. Its threshold was typically narrower than the entrances to shops and usually led to the *fauces*, whose elongated form buffered the inside from the outside. Rituals enacted at this boundary's crossing helped temper the two spheres' differences.[100] Decoration also played a role because this entry point received significantly more elaboration than other doorways. We have already witnessed the privileging of the access doorway at the Casa del Fauno. It benefited from a deliberate decorative syncopation in the façade's rhythmic arrangement: pilasters crowned with ornate composite capitals stood on the *inside* of its framing piers. Above and below, respectively, an entablature and the tessellated "HAVE" inscription distinguished the critical threshold. Paved with marble chips and recessed from the street, the serene *vestibulum* likely contrasted with the flurry of activity and mash of goods crowding the façade's shop entryways.

Other techniques for distinguishing the access doorway, although drawing on a limited architectonic palette, were far from subtle. At Herculaneum's Casa del Tramezzo di Legno (III.11–12; Fig. 44), for instance, two doorways pierced the house's front. Both spanned the same width, but the access doorway drew attention by its central location, its greater height (which was exacerbated by the house's sloping disposition), and a terra cotta architrave. Two benches flanking the door furthered the contrast and showed which door was worth waiting outside. Even on lightly adorned house façades, the access door received attention. Only one aperture opened along the staid façade of Pompeii's Casa dei Vettii (VI.15.1; Fig. 38), but the house's owners, in a technique common to modest and grand residences alike, emphasized the doorway with plasterwork pilasters that maintained the façade's measured spirit.[101]

These three examples differed extensively in their streetward aspect – one consisting mostly of open spaces separated by ashlar piers, the others relatively "closed-off" and decorated with plaster – but they together document a uniform drive to draw attention to the access door. Elsewhere, a careful array of single and double columns and its pictorial parallel in vertical strips of paint served the same goal.[102] It is telling that the spots where figural motifs appear – the rare breaks from austerity – cluster around the access doorway. Above the entrance to

[100] For sources involving the threshold, see Ogle 1911; Hallett 1980, 110 (on the doorway as the "metonymic representative of the entire *domus*"); MacMahon 2003. See "Doorways, Defense, and Domestic Priorities" in this chapter.

[101] For a humbler situation, see the Casa di P. Axius (I.17.1), where plaster pilasters capped by simple moldings single out the doorway.

[102] See, respectively, the Casa dell'Atrio Corinzio in Herculaneum (V.30) and the Casa di M. Vesonius Primus in Pompeii (VI.14.21–22) among others.

53. The Casa dell'Augustale at Pompeii (II.2.4) featured a rare bit of sculptural decoration above its doorway; its pilasters were also painted to evoke the appearance of precious stone, and its windows were symmetrically arrayed around the main entryway.
Photo: author. Courtesy: Soprintendenza Speciale per Pompei, Ercolano e Stabia.

Pompeii's Casa dell'Augustale (II.2.4), a plasterwork wreath evocative of the *corona civica* stood between paintings of garlanded trees[103] (Fig. 53). And we should not forget doors themselves, which – to judge from cuttings in the threshold, impressions left in volcanic material, and painted depictions – were typically double- or triple-leafed, divided into panels, and occasionally adorned with decorative, large-headed nails.[104] (We unfortunately cannot confirm that their wood was painted, as frescoed depictions suggest.) Spotlighting a house's main entrance, this diversity of decoration suggests, was not a matter of blind repetition of conventional forms, but represented a fundamental push in façade decoration expressed through many unique solutions.

House owners lavished decorative emphasis on access doorways for several reasons. First, it helped distinguish these doorways from and elevate them above others, particularly those leading to commercial and industrial spaces. When one doorway stood taller than the others, had a different form, and was surrounded by architectural motifs shared with temples and civic buildings, few would confuse it with the quotidian space of trade or production.

[103] Spinazzola 1953, 134–135. Cf. the Casa dei Capitelli Figurati (VII.4.57).
[104] Spinazzola 1953, 322–334; MacMahon 2003, 64–65. Such a doorway is preserved in plaster at the Casa dell'Augustale (II.2.2) at Pompeii. Similar depictions of doorways appear on Roman sarcophagi: Haarlov 1977. Horizontal divisions of the door likely emphasized the features' height.

54. At Pompeii, the Casa di Loreius (III.5.2) boasted a doorway flanked by engaged columns amid a unified façade spanned by benches and a low-slung roof.
Photo: author. Courtesy: Soprintendenza Speciale per Pompei, Ercolano e Stabia.

Second, if houses were architectural stand-ins for the owners and households they sheltered, as we read repeatedly, then decoration on access doorways offered a means of competing for visual prominence.[105] Along one block of Pompeii's Via dell'Abbondanza, for instance, three houses vied with one another. Eastbound travelers first saw on their left the engaged columns and extended benches flanking the door of the Casa di Loreius (III.5.2) (Fig. 54). On the right, the 5-meter tall double doors of the Casa di D. Octavius Quartio (II.2.2), raised on two steps and sheltered within a bench-lined recess, dwarfed its neighbor (Fig. 55). Last, streetgoers marveled at (or decried the ostentation of) the access doorway of the Casa dell'Augustale (II.2.4), which was capped with the wreath and trees, framed by pilasters painted to resemble exotic stone, and graced by symmetrically disposed benches (Fig. 53).

Third and finally, such doorway decoration aggrandized the experience of a house, heightening the expectations of those who would enter while leaving those who remained in the street with a favorable impression of the house's stateliness. In all, it was critical to signal externally that *this doorway* deserved special attention and that something or someone notable lay behind it. Tellingly, only access doorways are thus singled out and, in fact, almost exclusively those leading to an atrium. Streetgoers seeing these cues and drawing on their knowledge of house layouts might, therefore, have inferred

[105] Implicitly: Vitr. 6.5.1–2; Val. Max. 6.3.1; Cic. *Dom.* 101–102. More explicitly: Cic. *Off.* 1.138–139. See also earlier discussion in "House Exteriors: Display and Assessment" in Chapter 4.

55. Along the Via dell'Abbondanza at Pompeii, the Casa di D. Octavius Quartio (II.2.2) presented to the street an impressively tall entryway preceded by benches.
Photo: author. Courtesy: Soprintendenza Speciale per Pompei, Ercolano e Stabia.

something of a house's internal organization from its façade decor.[106] Phrased another way, such decoration around a doorway may have acted as architectural shorthand that alerted passers-by to an atrium's presence.

The marking of interior elements through exterior decoration is most evident where exterior changes corresponded with interior renovations. It appears, for example, that the Casa del Fauno had long been endowed with two atria, but, for some time, only the western one was accessible through the house's extremely regular façade[107] (Figs. 49, 50). At a later point, the shop that likely preceded the eastern atrium was removed and a *fauces*-like space was opened outward. The center pilasters on the piers flanking the doorway were carved away, and freshly cut stone was placed in the opening to narrow the entrance and to form pilasters similar to those flanking the existing access doorway (Figs. 43, 56). Thus, the façade's architectural unity was preserved, the visual supremacy of the western atrium entrance was maintained, and the owner realized his or her goal of signaling on the outside the presence of an atrium inside.

[106] That the access doorway could be understood as an external marker of interior events is suggested by the threshold's regular decoration at critical moments in a *domus'* life cycle. See earlier discussion in "House Exteriors: Display and Assessment" in Chapter 4.
[107] See earlier discussion in "Façade Functions on the Outside: Unity and Coherence" in this chapter.

56. When a secondary atrium was opened, doorway 5 of the Casa del Fauno at Pompeii (VI.12.1–6) was narrowed and endowed with pilasters. Central pilasters were also carved away from the flanking piers.
Photo: author. Courtesy: Soprintendenza Speciale per Pompei, Ercolano e Stabia.

If streetgoers read the presence of an atrium from a façade's form, a flood of associations with family and status might have rushed to mind. The atrium appears to have been part and parcel of the so-called *salutatio*, which could ritually define the relationship between the house owner and the outside world.[108] In particular, this supposedly daily greeting, in tandem with the atrium's architecture and decoration, spotlighted the master of the house and placed him in a position of authority over visiting clients. Our sources also tell us that many of the rituals of the life cycle unfolded in the atrium: a deceased family member lying in state, girls and boys dedicating childhood emblems to

[108] Friedländer 1907, 207–212 (ancient references); Wiseman 1982; Saller 1989, 57–61.

the household gods to symbolically mark their transition to adulthood, and the potential worship of household deities.[109] Study of the artifacts recovered from atria show these to be, in practice, multipurpose spaces, but in terms of ideology, the atrium was thus both the *locus* of the *paterfamilias's* status – the space where his identity was generated through bloodlines, his standing was underlined through ritual, and both were confirmed by performing his superiority to others – as well as a *symbol* of that status.[110] Although plans of "the typical Roman house" always include atria, and we hear Pompeii described as a "town of atrium houses," having this architectural feature was hardly universal.[111] In Wallace-Hadrill's sampling of Pompeii and Herculaneum, only 52 percent of the houses with areas greater than 50 square meters had atria.[112] Although the direct experience of these spaces and their rituals may have been limited to those who stepped inside, exterior decoration could make powerful modes of social presentation – related to ideas of abstract and ritualized authority – part of the street's public dialogue. Especially for streetgoers who did not enjoy such status, the dimensions of and decoration around the access doorway could form a crucial claim about who the owner was and where he stood within the hierarchy of Roman urban society.

The exterior articulation of interior architecture was not limited to what have been called the public areas of the house, but could also encompass other zones and activities as well. Prominent among these was the peristyle, which played host to a more intimate form of interaction and was marked on the outside by a considerably different means: a conspicuous *lack* of adornment. Streetgoers might have perceived the Casa del Fauno's massive rear peristyle, which occupied the house's entire width, while walking along either of the house's flanks. Windows peppered the front half of the house's east side, while a tall, windowless wall extended 40 meters toward the rear (Figs. 50, 51). A blank wall may not carry special meaning in our age of electric light, but Romans were undoubtedly more aware of how a building was lit and could have safely assumed that an interior light source illuminated the house's rear.[113] Here, where the owner left no doubt about the house's enormous size, the wall's extensive length alone suggested the presence of a peristyle within. And

---

[109] Rituals of life cycle: Orr 1973; Harmon 1978; Clarke 1991, 4–12; Fröhlich 1991, 28–37; Bodel 2008. Ancient sources: Vitr. 6.3.6; Polyb. 6.53; Pliny *NH* 35.6; Prop. 4.1.131–132; Pers. 5.30–31.

[110] Artifacts in atria: Berry 1997; Allison 2004, 65–70.

[111] "Town of atrium houses": Dwyer 1991, 25.

[112] Wallace-Hadrill 1994, 86–87, table 4.3, and figure 4.16. Wallace-Hadrill's sample includes Insulae III–VI at Herculaneum and Regio I, Insulae 6–12 and Regio VI, Insulae 9–16 at Pompeii. For the percentage given earlier, I have eliminated the lowest quartile from his extremely broad sample of "houses" because that quartile consists primarily of one- or two-room structures.

[113] On the lighting of buildings, see, e.g., Vitr. 1.2.7; 6.6.6; Pliny *Ep.* 2.17, 5.6; *Dig.* 7.1.30, 8.2.

the one architectural feature along the side – a narrow plaster pilaster that held no structural significance – was situated precisely at the juncture between the windowed southern half and the smooth wall to the north, a location that corresponded with the peristyle's southern extreme. Thus, for streetgoers who could not "read" the large windowless wall, the pilaster signaled where the substantial peristyle began.[114]

A peristyle, or any of the similar open areas often found in larger houses, was metonymic for a broader array of architectural forms and their associated social activities. That is, within the domestic realm, a peristyle existed in symbiosis with the rooms grouped around it: the reception spaces regularly called *triclinia* and *oeci* that soaked in views of the space's greenery, statuary, and fountains. As Wallace-Hadrill has shown, an increasingly fashionable means of domestic self-presentation in the decades before 79 CE hinged on managing access to the master of the house through the use of these very spaces.[115] For instance, Pompeii's Casa dei Vettii (itself enclosed by a tall, windowless wall), was graced with a variety of reception rooms of various sizes and shapes that allowed the house's owners to calibrate different social occasions, from grand dinners to more intimate one-on-one meetings. In this way, the external signaling of a peristyle provided a flag for a total spatiosocial assemblage: the presence of specific status-bearing reception rooms and the coordinate ability to host the meaningful (and potentially hierarchical) gatherings therein.

External indications of interior features on occasion extended beyond atria and peristyles. For example, on the western face of the grand Casa del Centenario at Pompeii (IX.8.1–7; Fig. 57), a circular window opened near the top of a wall projecting above the sidewalk while two apertures appeared below, at ground level. Round windows were rare in Roman domestic architecture, but they did appear in bath buildings, especially in *caldaria*, and may have signaled the private bath enjoyed by this house's owner.[116] Anyone passing along this thoroughfare likely saw slaves feeding fuel to the bath's furnace through the low openings or smelled the unguents dispelled with bath water from two streetside drains.

Even when an exterior wall was not available to broadcast such messages, streetgoers could have been alerted to household occasions in many ways – by smelling the aroma of meat braising for a dinner party, by overhearing the raucous laughter of revelers gathered around a plein-air *triclinium* (as at Pompeii's Casa del Efebo [I.7.10–12]), or by listening to notes plucked on

---

[114] The forces of time have erased, I suspect, a corresponding pilaster on the house's west side.
[115] Wallace-Hadrill 1994, 20–21, 51–60. Also, Clarke 1991, 12–19.
[116] Yegül 1992, 57–66 (on the characteristic circular window), 50–55 (this and other private baths).

57. Along the west side of the Casa del Centenario at Pompeii (IX.8.1–7), a projection adorned with a circular window (top) was one of several external cues that a private bathing suite lay within the structure.
Photo: author. Courtesy: Soprintendenza Speciale per Pompei, Ercolano e Stabia.

a lyre.[117] Or such cues perhaps emphasized what the architecture might already have suggested and thereby reinforced the cognitive link between exterior decoration and interior activities. Overall, because an owner could handpick visitors to participate in these rites, allowing some to gain intimate access to his person, power, and benefits while excluding others, any streetside perception

[117] Overheard sounds: e.g., Cic. *Rosc. Am.* 134.

of interior events held potency. Even when the house was shut tight, it acutely reminded passersby of a social event in which they were not partaking.

THE VIEW THROUGH AS FAÇADE ELEMENT

Such realizations of exclusion on the part of streetgoers – or, put another way, such assertions voiced by owners into the street – could have been even more forceful when these interior features were not just abstractly "legible," but also directly seen through open doors. Direct textual evidence for the position of doors during the day is scarce, but what survives suggests that the practice of leaving house doors open was routine. A telling passage comes from Livy's narration of the Roman general Camillus's scouting mission into the town of Tusculum in 381 BCE. Although a Roman attack is imminent, Camillus is surprised because life in Tusculum carries on as normal: house doors stand open, shops display wares, workmen toil, and the whole populace takes to the sidewalks. The scene Livy paints could just as well represent the atmosphere and signs of a peaceful city of his own time, suggesting that open house doors were, for him and his reader, an everyday fact of life.[118]

Leaving one's access doorway open usually required positioning a guard at this critical threshold. Ovid has the god of doorways, Janus himself, describe the task:

> Every door has a pair of fronts – this way and that – one of which looks toward the people and the other the *lares*; and just as your doorman, sitting near the house's threshold, sees who goes out and in, so I, the doorman of the heavenly court, simultaneously look both East and West.[119]

Although doorkeepers, in admitting or refusing visitors, need not have mastered many skills, they were frequently characterized as powerful and arrogant because of the influence they wielded in allowing or restricting access.[120] Sparing a member of the household (most likely a slave) to mind the door was also probably a sacrifice limited to Romans of a certain financial level, which made door-opening a social marker in itself. But the way that this act made interior architecture visible to the street provided more opportunities for scoring social points.

---

[118] Livy 6.25.6–11. Other examples of open doorways as a daily fact of life: Livy 5.41.7; Vell. Pat. 2.14.1. Closing the doorway was the typical sign that a noble house was in mourning: Wallace-Hadrill 1988, 46, n. 12 for sources.

[119] Ov. *Fast.* 1.135–140: *omnis habet geminas, hinc atque hinc, ianua frontes, / e quibus haec populum spectat, at illa larem; / utque sedens primi vester prope limina tecti / ianitor egressus introitusque videt, / sic ego perspicio caelestis ianitor aulae / Eoas partes Hesperiasque simul.*

[120] Specific names were given to this person, although there is no clear differentiation between them. *Ianitor*: Sen. *Dial.* 2.14.2; Mart. 5.22.10; Suet. *Vit.* 16 (*cellula ianitoris*). *Ostiarius*: Sen. *Ira* 3.37.2 (*ostiarius* among lowest slaves of household); Plaut. *Asin.* 273; Petron. 28.8.

58. A look from the street into the Casa del Menandro in Pompeii (I.10.4), when unobstructed, granted streetgoers a view through the house's main spaces.
Photo: Neg. D-DAI-Rom 59.1614.

It is widely remarked that houses in Campania were organized around a visual axis.[121] Pompeii's Casa del Menandro (I.10.4; Fig. 58), for instance, offered an axial vista that passed straight through the frames of the *fauces*, atrium,

[121] Among others, Drerup 1959; Bek 1980; Clarke 1991, 2–6; Wallace-Hadrill 1994, 44–45.

and *tablinum* before continuing back to the peristyle and an array of niches. Intercolumniations were twice adjusted in the sprawling and asymmetrical house to achieve the highly organized view. What we see on site can leave the mistaken impression of an "empty house," however, since many potential barriers – such as doors, screens/partitions, and curtains – are no longer visible. In the Casa del Menandro, a wooden partition and folding doors could close off the view across the front and rear of the *tablinum*, for instance.[122] And the atrium-end of the *fauces* of many large houses could be blocked by another barrier, either solid or more fencelike, which would have restricted sightlines into the house at a still earlier point.[123] With these barriers (to sight and access) available for manipulation, the houses of Campania were more flexible spatially than has often been acknowledged. From the perspective of hosting outsiders, such adaptability should come as little surprise, given Romans' desire to shape the experience of visitors. And it also makes sense when the house is considered as a lived space because it allowed for the separation of activities, preservation of heat in smaller spaces, and other goals.

At the same time, houses' organization around a distinct visual axis nevertheless points to a desire to enable someone to look through the entire structure – perhaps not always, but certainly from time to time. When the access doorway was open and other barriers were removed, such "visual transparency" provided those looking in from the street a view across the front areas of the house through to the structures' innermost portions.[124] The exterior cues discussed earlier not only hinted at what lay within the house, but also aided in alerting streetgoers to and aligning them with a visual axis. Although not all of a house would be in view, an owner could exhibit the locations and dimensions of the house's spatial nuclei, allowing on-lookers to form a mental blueprint of the dwelling's composition and amenities.[125] In fact,

---

[122] "Empty house": Lauritsen 2011, 59. Casa del Menandro barriers: Lauritsen 2013. Of twenty-one houses in Lauritsen's sample where the atrium and peristyle were aligned axially, eighteen had barriers that could in part or fully isolate the two spaces from one another: Lauritsen 2013, table 5. Maiuri (1958, 213) anticipates some of these considerations. I thank Evan Proudfoot for sharing this reference.

[123] Proudfoot 2013 for this and related issues of permanent or semipermanent blockages.

[124] "Visual transparency": Wallace-Hadrill 1994, 44–45.

[125] Personal autopsy of Herculaneum and Pompeii revealed that the average access doorway was 1.7 meters in width. It is possible, however, that organic impediments, such as wooden furniture or hanging cloth, would have blocked this view, but they have generally not survived in the material record. Wooden furniture: Mols 1999. Cloth as disrupter of physical or visual passage in Roman houses of North Africa: Thébert 1987, 388–389.

Other goals of exterior decoration, such as demonstrating a house's magnitude, could also be achieved by the view-through. An extreme case is Pompeii's Casa dei Capitelli Colorati (VII.4.31/51), a house that, despite opening onto streets at its north and south, was "buried" within its city block. Anyone peering through either access doorway, however, was granted a 75-meter long door-to-door sightline that crossed an atrium and two peristyles.

the sunlight beaming down into atria and peristyles highlighted them and offset the difficulties of looking from a bright street into a dark structure.

A directed gaze also had utility in less opulent settings. Even when the means to construct grand peristyles were beyond reach, house owners nevertheless sought to draw attention to the gardens or open areas that played similar roles.[126] For example, two neighboring Pompeian houses that were considered sufficiently humble by excavators to remain unnamed forged street-oriented displays. Neither had an impluviate atrium, but one (I.11.13) proudly flaunted its garden shrine at a sightline's terminus, while the other (I.11.17) neatly framed a triclinium within a perfectly symmetrical viewshed. Pompeii's Casa di Fabius Amandio (I.7.2–3) and Herculaneum's Casa di Nettuno ed Anfitrite (V.6–7), both small but well-appointed houses, featured views from the street: in the former, outsiders saw an uncolonnaded, unroofed garden and two reception rooms, while the latter's handsome eponymous glass mosaic was visible through a window (Fig. 59). Although it is unclear how often modest houses kept their doors open, both of these dwellings apparently had rooms

59. A stunning mosaic was perfectly framed for streetgoers looking into the relatively small Casa di Nettuno ed Anfitrite at Herculaneum (V.6–7).
Photo: Alinari Archive, Florence.

[126] Wallace-Hadrill 1994, 82–87. For peristyle elements elsewhere in the house, see George 1998.

for doormen, which presses us to recognize the strong social diffusion of this desire to make resplendent interior features visible to those in or entering from the street.[127]

In sum, we began this section with two extreme modern examples of how those outside a house could (or could not) perceive a structure's interior. We can now better understand where Roman houses stood between the poles. It is hard to imagine how houses could make their essential armature, particularly status-bearing architectural forms, more visible for external viewers. One possibility – opening more windows or doors onto the street – would have threatened to compromise the careful control of outsiders that a lone, primary entrance permitted and would likely have diminished the *appearance* of security. There was clearly a balance to be struck between displaying a house's inner goods – whether architecture, decoration, virtuous kin, copious visitors, or plentiful slaves – and the opposing desire not to endanger those goods or to project streetward the impression that they were vulnerable. The Roman solution drew the line cleverly: streetgoers' penetration was limited *physically* and could be granted *visually*.

CONCLUSION: DECORATION INSIDE AND OUTSIDE REVISITED

As we consider the visual and social interplay between "the in" and "the out," we must consider not only a potential view *into* the house from the street, but also what framed that view – the façade itself. For visitors who entered a house or pedestrians who glanced in an open door, the façade and view-through were part of one experience. In a curious feature of this relationship, similar decoration sometimes adorned both outside and inside, such as at the Casa Sannitica in Herculaneum (V.1–2; Figs. 41, 45). Amid its façade's broad panels of colored plasterwork, the main doorway was framed by pilasters with vegetal capitals and capped by a dentiled architrave.[128] When the large doors were open, a passerby could have recognized similar elements inside: the first-style array of the *fauces* added colors and patterns to create a more ornate and varied ensemble. Pilasters at the far end (identical to their exterior counterparts except for their more intricate capitals) and a dentiled molding atop the first-style panels also enriched the exterior's motifs while drawing together the length of the

---

[127] It is difficult to securely identify rooms specifically assigned to porters because the criteria for this classification are not clear. A solitary room adjoined to the *fauces* and containing a bed or other sitting spot would seem to provide the strictest and safest definition. Other spaces not meeting these requirements could, of course, have been used for the same purpose; witness the wool-combing implements found beneath a stairwell adjacent to the entrance of the Casa di Fabius Amandio at Pompeii (I.7.2–3; De Vos and De Vos 1982, 112–113). Potential *cellae ostiariae* at Herculaneum alone: the Casa dello Scheletro (III.3), Casa dell'Alcova (IV.3–4), and Casa di Nettuno ed Anfitrite (V.6–7).

[128] See Laidlaw 1985, fig. 76 for a diagram of the arrangement.

fauces.[129] Similar patterns can be seen elsewhere: the white plasterwork façade "blocks" of Pompeii's Casa degli Suettii (VII.2.51) were echoed polychromatically within the doorway, and the large marble pieces in the sidewalk outside the Casa dell'Atrio Corinzio at Herculaneum (V.30) were refined inside the threshold, where chips of the same stones, but more regular in size, were arrayed in a grid. We cannot know with certainty how widespread the phenomenon of inside–outside mimicry was; to be detected, it requires more than the sporadic preservation we encounter.

Even this practice's occasional deployment points to important considerations about interior–exterior interaction. First, only rarely did an austere façade match much more than the *fauces* and any other areas that were adorned with similarly severe motifs. Indeed, a view-through regularly presented luxuries – gardens and sculpture in addition to figural paintings – that contrasted markedly with the stark façade. When exterior elements were repeated inside, two tasks were potentially accomplished. Such an arrangement provided a transition zone between the austere façade and the more sumptuous interior. But, by borrowing directly from, but also elaborating pointedly on, the exterior, the transitional decoration pulled the eye in and invited a comparison. Viewers could only come to the conclusion that what lay inside the house was a more splendid version of what stood outside.

Even where matching was not present, the view-through became another façade element that, in tandem with the façade's severe decoration, had significant social effects on those passing by the house or entering it. Viewers could look through a number of areas, each of which, if we follow the arguments of Wallace-Hadrill, might privilege a more limited group of visitors than the previous.[130] For the street-side viewer, yet another boundary – the house's front threshold – stood in the way, demarcating another level of access or exclusion. The façade and view-through underscored that some people who were encouraged to look into the house were physically shut out from it altogether. Those allowed to enter after first seeing the austere façade amid the street's bustle may have been struck by the comparatively lush ornament and relative tranquility that reigned in the interior. In fact, a house's inside likely seemed all the more opulent to visitors *because* of the contrast. In other words, like strategies we encountered in the previous chapter – sidewalk decoration that claimed streetspace or street-axis views from afar and expanded the impression of a house and its owner into the city – decoration inside and outside could work together to extend a house's fundamental program of differentiating visitors (or nonvisitors) into the space traversed by streetgoers.

[129] Maiuri 1958, 199–201; Clarke 1991, 85–89.
[130] Wallace-Hadrill 1994, 3–61.

Amid the street's contentious surroundings, houses thus sought to create a hierarchy of sorts.

The disparity between interior and exterior encourages us to revisit a fundamental issue in domestic decor. Previous scholars ignored the façade in part because it paled in comparison with the interior's richness. We can now understand how, in the public realm of the street, house owners applied a markedly different set of aesthetic criteria to their façades and chose a more restrained mode of expression. The difference in context alone might call into question prior assessments of façade architecture. But separating façades and interiors into two distinct arenas of activity may risk perpetuating the conceptual gap between "the in" and "the out" in the Roman city. In other words, it is not enough to agree with Lucretius's claim that the interior and exterior represented different types of spaces and thus to conclude merely that these two decorative zones served diverse purposes. Rather, the very impulse to cater to these two spaces in different but connected ways was in itself part of the larger project of houses and their owners.

Demosthenes, the Athenian orator, was fond of saying that, in the time of Themistocles and Miltiades, one could not distinguish a politician's house from those of his fellow citizens.[131] We can now appreciate just how differently Roman sensibilities were attuned. People walking along a street would not sense that they were passing through a faceless corridor. To Romans, a wall was never just a wall, but was connected to and could tell them something about an individual or a group of people. In some cases, such as when a wall was covered with electoral *programmata*, it literally carried messages. But the architecture and decoration made statements as well: about owners and what they possessed, about streetgoers and whether or not they were accepted within houses, and about the social hierarchy and how it should stack up.

The house was not alone in exerting pressure. In the defensive posture struck by houses, we have seen the influence of the street and its denizens. This counterbalance offers a reminder that space is created and edifices designed because of a confluence (or even collision) of multiple pressures. Chapter 6 focuses on this sometimes contentious discourse. It maintains attention on the edifice–street boundary by investigating a still more telling artifact of the tension between "the in" and "the out" – the streetside benches that fronted many buildings (including houses) and that therefore occupied the collective space of the sidewalk while being physically connected to buildings that were anything but communal endeavors.

---

[131] Dem. 3.25–26; 13.29; 23.207. But see Nevett 2009.

SIX

THE "IN" AND THE "OUT"

Streetside Benches and Urban Society

A CENTRAL CONCERN OF THE PRECEDING CHAPTERS HAS BEEN THE relationship between the street and the buildings that faced it: in other words, the exterior and the interior. We have seen this dialogue manifested socially, as façades functioned as outward showpieces that sought to impact urban residents while also offering, in return, a stage where aggrieved street-goers could reply through acts, scrawled words, or song. Part and parcel of the discourse has been architecture, as façades mediated between a property and the thoroughfare, at times opening shops interiors to the passing crowds and at other times guarding what lay within. This chapter continues such a dialectical inquiry between exterior and interior but expands its scope by considering the city of Pompeii, its street system and urban social dynamics, as a whole. It does so, however, by concentrating on one seemingly ephemeral form of Pompeii's urban environment – the streetside benches that stood along building fronts and were available for the public to sit upon.[1]

Streetside benches constituted a significant urban phenomenon. In the excavated portions of Pompeii, at least 100 benches fronted 69 different properties (Plate I).[2] Rectangular in form and constructed using many masonry techniques, the benches typically measure approximately 0.4 meters in height and depth,

---

[1] This chapter draws extensively on my article of a similar name: Hartnett 2008a. See also Gesemann 1996, 142–145.
[2] I define a bench as an intentionally built masonry construction for sitting available to the street. This filters out the random ashlar blocks apparently left in front of buildings by excavators as

while their lengths vary from less than a meter to nearly 10 meters.[3] Some stood flush against building façades (Figs. 39, 44, 53, 54); others were tucked into corners where one building projects further than another (what I call "indented," Fig. 60); a smaller group was situated against the walls of recessed areas open to the street (thus "subsumed" within properties, Fig. 61). Stone benches were not alone in offering Pompeians places to perch, since spots such as temple steps could have served as improvised seats. Moreover, frescoes from the Praedia of Julia Felix show scenes of life in the forum, including what appear to be wooden stools and benches supporting five figures: a salesman of metal tools and four women in front of a sandal maker.[4] Such furniture undoubtedly lined the streets on occasion as well, yet it is now largely lost to us.[5] That these other options existed does not undermine a study of masonry streetside benches, but instead underscores the intentions and choices that preceded a builder's decision to construct a more costly and more permanent form of seating.

well as benches immediately within a structure. For a catalog of Pompeii's 100 benches, their dimensions, and placement, see Hartnett 2008a, table 1.

Two benches are known only from reports of their re-excavation in the 1930s: Della Corte 1936, 335. We do not know their measurements, nor were the benches drawn before the collapse of a modern retaining wall reburied them: Van der Poel 1986, 64.

Archival photographs confirm that some benches have changed form since their original unearthing; for example at the Casa del Moralista (III.4.3). Photographs C1116 (1918), C1313 (1922), and A351 (1946) document that the two benches currently visible on site are the remains of a reworking of a reconstruction. Consequently, I focus less on problematic aspects of benches – bench height, for instance – and instead concentrate on features that are less likely to have changed, such as their positioning and "footprint" (length and depth).

[3] Romans had two names for a multiseat bench without arms or back: *subsellium* and *scamnum*. Which they used for streetside benches is not clear, since no source, to my knowledge, describes the constructions by name. For discussions of these two words and their meanings, see Mols 1999, 52–54; Daremberg and Saglio 1877–1919, 4:1111–1113 (*scamnum*), 4: 1551–1552 (*subsellium*); *RE* 4.A.1.502–504 (*subsellium*).

Subsellium is the more common term; it regularly describes the wooden seating arranged for groups of people, such as audiences at poetic recitations (Juv. 7.45, 7.86; Pliny *Ep.* 2.14.6; Tac. *Dial.* 9.3; Suet. *Claud.* 41.1), jurors at trials (Cic. *Brut.* 289–290; *Fam.* 8.8.1; *De or.* 1.32, 1.264; Aul Gell. 13.11.3, 14.2.11; Juv. 16.44), and senators in the curia (Cic. *Cat.* 1.16; *De or.* 2.143; *Phil.* 2.19, 5.18; Livy 3.64.6; Suet. *Aug.* 44; *Claud.* 23). This term, however, is not limited to wooden furniture, since it also regularly describes the masonry seats of a theater: Plaut. *Amph.* prol. 65; Mart. 1.29.2, 5.8.2, 5.27.3; Suet. *Aug.* 43.4, 44.1; *Nep.* 26.2. (See also *CIL* 6.2104, which mentions *subsellia marmorea*.) Households also appear to have owned *subsellia* as a matter of course; when their use is specified, it is often as seating that supplements the couches at dinners: *Dig.* 33.10.3, 1.14.31, 20.11.9; Sen. *Dial.* 4.25.4; Plaut. *Stich.* 93–95, 488–489, 703–704; *Capt.* 471.

By contrast, *scamnum* is both a less distinct and less frequent term. It is at times used interchangeably with *subsellium*, such as to describe the theater seats reserved for *equites* (Mart. 5.41; marble *scamna* are mentioned in *CIL* 4.1066), yet it also describes a footstool as well as a bench and therefore *can* epitomize humble furnishings (Varro *Ling.* 5.168; *Cod. Theod.* 3.1.2: *subsellia vel, ut vulgo dicunt, scamna*; Val. Max. 4.3.5; Ov. *Fast.* 6.305).

[4] Nappo 1991.

[5] At Herculaneum, for instance, four wooden benches have been found: Mols 1999, 52–55, nos. 24–26.

60. In front of an eating and drinking establishment at Pompeii (VI.1.5), one bench is "indented," where one building projects further into the street.
Photo: author. Courtesy: Soprintendenza Speciale per Pompei, Ercolano e Stabia.

61. Two benches stand in front of a doorway to the Casa di M. Obellius Firmus at Pompeii (IX.14.2); embraced by the house's walls, they are "subsumed" within the entryway.
Photo: author. Courtesy: Soprintendenza Speciale per Pompei, Ercolano e Stabia.

An additional value of examining streetside benches derives from the swivel-like role they played.[6] Because benches formed part of the architectural interface between the realms of interior, privately financed architecture and the exterior space of the street's public domain, their study holds special potential for understanding the negotiation of individual and urban desires. At the fulcrum between these counterbalancing forces, benches offer a starting point for thinking not just about the owner-centric insides of buildings or the chaotic outsides, but about the push and pull between these spheres. As such, they testify to the many agents – many of whom typically remain invisible – that gave shape to the urban streetscape.

ASSUMPTIONS AND AGENCY IN THE STUDY OF BENCHES

Previous generations of scholars have considered benches but have usually imagined them from only one side of the wall – namely, the house owner's. We can gain a sense of traditional assumptions about benches and methodological issues surrounding their study by considering the Casa Sannitica at Herculaneum (V.1–2). The great Amedeo Maiuri, in his 1958 publication on Herculaneum, assigns the house a paradigmatic importance because it "constitutes our noblest example of Herculaneum's domestic architecture as well as one of the best exemplars of the ancient house"[7] (Fig. 41). Today, two benchlike structures run the width of the house's frontage, but this was not always the case. Along the short stretch south of the main door, there once stood only a sloping, red-plastered masonry "hump," which the house's owner later "squared-off" into a bench.[8] Excavation diaries from September 1928 and subsequent archival photographs suggest that excavators restored this bench and lengthened it by more than a meter[9] (Fig. 62). On the other side of the house's entryway, a long, low bench has been reconstructed, even though archival photographs show only "humps" here and the excavation diaries make no mention of benches.[10] A fair

---

[6] For a similar treatment of benches in Renaissance Florence, see Elet 2002.

[7] Maiuri 1958, 198–199: "costituisce l'esempio più nobile che abbiamo dell'architettura della casa ercolanese ed uno dei più perfetti e compiuti che si hanno della casa antica."

[8] The smooth red plaster indicates that the hump was meant to blend visually with the red field of the façade socle above. Although similar humps exist elsewhere, their purpose is unclear; perhaps they protected the base of the wall and any water lines running along it. At other properties (e.g., along the south side of the Casa dei Vettii at Pompeii [VI.15.1]) comparable humps cover nearly the entire surface of the sidewalk, essentially rendering it impassable.

[9] The *Giornali degli Scavi* record this second phase, describing a bench covered in red plaster and measuring .44 (h) by .42 (d) by 1.90 meters (l). As reconstructed, the bench stretches to a length of 2.85 meters, while the hump terminates at precisely 1.90 meters. Compare archival photographs C182 (1931) and C223 (1932).

[10] The *Giornali degli Scavi*, describe the suspension of work on this house on September 12, 1928, and its recommencement on January 19, 1931. No mention of benches is made as work passes the façade window (May 29) and second door (V.2: June 23). A fair portion of the wall above the northern bench is likely modern reconstruction: Ganschow 1989, 221.

62. Two photographs of the Casa Sannitica at Herculaneum (V.1) reveal the changes made to its frontage between 1932 (the date of the archival photo at left) and the present day (at right). The arrow indicates the location of the "hump" that was reconstructed as a bench.
Photos: Soprintendenza Speciale per Pompei, Ercolano e Stabia, Archivio Fotografico degli Scavi, C223; author. Courtesy: Soprintendenza Speciale per Pompei, Ercolano e Stabia.

portion of what is currently visible in front of the Casa Sannitica, therefore, is most likely fanciful enlargement.[11]

Questions thus arise about expectations and choices, both ancient and modern: What drove the owner of the Casa Sannitica to abandon the hump and install a bench, at least on the south side? What meaning or purpose did a bench carry for him or her and other Romans? Later, when the south bench was apparently lengthened and the north bench was likely constructed *de novo* by Maiuri and his contemporaries, what impelled them? What meanings and uses did they expect a bench to have?

Potential answers to questions about modern sensibilities emerge elsewhere in Maiuri's publication on Herculaneum. We gain a sense of the common conception of benches; namely, that they were linked to an "elite character" and the reception of clients at the *salutatio*. When discussing the expansive Casa dell'Atrio a Mosaico (IV.1–2), for example, Maiuri expresses surprise that the streetward appearance of this seaside villa-in-miniature does not present the structure's true noble character.[12] The only index of refined prosperity is "the accustomed masonry bench dressed in *opus signinum* that stands to the

[11] For a similar phenomenon, see Monteix 2010, 1–39.
[12] Maiuri 1958, 282.

left of the door."[13] The same connections arise elsewhere, such as when we read about the small Casa dell'Ara Laterizia (III.17). In answer to the shabby interior decoration, Maiuri uses the presence of an exterior bench to argue that the house was considerably more elegant than its decor would suggest.[14] Yet such links are problematic. At Herculaneum alone, benches stand not just in front of the small Casa del Papiro Dipinto (IV.8–9) but even in front of the Casa a Graticcio (III.13–15), a building explicitly contrasted with "patrician" housing because of its flimsier construction technique and multiple inhabitants.[15]

It is not the case that there were no connections between benches and large houses, nor between benches and the reception of clients. Rather, as I argue later, the matter is not a simple one-to-one relationship because benches appear outside all manner of buildings. For now, however, we must recognize the shortfall of focusing only on these particular aspects of benches: in doing so, we overlook other factors that might have motivated and governed their placement as well as other social activities that may have played out on or around them. At Herculaneum, for instance, benches appear only on the *cardines*, but never on the *decumani*, a circumstance likely related to the width, traffic, and orientation of these streets. In fact, another feature of the Casa Sannitica and its street frontage expands our view further: directly above the southern bench, a graffito was scratched into the façade's plaster: *hic sitiet amor*, "here love thirsts."[16] Exactly what type of *amor* this bench and others might have hosted is suggested by a more detailed inscription from Pompeii. Above a bench near the Porta Marina, one graffito is explicit: "If someone sits here, he should read this before all else: if he wants to screw, he should seek out Attice – costs 16 *asses*."[17] Such declarations certainly open up many more possibilities about the type of clientele actually using benches.

These inscriptions prompt reflection about expectations, both ancient and modern, and can pave the way for a different approach. In the first place, benches could be used in ways different from what we have assumed. Builders, moreover, must have been cognizant of such alternative uses and understood

---

[13] Maiuri 1958, 282: "...solo indice qui, come a Pompei, di signorile agiatezza se non di nobilità, è la presenza del consueto sedile di fabbrica rivestito di signino che appare dal lato sinistro della porta." Shortly thereafter, Maiuri documents the projecting balcony at the front of the house and, in saying that it served to protect the waiting clientele, he ascribes a purpose to the bench as well.

[14] Maiuri 1958, 420.

[15] Maiuri 1958, 423–425 and 407–420, respectively. See esp. 409 (Casa a Gratticio): "un genere di edilizia che appare essere in pieno contrasto tanto con le pesanti strutture della casa patrizia preromama, quanto con la più robusta e solida costruzione laterizia dell'età dell'impero"; and 423 (Casa del Papiro Dipinto): "una modesta casa."

[16] *CIL* 4.10562.

[17] *CIL* 4.1751: *si quis hic sederit, legat hoc ante omnia; si qui futuere volet Atticen quaerat assibus XVI.* See also the following graffiti scratched near benches, which similarly carry a sexual tone: *CIL* 4.3710–1, 4.8364, 4.8512, 4.8877, 4.8883, 4.8931, 4.8933, 4.8939, 4.8940, 4.10241.

that, when they built benches on the street, this type of construction would
initiate a variety of interactions with that space and its denizens. Last, scholars
have tended to ignore such expectations of bench-building and to focus instead
on what they imagine were builders' original intentions. The architectural
historian Spiro Kostof offers some guidelines for understanding this relationship between the intended uses of the built environment and its actual
employment. He stresses "the total context of architecture," the temporal,
spatial, decorative, and ideological setting of a structure.[18] Within this framework, he contends that buildings are social artifacts "of specific impulse,
energy, and commitment," the embodiments of decisions, choices, compro-
mises, and motivations.[19] The impulses and energies behind any given construction must ultimately emerge from those who pay for it, but other players
are involved, too. As with façades, so with benches: the potential reactions to,
perceptions of, and uses by other urban inhabitants also have an impact on
what, when, and how someone will build.

In this sense, a bench cannot be viewed simply as the result of an owner's
architectural need or whim, but also must be seen as the manifestation of
a much more complex set of influences and pressures: legal, social, and others.
Amatory inscriptions and acts, for instance, will have weighed on a builder's
mind alongside *salutationes*. Moreover, imagining benches as "social artifacts"
opens new possibilities for examining the built environment. If each structure
in a city is the concrete materialization of multiple contexts, processes,
impulses, and pressures, then – by turning the process around and studying
that one feature, including under which circumstances it was built – we might
illuminate a host of issues that were important in its formation.

BENCHES AND BUILDINGS

We have a variety of sources at our disposal for determining who constructed
benches. The Tabula Heracleensis, as we have seen, assigned owners of property bordering the street responsibility for constructing and maintaining the
roadbed and sidewalk in front of their buildings. Moreover, the previous
chapters have shown both that owners understood the power of manipulating
this liminal sector and that they thus took an active interest in the décor and
form of the precise space where benches were built. Benches' actual placement,
decoration, and form highlight owners' responsibility and strategies of display.
At the Casa di D. Octavius Quartio (II.2.2), the Casa di M. Obellius Firmus

---

[18] The case for total context: Kostof 1985, 7–19. Kostof (1985, 15 and 632) argues, for example,
that one cannot understand plantation mansions of the eighteenth-century American South
without also studying slave shanties.
[19] Kostof 1985, 7.

(IX.14.2), and the Casa delle Colombe a Mosaico (VIII.2.34), for example, an open area in front of the main entryway is lined by benches (Fig. 55, 61). Thus separated from the street and embraced within the houses' boundaries, the benches must have been the products of an owner's initiative and were meant to express the same to streetgoers.

When benches face directly onto the street, they routinely show signs of blending visually with the rest of the property, most often by being painted the same color as street-facing walls.[20] But owners also used benches in well-orchestrated streetward presentations. At the Casa di Loreius along the Via dell'Abbondanza (III.5.2), for instance, benches were deployed alongside other elements – engaged columns, projecting balconies, a decorative molding, and possibly also a painted ensemble – to form a carefully conceived façade (Fig. 54). We also see benches aiding in other common goals of façade architecture, as enumerated in Chapter 5: by flanking a residence's principal entrance, they help to distinguish it from other streetside openings. The main entryway of the Casa del Augustale (II.2.4) stood out because of its height, stucco wreath, framing pilasters, symmetrically arranged windows, elevated threshold, and also benches of equal dimensions on each side (Fig. 53). These decorative ensembles both confirm that benches were conscious constructions and show that, among the street's many other architectural claims, benches both helped garner attention for specific doorways and made the claim that these openings were truly important.[21]

Benches not only stand in front of grand houses, but in front of virtually all other types of structure as well. Two benches alongside the Via Consolare near the Porta Ercolano (VI.1.5; VI.1.2), for example, document another useful setting for benches (Figs. 60, 63): they both front spaces dedicated primarily to offering food and drink, as indicated by the marble-covered countertops inside. Of the fifty bench-fronted properties to which we can with some degree of confidence assign a primary purpose, twenty-one were commercially or industrially oriented to judge from their broad doorways and other diagnostic

---

[20] Red paint once covered both the socle of the Casa del Menandro (I.10.4) and the two benches flanking its main doorway. The eastern bench also fit perfectly into one of the four broad panels that spanned the façade: photo C1351 (1926).

[21] The owners of several benches at Pompeii are not always so clear. The bench along the north side of insula IX.1, for instance, appears to abut the plot of property IX.1.22, yet it lies far away from any doorway to that property. On the other hand, it is closer to IX.1.30 (what appears to be the back door of the large house at IX.1.20) and almost directly across the street from IX.2.16, the main entrance to the Casa di T. Dentatius Panthera. Similar complications arise with a bench on the east side of insula IX.8 and a bench near doorway VIII.7.16. Another example, however, makes clear that owners at times had curious priorities when it came to benches. Although the narrow alleyway between insulae VI.5 and VI.7 was apparently unpaved and almost entirely unadorned with sidewalks, a bench sits atop a short section of sidewalk near doorway VI.5.22, the back entrance to a house.

63. Just inside the Porta Ercolano at Pompeii, a bench juts into the sidewalk in front of a bar/tavern (VI.1.2).
Photo: author. Courtesy: Soprintendenza Speciale per Pompei, Ercolano e Stabia.

features such as masonry countertops, amphorae, or industry-specific equipment.[22] Of these, nine were bars/taverns. Two others were bakeries.

Two benches back onto buildings of civic character. One lies against the north face of the Forum Baths and faces the large arch at the intersection of Via di Mercurio and Via delle Terme. One block away, the Macellum at the forum's northeast corner also boasts a bench along the south side of the Via degli Augustali. Interestingly, those sitting on either bench were rewarded with views of broad and active thoroughfares.

Major arrays of benches in Pompeii occur at yet another type of property, which might best be described as semipublic. Three long stretches of benches stand outside both the Praedia Julia Felix and the Sarno/Palestra Baths. The former structure, located near the amphitheater, offered apartments, shops, baths, and dining areas for rent (in addition to a food/drink establishment along its front) (Fig. 64). The latter incorporated baths, a palestra, a bar, and dining facilities into a multifloored complex overlooking the Sarno Gulf and Sorrentine peninsula.[23] Like the Praedia, it also appears not to have been open to the general public, but probably served only a select, perhaps paying, group.

[22] Assigning a single purpose to any structure at Pompeii is tricky business, both because of the realities of ancient life and the shortcomings of evidence. Commercial, domestic, and industrial spaces were often indistinguishable from or overlapped one another, especially in circumstances where means and space were tight.

In analyzing these structures, I have relied where possible upon close analyses of specific property types (such as Ellis 2004 for bars/taverns) and specific city blocks (such as Wallace-Hadrill's sample [1994, 187–216] of blocks from Regions I and VI). Ellis (2004, 373–375) notes that 81 percent of commercial spaces outfitted with masonry counters at Pompeii also had cooking facilities.

[23] Praedia: CIL 4.1136; Richardson 1988, 292–298; Parslow 1989. Sarno/Palestra bath complex: Koloski-Ostrow 1990. The relationship between the two parts of this latter complex are not

64. An array of three long benches fronts the semipublic space of the Praedia of Julia Felix in Pompeii (II.4.1–7).
Photo: author. Courtesy: Soprintendenza Speciale per Pompei, Ercolano e Stabia.

In view of these many contexts, one obvious yet significant point is that benches were often built far from the elite domestic sphere with which they are traditionally associated. Moreover, their frequent proximity to bars/taverns undercuts simplistic ties with prestige. For sustenance and entertainment, these locales drew many for whom cooking at home was problematic because of deficiency of space, not to mention the dangers and heat of fires. Links with the nonelite must have provided one reason that elite authors portrayed such establishments as nodes of moral depravity, the anti-type of the proper house.[24] In sum, citywide archaeological evidence suggests that Roman conceptions of benches were not nearly so monolithic as – and often ran counter to – modern scholarly constructions.

MEANINGS AND PURPOSES OF BENCHES

A survey of Latin literature suggests that benches as places to sit conjured complex and even contradictory associations for Romans. Beyond its most literal definition, the verb *sedere* and its derivatives circumscribe two divergent meanings. *Sedere* may imply an admirable authority (a magistrate "sits" when appearing in his official role), yet the same stationary sense may entail lethargic entrenchment – to sit is to do nothing. In an anecdote illustrating suspicion toward sitting, Valerius Maximus describes a decree of the senate that no one in

---

clear. Arguments have been made for its having been a complex that was later divided (Koloski-Ostrow 1990, esp. 55–58), and vice versa (Richardson 1988, 298–301).

[24] Among other sources, Petron. 95; Hor. *Sat.* 2.4.62; Cic. *Phil.* 13.24; Juv. 8.146–171. Elite anxiety about these establishments: Kleberg 1957, 91–107; Hermansen 1982, 196–203; Toner 1995, 74–77; Monteix 2007a.

Rome be allowed to erect benches or seek to watch *ludi* while sitting, so that "the virility of the Roman people's characteristic standing posture might be joined with mental relaxation."[25] Though lacking Valerius's sexual overtones, Cicero draws a similar nationalistic link by contrasting the ordered Roman *contio* (political meeting) with Greek assemblies, whose seated members fall victim to "immoderate liberty and licentiousness" and give rise to "those bent on sedition."[26] On the other hand, sitting is portrayed as a proverbially Roman act early in Varro's *De re rustica*. As several characters await a temple's sacristan, one inquires, in a reference to Q. Fabius Maximus, "Do you want us then to practice the old proverb, 'the Roman conquers by sitting,' in the meantime, until he arrives?"[27] In this context, the evocation of the *Cunctator* served as a joking mockery of one's own inactivity, but, viewed more broadly, the *sententia* also extolled patience, perseverance, and commitment to a task, virtues that Romans considered essential to the success of their farming forefathers.[28]

A seated posture occupied one place on a rough scale of more or less desirable bodily positions, but the type of furniture afforded to sitters often served to rank them.[29] In official meetings, for instance, the presiding magistrates (consuls in the senate, judges in judicial proceedings) enjoyed *sellae*, individual seats lacking arms and backs, while all others sat on benches, *subsellia*.[30] The *solium*, having both arms and a back, seems to have suggested a more enduring character than the connotation of terrestrial power claimed by

[25] Val. Max. 2.4.1–2: . . . *ut scilicet remissioni animorum standi virilitas propria Romanae gentis iuncta est.*

[26] Cic. *Flac.* 15–16 (16: *Graecorum autem totae res publicae sedentis contionis temeritate administrantur. itaque ut hanc Graeciam quae iam diu suis consiliis perculsa et adflicta est omittam, illa vetus quae quondam opibus, imperio, gloria floruit hoc uno malo concidit, libertate immoderata ac licentia contionum. cum in theatro imperiti homines rerum omnium rudes ignarique consederant, tum bella inutilia suscipiebant, tum seditiosos homines rei publicae praeficiebant, tum optime meritos civis e civitate eiciebant.*).

[27] Varro *Rust.* 1.2.1–2 (1.2.2: *voltis igitur interea vetus proverbium, quod est 'Romanus sedendo vincit', usurpemus, dum ille venit?*). Livy (22.39.15) portrays Fabius himself explaining the strategy to the consul L. Aemilius Paulus: *dubitas ergo quin sedendo superaturi simus eum qui senescat in dies, non commeatus, non supplementum, non pecuniam habeat?* For the same strategy using a form of *sedere*, see Livy 22.24.10; Sil. *Pun.* 7.151, 16.673. To judge from Erasmus's inclusion of this saying in his *Adagia* (1.10.29), it was a well-circulated dictum.

[28] For example, Cicero (*Sen.* 56) offers an encomium to agriculture and *agricolae* (even mentioning Cincinnatus by name) and claims that no other life is *beatior*, especially for the *boni assiduique* who gain storerooms full of food. *Assiduus* is at times contrasted with *proletarius* precisely because of its agrarian connection: Varro as quoted in Non. 67M.

[29] Posture and power in Roman society: Newbold 2000; Roller 2006. For sitting preferred to standing, see Verg. *Aen.* 8.175–178; Aul. Gell. 2.2.1–10. At dinner parties, parasites had to sit and servers stood while most guests reclined on *lecti* (Plaut. *Stich.* 486–493; *Capt.* 471). Even when all those present received similar accommodations on masonry benches, as at the theater or venues for spectacle, Romans found other ways to create a pecking order. On the *Lex Iulia Theatralis* and the issue of reserved seating, see Rawson 1987; Edmonson 1996; Rose 2005.

[30] Senate: Dio Cass. 43.14 (Caesar sitting between the consuls). Law courts: Cic. *Verr.* 2.102, 4.85; Tac. *Ann.* 1.75. The *sella* was a perquisite of only specific magistracies, although foreign dignitaries also received it under extraordinary circumstances: Livy 9.34.5, 23.23.5, 29.37.1, 34.44.4, 38.28.1. Among other honors, Caesar received a *sella aurea*: Dio Cass. 45.6. A double-wide *bisellium* was a special honor for an individual: e.g., *CIL* 10.1026, 11.3805.

the *sella*. Deities were seated on *solia* within temples and when they were "fed" at *lectisternia*, meals for the gods; kings sat on *solia*; and a similar shade of permanence may lie behind the use of the *solium* by a *paterfamilias* when he received clients during the *salutatio*.[31] Types of seating could even carry enough meaning that their very names were proxies for broader ways of life. In Cicero's *De oratore*, several characters complain about the disorder of the civil law and anticipate the day Crassus retires and rectifies the situation. Cicero has Antonius say: "We will learn these things from Crassus when, as he is planning on doing, he takes himself from the crowd and benches to leisure and the armchair."[32] Whereas benches were metonyms for the courts and public life in general, the *solium* indicated a domestic existence marked by counsel-giving.

Given this background, what are the implications for sitting on streetside benches? First, despite its connections to civic life, a bench is clearly a humble form of seating. Whenever other provisions for seating are present, it appears to rank lowest in the hierarchy. This position likely derives from the collective nature of seating it provides: it does not accommodate one person, but many, distinguished and undistinguished alike.[33] Second, lacking arms and having only the rigid façade as a backrest, a streetside bench was comparatively uncomfortable. Last, its masonry construction did not measure up to other materials, such as marble or bronze, which we know were used elsewhere.[34] In the end, how streetside sitters felt about their posture and how others viewed them depended on what those sitters were doing. Were they merely resting, wasting time, discussing important affairs, waiting, or, like Valerius Maximus's characters, being forced to wait? In other words, the circumstances were key, and bench-builders undoubtedly had wide-ranging goals in mind when they constructed such streetside seating.

Shop owners facing space constraints may have employed the street as supplemental room for their business. The three benches of the bakery at I.12.1–2 – two facing the street and a larger one in its forecourt – offered those waiting for bread a place to pass the time and avoid disrupting the workspace inside.[35] For bars and taverns, similar provisions supplemented interior seating, as at the establishment

---

[31] Deities: Suet. *Calig.* 57.3; Val. Max. 2.1.2; Tac. *Ann.* 15.44. Kings: Cic. *Fin.* 2.21.69; Ov. *Fast.* 6.353; Isid. *Etym.* 20.11. Heads of household: Cic. *Leg.* 1.10; *De or.* 2.143, 3.133. See also Cic. *De or.* 2.226, where Brutus's willingness to sell off his *paternum solium* provides fodder for Cicero's attacks on his character. Cf. Mart. 4.78; Verg. *Aen.* 7.169.

[32] Cic. *De or.* 2.143: *"ergo" inquit "ista" Antonius "tum a Crasso discemus, cum se de turba et a subselliis in otium, ut cogitat, soliumque contulerit."*

[33] For example, the united identity and lower stature of the college of tribunes was emphasized by their sitting together on a bench: Cic. *Fam.* 3.9.2; Livy 3.64, 42.33; Suet. *Iul.* 78.2; *Claud.* 23.2; Val. Max. 2.2.7.

[34] Marble: *CIL* 6.2104. Bronze: *CIL* 10.818.

[35] Mayeske (1972, 95) found that at least two other bakeries had benches on their interior: VI.3.3/27 and VII.12.13. Additionally, of the thirty-one bakeries that she catalogs for Pompeii, at least six others were outfitted with what she identifies as *triclinia*.

along the front of the Praedia of Julia Felix, which featured, in addition to the benches along its façade, a small triclinium as well as two boothlike sets of masonry tables and benches on its interior. Elsewhere, however, this impulse to provide seating options went unanswered, at least on the interior (largely for reasons of space), and bars outfitted with exterior benches presented eaters and drinkers with an open-air alternative to interior smells, heat, and crowds.[36] It is tempting to extend such a practical vision of benches from taverns and shops to houses. Indeed, this is clearly what Maiuri and others have done in understanding the presence of benches as a direct artifact and indicator of the *salutatio*'s actual practice and clients' real visits to their *patronus*.[37] Yet such an understanding is too strict because it conflates the presence of architecture with its prescribed use and thereby mistakes ideology for practice. For Roman interiors, we have long appreciated the *symbolic* power of domestic decoration; wall-painting, we understand, traffics heavily in the art of impression and evocation, rather than representation.[38] As I argued in Chapter 5, we may extend this conception of the built environment to Roman exteriors as well.

We can better understand the motivation for domestic bench-building by recognizing that the ideology of patronage enjoyed a persistent social and cultural currency into the principate. Ancient authors, in discussions related to patronage, routinely discuss the physical presence of *clientes*, sometimes showing them packing the house's interior to render the *domus frequentata*.[39] More importantly from our perspective, however, is that these visitors, waiting to be received, are repeatedly linked to the space *in front of* a house's door. In the words of Aulus Gellius:

> Those who long ago built spacious houses left in front of the entryway an empty space, which is midway between the house's doors and the street. In that place those who had come to greet the master of the house amassed before they were admitted, neither standing in the street nor being within the house.[40]

---

[36] These constructions were perhaps not simply places to sit; for shops, "benches" could have also conspicuously displayed merchandise, just as the steps of a church, S. Nicola a Nilo, are used by a second-hand goods dealer in modern Naples. See De Crescenzo 1979, 9.

[37] In an influential series of lectures given for a *Corso di Antichità Pompeiana ed Ercolanese* at the Università di Napoli (which have since been republished), Maiuri (2000, 20–21) attributed the paucity of *vestibula* at Pompeii to the gradual decline of the system of *clientela* and then turned his attention to benches: "But a residue of the ancient custom of waiting clients can be seen in the seats, those masonry podia that flank the entryways of elite houses and that, sheltered by balconies of upper-floor roofs, could offer spots for waiting and rest to clients, the people who had to wait patiently on the sidewalk, until they were either admitted or the patron emerged."

[38] See Scagliarini 1974–1976 for the seminal work on this issue.

[39] See, for example, Sen. *Ep.* 19.11, 76.11; Ov. *Met.* 1.168; Cic. *Att.* 1.18.1; *Brut.* 2.4.1. Also, by contrast, Sen. *Dial.* 10.14.10; *Ep.* 22.9.

[40] Aul. Gell. 16.5.8–9: *qui domos igitur amplas antiquitus faciebant, locum ante ianuam vacuum relinquebant, qui inter fores domus et viam medius esset. in eo loco, qui dominum eius domus salutatum*

Other authors grant us a sense of the power of seeing such expectant *clientes*. Seneca lists those things that gleam. Within a catalog that includes children, honors, wealth, spacious atria, a famous name, and a noble or beautiful wife, he adds "vestibules thronged with unadmitted clients."[41] Cicero likewise illustrates that an exterior view of waiting counsel-seekers was a potent outward manifestation of one's standing. If one of his characters has any doubts about an old man's continued prominence, Cicero has Crassus say in the *De Oratore*, "the proof is the doorway and vestibule of Quintus Mucius, since, even though he is now in very poor health and of advanced age, they are filled on a daily basis by a huge crowd of citizens and with the sheen of people of the highest rank."[42] Last, in a countercultural epistle, Seneca disagrees with conventional values and argues that riches, pleasures, and quests for office should be abandoned in favor of wisdom. He asks his reader, "Do you gaze at those homes of the powerful, those thresholds riotous with the quarreling of the ones paying their respects?" before advising, "Go past the steps of rich men's houses, and the lofty vestibules with their huge horde."[43]

Along with other features of street-facing décor, the presence of clients also conferred or underlined status. Exterior benches, whether or not there were actually clients sitting on them, partook in the visual rhetoric of patronage and the *salutatio*.[44] That is, they gave the impression that there *could* be visitors to the

---

venerant, priusquam admitterentur, consistebant et neque in via stabant, neque intra aedis erant. Cf. Macrob. *Sat.* 6.8.15–23. Gellius's immediate concern lies with the meaning of *vestibulum*, a word "encountered often in conversations, but not quite considered enough by all who use it without hesitation" (16.5.1). Gellius interestingly offers an etymological explanation of *vestibulum* that implies a given posture for the *salutatores*. *Ve-* he understands as possibly intensive or weakening (16.5.5–7), while the remainder of the word comes "from that standing (*consistio*) in a large space, and from a sort of standing place (*stabulatio*)." *Vestibula*: Leach 1993, 1997, esp. 53–56; Lafon 1997. Gellius may not be immune from the pitfall he describes, since he later contradicts himself by locating the *vestibulum* within the house – a mistake that reminds us of the dangers of nomenclature. For authors who place the *vestibulum* outside the house, see, in addition to the works listed here, Varro *Ling.* 7.81 "*ante domum*"; *Dig.* 10.3.19.1; Plaut. *Mostell.* 817–829; Stat. *Silv.* 4.4.41–42. Cf. Serv. *A.* 6.273. Vitruvius 6.5.1 links *vestibula* directly with elevated status and the reception of clients.

41 Sen. *Marc.* 10.1: . . .*exclusorum clientium turba referta vestibula*. . .

42 *De or.* 1.200: *testis est huiusce Q. Mucii ianua et vestibulum, quod in eius infirmissima valetudine adfectaque iam aetate maxima cotidie frequentia civium ac summorum hominum splendore celebratur.* See also Verg. *G.* 2.461–465, which focuses on the external view of the *salutatio* in comparing an urban lifestyle unfavorably to a rural one. Cf. Cic. *Att.* 4.3.5.

43 *Ep.* 84.11–12: *intueris illas potentium domos, illa tumultuosa rixa salutantium limina?. . . praeteri istos gradus divitum et magno adgestu suspensa vestibula.*

44 I know of no passages depicting *salutatores* or *clientes* sitting on benches awaiting their patron. See, however, Juv. 10.159–162, where Hannibal is described as a client of the king of Bithynia. Cf. Prop. 3.3.19; Livy 5.41.

Evidence from amphitheaters in Arles and Pola suggests an average seat width of 0.4 meter per person, a figure that P. Rose, in his study of spectator comfort in Roman entertainment venues (2005, 114–119), accepts as a medium value. Domestic properties fronted by benches had, on average, 3.77 meters of sitting space, which potentially accommodated as many as

house and that, therefore, the owner could marshal this social ritual fundamentally concerned with status and hierarchy. But if clients did, in fact, sit on them, streetside benches could take on still more shades of meaning. Benches could represent a concession to clients' comfort. This accommodation might have been welcomed by clients, but – like the small gifts of money or food (*sportulae*) distributed by patrons – a place to sit constituted an offering whose acceptance implied clients' admission of a social position both inferior to and dependant upon that of their patron. Moreover, clients waiting on a bench alongside others likely knew that their patron was simultaneously taking his place in the customary *solium*, which, if all went according to plan, he had received from his father and would pass on to the next *paterfamilias*. The difference in seating and posture was only exacerbated when clients stood and entered the house, where they might walk toward their patron whose throne-like seat was positioned on his house's visual axis.

The two potential meanings of benches I have outlined – as simple sitting spot outside shops and as symbolic claim along house façades – were anything but distinct. At the Casa di D. Octavius Quartio (II.2.2), for instance, two benches lined the entryway; one then also extended westward along the façade, stopping just short of the broad doorway to a bar (Fig. 55). Here, the bench openly did double duty, and the overlap demonstrates the intertwined natures of the practical and the symbolic for bench-sitters. Even as the bar's customers may have been happy to have a place to sit while eating, they were, in some senses, revealing their inferior socioeconomic position by putting their mundane activities on show for the street – a distinct contrast to the relative seclusion and controlled view enjoyed by elites dining in the opulent house next door. Thus, nondomestic benches may have inadvertently reinforced status distinctions because they hosted activities from which the elite could choose to be insulated, such as streetside dining, waiting or resting in public, and the procurement of foodstuffs and other goods. At the same time, streetgoers taking a rest on a domestic bench potentially put themselves in the position of clients and could thus aid the streetward display of the bench's owner.

In conclusion, although benches were not a *sine qua non* of any type of building, they advanced the causes of their owners in multiple ways across their various contexts. From contributing to commercial success to aiding other façade features in marking a property's dimensions, making an impression on those passing through the street, or lending an air of social distinction, they were useful elements of a property's streetface.

nine people. Bars/taverns averaged 2.21 meters of sitting space (five people), commercially oriented properties averaged 1.81 meters (four people), and the semipublic venues had the longest arrays of sitting space at 13.73 meters of bench space (thirty-four people).

BENCHES AND THE STREET

To this point, we have been considering the relationship between benches and the properties they faced. But what about their interaction with the street? As the suggestive graffito from the Casa Sannitica reminds us, benches were not solely the dominion of the owner, but were also elements of the urban landscape. They bruised shins, hosted weary walkers, and enabled amorous encounters. As such, pressures to construct or not to construct benches undoubtedly weighed on owners. Some of these, as we shall see, were legal: concern for disrupting traffic runs deep through municipal charters. Others were social or practical, such as the paucity of (and desire for) sitting spots in the city and the potential gratitude felt for those who provided places to rest. This convergence of influences must have been complicated, and some of its details remain murky. The remains of Pompeii fortunately furnish a rare opportunity to view and study the concrete results of such a union of desires and reactions on the part of owners and the civic population. What emerges is a tension between bench-owners' wishes for visibility and prominence on the street and the nuisance their constructions created for the broader population.

Benches covered a portion, sometimes a sizable one, of the walkway along streets and thus could interfere with the passage of pedestrians, with domino effects on wheeled and animal traffic. Such intrusions could be inconvenient because, as we have seen, even sidewalks along fairly busy streets such as the Via dell'Abbondanza could be so narrow as to make it difficult for more than two pedestrians to pass comfortably. If shop wares crept into sidewalks, then poetic descriptions of thoroughfares choked with traffic do not seem outlandish.[45]

Similar to the legal protection of universal access to the street that we witnessed in Chapter 3 was a cognate concern for threats to passability on urban thoroughfares, which regularly found expression in early imperial legal sources. The Tabula Heracleensis, for instance, compels aediles to prevent any constructions that block or close off streets or other public spaces.[46] The sentiment was paralleled in contemporary municipal charters from elsewhere in the empire, such as the so-called *Lex Coloniae Genetivae Iuliae* from Spain, and similar issues are treated in still more detail in the *Digest*, where the jurists ascribe the care of streets and public places to magistrates, asking them to intervene if anything is constructed to narrow or obstruct those spaces.[47] Most notably, worsening a thoroughfare is defined as impairing its usefulness for walking or driving, a charge under which bench construction could surely

---

[45] Merchandise in street: see "The Street as an Economic Space" in Chapter 2.

[46] *Tabula Heracleensis*, ll. 68–72.

[47] *Lex Coloniae Genetivae Iuliae* 104 (*FIRA* 21). For bibliography, see Crawford 1996, 393–394. A similar provision appears in the *Lex Iulia Agraria* 4 (*FIRA* 12), on which see Crawford 1996, 763–772. Cf. Livy 39.44.4; *Dig.* 43.8.2.25.

be placed.[48] One particular text preserved in the *Digest*, authored in Greek by Papinian, links sidewalk obstructions directly to traffic. It charges the *astunomikoi*, or city overseers, with magisterial responsibilities paralleling those described elsewhere, but it is more explicit: nothing may be left outside of workshops, save two exceptions (fullers' drying cloth and carpenters' wheels), and these cases are allowed only if a vehicle is not prevented from passing.[49] How applicable these municipal charters and legal wranglings (especially Papinian's) were to first-century Pompeii is debatable.[50] The existence, prevalence, and terms of the legal debate make clear, however, that passability was a real issue, not just in legal-academic circles, but in cities throughout the empire.

An initial assessment of the actual positioning of benches documents such concern at Pompeii. We have already witnessed benches placed within the outer limit of a house façade and thus removed from the flow of traffic (Fig. 61). This category of "subsumed" benches encompasses a fair portion of the sample: twelve benches at six properties. Elsewhere, a similar phenomenon occurs; some benches stand in locations where the distance between the edge of the sidewalk and the façade grows larger (Fig. 60). Owners of thirteen "indented" benches at thirteen properties similarly avoided the interruption of traffic or, stated differently, maximized the passability of traffic while still constructing benches. Preliminarily, then, we may make two conclusions: that Pompeians were broadly aware of the obstructions that benches could present along a street and that some owners tried to prevent interference. The sources typically pinpoint aediles as the enforcers or adjudicators of street-related issues, but it would be incorrect to view bench-building or nonbuilding as a phenomenon solely resulting from their particular charges and whims. Rather, private suits could be brought against offending builders, and aediles as well as owners of street frontage could have been pressured informally by urban inhabitants as well. In view of the legal evidence and the poetic complaints about crowded streets, general public interest likely pushed against the blockage of streets and toward the easy passage of traffic. Thus, even in the constructions of a few (or lack thereof), we might witness the pressures of many.

One key factor in gauging the level of obstruction along a street is the thoroughfare's width. As we have seen, the approximately 7 kilometers of

---

[48] *Dig.* 43.8.2.32. According to the praetor's edict, owners must remove any offending obstructions or pay rent to the public purse: *Dig.* 43.8.2.17. For possible parallel concerns at Pompeii, see *CIL* 10.1018. Cf. *CIL* 10.821. For examples of the cooption of the street throughout the empire, see Zaccaria Ruggiu 1995, 260–263.

[49] *Dig.* 43.10.1.

[50] Especially problematic is the late date of some of the jurists, although the conservative nature of Roman legal practice suggests that their writings likely reflect prior principles and sentiments. Jurists' frequent appeals to the authority of the praetor's edict also suggest a strong degree of continuity, since this document underwent only incremental changes until it assumed a permanent form under Hadrian. For Campanian parallels to broader legal principles, see Saliou 1999: esp. 174–185, 198–200; *CIL* 10.787.

TABLE 2 *Number of benches and properties fronted by benches along streets of various widths*

	Width			
Street Width by Quartile	Quartile 1 (17% of streets) 2.5–3.5m	Quartile 2 (29% of streets) 4–4.5m	Quartile 3 (28% of streets) 5–7m	Quartile 4 (26% of streets) 7.5+m
Number of Benches	3	24	32	37
Number of Properties	3	18	24	22

Pompeii's urban streets vary in width, ranging from about 2 to more than 12 meters and averaging between 5 and 6 meters. Street widths do not follow an even distribution, but concentrate at two predominant measurements: (1) between 4 and 6 meters; and (2) at roughly 8 meters. Typically, the former consists primarily of the streets running between the long sides of narrow urban blocks, while the latter represents the main avenues of the urban armature, leading from one city gate to another. We can gain a more finely tuned assessment of how much street width was a factor in bench-building by dividing all the city's streets into four quartiles according to width, with each quartile representing approximately an equal amount of street frontage (Table 2).[51]

Aside from the greater space that wider streets offered, another reason for the greater desirability of benches along broad thoroughfares could lie in Romans' interest in the external visibility of their urban properties. In Chapter 5, we saw how Pompeians whose property faced two (or more) streets routinely chose the more monumental thoroughfare for their principal façades. Such a practice aligns with evidence we encountered in Chapter 4: the many properties that were positioned at the visual focal point along a street's axis and Cicero's boasts of how his house stood in view of the city's busiest and most prestigious zones. It would appear, then, that property owners, in concentrating their bench-building on the wider streets, were also seeking out a degree of monumentality.[52]

A street's width provides but one indication of how much (or how little) benches would prove an interference. For instance, eighteen of the twenty-five

[51] Due to the distribution of widths across the length of Pompeii's streets, these quartiles are not of precisely the same size. Quartile 1 represents 17 percent of the city's streets by length; quartile 2: 29 percent; quartile 3: 28 percent; and quartile 4: 26 percent.

[52] Benches also appear more frequently along streets that are well integrated within the city's street network, both by the measure of their "depth" from city gates as well as the number of intersections their streets share with other thoroughfares: Kaiser 2011a, tables 3.3, 3.7.

TABLE 3 *Number of benches on streets with different levels of activity (as measured by doorway frequency) and deviation from an even distribution of benches*

Street Activity by Doorway Frequency	Group 1: Least busy streets (doorways every 15+ m)	Group 2: Less busy streets (doorways every 11–15 m)	Group 3: More busy streets (doorways every 6–10 m)	Group 4: Most busy streets (doorways every 0–5 m)
Raw Number of Benches	3	6	39	43
Percentage of All Streets Represented	14.6%	15.3%	26.2%	43.8%
Expected Number of Benches (Assuming Even Distribution)	13.3	13.9	23.8	39.9
Deviation from Even Distribution	−10.3	−7.9	+15.2	+3.1

"indented" or "subsumed" benches stand along streets in the two widest quartiles, which suggests that traffic was still very much an issue even for wide streets. I now want to consider, as best we can, the amount of action bustling along the street – the volume through the channel. Ray Laurence outlines two means of assessing the relative level of activity along urban thoroughfares. Working from the assumption that the presence of doorways and street-facing "messages" (essentially inscriptions, including dipinti and graffiti) reflects the presence of urban inhabitants in their vicinity, Laurence measures the frequency of both elements on a street-by-street basis to build citywide maps of Pompeii's more and less busy zones.[53] While his approach is not unproblematic, Laurence's street activity data may be profitably merged with my bench database to illustrate the effect of street traffic on bench construction (Tables 3, 4).

The first line of Tables 3 and 4 shows that, according to both indices of activity, benches were built primarily along busier streets. Laurence's data, however, are divided into four groups by absolute measures of doorway or message frequency (group 1 contains streets with doorways every 0–5 meters, group 2 every 6–10 meters, etc.) with the result that the group with the greatest concentration of doorways (every 0–5 meters) comprises 43.8 percent of the sample, whereas the group with the lowest concentration (every 15 meters or more) comprises 14.6 percent (second line of Tables 3, 4). The data may therefore give the mistaken impression that owners built benches along busy streets because these settings made up so much of the city and were hard to avoid. We can determine, on the contrary, that busy streets were actively desired by builders: the third line of Tables 3 and 4 shows

[53] Laurence 2007, ch. 6, "Street Activity and Public Interaction," especially maps 6.1–6.8.

TABLE 4 *Number of benches on streets with different levels of activity (as measured by "message" frequency) and deviation from an even distribution of benches*

Street Activity by Message Frequency	Group 1: Least busy streets (messages every 12+ m)	Group 2: Less busy streets (messages every 9–12 m)	Group 3: More busy streets (messages every 5–8 m)	Group 4: Most busy streets (messages every 0–4 m)
Raw Number of Benches	11	6	18	47
Percentage of All Streets Represented	30.6%	6.5%	17.2%	45.8%
Expected Number of Benches (Assuming Even Distribution)	25.0	5.3	14.1	37.7
Deviation from Even Distribution	−14.0	+0.7	+3.9	+9.3

what the bench count would have been if benches were evenly distributed across all streets, regardless of activity level, and the fourth line of Tables 3 and 4 shows how much the actual bench count differs from that number. For the first measure of street activity (doorway frequency), these adjusted results indicate a strong correlation of benches with more lively streets, while the modified figures for the second index (message frequency) follow a similar pattern, with a much lower concentration of benches on the least busy streets and vice versa. In sum, property owners sought out more prominent positions for bench-building, where their efforts would be visible, not merely in grander and more impressive settings, but wherever there were more people to see and experience them.

More activity along the streets not only meant more spectators, but also potentially more crowding and greater obstruction of traffic. How much space did these streetgoers have to maneuver? Table 5 shows the number of benches found on streets of various widths and activity levels.

On the one hand, the data illustrate one impression of the independent examinations of width and activity: the widest streets where benches are present also hosted much traffic. Streets in the top half of widths and in the two top classifications for activity account for 67 of the 88 benches for which we have data (lower right portion of Table 5). On the other hand, 19 benches were built on relatively busy, but also narrow streets (lower left portion of Table 5). Thus, aside from a few outliers, benches are grouped in two contexts: wide, busy streets and narrow, busy streets.

In the first setting – wide and busy – it is difficult to gauge just how obstructive benches would have been. Did space or volume of traffic win? One additional factor to consider is the intensity of wheeled traffic. In the late 1980s, Japanese scholars conducted a citywide survey of the location and depth

TABLE 5 *Number of benches on streets of various widths and degrees of activity (as measured by doorway frequency)*

		Width			
		Narrowest (2.5–3.5m)	Narrower (4–4.5m)	Wider (5.5–7m)	Widest (7.5+m)
Street Activity (As measured by doorway frequency)	Least Busy (Group 1)	0	3	0	0
	Less Busy (Group 2)	1	2	3	0
	More Busy (Group 3)	1	17	15	6
	Most Busy (Group 4)	1	0	11	31

of wheel ruts throughout Pompeii's urban network[54] (Fig. 65). If patterns of wear reflect vehicular use of streets, the results appear to demonstrate that, for the most part, the widest streets carried the most wheeled traffic. The segment of the Via dell'Abbondanza east of the Via Stabiana, for instance, averages roughly 8 meters in width, placing it in the quartile of widest streets at Pompeii; it also falls into the category of streets with the deepest ruts. This higher concentration of wheeled traffic likely forced pedestrians onto sidewalks, thus intensifying the density of activity there. Yet the built environment was generally ready to accommodate the load.

Along the streets belonging to the widest two quartiles, benches face onto the widest sidewalks. On average, sidewalks fronted by benches in these quartiles span 2.1 meters, a considerably greater width than in the lower two quartiles, so that benches on average occupy 18.4 percent of the sidewalk and thus leave 1.71 m for pedestrians[55] (Table 6). In this setting, then, it would appear that a social bargain had been struck: owners could gain visibility and a more monumental setting for their benches while placing these constructions where they would not crowd out foot traffic.

---

[54] Tsujimura 1991.
[55] This figure takes the greater width for "indented" benches.

TABLE 6 *Degree of sidewalk blockage by benches across streets of different widths*

	Width	
	Quartiles 1 and 2 2.5–4.5 m w	Quartiles 3 and 4 5–7.5+ m w
Average Bench Blockage of Sidewalk	.38	.39
Average Sidewalk Width	1.44	2.10
Percentage of Sidewalk Blocked	26.1%	18.4%
Width of Passable Sidewalk Space	1.06	1.71

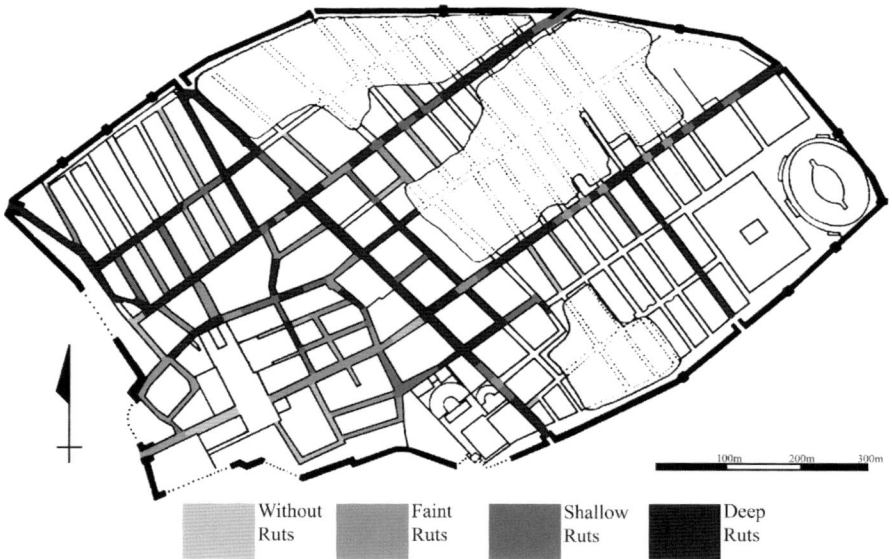

Without Ruts   Faint Ruts   Shallow Ruts   Deep Ruts

65. The depth of wheel ruts throughout Pompeii offers one indication of which streets were the most heavily trafficked by vehicles.
Drawing: Miguel Muñoz (adapted from Tsujimura 1991, fig. 5).

TABLE 7 *Number of benches on streets of various widths and degrees of activity (as measured by "message" frequency)*

		Narrowest (2.5–3.5m)	Narrower (4–4.5m)	Wider (5.5–7m)	Widest (7.5+m)
Width					
Street Activity (As measured by "message" frequency)	Least (Group 1)	1	4	5	1
	Less (Group 2)	0	6	0	0
	More (Group 3)	1	2	3	12
	Most (Group 4)	0	8	19	20

In the other setting – narrow and busy – the volume of street activity may have been of a comparable magnitude, but narrower streets packed it more tightly. On streets in the narrowest two quartiles, benches on average occupied 26 percent of a sidewalk 1.44 meters in width, leaving just over a meter of passable space (Table 6). A first glance, then, appears to show a somewhat different balance between individual and collective interests in these settings, since benches constituted greater obstacles. The story grows more complicated, however, when we examine a cross-tabulation of street width with the other measure of street activity, the frequency of streetside "messages" (Table 7).

In comparing this measure of activity versus width with that for doorways (Table 5), the distribution of benches on wide and busy streets is fairly coherent aside from a small aberration in the second widest quartile. Yet there are notable differences for the streets in the second narrowest quartile. Benches on narrower streets, rather than being clustered heavily along streets with greater activity, are present along a wider spectrum of frequencies of "messages." This suggests that, whereas bench-builders do not seem to have been very troubled by disrupting the type of traffic measured by the frequency of doorways (building seventeen benches in the second most-heavily trafficked group of streets), they were more concerned with interfering with the type of traffic measured by message frequency and were therefore more likely to build benches where this second type of traffic was less intense. Laurence contends that messages "highlight the interaction of those traveling through the streets" while doorways appear to indicate "localised patterns of social interaction."[56] That is, doorways show the likelihood of people entering and exiting the street, while graffiti and dipinti testify to the general presence of those moving through the city. If Laurence is correct, then my data for benches would suggest that, for narrower streets, bench-builders were less inclined to interfere with moving traffic or, when viewed from the opposite side, were more prone to obstruct local activity. Can we discern which of these was the case?

The intraurban distribution of benches may support the conclusion that avoiding the disruption of traffic between one part of the city and another was the greater concern. Several sectors of the city, such as the densely packed neighborhood immediately east of the forum, have relatively few or almost no benches along their streets (Plate I). Moreover, there is a striking paucity of benches along some major arteries – such as the Via delle Terme/Via della Fortuna and the Via Stabiana – a pattern that contrasts markedly with the heavy concentration toward the further portions of the Via di Nola and Via dell'Abbondanza. In other words, even if they lie along main and much-traveled routes, benches appear more frequently toward the margins of the city, where they were less likely than centrally located benches to be passed on errands within the city. The distribution pattern and the width versus traffic data for messages thus both testify to the same social pressure against obstructing *passage between points within* the city.

BENCHES AS OBSTRUCTIONS

While the material record suggests that the balance between potential bench-builders and the general public may have swung somewhat toward the latter in some locations, there were plenty of other points in the city where benches did obstruct activity, even intentionally. An egregious example is presented by the bench outside the bar at VI.1.2, which does not simply run along the façade, but juts at a right angle into the sidewalk near the Porta Ercolano (Fig. 63). What did owners have to gain by providing an obstacle in this public space under their control? Benches that proved to be impediments had much in common with other examples of owners' efforts to distinguish buildings from the urban fabric. We have already seen properties aligned on a street axis, façades decorated in a striking manner, and the addition of steps or ramps in the sidewalk.[57]

In light of these efforts, it becomes clearer that, even as public pressure may have restricted bench construction, some property owners likely sought to gain

---

[56] Laurence 2007, 110.
[57] See "Visibility and Intra-Urban Views" in Chapter 4.

notice by building benches that disrupted traffic. For instance, the two benches
flanking the doorway of the Casa degli Aufidii (I.10.18) – whose well-planned
façade of matching benches, plaster pilasters, and a second-floor projection
testifies to a careful street presence – occupied about 0.4 meters of the
1.45 meter-wide sidewalk and thus left slightly more than a meter for pedestrians to pass along this busy route. In the same way, the benches outside
a bakery (IX.3.20) and the just-mentioned bar (VI.1.2) were likely also meant
to obstruct pedestrians' passage – since they spanned 74 percent and 67 percent
of their respective sidewalks, how could they not? – and thereby to have an
impact on streetgoers.[58] In the important meeting point that the street offered
Roman society, many voices competed for attention and symbolic control
through many media. Inconveniencing others was one means of accomplishing
these goals. Someone stumbling over or forced to move around a bench was
more likely to look up and see who was responsible for this nuisance and who
also happened to be selling lunch. In this contest, the bench builder won, since
his or her image was extended into the arena of the street, thus capturing, if on
a smaller scale, the same power of intraurban recognition that Cicero craved
and that street-axis vistas and other tactics likewise provoked.

BENCHES AS PUBLIC WORKS

This view of benches presupposes that bench-builders, in their willingness to
disrupt others for their own benefit, were primarily self-serving. But, in
a typically Roman combination of self-interest and civic benefit, property
owners may have also sought to profit by accommodating street-sitters and
thereby gaining their favor. Given the scanty textual scraps about sitting in the
street, we have few tools at our disposal to detect any such attempts at low-scale
euergetism. But we know that Roman architects, in the face of soggy Italian
winters and stifling Mediterranean summers, were intimately concerned with
managing sunlight to moderate temperature. Vitruvius, for example, considers
the direction of the sun in laying out any number of different features, from
cities to houses and farms.[59] Repeated references across multiple authors,
especially Pliny, to seasonal rooms and the influence of sunlight also point to
the same concern.[60] And, most interestingly, in the wake of Rome's Great Fire

---

[58] Spinazzola (1953, 248–249) discusses the eye-catching display of the *popina*. In addition to the
typical red fields, it featured a depiction of Mercury, several niches adorned with masks, and
an apotropaic figure.

[59] E.g., Vitr. *De arch.* 1.2.7, 6.6.6. Interestingly, wind is perhaps his overriding concern.

[60] Seasonal dining rooms: Vitr. *De arch.* 6.3.10–11, 6.4.1–2. Pliny's villa and townhouse: Pliny
Ep. 2.17, 5.6. Legal sources are also concerned with light: e.g., *Dig.* 7.1.30, 8.2 (where
servitudes or light are considered within a section concerned with infringements on one's
enjoyment of property, *De servitutibus praediorum urbanorum*). Cf. Mart. 5.20 for shade as
a desideratum of someone living an urban life of leisure.

in 64 CE and Nero's subsequent building code that restricted building heights and required broader streets, Tacitus characteristically claims that some people did not welcome the change because "the broad expanses, with no protecting shadows, now glowed under a more oppressive heat" than when narrow streets and tall structures had shielded the sun's rays.[61] One strategy for gaining insight into owners' possible efforts to gain street-sitters' good graces, then, is to investigate the disposition of benches with respect to the cardinal directions and the amount of shade that was provided to sitters.

As we saw in Chapter 2, the orientation of Pompeii's benches indicates that their exposure to summer sunlight was very much operative in bench distribution. Benches on the south-southeast side of the street are collectively longer and outnumber those of other orientations by a healthy margin (Table 1). Now, this count could be misleading because Pompeii did not feature equal lengths of streets running in each direction.[62] But we may confidently gauge the relative preference for bench orientation along parallel thoroughfares because virtually all other variables – amount of traffic, location in city, and the like – are equal for both sides of any given street. The distinct preference is for the SSE side of WSW–ENE running streets, while there is a less striking difference among the sides of NNW–SSE running streets.

All in all, within the possibilities that Pompeii's street grid presented, the distribution pattern favors the comfort of streetside sitters over the course of the day. For the first set of streets, benches on the SSE side were shaded from the sun from sunrise through the mid-afternoon; only as daylight faded did they receive exposure to the rays that had bathed their NNW-side counterparts through the heart of the day. (The narrowness of the second set of streets would have produced shade for much of the day and thus mitigated the difference between the sides.[63]) This conclusion, from the viewpoint of the urban population at large, demonstrates their greater tolerance for shady intrusions into the sidewalk. From the builder's perspective, we see bench-building as an act aimed simultaneously outward and inward: one that considered the comfortable use of benches by urban dwellers but with an eye to how an owner might gain.

Although a considerable portion of Roman cities like Pompeii was given over to public architecture, areas of leisure were not always convenient for

[61] Tac. *Ann.* 15.43: *at nunc patulam latitudinem et nulla umbra defensam graviore aestu ardescere*. See also contrasts between sunny spots in the city and shady ones, "Spots for Congregating" in Chapter 2.

[62] In the eastern portion of Pompeii, for instance, the city's layout of a series of long, thin blocks created more frontage on the east and west sides of the blocks while also channeling a greater amount of traffic along east–west streets, such as the Via dell'Abbondanza.

[63] Additionally, benches could also have been sheltered by projecting balconies or roofs, as at the Casa di Loreius (III.5.2, Fig. 54), although the fragmentary evidence does not permit a careful consideration of this phenomenon.

a short break from one's urban business because they could be distant, open only during specific hours (baths, e.g.), or inhospitable to the general population.[64] In other words, amid the normal urban fabric of Pompeii, there are, by our standards, few elements of the built environment – and especially the streetscape – dedicated to people's comfort.[65] Unlike some modern cities, in which civic campaigns are responsible for benches along sidewalks, nothing comparable existed at Pompeii. My point is not about city government, however, so much as simply where people would pass the time or sit to catch their breath amid the bustle of urban life and errands. Romans undoubtedly improvised places to sit in the city, but masonry benches could also have been sites for sore legs.[66] Scattered throughout the city, but clustered especially along the streets between the theaters and the amphitheater, they offered a small public service.

Other benches found at Pompeii suggest that providing seating was considered an act of beneficence. Three bronze benches discovered in the *tepidarium* of the Forum Baths, for example, were quite elaborate, sporting legs in the shape of animal shanks and hoofs, as well as cow-headed features along their sides. These bovine motifs visually pun on the cognomen of the benches' donor, Marcus Nigidius Vaccula ("little cow"), who also proudly inscribed his name.[67] Provision of seating as euergetism extended, of course, to the construction of theaters and amphitheaters,[68] and we might view the semicircular benches-cum-tombs, the so-called *scholae*, outside Pompeii's city gates in this same vein. The nine tombs, standing immediately outside five gates, were given to deceased city benefactors and offered public spots for relaxation and escape from the urban chaos.[69] Especially in light of the orientation of streetside benches and the legal and architectural connections between property owners and their street frontage, masonry benches in front of houses and shops were likely understood as intraurban examples of euergestistic acts, providing

---

[64] For a discussion of urbanites passing time on the streets and benches' potential roles in shaping or reflecting this phenomenon, see "Spots for Congregating" in Chapter 2.

[65] Multiple sources make the obvious point that sitting provided a welcome break: e.g., Pliny *Ep.* 5.6.40; Celsus *Med.* 1.3.9.

[66] I suspect that the rear molding of the Temple of Jupiter, which was shaded, removed from traffic currents, and enjoyed a view of a bath, was a popular spot for city-dwellers.

[67] *CIL* 10.818: *M. Nigidius Vaccula S. P.* This benefactor also dedicated a bronze brazier in the *tepidarium*; it had the same inscription, with a low relief calf in place of his cognomen: *CIL* 10.8071, 48.

[68] Theater and amphitheater construction at Pompeii: *CIL* 10.833–834, 10.844, 10.853–855, 10.857a, d.

[69] To judge from the epigraphic evidence, *scholae* were given exclusively by the decuriones and appear to be among the greatest marks of distinction a Pompeian could receive posthumously. Outside the Porta Ercolano: *CIL* 10.816, 10.996; Porta Vesuvio: *NSc* 1910, 405; Porta Nola: *AE* 1911, 71; Porta Stabia: *Eph. Epigr.* VIII, nos. 318, 330; *CIL* 10.1065. Two other *scholae* lack inscriptions, one each outside the Porta Nola (on which, Pozzi 1960) and the Porta Nocera. For *scholae* tombs in general, see Richardson 1988, 254–256, 365–366.

a service for the urban population and garnering a degree of gratitude and prestige for their owner.

CONCLUSION

In conclusion, a focus on streetside benches has further corroborated much of what our preceding examination of the house–street boundary – in concept and in actual form – demonstrated. This chapter confirms both *that* owners sought to make an impression or establish control in the street as well as *how*: through decoration and architectural organization, the display of meaning-rich constructions, the hosting of visitors, the attainment of visual prominence, and even the obstruction of traffic. If we have been imagining houses as inward-looking, then the three preceding chapters suggest that we ought to think again. From benches and façades to sidewalk ramps and other features of the built environment, none were neutral architectural elements or mere contain-ers of interior space, but stood as individuals' entrees in contests along the street, attempting to impact, control, and outstrip other buildings and people in that social arena.

Yet a leitmotif of Part II has been the numerous ways that exposure to the street entailed a pushback from this space. The form of façades, with their defensive posture and ponderous decoration, for example, reflects pressure imposed by the street's dangers. And outraged nay-sayers threatened to retaliate in words and deeds in the exact spot where owners made statements about their status and reputation and where such counterclaims thus carried the greatest potential sting. This chapter has added to the pushback by showing, very much more in the aggregate, the additional pressures that were brought to bear on frontagers. That is, patterns of bench distribution have underscored how these constructions were subject to reactions and demands from the street and streetgoers who discouraged, encouraged, or tolerated bench-building at dif-ferent points in the city. If this investigation of one apparently simple streetside construction has not been a clean-cut story with a tidy ending, it is in many ways a reflection of the character of Roman urban environments, if not cities more generally. They were formed by and resulted from many impulses, motivations, and desires, and could take on vastly different meanings depend-ing on the beholder. Being attentive to such a multiplicity of voices entails moving beyond one-dimensional explanations of urban phenomena and espe-cially considering constructions from something other than a builder's perspective.

Along those lines, the dialogue we witnessed in Part II has largely been structured along the lines of "the in" and "the out," between owners and streetgoers. Yet certain aspects of that discourse – such as decorated sidewalks, contrasts between adjacent façades, and efforts to gain visibility – push us to recognize that competitions and contrasts were also more rooted in specific locations, with neighbors as audiences and potential rivals. All manner of buildings and people stood in close juxtaposition and deep conversation. Thus, if Part I was primarily concerned with describing the activities, sensations, characters, and social atmosphere of the street's "void," and if Part II has been interested in seeing how the "frame" shaped and reflected that interaction, then Part III rejoins the two realms by digging deeper into the stories of neighborhood residents and their efforts at shaping the built environment at two particular locations.

PART III

THE STREET IN MICROCOSM

IMAGINE ONE CORNER IN A ROMAN CITY. A FREEDMAN, ADJUSTING HIS toga, emerges from his newly bought house and steps into the street, head held high, for a dinner at an associate's house, a handsome slave in tow. Meanwhile, a girl pours murky dishwater from a nearby apartment, narrowly missing the priestess drinking from a fountain. Family members attend to an ancestor's bronze statue on his birthday, carefully polishing it as he prescribed, but vendors hawking goods and sharing gossip force the mourners to raise their voices. Young men linger around a tavern sipping wine; one makes eyes at the barmaid; another scratches a face in the plaster façade; two more share their dislike of an arrogant entrepreneur down the street.

Among these streetgoers, there are certainly profound differences, most obviously status, gender, and age. Yet they are all united by their shared use of the same space, a corner common to their lives. In Roman Italy, similar scenes played out daily on innumerable corners and along countless streets. But so much of that quotidian texture remains beyond our reach; the evidence rarely permits even an impressionistic sketch. On occasion, when it does, however, a unique glimpse of urban life emerges, one that grants us insight into the strategies of and the contests among a neighborhood's inhabitants. Part III of this book presents two such cases, one near Herculaneum's monumental heart, the other along a more commonplace Pompeian thoroughfare. The next two chapters – as they each present the story of one slice of urban life – are not meant to be stand-ins for all corners and all Romans, but only what they are: cross-sections as closely examined as the evidence allows and reasonable reconstruction permits.

In urban sociology and anthropology, an in-depth investigation of one specific section of a city represents a powerful method of inquiry. One of its most successful practitioners is Mitchell Duneier, who worked among the scavengers of used magazines and books near the intersection of Sixth and Greenwich Avenues in Greenwich Village. His book *Sidewalk* – almost a location-specific ethnography – opens an alternative world on Manhattan's streets and thereby disrupts normal assumptions about joblessness, the homeless, and their interactions with other New Yorkers, be they police, female pedestrians, or lawmakers.[1] That is, examination of one corner grants Duneier insight into a number of issues that are central to the social make-up and dynamics of Manhattan's streets and that may have been invisible if he had structured his work around a single person or property.[2]

Studies of individual monuments – houses, baths, temples, and the like – are, of course, de rigueur in Classical Archaeology. But parallel approaches to more pedestrian parts of ancient cities have, to my knowledge, rarely been attempted.[3] Historical studies of social life will rarely be as complete as what Duneier and others can discern from direct observation. As a result, some aspects of the following "microhistories" are necessarily written, as Natalie Zemon Davis has put it, in the subjunctive and conditional moods.[4] When necessary, I traffic in likelihoods and draw on broader patterns or better-documented circumstances to suggest possibilities for lacunae. Nevertheless, at Herculaneum and Pompeii, the rich data do offer opportunities for putting Roman street dynamics under the microscope. They prompt us, in the words of one practitioner of microhistory, to ask "large questions in small places."[5] Part III thus reunites the people and the buildings that have, respectively but not exclusively, been the focus of Parts I and II. We will look at a broad range of street performances, presentations, and conflicts among various actors and across manifold means. As our corners come to life, what emerges is rarely pleasant bonhomie, but strong contestations for standing and status.

[1] Duneier 1999.
[2] In fact, Duneier returned to this neighborhood to expand his inquiry after completing a manuscript about just one of this corner's figures, a book salesman named Hakim Hasan. The afterword to Duneier 1999 (319–330), written by Hasan, discusses the ways in which such a figure-centered approach was unsatisfying and how he urged Duneier to see the broader picture that could be attained by studying the neighborhood in its totality.
[3] One interesting exception is Franklin 1986, a study of the wall inscriptions at one Pompeian *piazetta* located near the city's famous *lupanar* (VII.12.18–20). Using these graffiti, Franklin is able to piece together something of the social life of this lone open space in a dense urban neighborhood, painting quick portraits of several figures.
[4] Davis 2006, 13.
[5] Joyner 1999, 1. For more bibliography, see http://microhistory.eu.

SEVEN

ON THE EDGE OF THE CIVIC

A Herculaneum Street

As the great Italian archaeologist Amedeo Maiuri led his team in excavating Herculaneum in the mid-twentieth century, they encountered obstacles both modern and ancient. While they dug, they commandeered houses along the alleys of modern Resina, tore them down, and then slowly unveiled the town's ancient predecessor below. This was no small task because the eruption of Mount Vesuvius inundated Herculaneum, entombing it under approximately 20 meters of pyroclastic flow. Digging through the petrified material was expensive and troublesome but full of compensation. An ancient city was coming to life, as houses, bars, bakeries, shops, and splendid public buildings again saw the light of day. By the time World War II slowed Maiuri's excavations, a huge palestra, two sets of baths, a host of elegant seaside mansions, a pair of temples, and much more had been unveiled[1] (Fig. 66). Unfortunately for Maiuri, he was hardly the first to understand Herculaneum's lure. Starting in the early eighteenth century, after townspeople in Resina started pulling up marble from wells, the site drew the interest of the rulers of Naples. Especially influential was the Bourbon royal house, which funded subterranean exploration that tunneled through the city, yielded many treasures to decorate the family's palaces, and was documented

---

[1] Maiuri 1958 offers the major publication of this campaign. An intended second volume dedicated to decoration, finds, and inscriptions was never published. For assessments of Maiuri's approach to the site, see Camardo 2006; Monteix 2010, 1–40; Wallace-Hadrill 2011a, 73–86.

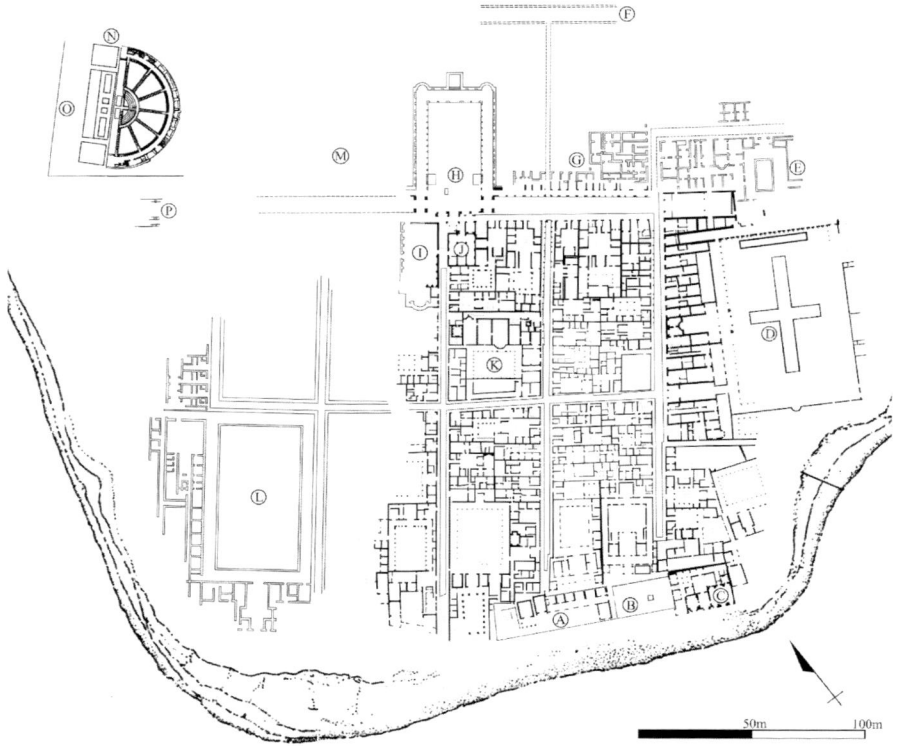

66. Plan of Herculaneum incorporating excavated area (solid lines) and monuments known from Bourbon tunneling (double lines).
Legend:
A, Sacred Precinct, with Temple of Venus; B, Altar of M. Nonius Balbus; C, Suburban Bath; D, Palestra; E, Rooms Associated with Palestra; F, So-called *Decumanus Superior*; G, Insula-like Building; H, Porticus; I, Basilica Noniana; J, Headquarters of the Augustales; K, Forum Baths; L, Large House (?); M, Potential Location of Forum; N, Theater; O, Porticoed Space; P, Temple (?) Substructure
Drawing: author.

intermittently with maps – no small task because the tunnels did not always connect.[2] Maiuri's excavation notebooks often lament the subsequent problems posed by the Bourbon *cunicoli*, "rabbit holes."[3] Despite these frustrations, Maiuri's excavations between 1927 and 1961 increased the exposed area fivefold.

The unearthed city of Herculaneum matched and even occasionally outstripped its more famous cousin of Pompeii. For one, Maiuri had seen and even

---

[2] Ruggiero 1885 collects many of the records of these early campaigns. See also Allrogen-Bedel 1974, 1983, 1993, 1996; Pannuti 1983; Parslow 1995.
[3] For example, the *Giornale di Scavo* (henceforth *GdS*) for March 16, 1939 laments about an upper floor: "La muratura è abbastanza sviluppata, ma è del tutto marcita e mancante della parte inferiore perché attraversata da cunicoli ... "

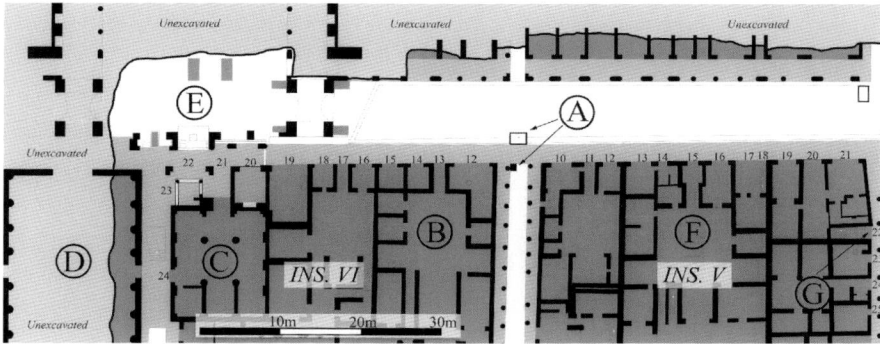

67. The segment of the *Decumanus Maximus* under consideration in Chapter 7 stands at the threshold between civic space and more quotidian urban fabric.
Legend:
A, Fountain and Water Tower; B, Casa del Salone Nero; C, Headquarters of the Augustales; D, Basilica Noniana; E, Porticus; F, Casa del Bicentenario; G, Doorway of L. Cominius Primus
Drawing: author.

improved on techniques pioneered at Pompeii, such as the preservation of upper floors, because the pyroclastic flows at Herculaneum encased and thus preserved many organic remains. Enclosed within the volcanic matrix were projecting balconies, furnishings of wine shops, beds, and a cradle.[4] And the organic material extends to a nearly singular collection of wooden tablets that Herculaneans kept as documents of legal cases and hearings. As Wallace-Hadrill describes them, the tablets complement the physical "stage" of excavated buildings by granting some idea of the "script" that characters followed.[5] The combined lure of unveiling grand edifices and gaining a fine-grained picture of social life fueled excavation in the late twentieth century that left us with nearly all the urban fabric currently visible. Since 2001, the Herculaneum Conservation Project has strived to stabilize what has been revealed and to deepen knowledge of the site.

This chapter examines one stretch of street initially touched by Maiuri and fully revealed in the 1960s – the segment of the *decumanus maximus* between Cardo III and Cardo IV (Figs. 67, 68). The broadest thoroughfare yet unearthed in Herculaneum, the *decumanus maximus* presents a striking streetscape of fountains, upper stories, façade paintings, formal inscriptions, and the most intriguing wooden tablets. Beyond its state of preservation, the *decumanus maximus* also offers striking juxtapositions. Some affairs and people here, as we shall see, were grand civic ones, and this street shows how authority was expressed or sought. Others were more run-of-the-mill – bars and barkeeps,

---

[4] Publications of some of these features: Scatozza-Höricht 1986, 1989; Budetta and Pagano 1988; Mols 1999; Andrews 2006; Monteix 2010.
[5] Wallace-Hadrill 1994, 182.

68. Reconstruction of westward view along *decumanus maximus* from vantage point near fountain.
Drawing: James Kennedy.

houses and upstart owners, fountains and those drawing water – which thus reveals how realms high and low mixed, mingled, and sometimes clashed.

CONTEXTS AND DEVELOPMENT OF THE STREET

Before watching the posturing and responses of individuals, groups, and more shadowy figures, it is helpful to situate our street in space and time. Herculaneum was squeezed onto a narrow spit of land between two rivers flowing into the Bay of Naples. Strabo mentions both the salubrious breezes that the site enjoyed as well as the succession of six different peoples that supposedly inhabited the location. The site enjoyed stunning views over the bay, and Herculaneum's position on a road to Campania's fertile interior helps explain its perpetual attraction. In 89 BCE, Herculaneum became a Roman *municipium*, likely in its sixth century of existence and third century under heavy Roman influence.[6]

This chapter's stretch of street stands near the edge of the site's excavated area, but once helped constitute Herculaneum's beating heart. Houses, frequently outfitted with apartments, lined the *decumanus maximus* from an early date, and many shops open along their façades. By the Augustan period, public monuments began to proliferate: at the intersection with Cardo V, a columned entranceway to a multipurpose complex dominated the street's endpoint;

[6] Location and harbors: Dion. Hal. 1.44; Sisenna fr. 53. Breezes and peoples: Strabo 5.4.8. Cf. Sen. Q *Nat.* 6.1.2. The city's ancient history: De Kind 1998, 19–26. Roman presence on the Bay of Naples: D'Arms 1970. Villas near Herculaneum: Scatozza-Höricht 1985; Wojcik 1986; Pagano 1991.

fountains were installed nearby and at the junction with Cardo IV. Herculaneum's *patronus*, Marcus Nonius Balbus, erected a basilica at our street's other end, and a civic building associated with the Augustales rose across Cardo III[7] (Fig. 66). The following decades saw further monumentalization, as the street's north side hosted a tall insula-like building that loomed over the sidewalk on hefty brick piers. By this time, the roadway was paved with packed pozzolana earth intermingled with limestone chips (rather than the typical basalt flagstones) and was outfitted with drainage canals along its sides; all in all, it spanned twice the width of other streets.[8] Several post holes ran down the middle of the street, likely to create a tented area, perhaps for a market. Nearby, two heavy *cippi* limited wheeled-vehicle access to the *decumanus* from Cardo V and thus protected the canopy system[9] (Fig. 69). Within a couple decades, another major civic structure arose near the basilica and other civic building. Consisting of a large paved piazza surrounded on three sides by porticoes, the Porticus engulfed the *decumanus* and marked its southern corners with quadrifrontal arches positioned squarely on the roadbed.[10]

This stretch of the *decumanus maximus*, with its width and civic sensibility, undoubtedly enjoyed prominence within Herculaneum. Maiuri even considered it the city's forum. Archival records locate the forum further to the northwest, and some scholars have noted that we do not know how far north the city stretched.[11] Since a significant portion of the city remains buried – perhaps as much as three-quarters – what we encounter on site may well be a misleadingly small and muted slice of a larger and more dynamic city than Maiuri imagined.[12]

[7] Excavation suggests that a street was in place by the middle of the fourth century BCE and that it had been monumentalized by the Augustan period. Construction history and shops: Monteix 2010, esp. 312–345. Fountains: Hartnett 2008b. Complex: Maiuri 1958, 113–143; Yegül 1993; Pagano 1996, 243–246. Basilica Noniana: *CIL* 10.1425 = *ILS* 5527; Pagano 1990; Allrogen-Bedel 2008b; Wallace-Hadrill 2011b, 133–135. Throughout this chapter, I follow the conventional cardinal directions for Herculaneum rather than true ones. "North" is thus uphill.

[8] Maiuri 1958, 40–43; Pagano 1993, 597.

[9] Structure: Cerulli Irelli 1975; Pagano 1987, 141. Street and post holes: Maiuri 1958, 43. Wheeled traffic from Cardo IV was also blocked, probably from an earlier date, by a precipitous drop in the pavement.

[10] Najbjerg 1997, 2002; Allrogen-Bedel 2008a; Wallace-Hadrill 2011b, 141–156. Statues (now lost, likely equestrian) stood on high bases on the east and west sides of both archways.

[11] Location of forum: Maiuri 1958, 27–32, 85–87; Adamo-Muscettola 1982, 5–6; Pagano 1996, 235–236; De Kind 1998, 55–57; Wallace-Hadrill 2011b, 128–131. Inscriptions mention other buildings that would be appropriate for a forum but have not yet been discovered: *macellum* (*CIL* 10.1450, 1457), *Capitolium* (Camodeca 2008). Cf. *CIL* 10.1453 (*schola, pondera, chalcidicum*). The Naples-Pompeii-Nucera road likely passed through Herculaneum as another east–west *decumanus*; whether it is to be identified with a double-wide and porticoed street found in 1756, another found in 1754, or neither, is not clear: Ruggiero 1885, 154, 208. Implications for the city plan: Allrogen-Bedel 1983, 154, n. 87; Scatozza-Höricht 1985, 142; De Kind 1998, 55–58.

[12] The city seems to have been bounded by the ancient shoreline and the palestra complex on the south and east, respectively. That said, it is unclear how far to the east the city stretched north of the Palestra complex because Bourbon plans show that Cardo V turned east: Pagano 1996. A group of eight rectangular blocks, four east–west by two north–south, likely separated

69. Archival photograph of the so-called *decumanus maximus* from the northeast, showing two large *cippi* that restricted access by wheeled vehicles and a row of post holes that may have held a canopy over part of the roadbed.
Photo: Maiuri 1958, Libreria dello Stato, Rome, Fig. 40.

Forum or not, the *decumanus* serves as a pivot point between the civic realm and more quotidian spaces. It swarmed with people drawn by this mix of destinations. Space was tight, onlookers many, and prestige high. This conspicuous yet liminal character is key as we investigate, in turn, a pair of monuments associated with the city's establishment, a group that strove for legitimacy, and an individual who climbed from servitude to civic honor.

STORY ONE: AMENITIES, APHRODITE, AND AN AEDILE

During Augustus's reign, Herculaneum benefitted from the arrival of an aqueduct. The new amenity's effects were keenly felt throughout the city and visible along our street.[13] The corner of the *decumanus* and Cardo IV gained

the palestra from the city's western extents, where the *decumanus inferior* terminated in an elongated city block. Near the western end of the *decumanus maximus* stood a large mass that one eighteenth-century mapmaker identified as a temple. Just to its north was a theater. Of special importance to identifying these features and understanding their interrelation is the plan of the site by Pietro La Vega published in 1797 and first reproduced by Ruggiero (1885, tav. 1). For a history of plans made of the city, see Pagano 1996, 229–234.

[13] Water provisions at Herculaneum: Maiuri 1958, 51–53; Jansen 1991, 2002; Camardo, Castaldi, and Thompson 2006; Camardo 2007. Aqueduct: Sgobbo 1938; Potenza 1996.

70. At the intersection of Cardo IV and the *decumanus maximus* stood two monuments related to Herculaneum's water supply: a two-spigot fountain (foreground) and a pressure-control tower, which does not survive to its full height (left background). Magistrates' decrees were painted on the east side of the tower (where their protective glass is visible). A compital altar is also visible behind the fountain.
Photo: author. Courtesy: Soprintendenza Speciale per Pompei, Ercolano e Stabia.

a pressure-control tower – a brick shaft outfitted with grooves to protect the lead pipes than ran up to and down from a small basin about 5 meters above the roadbed – and, in the tower's shadow, a fountain consisting of four limestone slabs. On its shorter ends, water jetted through reliefs depicting deities. It spilled its overflow into the drainage canal it straddled (Fig. 70).

It is unclear exactly whom Herculaneans credited for the water system. In Rome and throughout Italy, Augustus and Agrippa were renowned for constructing aqueducts, and Herculaneans would have recognized an imperial role if water was diverted to their city from the main Serino-Misenum artery. No immediate evidence points to which local benefactors were responsible for creating and maintaining the intraurban system that carried water to fountains, baths, and houses. And few patterns emerge from other cities.[14] Nevertheless,

Further chemical investigation may prove conclusively whether the aqueduct carried water from the mountain spring at Serino along a grand imperial aqueduct or was sourced more locally from the slopes of Vesuvius.

[14] Augustan-era aqueducts: Zanker 1998, 121. Cf. Eck 1987, 72 and ns. 124–125. Magnitude of the undertaking: Shaw 1984, 134–135; 1991, 68–69; Eck 1987, 75–79. Benefactors: *Dig.* 22.6.9.5 (designating aqueducts and water supply as appropriate destinations for individuals' legacies). Magistrates: *CIL* 10.480 = *ILLRP* 636 (Paestum); *CIL* 10.4842 = *ILS* 5743 (Venafrum). Variety of circumstances: Eck 1987, 87–92. In Rome, our knowledge is greater: Robinson 1992, 95–105.

streetgoers likely associated the water tower and fountain with someone locally, and their impression would have been very favorable because the two monuments signaled a vast improvement in quality of life. Before the aqueduct's arrival, city dwellers drew water from cisterns and deep wells. Now, fresh water not only flowed to streetside fountains (three of which have been discovered) for drinking, cooking, and cleaning, but also to some houses, where fountains might bubble away in gardens. Citywide, baths were improved and built *de novo*, and a swimming pool could be added.[15] In sum, these two monuments, on one level, offered a public convenience, but, on another, they symbolized the care someone – from a local official to perhaps the emperor – took for the urban population. Their presence was itself a statement, and their adornment further solidified a place in Herculaneum's power structure.

The Fountain

Decorating the western end of the fountain was a relief of Venus/Aphrodite (Fig. 71). Shown nude and wringing out her hair, she recalls Aphrodite Anadyomene, the goddess emerging from the sea after her birth. Water gushed forth from a shell to create a multimedia narrative.[16] The fountain's other end featured an archaizing and planar relief of Minerva's head, her round face crowned with a crested helmet.[17]

The specific depiction of Aphrodite Anadyomene subtly evoked the city's heritage and history through a multilevel system of references. As an artistic subject, this incarnation enjoyed its strongest ties to Hellenistic Greece and especially Apelles, who painted a panel of the goddess for Alexander the Great. Herculaneans welcomed such an alignment with high Greek culture, not least because of the long-standing Greek presence around the Bay of Naples, which was still felt locally. As one example, a block to the West, Greek captions explained a public cycle of paintings depicting the labors of Hercules, the city's mythical founder. With its sense of historical depth and maritime theme, the relief also echoed Herculaneans' time-honored veneration of Aphrodite/Venus. An Oscan dedication to Herentas of Eryx, an Italic nature goddess affiliated with Venus Erycina, was discovered in the city, and dates to the second century BCE if not earlier, thus indicating the cult's deep local history. Moreover, at Eryx, the goddess was a protectress of sailors, a nautical connection also in evidence at Herculaneum,

[15] According to Maiuri (1958, 51), wells had to be dug 8 to 10 meters deep to reach a suitable volume of water. Fountains: Hartnett 2008b. Houses: Jansen 1991. Baths: Guidobaldi 2008b.

[16] Hes. *Theog.* 188–99 for the story. Kapossy 1969, 12–19 for other depictions of Venus/Aphrodite on fountains.

[17] For the identification, see Hartnett 2008b, 83 (previously, it was thought to be a gorgon). In general, this section draws on Hartnett 2008b.

71. On the west end of the fountain at the corner of Cardo IV and the *decumanus maximus*, a relief of Aphrodite Anadyomene offered a multiregister appeal to Herculaneum's sacred heritage. Photo: author. Courtesy: Soprintendenza Speciale per Pompei, Ercolano e Stabia.

where an epigraphically attested group of *Venerii*, or Venus-worshippers, likely made their base near a seaside temple of Venus.[18] Thus, this subject, beyond Greek ties, evoked the particular history and form of the goddess's deep local worship.

Beyond celebrating Hellenism and local heritage, this depiction also conjured imperial connections. As is well-known, Caesar and Augustus claimed Venus as their matronly ancestress. To make the shift from the erotic Greek goddess, the emperors sometimes adjusted Venus's iconography, but mere context was often sufficient to transform her. In fact, after Augustus took Apelles's painting of Aphrodite Anadyomene to Rome and displayed it in

[18] Apelles painting and its reception: Pliny *NH* 9.91, 35.27, 35.87, 35.91; Antipater of Sidon, *Anth. Pal.* 178–182; Ov. *Am.* 1.14.33; *Ars am.* 3.401, 3.224; *Pont.* 4.1.29. For more on the Anadyomene, its various manifestations, and their relative dates, see Havelock 1995, 86–93. Greek inscriptions: e.g., Della Corte 1958, nos. 28, 264, 288, 601, and 654. Captions at Basilica: Pagano 2001, 918–919. Oscan inscription: Catalano, García y García, and Panzera 2002, 138–139. Eryx: Schindler 1998, 16–17, 108–113. Cf. Paus. 2.34.11; *IG* 14.745 (Naples); Stat. *Silv.* 2.2.73–82, 3.1.147–53. *Venerii*: Della Corte 1958, no. 851; Camodeca 2008, 59, no. 2; Hartnett 2008b, 82 and ns. 42–44. Cf. *CIL* 4.1146, 4.7791 (Pompeii). Temple and decoration: Maiuri 1958, 181–182; Balasco and Pagano 2004; Guidobaldi 2008a; Moormann 2011, 64–67.

the Temple of Divus Julius, the geographer Strabo offered a common reading: he writes that Augustus had given his father an image of their divine predecessor.[19] In Herculaneum – on a fountain built during Augustus's reign and spouting water from an aqueduct he possibly funded – Aphrodite could similarly transform to Caesar and Augustus's *progenetrix*, especially since viewers looking would have seen the relief against the backdrop of Herculaneum's civic center, where statues of both of Venus's descendants, now *divi*, soon stood within a civic edifice less than a block away.[20] This manifestation of Aphrodite/ Venus was, then, a polysemous one, referencing strong beliefs and images through its form and content.

If the relief's manifestation of Aphrodite/Venus referenced manifold strong beliefs, then the fountain's placement within Herculaneum's sacred landscape paralleled this aim because it formed one point in a citywide constellation of cross-references involving fountains. What is intriguing, first, is that all four subjects depicted on the city's fountains were deities, and, moreover, ones revered somewhere in Herculaneum. As noted, Venus had her own temple and confraternity, Minerva and Neptune appeared in archaizing reliefs that likely stood near Venus's temple, and Hercules featured in multiple civic buildings. Second, each fountain stands down the street from a key landmark for its deity. A viewer of the Neptune relief on Cardo V, for example, looked south and thus saw the marine god with the sea as a backdrop. The fountain showing Hercules enjoyed connections along the *decumanus maximus* in the Basilica's cycle of paintings as well as murals in two other civic structures. And the reliefs of Venus and Minerva stand up Cardo IV from the seaside precinct where both goddesses were worshipped.[21] Overall, this web suggests a sophisticated conception of streets and fountains, one that linked across the urban fabric while appealing deeply to Herculaneum's sacred heritage and topography. In the end, for anyone fetching water, rinsing off, or chatting with friends, the fountain's images, imbued with intense local meaning, raised a simple water trough and its creator to a more rarified standing.

The Water Tower

Subsequent officials took advantage of this prominent location and popular amenity by splashing their names on the water tower. In 79 CE, carefully rendered black letters stood out against a whitewash at eye-level on the shaft's east side:

---

[19] Caesar, Augustus, and Venus: Zanker 1988, 195–201. Dedication in Rome: Pliny *NH* 35.27, 35.87, 35.91. Reactions: Strabo 14.2.19; Ov. *Tr.* 521–532.

[20] Caesar and Augustus statues: *CIL* 10.1411–1412. In subsequent years, a portrait of Augustus featured in the Porticus's sculptural program: Najbjerg 1997, 138–252; Allroggen-Bedel 2008a.

[21] For the fountains and their topographical relationships, see Hartnett 2008b, esp. 83–85, which should now be read with Guidobaldi 2008a.

M(ARCUS) • [ALF]ICIVS PA[UL]VS
AEDIL[IS]

[SI QU]IS • VELIT • IN HUNC • LOCVM
STERCVS • ABICERE • MONETVR • N[ON]
IACERE • SIQVIS • ADVER[SUS EA]
I(U)DICIVM • FECERIT • LIBERI DENT
[DENA]RIUM • N(UMMUM) • SERVI • VERBERIBUS
[I]N • SEDIBVS • ADMONENTVR[22]

[Marcus Alficius Paulus, the Aedile (decrees the following):
Whoever wishes to jettison *stercus* into this spot is warned not to throw it.
If someone should act contrary to these orders, let him, if free, pay a fine of
(some amount of) denarii; if slaves, let them receive lashes at the spot of
their infraction.]

The inscription records a local magistrate's decree, which forbids the dumping
of *stercus* – likely fecal matter, human or animal – into this spot. Alficius also
warns of potential punishments, fines or floggings, depending on the perpe-
trator's status. Here, so close to the water supply, the inscription logically aims
to prevent contamination from the dumping of chamber pots. Yet the decree
also served to promote Alficius in several ways.

When excavators came across the aedile's decree, they noticed several letters
beneath and, scraping it away, discovered another, more fragmentary decree.
Issued by the city's two *duoviri*, its precise subject is unclear, but it also leveled
a bifurcated structure of penalties[23] (Fig. 72). The original editors explained the
collocation of decrees as a public bulletin board, yet such an interpretation
oversimplifies matters. Most obviously, the officials benefited by attaching
their names to an amenity that the city's inhabitants deeply valued.
The decrees' layout and content may have even implied the magistrates' responsibility for providing water, since – in listing their names and offices first, in the
largest letters, and in the nominative – they replicated the opening formula of
dedicatory inscriptions. Inattentive readers may thus have concluded that Alficius
or his predecessors were to be thanked for the water system.[24]

[22] Originally published as Della Corte 1958, no. 723. Later as *AÉpigr* 1962, no. 234, *CIL* 4.10488.
[23] Della Corte 1958, no. 730; *CIL* 4.10489: *M(arcus) Rufellius Robia A(ulus) Tetteius Se[verus] / IIvir[i iure] dic(undo) / b(onum) f(actum) ad laev[and –]pu[–]erte ut[–]ipe[–]e / [e]dicemus HS XX si [prim]os(?) t[–] praesent[–] HS n(ummum) servom verberibus coercueramus*. See also Falcone et al. 2008. A. Tetteius Severus also appears on two wooden tablets: as a signatory on *TH* 1, found in the Casa del Bicentenario (V.13–16) dated to 55 CE; as the renter of rural property and personnel on *TH* 4, which is datable to 60 CE but unprovenanced. The other two officials are not otherwise known in the epigraphic record. See also Della Corte 1958, no. 721–722 for another name painted on the south side of the water tower.
[24] Bulletin board: Della Corte 1958, 292, followed by Falcone et al. 2008. A column near Pompeii's Temple of Apollo offers a parallel, recording the generous gift of two officials through the same formula: *CIL* 10.802. Other Campanian examples: *CIL* 10.844 and 10.852 (*theatrum tectum* at Pompeii); *CIL* 10.1425 (M. Nonius Balbus's gifts at Herculaneum).

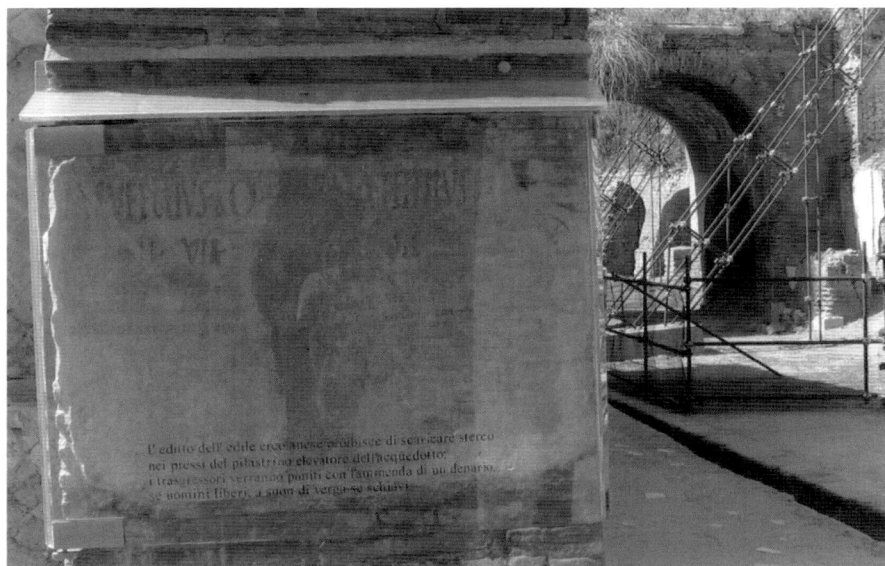

72. On the east side of the water tower, a series of inscriptions announced decrees of municipal magistrates. In both, transgressors were treated differently depending on their legal status (slave or free). In the background is visible part of the quadrifrontal arch that marked the southern edge of the Porticus.
Photo: author. Courtesy: Soprintendenza Speciale per Pompei, Ercolano e Stabia.

Additionally, Alficius simply placed his name in a conspicuous and strategic spot. On the tower's east side, the inscription's white background stood out from the brick surface and drew the attention of westbound pedestrians. Moreover, readers faced Herculaneum's civic center, which underscored Alficius's role as magistrate. Here streetgoers witnessed evidence of Alficius in action, carrying out his aedilician duties and issuing a fairly unobjectionable directive, a key point if readers encountered it en route to the most distinctly political area of the city. Yet Alficius was as concerned with demonstrating his power as appealing broadly for support. Offenders of different ranks, we noted, were punished differently – slaves beaten and free people fined. This split treatment, on the one hand, reconfirmed the social order, even doing so performatively when slaves were flogged in the street. It thus legitimized the hierarchy, which was important amid the street's threats to social boundaries. Within this pecking order, Alficius plays a double role: listed as an elected official, he advertises his elite status; as the decree's issuer, he casts himself as that hierarchy's creator, the one deciding who merits what.[25]

Another aspect localizes Alficius's authority. The decree is place-specific, forbidding *stercus*-throwing into the street (*in hunc locum*). Managing street

[25] For a broader discussion of the phenomenon, see Garnsey 1970, esp. 138–141. The differentiated penalties were not unusual for acts in the street: e.g., *Dig.* 43.10.1.2.

cleaning fell within an aedile's duties, so Alficius's involvement is expected.[26] Yet, in context, *in hunc locum* takes on more meaning because it refers to the very space in which readers were standing. Alficius reminds streetgoers that he governs both this particular intersection and the street generally. This facet falls in line with the innocuous assessment that the water tower was a public bulletin board because the decree was applicable here. Yet, by the same token, it is precisely Alficius's exactness of location that asserted his authority, linked him closely to the water system, and underlined the personal promotion central to his inscription and to self-presentation in streets more generally: name, status, and control were key.

STORY TWO: THE AUGUSTALES CLAIM A PLACE

Over the last half-century of Herculaneum's ancient life, a new institution appeared on the scene and along our street – the Augustales. This group, which arose during Augustus's reign, thrived in Roman cities through the third century CE largely because it filled a sizable social gap. The overwhelming majority of Augustales were former slaves whose servile origins barred them from holding magistracies or becoming local senators (decuriones). Yet some freedmen became quite rich and understandably aspired for the trappings of standing. The institution of the Augustales struck a compromise. Apparently after passing a review and paying a fee, members undertook acts of euergetism (such as sponsoring events, distributing money, and constructing or repairing buildings) or other tasks of civic importance (such as the imperial cult). A social bargain was thereby struck: rich freedmen and others were able to gain prestige by benefitting civic life while remaining outside the magisterial *cursus*.[27] By the mid-first century CE, the Augustales' position was significant but limited. In the pecking order expressed at public distributions of money, for instance, their amount outstripped what the common folk received but was typically less than the decuriones' sum.[28] Even if they reached a ceiling, Augustales might find consolation in their progeny's prospects; as freeborn citizens, they could hold magistracies and become members of the decurional class (which they did in disproportionate numbers).[29]

[26] The *Lex Irnitana* (19; González 1986) assigned the following duties to aediles: *annonam, aedes sacras, loca sacra religiosa, oppidum, vias, vicos, cloacas, balinea, macella, pondera mensurasve exigendi aequandi, vigilias cum res desiderat exigendi*. Similar responsibilities are granted by the *Tabula Heracleensis* ll. 20–55 (with Crawford 1996, 355–392). See also Mommsen 1887, 2.1.480–483; Robinson 1992, 59–82; Wallace-Hadrill 1995, 43–55.
[27] On Augustales, see Duthoy 1978; Ostrow 1985; Woods 1991; Abramenko 1997; Laird 2002; Mouritsen 2011, 249–260.
[28] Duthoy 1978, 149–150, esp. n. 168. Guadagno 1977, 119, n. 12 for additional parallels.
[29] For the classic study of the phenomenon, see Gordon 1931.

But this is the end of the story. If we start at the beginning, the account is not so much about success and acceptance as about striving to attain and maintain that position. In the decades after their founding, the Augustales sought to establish themselves as one of Herculaneum's civic institutions through dedications, building projects, and appearances en masse along the *decumanus maximus*.

The Headquarters of the Augustales

This campaign began not long after their founding, as the Augustales made an architectural mark on Herculaneum. Since its discovery in the early 1960s, one well-preserved building at the *decumanus*'s intersection with Cardo III has traditionally been identified as the group's meeting spot[30] (Figs. 73, 74). On the interior, it was a nearly unified prism of space arranged

73. The front of the edifice at the corner of Cardo III and the *decumanus maximus* (here viewed from the north) was differentiated from the rest of the streetface by its polychrome paving, extensive use of marble, and encroachment on the sidewalk. On either side of its *fauces*-like entryway, it also offered publicly accessible spaces, which may have had a religious character. Photo: Andrew Wallace-Hadrill.

[30] Guadagno 1983 represents the original formal identification of the edifice as the headquarters of the Augustales, or, as he calls it, the *aedes Augustalium*. For the circumstances of Guadagno's article and the history of identifications, see Wallace-Hadrill 2011b, esp. 135–141.

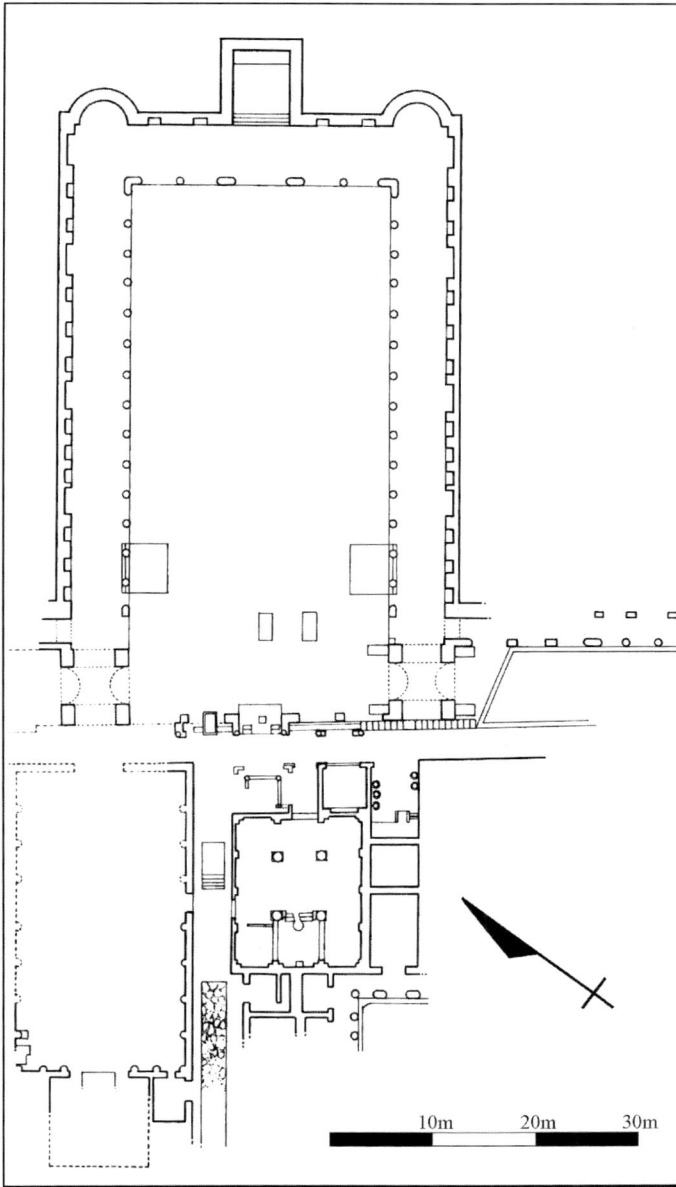

74. A careful architectural interplay existed among the three civic buildings at the west end of the visible portion of the *decumanus maximus*, as the Basilica Noniana (lower left) and possible Augustales headquarters (lower center) were symmetrically arrayed along Cardo III, while the Porticus (top) was physically linked to the latter.
Drawing: author.

around four large Tuscan columns. The one exception was an elevated alcove on the building's axis: *opus sectile* paving, marble veneer, and mega-lographic paintings of Hercules signaled its special status. The Augustales dedicated statues of Caesar and Augustus, both *divi*, that adjoined two of the columns.[31] Although scholars have raised questions about the building's identification, the preponderance of the evidence, both epigraphic and architectural, points to the building's fundamental connection to the Augustales.[32]

How might Herculaneans have experienced and understood the Augustales' structure, particularly from the street? The south side of the *decumanus maximus* was a picture of architectural order, with building façades aligned and evenly set back from the sidewalk (Fig. 73; see also Figs. 67, 68). Such a clean organization changed, however, when one moved toward Cardo III because the Augustales' home was distinguished by its intentional blurring of two related boundaries: that between interior and exterior and that between public and proprietary space. The structure's central brick core was set back from the streetface, and, across the three areas of the building's streetward aspect, the Augustales cultivated opulence and openness. On the east was a nearly square space paved in polychrome marble, decorated with simple murals, and equipped with a marble threshold without cuttings. On the west was another open area delimited by two L-shaped pilasters. Within a chest-height wall, a marble counter ran in a U-shape, and miniature pink marble columns at its corners supported an architrave.[33] Concessions in the main edifice – particularly, its off-center

---

[31] Paintings: Moormann 1983; 2011, 120–124. *CIL* 10.1411 (Augustus); 10.1412 (Caesar).

[32] The negative impression of an inscription in Herculaneum (*CIL* 10.1462: *[D(ecreto)] d(ecurionum) locum ab inchoato / [c]um tectoris p(ecunia) p(ublica) Augustalib(us) datum*) records a decree of the decuriones that granted a *locus* to the Augustales for the erection of a structure from the foundations to the plasterwork. If the building were completed, it may be the one on the *decumanus maximus*. One issue in the identification is the problematic nature of another inscription found within the building. It records a dedication sacred to Augustus by two brothers, which was celebrated by a dinner held for the Augustales and decuriones: *AÉpigr* 1979, 169 (*Augusto sacr(um) / AA(uli) Lucii A(uli) filii Men(enia) / Proculus et Iulianus / p(ecunia) s(ua) / dedicatione decurionibus et / Augustalibus cenam dederunt*). Guadagno (1983, 172) argued that the dedication was the building itself and that it occurred during Augustus's lifetime. However, the inscription was found in the volcanic material 3.5 meters above the building's floor (Allroggen-Bedel 1974, 105 citing the *GdS* of 25 November 1960), it would best fit a statue base or altar, and there is no logical place for it within the structure. Wallace-Hadrill (2011b) represents a recent questioning of the building's identification. Beyond the preceding objections, he notes graffiti on one column that refer to a *curia August(i)an(a)*, which Guadagno (1988) understood as a toponym for this building, but which for Wallace-Hadrill (2011b, 137–139) suggests a possible identification of the structure as the meeting spot of the decuriones. Another issue is the paucity of suitable architectural comparanda for buildings belonging to the Augustales: Bollman 1998, 237–431. The most secure is in nearby Misenum, which had a similar tripartite structure but faced onto an open courtyard: De Franciscis 1991. If, as Wallace-Hadrill (2011b, 136–137) and others (Etienne 1993; Torelli 2004, esp. 121–125) have contended, the cella of the Herculaneum structure was dedicated to Augustus, then several inscriptions from Misenum suggest that the presence of an imperial shrine within a structure belonging to the Augustales was not unusual because they could hardly be clearer in naming the structure: *in templo Aug. quod est Augustalium*, "in the temple of Augustus which belongs to the Augustales": *AÉpigr* 1993, 468; 1993, 473; 2000, 344; D'Arms 2000, Text C.

[33] Guadagno 1983, 164–165 calls the two spaces "ufficiale" and "pubblico" (east) and "sacra" (west).

entryway, trapezoidal shape, and projection into Cardo III – suggest that the western space predated the structure's central core[34] (Fig. 74). An inscription found nearby hints that the *genius municipi Herculanei* was venerated in this "sacred area."[35] Between east and west was the building's entrance; bordered by a solid wall and a spur wall of the apparent sanctuary, its channel replicated the corridorlike feel of a *fauces* while still being open to the street.

The streetward appearance, while opening up these areas, also sought to unify the structure's disparate parts and to claim streetspace. The campaign began at the ground: after a step that separated the structure from the simply paved sidewalk to the east, polychromatic marble chips were tightly packed in the sidewalk and within its entrance. As pedestrians stepped down, they also entered a tunnel-like construction, for overhead the structure continued atop wooden rafters that spanned the sidewalk to rest on a heavy beam that itself was supported by four masonry supports.[36] What exactly they carried is not clear, but the sidewalk covering helped to integrate the preexisting "sacred area" into a coherent architectural image that also remained distinct from the rest of the streetscape.[37]

The structure, then, from sidewalk and architecture to decoration, did not blend seamlessly and quietly into its street. Rather, it aggressively sought attention and signaled a special status amid more mundane surroundings. This campaign can be seen as metaphorical for the social aspirations of the Augustales, who sought to differentiate themselves from other urbanites. The building likewise drew eyes as a structure apart from the rest of the streetscape. Anyone passing by saw a notable degree of opulence in the paving and extensive marble work. Like the encroachment on the sidewalk, such richness helped to elevate the edifice to the realm of temples and civic structures. Yet the luxuries, in euergetistic acts parallel to the Augustales' other benefactions, were also publicly accessible and enjoyable. Last, the building gained legitimacy through association with prominent landmarks (Fig. 74). First, of course, was the preservation and incorporation of the "sacred area" into the building, which showcased the group's *pietas* and more closely linked the civic touchstone, the new structure, and its chief protagonists. Second, the Augustales' headquarters stood symmetrically across Cardo III from the Basilica Noniana, a product of the beneficence of M. Nonius Balbus, Herculaneum's Augustan-era patron. (In fact, the two structures even projected equally into that street.)

[34] Guadagno 1983, 164–166.
[35] *AÉpigr* 1979, 170; Guadagno 1995, 119–120.
[36] The four supports corresponded with the structure's streetward walls. Najbjerg 2002, 143–145 (esp. fig. 30, which shows an axonometric drawing of the reconstructed beams from the time of the building's excavation). See the *GdS*, 30 Sett.-14 Nov. 1961.
[37] Remains of a bed were found here (*Giornale di Scavo* 16 Ott 1961), and a toilet is built into the northwest corner of the structure's masonry, which suggests a possible apartment.

The pairing linked the two buildings, to the benefit of our structure's creators and users.[38]

The Augustales and the Porticus

About forty years later and just across the street, the Augustales helped construct and decorate the Porticus, which had a still greater impact on the *decumanus maximus*[39] (Figs. 67, 68, 74). A three-sided portico accessed by two quadrifrontal arches that framed an arcaded porch, the Porticus is the most lavish public building found in the city. Stuccowork adorned the structure's few parts not reveted in marble, while mythological paintings supplemented a cycle of imperial portraits inside the building. Herculaneans entering the Porticus likely concluded that the Augustales deserved credit for part of this rich assemblage because the inscription *Augustales S(ua) P(ecunia)*, "the Augustales (made this) with their own money," appeared above one of the Porticus's lateral archways.[40] That the inscription was integrated into the building's architecture suggests that the Augustales paid for a substantial feature.[41] Supplementing the group's dedicatory voice was that of L. Mammius Maximus, an individual Augustalis whose payment for the building's initial sculptures was recorded on their bases.[42]

If streetgoers were unaware of these internal links to the Augustales, a walk down the *decumanus* eliminated any ambiguity, for the Augustales' headquarters was physically bonded with the Porticus. A five-opening arcade marked the latter's southern boundary; its two central piers bonded with columns in front of the former's "sacred area" to frame a podium.[43] In other words, the two structures were built into one another, and, moreover, the Porticus stood in a strict axial relationship with a feature of the Augustales headquarters. In sum, between the two buildings, streetgoers wishing to move along the *decumanus* were forced to pass through a space associated with the Augustales. Though the Augustales headquarters strongly suggested a place in civic life, the group's

---

[38] Wallace-Hadrill 2011b, 133–135 for the definitive identification. Previous work: Allrogen-Bedel 1974, 1983; Pagano 1990; 1996, 238–240.

[39] On this structure, its purpose, and the history of identifications, see Najbjerg 2002; Allroggen-Bedel 2008a; Wallace-Hadrill 2011b, esp. 141–156.

[40] A drawing by the eighteenth-century explorer Pierre Bardet appears to show *CIL* 10.977. The drawing and inscription do not match perfectly because Bardet omits the *S.P.*, but Najbjerg (2002, 158) contends they are one and the same. The inscription is sizable, measuring more than 2.5 meters in length.

[41] Najbjerg (2002, 157–163) contends that the whole structure represented "an extension of the Collegio degli Augustali because of the group's rapid growth in the middle of the 1st c. A.D." (157) while serving additional civic purposes.

[42] Allroggen-Bedel 1974, 107–108. Statue bases: *CIL* 10.1413, 10.1417, 10.1418; Guadagno 1978, 138–139, no. 7 and 142, no. 11. The dedicator's identity as an Augustalis: *CIL* 10.1459.

[43] Najbjerg 2002, 145–146; Wallace-Hadrill 2011b, 143–145.

affiliation with the Porticus, whatever the structure's exact purpose, unabashedly claimed recognition in precisely the sphere in which the Augustales craved distinction but from which they were legally excluded.[44]

Augustales in the Street and City

The public actions of the Augustales along our street and throughout Herculaneum rounded out the group's civic presence. A public ceremony along the *decumanus maximus* surely commemorated the Augustales' collective funding of the Porticus (itself an act akin to decurional financing of Herculaneum's Basilica or theater), and we know of other public rites. One was a joint dinner with the decurions on the occasion of a dedication to Augustus.[45] We do not know where it was held, though the Augustales headquarters did offer substantial interior space, and inscriptions of Augustales at Misenum, which refer to *epulae* and record gifts of dining furniture, suggest the importance of group dining in or around their headquarters.[46] Another conspicuous performance involved annual distributions of money to Augustales from the legacies of deceased members. At Ostia, the interest accrued from large endowments perpetuated certain activities: the Augustales decorated the deceased's statue on his birthday and then split the remaining sum among present members.[47] If a similar event played out at one of the many statues added to the Porticus in Herculaneum, its optics and effects could have been striking. As toga-clad individuals clustered around the sculpture and saw to its maintenance, their shared activity amid the everyday urban flurry encouraged group unity. For witnesses, it demonstrated an individual member's euergetism and all members' special status.

A parallel event at Herculaneum demonstrates another goal of the Augustales. At a public allocation of money that celebrated the rededication of the temple of Venus, everyday citizens who were present received four sesterces each, while Augustales and decurions were given twenty.[48] The cash layout undoubtedly drew a crowd to the seaside sanctuary, and if the Augustales moved there en masse, they likely started from their headquarters and processed along the *decumanus maximus*. If they walked individually, then they were probably indistinguishable from the decuriones. The Augustales would have welcomed such a treatment since, like the undifferentiated sums of money

---

[44] On the various labels applied to the Porticus, including *Augusteum* and *forum*: Wallace-Hadrill 2011b, 141–156.

[45] *AÉpigr* 1979, 169.

[46] *AÉpigr* 1993, 434, 477, and 478. Cf. *CIL* 10.114.

[47] Distributions at Misenum: *AÉpigr* 1993, 467, 468 = *AÉpigr* 1994, 426a, b; *AÉpigr* 1993, 474, 477; D'Arms 2000 A–C. Ostia: *CIL* 14.367, 14.431 (on which, see Laird 2006).

[48] Two Herculaneans, apparently mother and son, funded the temple's restoration and the distribution: Camodeca 2008, 59, no. 2.

received by the two groups, it blurred the boundary dividing them. Indeed, the banquet that included the decurions also smoothed over distinctions and allowed the Augustales rub elbows with the city's powerbrokers.[49]

Evidence from other cities suggests additional endeavors that put the Augustales in a spotlight of their own. One frieze of a funerary monument from Brescia, for instance, catalogs an Augustalis's civic actions, showing two combatants (apparently visual shorthand for *ludi* sponsorship), a sacrifice at an altar, a figure seated on a tribunal who distributes a sack's contents to people filing by on the ground, and a procession of togate figures approaching the tribunal.[50] All these activities, which stood outside magistrates' official duties, placed Augustales squarely in the public eye in a quasi-civic role. Food allocations held popularity and were regularly commemorated in image and epigraphy; if they occurred at Herculaneum, there were many suitable spots where the Augustales might bestow munificence against the prestigious backdrop of the *decumanus*.[51] Not all of these displays unfolded in streets, of course, but, amid the sea of Augustales-related inscriptions from the Roman world, a surprisingly common theme is the group's paving of streets and roads. In at least seven Italian cities, resurfacing or construction took place, thus granting this category of donation roughly the same frequency as giving *ludi*.[52] Such a generous undertaking is not surprising because it also put the Augustales in the patronal position the group longed for. Yet this concentration also prompts the question of whether the Augustales understood that visibility on the street was especially crucial to their self-presentation. Our stretch in Herculaneum felt the group's impact repeatedly and in proportion to their growing influence. Luxury materials and forms impressed, public space was coopted, and the group's ties to civic and religious landmarks were emphasized. In their headquarters and the Porticus, as in their appearances at distributions and banquets, the Augustales presented themselves as an established segment of the city's civic existence, claiming a space and carrying out duties aligned with the traditional elite.

---

[49] Other feasts for Augustales and decurions: *CIL* 9.4971; 10.1881; 14.2793. For Augustales sponsoring feasts, see Donahue 2004, 101–104 and Appendix 3. Augustales benefitting from meals: Donahue 2004, 124–125.

[50] Ryberg 1955, 100–101; Compostella 1989. This last episode is likely intended as a prelude to the distribution scene because the figures are identical.

[51] Images: for example, the Tomb of Naevoleia Tyche at Pompeii: Kockel 1983, 100–108, Tafel 28a. Epigraphy: *CIL* 2.4514; 9.4168, 9.4957; 10.114, 10.1887; 11.4582, 11.5222; *AÉpigr* 1981, no. 342. Potential Herculaneum locations: the platform linking the Augustales' headquarters to the Porticus, either of the tribunal-like structures within the Porticus, or the odd platform between the Basilica Noniana and the Augustales' headquarters at the northern end of Cardo III.

[52] Ateste: *CIL* 5.2535; Aquilonia: *CIL* 9.6259; Saepinum: *CIL* 9.2476; Concordia: *CIL* 5.1894; Puteoli: *CIL* 10.1885; Tarvisium: *CIL* 5.2116.

STORY THREE: L. VENIDIUS ENNYCHUS AND THE CASA DEL SALONE NERO

Posted within the Basilica Noniana were several marble slabs engraved with hundreds of names.[53] It was long suspected that they listed members of the Augustales; it now appears that the so-called *alba* concerned citizenship. As such, their rich data open a broad view into Herculaneum's demography. But, by the same token, focusing on the big picture might obscure the individuals behind the names, their particular experiences, and the many paths they took to achieve (or be born into) citizenship. On occasion, the evidence allows us to put a face on a name and to piece together a three-dimensional social existence. Among the inscribed names is L. Venidius Ennychus, a figure whose path from slave to Augustalis we can trace thanks to a dossier of wooden tablets found in a house along our stretch of street.[54] We thus encounter another figure in this space's social life whose self-presentation sheds light on how individuals impacted the built environment and linked their personal image to group membership.

Ennychus's early years are obscure. His Greek cognomen hints at his ethnicity and perhaps foreign birth. How he became a slave – by birth, exposure, piracy, or some other means – is unclear. Given the almost total lack of other Venidii at Herculaneum, he may have come to the city only after his manumission.[55] Ennychus was likely emancipated either by an informal process or before the age of thirty; either would have made him a member of a particular class to which we know he belonged, the Junian Latins. Junian Latins were free and could use the *tria nomina* normally associated with citizens, but were not yet full citizens. They had *libertas* but not *civitas*.[56]

With this legal status, Ennychus could not inherit or write a legal will, but he could circulate freely in the business world, which the archive suggests he did. The earliest tablet (40–41 CE) records a loan Ennychus made of 1,800 sesterces; others record more loans in 52 and 59.[57] He was thus freed before the prior date. The elaborate provisions of the *Lex Aelia Sentia* allowed Ennychus to become a citizen, and the tablets detail this process. As was required, he got married (to a freedwoman named Acte Livia), and a tablet dated July 24, 60

---

[53] These were found in pieces over the centuries: *CIL* 10.1403 a-l; *AÉpigr* 1978, 119a-d; *AÉpigr* 1992, 286a-d. For the most recent treatment, see de Ligt and Garnsey 2012. Latest edition: Camodeca 2008. Location: Wallace-Hadrill 2011b, 133–135. Additional names were written in ink: Pagano 1992.

[54] Ennychus appears on fragment *AÉpigr* 1978, 119b of the Album. Reeditions of the tablets: Camodeca 2002, 2006. Findspot: Camodeca 2009, 36–39. The following account draws on these sources together with the synthetic work of Arangio-Ruiz 1974, 535–551; Weaver 1990, 1991, 1997; Wallace-Hadrill 1994, 179–182.

[55] Only one is known, *L. Venidius L. l. Chronius* (*CIL* 10.1403g), who was probably a freedman of Ennychus himself: Camodeca 2002, 264.

[56] On Junian Latins: Weaver 1990, 1991, 1997; Lopez Barja de Quiroga 1998. Relevant ancient texts: Gai. *Inst.* 1.17–18, 35.

[57] *TH* 44, 45 and Camodeca 2002, esp. 266–275.

declares a daughter's birth. One year and one day later, in the Basilica Noniana, magistrates and the decurions ruled positively on his petition for citizenship, following a procedure called *anniculi causae probatio*, which required the survival of a Junian Latin's child to one year of age. The following March, in 62 CE, a contingent from Herculaneum met the urban praetor in Rome for final approval of Ennychus's citizenship.[58]

This step did not satisfy Ennychus's ambition. Sometime later, he sought a *ius honoris*, a "right to honor," which was likely membership among the Augustales. A detractor challenged him, however – on what grounds we do not know. Tablets document his appeal: Ennychus offered testimony to L. Annius Rufus, a preeminent Herculanean, and invited him to select one arbiter from a list of ten decurions and Augustales to investigate the claim. The offer was apparently not acceptable, but another arbiter was agreed upon.[59] Ennychus's ascent is impressive: from slavery to contending for (if not also reaching) the highest municipal honor for freedmen. And the climb was not easy because present at every step were barriers – some legal or biological, others social – and each ladder rung was contingent on the previous. Such perpetual straining is not unique to Ennychus – others who made similar strides populated the *alba* – but its degree is rarely clearer.

The Man and the House

For Ennychus, the quest for recognition extended to realms where he could operate outside legalistic strictures. Somewhere along his long path, it appears that Ennychus took up residence in a well-appointed house, which excavators termed the Casa del Salone Nero and which stood at the intersection of the *decumanus* with Cardo IV, close by the fountain and water tower (Fig. 75). In a room on the upper story overlooking the house's peristyle, the cache of Ennychus's tablets was found.[60] Maiuri thought that Ennychus, since he was a freedman, was the house's *procurator* and not its owner.[61] The resplendent houses of other freedmen, however, unveil the prejudice in Maiuri's reasoning.[62] Another argument holds that, because the dossier was found upstairs, Ennychus was perhaps only a lodger in an apartment.[63] The sure

---

[58] *TH* 5, 89 and Camodeca 2006.
[59] *TH* 83, 84. L. Annius Rufus is known to have held the duumvirate and contributed to the reconstruction of Herculaneum's theater: *CIL* 10.1443–1445.
[60] The tablets were found on August 16, 1939, on the pavement, but had rested on a wooden shelf attached to the northern wall of a room to the north of the peristyle: Camodeca 2009, 36.
[61] Maiuri 1958, 472, n. 51. The principles on which houses have been attributed to owners has rightly come in for criticism ever since Della Corte's work at Pompeii (1965): Castrén 1975, 31–33; Mouritsen 1988, 13–27.
[62] Wallace-Hadrill 1994, esp. 179.
[63] Camodeca 2002, 265, nos. 33–34.

sign of an independent apartment is a stairway leading directly from the street, which is not present at the Casa del Salone Nero.[64]

Caution is necessary in assigning houses to owners, but here we have the type of house we would expect of an aspiring Augustalis. For the *summa honoraria* required of membership, Ennychus would have a significant amount of money, and all the tablets' evidence shows a man who, two decades earlier, was already making his way in the world of finance, and several undatable tablets point to additional loans. In 66, Ennychus was considered worthy to stand as a woman's tutor, and, in 69, he was still alive and signed another document in Herculaneum.[65] In sum, Ennychus enjoyed considerable standing and, although we cannot be certain, the simplest explanation is that Ennychus owned this house in Herculaneum's final (ancient) years.

It is easy to see why this structure appealed to Ennychus.[66] At the corner along a high-prestige street, the edifice was conspicuous and perhaps gained an additional dignity from nearby structures like the Porticus. Outfitted with a spacious atrium, a well-decorated tablinum, and a four-sided peristyle, the

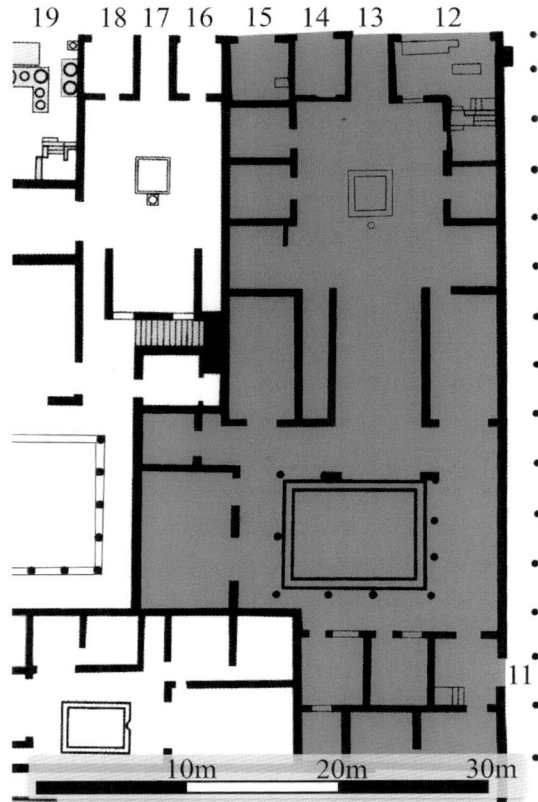

75. The Casa del Salone Nero boasted a traditional plan that aligned the *fauces*, atrium, *tablinum*, and peristyle along a visual axis.
Drawing: author.

[64] One must enter the rear door before gaining access to the stairway, so it is not clear an apartment existed. Given the stairs' location in the back of the house near its service quarters, lodging for the house's broader *familia* is more likely. On upper-floor apartments in general: Pirson 1999, esp. 75–84, 139–144. Independent entrances: Pirson 1997, 175–178; *Dig.* 32.91. 4–5, 43.17.3.7.

[65] Evidence of financial activity: *TH* 72, 88, 58 and Camodeca 2002. Alive in 69: Camodeca 2002, 262–263 with *TH* 53, 77, 78, 80, 92.

[66] No comprehensive publication of the house has been undertaken. It was originally explored by Bourbon tunnelers, then excavated intermittently between 1933 and 1948 (Maiuri 1958, 239–242), and finally brought to its current state by work in 1961. Notebooks from the early twentieth-century excavations report substantial damage by Bourbon tunnels: e.g., *GdS* 16 Marzo 1939. Locating the records for the 1961 excavations has proved difficult, although Pagano (1988, 209–210) reproduces a personal notebook of Maiuri, which he supplements with interviews with workmen. For a broad survey of the house, see Guidobaldi 2006, 190–199. Monteix (2010, 332–345) offers a construction history of Insula VI.

76. The façade of the Casa del Salone Nero drew together its own entryway and three shop-style doorways through a projecting roof and a façade-spanning molding (each preserved/reconstructed only in part) as well as through a sidewalk inlaid with large marble pieces.
Photo: author. Courtesy: Soprintendenza Speciale per Pompei, Ercolano e Stabia.

house was the picture of traditional Roman domestic forms and offered Ennychus a fashionable variety of rooms for hosting guests. Most notable was the house's eponymous "salon" with its elegant black walls. Diners here looked onto the garden, while smaller and still elegant rooms communicated greater intimacy. The house's exterior realized many goals discussed in Chapter 5. Along its east, a series of columns ran from the house's façade to its rear property line and demonstrated the depth of Ennychus's holdings. Meanwhile, a projecting roof, plaster molding, and distinctive sidewalk decoration spanned the house's breadth (Fig. 76).

This façade ensemble embraced three shops. At the corner, a metalworking shop equipped with an L-shaped counter opened wide (V.12). To judge from the finds – among others, a bronze candelabrum, lead ingots, simple tubing, and a semiprecious statuette – the craftsman's talents were wide-ranging. A set of stairs led to additional space above the shop's rear room and the construction atop the columns. On the west were two other shops (V.14, V.15). Of roughly equal dimensions and boasting lintels at the same height, they both featured wooden mezzanines for sleeping or storage. Between the eastern shop and the house's main doorway were two paintings, the lower of which is labeled *AD CUCUMAS* and shows four vessels of different colors, each with a price (Fig. 77). These may indicate a shop for wine, but paltry finds complicate the

77. The entryway of the Casa del Salone Nero presented streetgoers with two paintings: one apparently a sign for a wine shop, the other a figure (enhanced in this photograph) whose identity has not been firmly established. It may represent the god *Semo Sancus*, but its closest iconographic parallels are found in *genius* figures.
Photo: author. Courtesy: Soprintendenza Speciale per Pompei, Ercolano e Stabia.

identification of either spaces' use.[67] Part of this house's allure for Ennychus may have been the income he could derive from the shops, whether by

[67] The western shop was undergoing work at the time of the eruption, which makes its enigmatic finds especially difficult to interpret; its mezzanine level contained a number of ceramic and metal vessels, while on the ground floor was a marble head depicting a woman. On the shops along the frontage and their finds, see Monteix 2003; 2005; 2006, 19–23, 27–29,

entrusting their management to members of his household, leasing them to live-in tenants, or some other arrangement.[68] But demonstrating his position of authority over others may also have appealed. That is, the house's architecture made clear that the shops and keepers were within his sphere of influence, and streetgoers were left to conclude that Ennychus was a man others relied on for support, backing, and decisions.

The main doorway and the view that it framed pointed in the same direction. Carved wooden jambs flanked the entryway, and its crowning cornice rose above the façade-spanning molding. If the door stood open and no obstructions intervened, those peering in gained an architectural narrative of Ennychus's house, from the *fauces* all the way to the peristyle and the rooms behind – a sightline of some 30 meters. The vista alone encouraged streetgoers to draw favorable conclusions about social rituals Ennychus might host, which only gained strength if tenants or dependents were waiting outside or members of Ennychus's social circle were visiting the house. Those contacts embedded him within his neighborhood; among other evidence, he signs two documents in the L. Cominius Primus dossier, which was found several doors down the *decumanus maximus* (V.22).[69] Serious diplomatic efforts probably preceded Ennychus's selection of potential arbiters among the Augustales and decurions, and we can expect that he cultivated those relationships carefully. Indeed, the tablets document Ennychus's connections to many established and recognized families. For instance, M. Nonius Hermeros, likely a freedman of the family that claimed the city's *patronus* among its progenitors, appears as a signatory for Ennychus and also sold Ennychus a slave girl, vowing that she was in good health.[70] The links to leading families continued with signatories among the freed slaves of L. Mammius Maximus, the Augustalis who commissioned the Porticus's sculptural program.[71] All told, these were his associates in business and leisure; they signed his crucial documents. Negotiations for the transactions and testimony recorded on the tablets likely unfolded within

---

34–37; 2007b; 2010, esp. 401–404. Shop sign at VI.14: Pagano 1988, 212–215; Monteix 2010, 49–50.

[68] Although the shops' inclusion within the façade scheme linked them to Ennychus's street presentation, it does not clarify his relationship to their ownership and management. Doorways had once linked two shops with the house's atrium, but were later closed off, possibly during the 70s CE: Monteix 2010, 342–345. The separation may indicate less immediate control, and it adds to the hypothesis suggested by the mezzanines that the shops at one time doubled as dwellings.

[69] *TH* 2, 53. For others in the potential web of neighborhood relations, see *TH* 50, 102, in which C. Petronius Stephanus appears as a signatory on Venidius's documents. He may also be involved in the famous Petronia Justa dossier found in the nearby Casa del Bicentenario (V. 13–16) since he shares his name with one of the figures listed there. Those disputants and L. Cominius Primus appear in one another's documents: *TH* 2, 29, 33, 66, 68.

[70] *TH* 98 (signatory), 62 (slave girl). *TH* 101 featured a certain M. Nonius Tryp<h>onis.

[71] L. Mammi: *TH* 81. C. Novi: *TH* 2, 58. Q. Iuni: *TH* 50, 101.

Ennychus's house, over meals or in private meetings. The comings and goings of this well-connected circle, any of Ennychus's fellow Augustales or even the decurions with whom he on occasion shared a meal, helped to make this elegant house seem less like that of a striving new arrival and more like that of an established member of society.

Façade Painting and Image Making

One painting on Ennychus's façade may have offered a quiet reminder of his ascent. Directly above the image of the four vessels, a male figure appears half life-size against a red background (Fig. 77). He wears a white toga and holds a silver patera in his right hand, while a scepter or staff slants across his body. A laurel crown tops his bushy hair and bearded face. Above is the painted inscription *AD SANCUM*, the tiny *UM* written appearing within the C's curve. From the inscription Mario Pagano identified the figure as Semo Sancus.[72] A guarantor of oaths and good faith in business, Sancus was a suitable protector for a shop, since any customers who recognized his name were assured of fair treatment. The cult, however, is attested sparsely in Rome and Latium; it appears nowhere else, including Campania. Only one other possible depiction of Sancus exists, which Pagano contests. All of which raises questions: how many Herculaneans recognized this obscure figure? How else might they have understood the image?[73]

One possibility originates in the figure's posture, dress, and accouterments, which bear close similarities to images of the *genius* of the *paterfamilias* in household shrines. In fact, Maiuri initially identified Ennychus's painting as such.[74] The togate *genius*, typically framed by *lares*, stands before an altar; his toga often covers his head to emphasize his sacrificial posture, but he may also wear a wreath. His right hand always extends forward and holds a patera, while his left hand clutches several possible accessories, frequently a cornucopia.[75] In other words, while some details vary, the pose, clothing, and patera are remarkably consistent. If streetgoers recognized visual echoes of a *genius*, they would have imagined "the guiding *numen* of the family, its procreative force, and especially the living spirit of the *paterfamilias*."[76] At the Casa del Salone

[72] Pagano 1988, 211–212. The deity occasionally is called *Semo Sancus Dius Fidius* but appears in literature most often as *Sancus* Cf. Fröhlich 1991, 340–341; Monteix 2010, 49–50.
[73] Pagano 1988, 211 (esp. n. 10). Temple on Quirinal Hill of Sabine origin: Dion. Hal. 2.49.2, 9.60; Ov. *Fast.* 6.213–218; Prop. 4.9.74; *LTUR* 4.263–264 ("Semo Sancus in Colle, Aedes, Fanum, Sacellum, Templum," Coarelli; "Semo Sancus," Degrassi). See also *CIL* 6.568.
[74] Transcription of Maiuri's notebook in Pagano 1988, 209.
[75] See Pompeian examples such as at the Casa degli Archi (I.17.4; Fröhlich 1991, L37), the Casa dei Vettii (VI.15.1; Fröhlich 1991, L70), and an unnamed house adjacent to the Casa delle Nozze d'Argento (V.2.b/c; Fröhlich 1991, L49 with floral crown).
[76] Orr 1978, 1560–1575 (quotation from 1569–1570); Fröhlich 1991, 21–61. The *genius* was particularly venerated on the birthday feast and wedding day of the *paterfamilias*, and, upon his

Nero, the presence of a beard and shaggy hair (both rare attributes for *genii*) suggests an image tailored for a particular figurehead. Here, Ennychus, as a free Roman citizen with his own family and slaves, fulfilled that role.

Although figural scenes on house façades were rare, shop signs offered an appropriate location. In that sense, Ennychus likely welcomed the association with trustworthiness evoked in anyone who recognized Sancus, especially given his endeavors in money-lending. Yet, because the familiar image stood close to his house's main door, Ennychus perhaps enjoyed benefits beyond the commercial. For one, the image implied participation in the full *habitus* of Roman domestic religion. Individual elements had recognizable meanings: the laurel crown echoed magisterial insignia and the patera suggested dutifulness in religious affairs. But foremost is the figure's toga, a garment that Ennychus was forbidden to wear while a slave or a Junian Latin because of its special link to Roman citizenship, civic life, and, as the *Aeneid* reminds us, national identity.[77]

A *genius*-like togate figure offered a baseline image of *Romanitas*, but viewers perhaps conjured a more specific role if they, like Wallace-Hadrill, read the inscription as *AD SANC(T)UM*, "at the sign of the holy man."[78] While the letter's insertion represents a considerable leap, this identification meshes with the painting's dominant iconography and could underscore Ennychus's presumed membership among the Augustales.[79] If Ennychus stepped out of this doorway, perhaps bearded and bedecked in a toga, on his way to the Augustales' headquarters or the Porticus, he walked directly in front of this painting. Through his own movements and appearances, he could embody what the façade painting suggested, not just that he was an Augustalis, but also a citizen and man who mattered in the city.

All told, what we can reconstruct of Ennychus's street persona pulls in two directions: building himself up while also striving to make himself indistinguishable from Herculaneum's elite. Streetgoers saw a large house, in a prestigious location, with well-appointed reception spaces and possible commercial revenue. They viewed a painting suggesting the proper cultivation of household gods and perhaps reflecting the owner's citizen status. Visits by dependents, the comings and goings of social and business contacts, and the emergence of Ennychus himself and his activities, either alone or with other Augustales – all were additional cues, and they sought a visual and performative parity with the decurional class. In the ultimate tally, the first

---

death, the *genius* was said to pass to another person. Birthday: *CIL* 10.860–861; Tib. 2.2.1. Death: Hor. *Epist.* 2.2.188.

[77] Shop signs could carry a personal sensibility: e.g. *CIL* 4.806–807 (*Sittiius riistituit iiliipan* along with an image of a pygmy leading an elephant to a wine jug). Laurel crowns: Woods 1991, 111–112, 141–142, and table 3. Toga: Verg. *Aen.* 1.282; Stone 1994; Edmondson 2008.

[78] Wallace-Hadrill 1994, 181.

[79] It should be pointed out that both that the characters forming the UM are much smaller than the other letters and that the whole ensemble stood about 3 meters above the pavement.

portion of this story charted Ennychus's rise in status, while the second showed how he largely tried to mask that ascendance and, by emulating elite emblems and actions, to blend seamlessly into that social stratum.

CONCLUSION: MORE STORIES

As much as our street's social life has come into focus – especially how individuals and groups used architecture, decoration, decrees, and rituals to make their presence felt – the material record signals still more dramas and performances. For instance, an inscription on the tomb/funerary altar of M. Nonius Balbus mentions an annual parade honoring Herculaneum's *patronus* that likely passed along the *decumanus maximus*. We know that it departed from the seaside monument on the festival of the *Parentalia*, but little else.[80] However, the honorific cortege would not have missed the opportunity to pass by or through Balbus's most conspicuous donations to the city, including the Basilica Noniana. If the procession followed the showiest route, then it passed through the gates and city walls (which received Balbus's financial attention), advanced along Cardo V, turned west along the *decumanus*, and moved by the monuments I have discussed in this chapter, thus annually re-emphasizing the street's prestige.[81] As it moved along, the procession offered onlookers an idealized remembrance of a man who crowned Herculaneum's social pyramid as its most generous benefactor and prime representative in Augustan circles. Meanwhile, before that abundant audience, the parade's participants enjoyed a conspicuous connection to Balbus against a charged backdrop.

If we expand our scope even slightly, such grand civic affairs feel distant. It seems that L. Cominius Primus, the central figure of tablets found upstairs from doorway V.22, had his share of enemies. Three separate quarrels about real estate are attested, one involving his cutting of boundary stakes.[82] Herculaneans familiar with his disputes (and any reputation he perhaps earned from them) probably looked askance at Primus when they encountered him in the street, while others passed him by unaware. Everyone would have suspected something was awry, however, when a gang of at least eight slaves came to Primus's door and bombarded it with stones, according to testimony on one of Primus's tablets.[83] We have no other information about what provoked the action, but

---

[80] Maiuri 1942; Schumacher 1976; Guadagno 1978, 144–147; Hartnett 2008b, 85.
[81] Rogers 1991 offers a nice example of the care that went into selecting the route of civic processions.
[82] *TH* 76–80. For this and the other disputes, see Wallace-Hadrill 1994, 178–179, on which this summary draws.
[83] *TH* 2: *Cominius Primus testaus est et oste[n] / dit ianuas sibi lapidates quod tran[s]- / paruit, quod factum diceret ab [- / rio et Agatho et Phileto et Epagat[ho] / ser(vis) C[a]riae Longinae et Polluce [et – / [c]o et Xenodoro et Actiaco et Pat[r-.* The tablet leaves off at this point, and it is unclear how much

78. The streetface of the Casa del Bicentenario (V.13–16) shows evidence of once being a unified edifice that was later divided up because its eastern portion (at left) was distinguished from the main structure by its sidewalk and architecture.
Photo: author. Courtesy: Soprintendenza Speciale per Pompei, Ercolano e Stabia.

the attack, beyond its physical destruction, likely had a profound symbolic fallout because the threshold was so highly charged in the Roman sphere. And the humiliating act certainly would have occupied the neighborhood for some time.

Somewhere between the poles marked by the parade and door-stoning stand two other events. Next door to Primus's lodgings, the façade of the mammoth Casa del Bicentenario (V.13–16; Fig. 78) invites speculation about what brewed within the house. The structure's plan makes clear that a strict symmetricality once governed the façade, but in 79 CE what faced the street departed from unity and order because the property was apparently divided in two. A jetty was segmented, different paint decorated the split section, and a more elegant sidewalk was laid before it. Perhaps the new portion was merely sold off, but the determined effort to distinguish it from the house's original core suggests more dramatic possibilities. This house's tablets supply intense events but they do not map cleanly onto the architecture. Was there a dispute over an inheritance or a rift between freedman and patron? Whatever the cause, whether

further it may have continued to list the slaves' names before it presumably listed the name of the second owner. The sense of *quod transparuit* may be, as Arangio-Ruiz (1974, 304) suggests, that the doors were so pulverized that the light shone through.

sensational or commonplace, the example underscores the vital importance of fashioning an independent architectural presence along the street.[84]

On that note, an altar shoehorned between the Casa del Salone Nero and the water tower showcases others who yearned for visibility in this charged environment (Figs. 67, 68, 70). Paintings of snakes make this short mass of masonry identifiable as a shrine of the *compita* or crossroads gods, where Herculaneans propitiated protective deities. I will say more in Chapter 8 about such urban features when we consider a more elaborate example. What is notable now is that the figures who presided at annual ceremonies here, most likely slaves or freedmen, were able to assume a fleeting moment of prominence close to where aediles, Augustales, and others jockeyed for position.

These four additional vignettes draw attention to issues both methodological and qualitative. First, while they add dramas and players to our street, they offer less volume and precision of information than the main sections of this chapter. As a result, they reminder us both of how little we actually know and of how many questions about this street remain unanswered: What led to the segmentation of the Casa del Bicentenario? Who was throwing *stercus* near the fountain? What kind of commerce unfolded under the awnings in the street? Who was depicted on horseback in front of the quadrifrontal arch? Who dedicated the statue? Who maintained it? Few streets from Roman antiquity furnish more answers than this one. That we do not know close to everything, however, is telling: this chapter pushes us to recognize the immense *density* of claims made on a street. In prominent spots such as this, many individuals and groups vied for attention, and virtually everything that transpired was loaded with consciously constructed meanings.

Second, focusing on a particular street casts buildings, civic and domestic, in a useful light. Close-range studies of individual structures often take a building's setting into account. But when the context itself is the focus and the structure takes a place in a supporting cast, our perspective begins to shift. For example, if we were to compare Herculaneum's Porticus to similar buildings in cities across Roman Italy, such as the Eumachia building on Pompeii's forum, it might well appear striking for its decorative richness. But considering it amid its urban environment underlines how much it stood out in the cityscape, disrupting passage, dominating sightlines, outclassing neighbors in scale and materials, and melding into existing buildings. Equally, assuming a streetgoer's perspective permits us to see claims, whatever their form, in conversation with one another as products of and responses to local circumstances rather than

---

[84] For the original publication of this house, see Maiuri 1958, 222–38. There is reason to doubt both Maiuri's assumptions and conclusions, however: Wallace-Hadrill 1994, esp. 122–129; Monteix 2010, 17–18. The tablets document the famous case of Petronia Justa, on which see Weaver 1991, 166–172; 1997, 69–71; Lintott 2002; Camodeca 2009, 34–36.

simply as manifestations of broader phenomena and genres. At the edge of Herculaneum's monumental center, we understandably witness a concentration on civic life and formal recognition, especially in the grand structures around the intersection of Cardo III and the *decumanus*. But the sensibility bled outward to Alficius the aedile and the compital altar, as well as to Ennychus and his fellow Augustales. Diverse strivers were drawn magnetlike to this zone and sought to make their mark. If the previous chapters have shown urban dwellers seeking to tame the street's innate tendency toward chaos and to establish hierarchies, then it is no surprise to witness that impulse running especially strong in a prestigious city sector.

The question remains, however, of how much these characteristics reflect streets generally and how much they result from the specific character and location of the *decumanus*. Our additional stories, especially the episodes surrounding the Casa del Bicentenario and L. Cominius Primus, make clear that dramas independent of the civic realm also brewed. Chapter 8, by focusing on a street well-clear of Pompeii's forum, offers a counterpoint to this chapter. As we shall see, the contrasts are not as profound as we might expect.

EIGHT

A CONTENTIOUS COMMERCIAL
STREET IN POMPEII

S OON AFTER BECOMING THE DIRECTOR OF EXCAVATIONS AT POMPEII, Vittorio Spinazzola embarked on an ambitious project – the disinterment of nearly a half-kilometer of the Via dell'Abbondanza.[1] Much of this beautifully monumentalized avenue had long been exposed, from the Stabian Baths to the forum. Where its western end joined the forum, the colonnade encircling the civic heart was interrupted to receive this key artery, the widest in the city. The one city block that had already excavated east of the Via Stabiana boasted a towering house façade and tightly packed shops; it gave Spinazzola hope that the Via dell'Abbondanza remained prominent and busy as it ran eastward through a city gate.

The *scavi nuovi*, or "new excavations," as they were called, show a distinctly revisionist mindset on Spinazzola's part. His posthumous publication spells out the excavation's goals – to investigate, preserve, and reconstruct façades and their decoration, inscriptions, windows, balconies, roofs, and the like; to link the *scavi vecchi*, "old excavations," with the city's amphitheater; to excavate stratum-by-stratum, recording objects' findspots and documenting discoveries with photographs; and to examine one tract of urban thoroughfare, rather than one house or city block[2] (Fig. 2). Spinazzola did not intend to excavate much

---

[1] Spinazzola 1953, xiii. His term lasted from July 16, 1910 to September 4, 1923. For more, see Delpino 2001; Hartnett 2011b.

[2] Spinazzola 1953, xii–xiii, 9–32 (esp. p. 20 for a statement about streets as an object of study). See also earlier discussion, "Streets Past and Present" in the Introduction.

beyond building façades, but, for the first time, considered the street and its facing architecture an appropriate locus of investigation. He was confident that the street alone would reveal much about Roman life.

If Spinazzola hoped to unearth a vivid streetscape, his first trench did not disappoint. Within days of beginning digging, workers revealed the intersection of the Via dell'Abbondanza and the Vicolo di Pacquio Proculo that is this chapter's subject. Their first major find was a streetside fountain fronting a still-vibrant mural (Figs. 79, 80). As they continued east, they discovered a tavern blanketed with painted electoral endorsements. Over the following months, excavation progressed across from the tavern, and a large house emerged, its lofty façade topped by a balcony and its frontmost portions carpeted with mosaic.[3] Pleased with these results, Spinazzola joined his trench with the *scavi vecchi* to the west (Figs. 79, 81). A sizable fullery surfaced on the street's south side, while shops with elaborate paintings of deities appeared on the north. Ultimately, what he found along the street proved so tantalizing that Spinazzola dug past some façades to unveil their interiors. Subsequent work in the mid-twentieth century unveiled the remainder of the southern blocks, but no one after Spinazzola has dug on the north. While we see the streetface, the buildings' deeper portions remain buried beneath meters of volcanic material. Nevertheless, thanks to Spinazzola's vision of what counts as meaningful – not just what was *within*, but what was *between* buildings – we can approach the corner of the Via dell'Abbondanza and the Vicolo di Paquio Proculo as a space pulsing with life.

CONTEXT OF THE CORNER

Our intersection lay along an important and busy conduit in Pompeii's urban network. The Via dell'Abbondanza served, from the time of the construction of the city's circuit wall in the fourth century BCE (and perhaps earlier), as one of two major roadways running east from Pompeii's center, through fortified gates, and onward to a fertile plain and the towns of Nocera, Nola, and Sarno.[4] Stairs and a drop in the roadbed restricted wheeled traffic on the street west of the Via Stabiana. No such hindrance lay to the east, and the difference suggests the contrasting character of this street's two segments. To the west, the road – adorned with a quadrifrontal arch, widened to monumental stature, and bearing few signs of bars – likely offered a ceremonial route between the forum

---

[3] Entries in the *Notizie degle Scavi di Antichità* provided preliminary reports on the progress of the excavation: Della Corte 1911a, 1911b, 1912a, 1912b, 1912c, 1912d; Spano 1912.

[4] This was apparently the third circuit wall around the city: Chiaramonte 2007. Scholarly debates simmer about what stood along this roadway's eastern stretch before the establishment of the Sullan colony in 80 BCE. The arrival of Roman colonists, the construction of the amphitheater, and the refurbishment of the Stabian baths gave city dwellers more reasons to tread the street's length. Zanker 1998, 61–77 summarizes these and other changes.

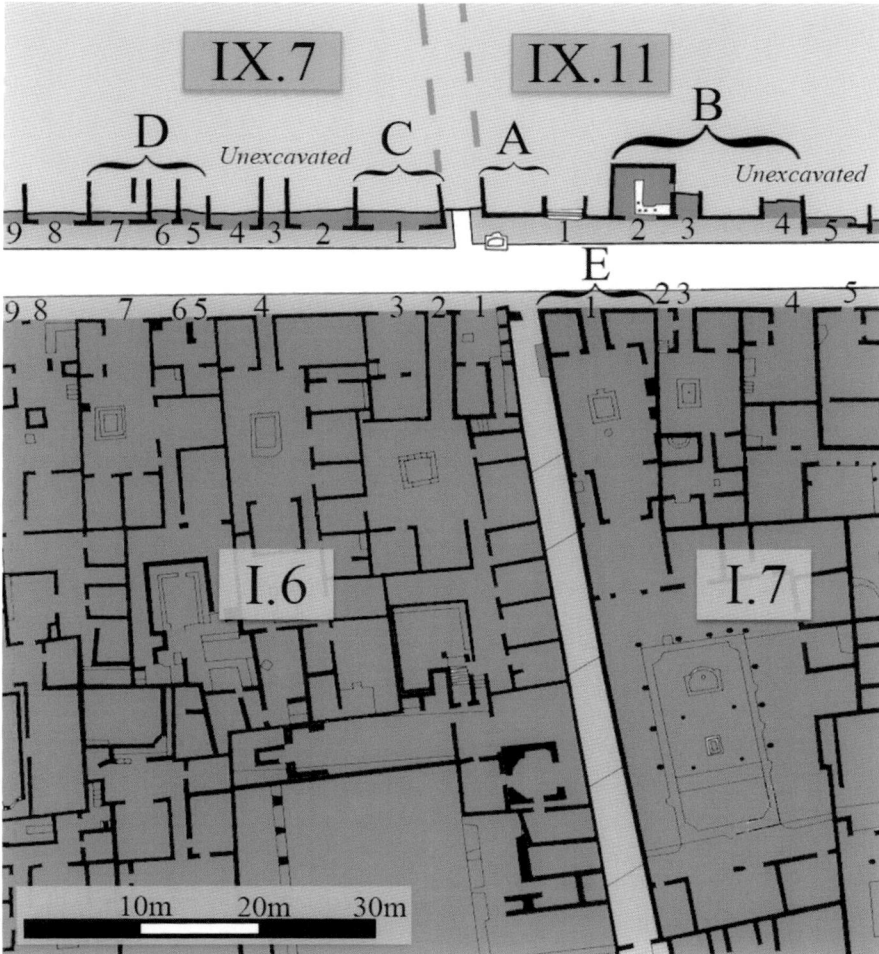

79. The stretch of the Via dell'Abbondanza studied in Chapter 8 boasts a number of fascinating properties and stories: a neighborhood altar, its murals, and the officials who curated those paintings (A); a bar, across whose frontage were painted electoral endorsements, apparently on the part of barmaids (B); frescoes of divine patrons – one a bit exotic, another very local – on the frontage of a possible feltmaker (C); a possible rival, in both cloth and iconography, just down the street (D); and the owner of a large house who sought to impress streetgoers and distinguish himself from his neighbors (E).
Drawing: author.

and the theaters with their cluster of temples.[5] To the east, by contrast, more than ten bars faced onto a similar length of roadway.[6] This stretch had fewer pretensions for elegance but plenty to attract regular traffic: a bakery and fullery, both among the city's largest; multiple residences, large and small; and an

[5] Tsujimura 1991, 65–68; Wallace-Hadrill 1995, 46–50; van Tilburg 2007, 136–144; Laurence 2008, 89–92.
[6] Ellis 2004.

80. Reconstruction of the view to the east along the Via dell'Abbondanza.
Drawing: James Kennedy.

eclectic admixture of commerce and industry, including an inn-for-rent and dyeworks. Measuring more than 8 meters in width, façade to façade, the street accommodated two-way wheeled traffic. Carts bearing heavy burdens had worn such deep ruts into the roadway that several intersections were repaved.[7]

This chapter's corner thus offers up a cross-section of quotidian circumstances along a heavily populated urban artery. A broad range of players – women with exotic names, a boastful house owner, a high-end textile merchant, slaves and freedmen wearing garments normally reserved for magistrates – vie for attention and, most interestingly, respond directly to one another. Their posturing, retorts, and squabbles played out before many: those running errands, bringing goods to market, scurrying to or from events in the theaters or amphitheater, fetching water, or making their way to cemeteries and suburban shrines along peripheral roads. This chapter examines five vignettes at this corner; collectively, they offer a rich document of urban

---

[7] Tsujimura 1991, 73–75. Other notable interventions included the installation of a fountain and water tower in the Augustan era. The fountain was placed half in the roadbed and half over the sidewalk at the southwest corner of insula IX.11, which forced wheeled traffic through a narrower passage and necessitated stone "bumpers" at its corners to prevent damage from passing carts. The tower obstructed enough of the alleyway between insulae I.6 and I.7 to make it impassable to wheeled traffic. After the water system was installed, concern for drainage led Pompeians to construct ramps or blockages where side streets met the southern side of the Via dell'Abbondanza. At this intersection, new curbstones were placed in the alley's opening, a masonry lintel was built above, and a wooden door was installed: Della Corte 1911a, 422–423; Tsujimura 1991, 85–86; Poehler 2012, 99–100. An architrave similarly spans the alleyway between insulae IX.1 and IX.7, one block to the west on the northern side of the Via dell'Abbondanza.

81. Reconstruction of the view to the west along the Via dell'Abbondanza.
Drawing: James Kennedy.

life, representing in tangible, human stories some sweeping dynamics of the
Roman world.

STORY ONE: AN ALTAR AT THE CROSSROADS

Pompeii's most prominent citizens constructed no public monuments at our
intersection. But a simple masonry altar, together with the murals surrounding it,
shows how a group of slaves or freedmen used a multiregistered appeal to seek
a social place akin the city's elite[8] (Fig. 80, Plate VIII). The mural is divided into
four sections. In the lower right, a painted garland encircles the actual altar, and
a snake slithers toward a small painted altar. Above, togate figures huddle around
another altar. Flanking them are two larger scale figures whose short tunics,
youthful faces, and rhyta identify them as Lares. On the left, a thin architectural
frame was painted around two stacked scenes. The lower depicted a *genius*, his
head covered for sacrifice, with more Lares. The upper register's twelve figures
are Olympian deities.[9] The altar's corner location, together with the snake and
sacrificers, make this monument recognizable as a shrine to the crossroads gods

---

[8] Although the simple forms of the altar made it an undistinguished cousin of marble specimens
in temple precincts, the roof projecting over the altar and its paintings, along with the sidewalk
paving of volcanic stone below them, helped to unite and to privilege this stretch.

[9] On this ensemble: Spinazzola 1953, 175–185; Fröhlich 1991, 335–337; Van Andringa 2000,
54–56.

82. In the upper-right scene of the mural above a compital altar (see Plate VIII), several neighborhood officials offer a sacrifice around a circular altar on the occasion of the *Compitalia*. Photo: Soprintendenza Speciale per Pompei, Ercolano e Stabia, Archivio Fotografico degli Scavi, C415.

(*compita*). Often called the *lares compitales*, these protective deities safeguarded and minimized the danger inherent in an urban contact point like an intersection. More than thirty similar compital altars have been found in Pompeii, and more certainly remain buried.[10] This is the grandest surviving ensemble.

Crossroad Officials

Let us start above the altar itself. The prime movers were neighborhood officials who sought legitimacy through the decoration they commissioned and the rites they performed here (Fig. 82). The four individuals' purple-bordered togas are pulled over their heads as they sacrifice at a cylindrical altar. One plays the double pipes, another pours a libation, and a third handles the entrails. To the altar's sides are affixed human-shaped figurines, while a pair of Lares bookend the scene.

Pompeii appears to have been divided, like Rome, into subdistricts, termed *vici*. A geographical and administrative unit, each *vicus* had a *compitum* as its religious focal point and was presided over by a group of officials, typically freedmen or slaves. Inscriptions document similar Pompeian officials (even if they deploy slightly different titles), and the fresco's sacrificing figures are certainly neighborhood submagistrates of this type. In Rome, where evidence is more abundant, their duties were multiple, ranging from administering directives from the aediles, such as distributing oil and grain, to controlling fires. A perquisite of the office was the ability to wear, and to be cremated in,

[10] Van Andringa 2000 with previous bibliography.

the *toga praetexta*, a purple-striped garment typically worn by official magistrates, decurions, and senators.[11]

Neighborhood officials especially enjoyed the spotlight at the annual winter rite of the *Compitalia*, when the crossroads *lares* were formally worshipped at the altar. Indeed, our officials unsurprisingly chose to depict the *Compitalia*'s climactic moment immediately above its actual location. Sources describe *vicus* households giving honey cakes at compital altars for the *Compitalia*. Although these are not discernable, the officials rendered the woolen objects that were hung by each household at the shrine or at their own thresholds.[12] Additionally, the officials listed their own names – Successus, Victor, Axclepiades, and Cosstas – in a small *tabula ansata* above the sacrifice.[13] Their desire for personal recognition at the altar was hardly unique because remnants of earlier painted scenes are visible.[14] In fact, the poor state of preservation here has revealed at least seven layers of paint covering this wall, and another representation of figures around an altar is detectable. In other words, successive office holders continually updated the painting and made it their own, even including their names here to personalize the image. Indeed, just around the corner, another painted inscription listed at least nine officials of the *Urbulanus* sector of the city.[15]

[11] Wards/neighborhoods at Pompeii: Van Andringa 2000; Laurence 2007, 39–45. An inscription dating to 47/46 BCE gives a title, *magistri vici et compiti*, that cements the bond between urban districts and their shrines: *CIL* 4.60. Later fragmentary evidence gives slightly different formulations: *mag[istri] lar[um]* in a dedicatory inscription (*CIL* 4.9807) and the word *vici* by itself atop a painted list of names near an altar (*CIL* 10.927). Duties: Dio 55.8.6–7; Suet. *Aug.* 40.2, *Claud.* 18.1–2. Toga praetexta: Livy 34.7.2–3; Cic. *Pis.* 8; Asc. *Pis.* 6–7C.

[12] Date and honey cakes: Dion. Hal. 4.14.3–4 (on which see Lott 2004, 30–37). Woolen objects: Festus (Paulus) 108L; 272–273L (shrine); Macrob. 1.7.34–35 (thresholds). See also Varro, *Ling.* 6.25. Only woolen dolls appear, emblematic of free members of a *familia*, not the woolen balls that were supposed to stand in for slaves. The *magistri vici* always appear as dedicators of carved stone altars in Augustan Rome (Lott 2004), and later epigraphical evidence shows that they paid for the cult as well as the monuments (*CIL* 6.449–452, 6.30960, 6.30958). For some doubts about the officials' agency behind all the altars at Pompeii, see Hasenohr 2003, 192.

[13] Spellings of two names are debated: Fröhlich (1991, 337) gives Sucuusus, Axcliipiadiis; Spinazzola (1953, 179) gives Concessus, Asclepiades. Other façade paintings at Pompeii also show officials: Fröhlich 1991, F17, F24, F29, F44, F66, F71. Lacking the standard *tria nomina* of citizens, these men were likely either slaves, who could be identified by one name alone, or freedmen, who for whatever reason (space, preference?) opted to represent themselves with only one name. Slave officials are documented at Pompeii: *CIL* 4.60, 4.7425. In Augustan Rome, only four of the ninety known *magistri/ministri vici* were definitely freeborn, whereas ten can be confirmed as slaves: Lott 2004, 92–94. Slaves' representation in the *toga praetexta* would have engendered still more criticism than a freedman's wearing of the garment Livy 34.7.3–10. Juvenal (10.103) apparently refers to a *vicus* official as a *pannosus aedilis*, "an aedile in rags." Cf. Cic. *Pis.* 8.

[14] One ghostly figure is apparent directly behind the altar and another on a smaller scale is detectable just to the right of the group.

[15] Layers: Spinazzola 1953, 179; Fröhlich 1991, 336–337; Van Andringa 2009, 172–173. Cf. Spinazzola 1953, 170 (five layers of paint at northeast corner of I.11). List of officials on the eastern face of insula IX.7: *CIL* 4.7807. Six seem to be freedmen, the other three slaves.

The depictions and lists of names were but reminders of activities that played out around the altar throughout the year. Local residents gave minor offerings (like the one found by Spinazzola) to implore the local *lares* to safeguard the neighborhood. Brides may also have left a coin during their weddings. On the *Compitalia*, however, the space became the principal stage of a wider observance. Our sources suggest that, as the gathered crowd craned their necks, the officials – clad in gleaming *togae praetextae* and accompanied by lictors bearing fasces – offered a sacrifice, perhaps of a pig that had been led around the neighborhood's boundaries. *Vicus* residents hung the woolen dolls in a ritual spotlighting the altar as a centripetal hub of neighborhood identity. Beyond the flute's airy notes, actors and mimes may have also performed in the street as part of this "solemn and sumptuous" festival. But even absent such events, the painting's details offered an idealized prompt of these occasions to passersby. The officials were proud of their position, which granted individuals outside Pompeii's political elite a rare public platform and allowed them to assume many of the trappings/duties and much of the visibility of magistrates.[16]

The August Lares

When the murals were uncovered in 1911, not all four panels were visible. In 78 or 79, someone whitewashed the lower left and painted an electoral endorsement.[17] When excavators cleaned off this final layer, three figures became visible: a central *genius* with a *toga praetexta* pulled over his head holds a cornucopia and pours a libation; flanking him, and on the same scale, are a pair of *Lares*[18] (Plate VIII). The officials, in depicting these three divine figures at the crossroads, chose a subject that resonated with developments in Rome's *vici* and that connected them to a grand imperial sphere.

In 7 BCE, Augustus reformed the neighborhoods of the *caput mundi*. He divided the city into fourteen regions, rehabilitated the *vicus* as an administrative division, and, most notably, granted statues of the *lares augusti* – "august/sacred *lares*," not

---

[16] Offering: Spinazzola 1953, 178. Cf. Spinazzola 1953, 169–170 (bones on altar at northwest corner of I.11). Brides: Varro apud Non. 531M. Lictors: Dio Cass. 55.8. Performances: Suet. *Aug.* 43.1. "Solemn and sumptuous": Dion. Hall. 4.14.3–4: μέγα . . . καὶ σεμνὸν. This might help explain the costs of the office: Patterson 2006, 252–263. Similar scenes may have played out at other times of the year, such as when flowers adorned the altar: Suet. *Aug.* 31.4 (perhaps on May 1 and June 27: Lott 2004, 115–116). Garlands were also a regular feature of *lares* veneration: Cato *Agr.* 143; Ov. *Fasti* 6.791–792; Pliny *NH* 21.11.

[17] CIL 4.7856: *C. Gavium Rufum II.V.I.D.O.V.F.* For the date: Franklin 1980, 61; 2001, 185–187.

[18] According to Fröhlich (1991, 337), this segment of the mural was likely commissioned by an earlier cadre of officials in the Augustan period. That it was later covered should not distract from the fact that generations of officials, while repainting the previous panel multiple times, recognized the continued appeal of the *genius* and *Lares* and retained this left side for the better part of a century.

"*lares* of Augustus" – to each neighborhood shrine.[19] If Ovid is any indication, then despite the adjective rather than the genitive, the new name resonated with the imperial figurehead himself: "The city has a thousand *lares* and the *genius* of the leader who handed them over, and the neighborhoods venerate the three spirits."[20] In this way, our Pompeian officials have layered different constituencies in the painting, celebrating their local prominence and affiliating themselves with the emperor's image, even granting it the most space in their composition.[21] The connection to Augustus was partly about gratitude because the *princeps* had emphasized their office, granting them and other individuals near the bottom of the social hierarchy prominence in their neighborhood and city. And the altar's context was also relevant because it stood directly behind the fountain, which dispensed water from an aqueduct that Augustus funded and that nourished Pompeii's baths, fed many of its houses, and allowed Pompeians to replace deep wells with streetside fountains as their primary water sources.

The Twelve Gods

Sheltered underneath the painted aedicula in the mural's upper left appear twelve representations of deities (Fig. 83). Alternating between men and women, their iconography identifies them, left to right, as: Jupiter, Juno, Mars, Minerva, Hercules, Venus, Mercury, Proserpina (?), Vulcan, Ceres, Apollo, and Diana. The group of twelve gods was encyclopedic in its evocation of divine authority. Yet subtleties in their selection and arrangement reveal an intentional curation for this location.

Another streetside representation of twelve gods adorned a façade near Pompeii's forum and sets our officials' choices in relief.[22] It featured, from left to right: Vesta, Diana, Apollo, Ceres, Minerva, Jupiter, Juno, Vulcan, Venus, Mars, Neptune, and Mercury. This selection of deities appears to be canonical; the same twelve "dined" at a *lectisternium* during the Second Punic War, for instance.[23] The ensemble evokes the Greek *Dodekatheoi*, but is more precisely identifiable as the Roman *dei consentes*, the supreme council that presided over human action, which was worshipped in sculpted form in the Forum

---

[19] Augustan reforms: Gradel 2002, 109–139 (esp. 121–125 for Pompeii); Lott 2004. Meanings of *augustus* in this sense: Lott 2004, 101–103.

[20] Ov. *Fast.* 5.145–146: *mille lares geniumque ducis, qui tradidit illos / urbs habet, et vici numina terna colunt.*

[21] There were few *genius* figures in Augustan Rome: Lott 2004, 110–114. However, at later periods and outside Rome, they grew in popularity: *CIL* 10.1269 (Nola), 10.3691 (Cumae), 10.4634 (Cales), 10.1581–1582 (Puteoli). Dedications to an imperial *genius*: *AÉpigr* 1989, n. 346a = Manganaro 1989: 191, n. 81; Lott 2004, 112;. See also Lott 2004, 206–209, 218–219.

[22] The painting is now largely known from drawings: *PPM* Suppl. 679, no. 131 (N. La Volpe, 20 December 1858) = Archivio Disegni della Soprintendenza Archeologica di Pompei 819; Fröhlich 1991, 330–331.

[23] Livy 22.9.10, 22.10.9. Another identical grouping: Enn. *Ann.* 1.62–63.

83. In the upper-left scene of the mural above the compital altar, a representation of the *dei consentes* took on a particular flavor by positioning deities with intensely-local relevance (Hercules, Venus, and Mercury) in the center.
Photo: Spinazzola 1953, Tav. D'Aggiunta 1.

Romanum.[24] Our officials' representation shuffles in two new divinities, but the other ten are the same, so it was also likely understood as the *dei consentes*. The order of the deities differs, and the change seems planned, since the other mural granted the Capitoline Triad primacy at the composition's center while, at our corner, Jupiter, Juno, and Minerva are kept almost as a unit, occupying first, second, and fourth positions, respectively. The middle position is occupied instead by Hercules, Mercury, and Venus – figures with intense meanings in Pompeii and along this street. After Vesuvius's eruption, Martial famously penned a mournful poem honoring Campania. He recalls Pompeii not by its name, but through its divine proxy and patroness, Venus.[25] The goddess's potency and primacy, particularly in the guise of Venus Pompeiana, will become still more apparent later in this chapter. Hercules is said to have founded Pompeii when he made a procession (*pompa*) here.[26] And Mercury, in addition to receiving formal cult in the city, was especially popular along this workaday street, where the god of commerce adorned at least six other façades, the most of any divinity.[27]

All in all, the contrast of the two paintings reveals that the neighborhood officials appealed broadly to divine authority while foregrounding the deities

[24] Dodekatheoi: *LIMC* III.646–658. Dei Consentes: Aug. *Civ.* 4.23.3; Sen. *Q Nat.* 2.41.2. Sanctuary: *CIL* 6.102; Varro *RR* 1.1.4; *LTUR* 2.9–10 ("Dei Consentes, Aedes," Nieddu).

[25] Mart. 4.44.

[26] Isid. *Etym.* 15.1.51; Serv. *A.* 7.662. As a further gauge of his local popularity, Hercules appeared at least nine more times in some form within the two excavated blocks to the south of our corner: Coralini 2001, 146–153, ns. 5–13.

[27] Mercury was worshipped alongside his mother Maia and later also Augustus. Inscribed plaques, given primarily by slaves and freedmen by decree of the decuriones and by the command of elected town officials, bear the imprimatur of civic authority in his worship: *CIL* 10.885, 10.887–888, 10.890. Mercury on façades: Fröhlich 1991: F6, F11, F14, F68, F69, F70. The trio of Hercules, Mercury, and Venus held a special place in the home of at least one neighborhood resident. Just down the street, in the impressive Casa di Trebius Valens (III.2.1), statuettes of the three deities were found, all on the same scale and apparently by the same artist: Spinazzola 1953, 281–296; Coralini 2001, 175–176.

with the greatest local appeal. In a way, this strategy characterizes the entire ensemble, which interwove multiple registers of identity, religion, and author- ity. The most cursory glance drew the composition together: throughout the three panels, figures hold *paterae*, have their heads covered, and strike similar poses. In this way, the neighborhood officials – relatively humble yet upwardly mobile – created a powerful hierarchy of images that funneled authority down from the heavens, through the imperial sphere and its figurehead, and into their very persons and city ward.[28] The mural offered a splendid backdrop for the officials' appearances, and, when they were absent, it offered an idealized aide- mémoire for those ceremonies, thus expanding the rare public spotlight to other times and audiences.

STORY TWO: BARMAIDS, POLITICIANS, AND NEIGHBORHOOD DRAMAS

A few meters east of the altar and just beyond an enormous entryway opened a one-room bar (IX.11.2) (Fig. 84). Its wide doorway illuminated a tightly packed interior: an L-shaped serving counter was topped by marble, inset with dolia, and furnished with a small oven.[29] Amphorae behind the counter were ready to accommodate the thirsty. The bar's small space – with 21 square meters of ground floor area, it was in the smallest 10 percent of Pompeii's taverns – may have pushed customers onto the sidewalk as they ate and drank.[30] Or they may have sought refuge from the tavern's heat and smoke by climbing the wooden stairs in the left rear corner.[31] A distinctive bronze tintinnabulum- cum-lamp hanging in the doorway drew streetgoers' eyes and ears. At its top was an ithyphallic pygmy who held a bell in his left hand and a razor-like object in his right. From his short perizoma emerged his giant member, itself topped by a smaller phallus. Additional bells and a lamp dangled from the pygmy's feet, scrotum, and phallus to make an arresting object that incited laughter and drove away the evil eye.[32]

About 5 meters further east, another broad doorway (IX.11.4) was tucked in front of a short spur wall decorated with a painting of several metal vessels, which may reflect goods on offer within (Fig. 85). As the spur wall closed off the structure's façade, it certainly drew welcome attention by standing directly in

---

[28] For a parallel effort on the part of a *magister vici* to appeal to local circumstances, see Lott 2004, 161–165.

[29] Original publication: Della Corte 1911a, 1911b. Recent work on these structures: Ellis 2004, 2008.

[30] Ellis 2008, figs. 14, 38.

[31] Opposite the stairs, in the back right, a doorway once connected to a hallway, which led in from the *fauces*-style doorway at IX.11.3.

[32] Spano 1912, 115; Conticello De Spagnolis and De Carolis 1988, 72; Clarke 2007, 69–81.

84. An archival photo shows the bar at IX.11.2 not long after its excavation. In the small space behind the marble-topped bar, numerous amphorae were resting against the wall. Many of the finds from the bar were put on display for visitors.
Photo: Alinari Archive, Florence.

the sightline of eastbound pedestrians.[33] The owner of this frontage endeavored to make it visually coherent. Unifying the streetface were a low roof projecting over the broad and distinctively paved sidewalk, as well as a façade-spanning red socle that replaced two different schemes of decoration.[34] The spur wall narrows the sidewalk's passable space to less than a meter, thus visually and spatially separating this stretch from other properties. Pedestrians passing through were inconvenienced by the construction, but it created an eddy in sidewalk traffic that could have hosted customers of the shop or the bar.

The façade and blockage constituted statements of dominion in themselves, but the messages painted on the wall offer more dramatic characters and events. Nineteen electoral endorsements are painted across this section of wall. They appear small and large, elegantly drawn and rather squiggly, and they span nearly a decade of electoral activity, to judge from the relative chronology of candidacies

[33] Fröhlich 1991, 337 (F67). A downspout embedded in the wall indicates that an upper story lay above, perhaps with small housing units for rent, although no traces remain today; the rest of the city block is buried. For the property's initial publication, see Della Corte 1911b, 1912a; Spano 1912.

[34] The sidewalk consists of a black *cocciopesto* dotted with small white stones and bits of colored marble. At the jambs to doorway IX.11.3, it is possible to see the earlier decoration: a black socle to the east and a white one to the west.

85. The bar at IX.11.2 was integrated into a street frontage that also featured a shop sign decorated with images of metal vessels standing in pedestrians' line of sight (right). Almost twenty painted electoral posters covered the streetface, although the only endorsers listed were women.
Photo: author. Courtesy: Soprintendenza Speciale per Pompei, Ercolano e Stabia.

that scholars have developed.[35] What draws our attention is not the posters' density (although they coat almost every surface), but the identities of those who made their mark on the street through them. Fourteen messages name no endorser, but the other five intriguingly list women as endorsers.[36] Four women individually support candidates: Maria, Zmyrina, Aegle, and Asellina.[37]

That the women endorsed candidates may initially seem odd since women were not able to vote or hold office.[38] But female endorsements represented a mildly widespread practice, with about fifty posters. Women's inscriptions follow similar patterns to endorsements by named men. They use the same formulae and abbreviations, are visually similar, and endorse candidates in comparable proportions. In other words, there is no "female way" to enter the political fray. But, even if female endorsements were not an unrelated phenomenon, our

[35] Pompeian electoral endorsements: Castrén 1975; Franklin 1980; Biundo 1996, 2003; Mouritsen 1999; Chiavia 2002. Relative dating: Franklin 1980, though see also Mouritsen 1988, 41.

[36] *CIL* 4.7862–7864, 4.7866, 4.7873.

[37] Immediately across the street, another poster lists Ismurna as an endorser, which could add another woman to our cast, but more likely is another spelling of Zmyrina: *CIL* 4.7221.

[38] *Dig.* 50.17.2: *feminis ab omnibus officiis civilibus vel publicis remotae sunt et ideo nec iudices esse possunt nec magistratum gerere nec postulare nec pro alio intervenire nec procuratores existere.*

corner nevertheless presents an interesting situation.[39] After all, Maria and her colleagues were visible participants in local politics – their posters were the only ones that listed an endorser here, and they also formed a large grouping within all the female endorsements citywide. These women seem especially engaged.

Who were they? We can say little with absolute certainty, but the women's names furnish a starting point. Three have a foreign character: Maria, now so common among Italians, signaled someone of Semitic origins; Zmyrina recalls the city of Smyrna on Asia Minor's Ionian coast; and Aegle is the name of several minor Greek mythological figures.[40] As such, the women's names broadly represented the eastern Mediterranean, a space rich with associations for Romans. Asellina, however, derived from Latin, meaning "little donkey," an affectionate diminutive.[41] Despite their diverse origins, the women constituted and occasionally presented themselves as an identifiable group. Their inscriptions mass at the tavern: three on its left doorjamb, one on its right, and another immediately across the street. Such proximity suggests an adherence to this location. Moreover, one inscription, to which I will return shortly, united the women. Supporting C. Lollius Fuscus for aedile, its last two lines read *Asellinas rogant nec sine Zmyrina*[42] (Fig. 86). The apparent use of the accusative for the nominative in *Asellinas* is unusual, but the plural verb implies a joint endorsement that is solidified by *nec sine Zmyrina*, "especially Zmyrina." Zmyrina endorsed another candidate at least six years before this inscription, thus marking a long-visible female presence on this street and its walls.[43] Ever since the bar's discovery, scholars have woven the various threads present into elaborate tapestries. They picture a bar owned by Asellina because she has the Latinate name and becomes the titular head of a collective presentation. And they imagine the women as foreign workers, possibly slaves, who furnished food, drink, and perhaps sex.

Our best guess is that the women indeed worked here. Whether their labor extended beyond serving food and drink, as we know happened elsewhere, is less clear.[44] In addition to the tintinnabulum, a graffito drawing of an ithyphallic figure offers the only other evidence for sexual activity, and phalloi are as much a sign of good fortune as a representation of sexual organs.[45] Our group's

---

[39] Savunen 1995, 1997, esp. 22–28; Bernstein 1988, 2007; Chiavia 2002, 197–204.

[40] E.g., Virg. *Ecl.* 6.20; Serv. *A.* 4.484; Pliny *NH* 35.40.

[41] *OLD*, s.v. *asella*.

[42] *CIL* 4.7863.

[43] Two of the women endorse the same candidate as well, C. Helvius Sabinus, for aedile: *CIL* 4.7862, 4.7866.

[44] *Dig.* 23.2.43.pr, 23.2.43.9.

[45] *CIL* 4.9097. The graffito was scratched into the red plaster just to the right of the door. It showed a nude man with ape-like features hurrying toward the tavern, arms spread wide, with a gigantic phallus. The image plays on shop-signs of Mercury, who appeared ithyphallic at the doorway of other shops, sometimes carrying a bag full of coins. Apparently in response to the drawing or some aspect of it, someone wrote *munificus*, "bountiful" or "generous," nearby.

86. This archival photograph shows several *programmata* that appeared to the left of the bar's entrance. Barely visible in the lower left is Zmyrina's endorsement of Gaius Julius Polybius. Clearer is a group backing of Gaius Lollius for duumvir, apparently by a group of women that included Zmyrina.
Photo: Soprintendenza Speciale per Pompei, Ercolano e Stabia, Archivio Fotografico degli Scavi, C436.

legal status is also in question; women – whether slave, free, or freed – use only their *cognomen* when endorsing candidates, so we lack helpful onomastic data, such as the *gentilicium* of a former owner that a freedwoman received upon manumission. It is not certain whether Asellina owned the bar or whether she was simply the most visible woman.

More than epigraphical records, the names reflected people whose daily lives unfolded here. Although the women's routine is largely lost, the material evidence allows us to stitch together some sense of their interactions. First, the space on the ground floor is very restricted, especially behind the counter, which likely put the women in close contact with one another and with customers, who may have spilled onto the extensive sidewalk or headed upstairs. The bar's wide entryway granted the women a view and perhaps knowledge of the neighborhood's workings. For instance, if the huge entryway next door preceded a sizeable house, then the women probably knew much about its activities by watching its denizens' comings and goings, by catching up with its dependents over a glass of wine, and by hearing sounds emanating from its doorway and courtyards. Similarly with a grand residence and smaller house across the street. In the latter, an industrious doorkeeper seems to have looked back across the street while carding wool.[46] In other words, even if these barmaids were stationary, they soaked in much.

At the same time, the bar's broad opening made Asellina, Aegle, and the rest visible to those passing along the busy thoroughfare. To newcomers, they might have offered suggestions on how to navigate the city's central alleyways or where to leave a cart for the night. For regulars at the fountain or altar, the women were a consistent neighborhood feature. Because of what they saw, what they learned from their substantial flow of customers, and their potential role as connectors among those diverse patrons, they likely had a strong involvement in and opinions about Pompeii's affairs. It is easy to imagine them having a stake in all matter of issues, both personal and civic – upcoming festivals, the rebuilding of the town, and not least the election of officials. Even if our elite literary sources disparage bars and bar-goers, we must remember both that such establishments were a ubiquitous urban feature catering to the daily needs of many and that the worlds of bars and townhouses were far from separate. They stood side by side, endorsements bridged the two spheres, and action from one could easily spill over into the other. Juvenal, for example, imagines a rich man trying to protect his household secrets by shutting his house, muting his slaves, and taking manifold other measures. But his efforts are in vain. In Juvenal's telling, the rumors head straight to the corner bar; the nearby barkeep soon knows all.[47] In sum, Maria and company could have dished out neighborhood knowledge with a side of legumes.

Such high–low interaction could be contentious, to judge from a series of events at our corner. One of the earliest posters still visible along this frontage was painted left of the bar's doorway (Fig. 86). In it, Zmyrina asked for support for Caius Iulius Polybius, a candidate for duumvir, whose name was famous enough to be given by its initials alone.[48] Such notoriety did not insulate his candidacy from a peculiar practice. Someone – we know not who – came along and white-washed Zmyrina's name out of the poster but left the remainder untouched.[49] This was not a one-off phenomenon, for one block away a *rogator*

---

[46] Two doorways fronted the smaller house. I.7.3 led across a travertine threshold to the dwelling's main residential space, whereas I.7.2, which connected to I.7.3, dead-ended underneath a wooden staircase. Wool-carding equipment was found here: Della Corte 1927, 7–15.

[47] Juv. 9.102–110 describes gossip spreading from a house to bar. See also *Apul. Met.* 1.7, 1.21. Gossip is also notorious around crossroads: Juv. 6.407–412; Hor. *Serm.* 2.6.50; Ov. *Am.* 3.1.18; Mart. 7.97.12; Prop. 2.20.22.

[48] He is also identified by his initials on two endorsements along this same façade: *CIL* 4.7872, 4.7888.

[49] *CIL* 4.7864.

named Cuculla also endorsed C. Iulius Polybius in the same election cycle and had her name covered.[50] Polybius's house stood two short blocks east on this very street, so the great man, surrounded by supporters, likely walked past both endorsements on his way to the forum for public business.[51] Did he not appreciate a barmaid's endorsement? Did he consider it below his station or harmful in some way?

The answers are not immediately clear, but the deletion of Zmyrina's name was not the end of the story. A few years later, her name appeared at least twice more at our corner.[52] In Pompeii's penultimate campaign season, a poster was painted just left of the bar's door and thus immediately above the cancelled endorsement. This is the endorsement of C. Lollius Fuscus that I mentioned earlier, the last two lines of which read: *Asellinas rogant / nec sine Zmyrina. Nec sine* literally means "not without," which emphasizes Zmyrina's inclusion; the phrasing thus intensifies the message: "and *especially* Zmyrina."[53] This sentiment appears to confirm what the location suggested; namely, that whoever painted this endorsement willfully reacted to the erasure of Zmyrina's name. You rub out our friend, the message says, and we will strenuously respond by pulling for someone else.[54] We can only imagine the reaction of whoever plastered over Zmyrina's name upon seeing this rejoinder. Zmyrina's colleagues, by contrast, seem emboldened: in separate endorsements, Maria and Aegle both supported Cn. Helvius Sabinus in the next election cycle. Overall, these endorsements, countertactics, and further responses show the stakes of self-presentation, as well as how a wide range of participants intersected in a sometimes-explosive push and pull.

STORY THREE: SHOP FAÇADES AND GODDESSES

The altar paintings and political endorsements were not alone in mixing different realms – human and divine, humble and elite. Across a narrow street from the altar, a wide doorway opens at the city block's southeast corner (IX.7.1; Fig. 87). Because the shop's interior remains buried, we do not know what wares it produced or offered. That it hosted felt-making, however, seems

---

[50] *CIL* 4.7841.

[51] It is difficult to know how much to make of Caius Julius Polybius's house, which presented a "throw-back" of sorts. Its façade, one of the most austere in the city, towered over the street with stucco molded to take the appearance of cut stone blocks; it presaged an impressive house rife with archaizing forms of decoration, such as a standalone vestibule boasting an unparalleled loggia: Leach 1993; Ciarallo, De Carolis, and Auricchio 2001.

[52] *CIL* 4.7221, 4.7863.

[53] The phrase *nec sine* is used in other endorsements as well: *CIL* 4.995, 4.1083, 4.6610, 4.7374, 4.7627, 4.7658, 4.9851.

[54] In fact, Lollius Fuscus appears to have had a special connection to whoever controlled this property, for the candidate's name appears no fewer than three times along this frontage, spelled out in some of the largest letters on the façade (*CIL* 4.7863, 4.7868, 4.7874).

87. Although only its front-most portions are excavated, the opening at IX.7.1 appears to have hosted work related to the felt industry. Above the entrance appear megalographic representations of the heads of deities, while flanking the doorway were paintings of Venus Pompeiana (left) and a procession in honor of Cybele (right).
Photo: Soprintendenza Speciale per Pompei, Ercolano e Stabia, Archivio Fotografico degli Scavi, C495.

likely because the *quactiliarii* (felters) endorse candidates on the right jamb.[55] The street-side furnace and an electoral endorsement from the *infectores* (dyers) suggest that a dye-works was located next door (IX.7.2).[56] The two businesses perhaps worked in concert or were owned by the same proprietor. A fascinating group of paintings surrounded the shop's entryway: megalographic paintings of four deities on the lintel, an ornately dressed Venus Pompeiana on the left jamb, and a procession of Cybele on the right. As we have seen, shops frequently boasted religious imagery because Romans perceived connections between commercial success and divine support. But this intriguingly catholic range of deities reveals the shop owner's careful associations, sheds light on events along this street, and opens a window onto local rivalries.[57]

[55] *CIL* 4.7809.
[56] *CIL* 4.7812.
[57] In general, on the façade and its paintings: Spinazzola 1953, 213–242; Fröhlich 1991, 182–184, 332–333; Clarke 2003, 87–94; Varone 2007, 129–131; Potts 2009.

Of all the paintings, those above the door and under the balcony's scalloped balustrade attracted the eye first. Each god's head and shoulders appear against a saffron background. Left to right, they are a youthful Apollo sporting a radiate crown of beams; the bearded Jupiter with a scepter (in the largest panel); Mercury with his customary caduceus and winged helmet; and Luna, the moon goddess, wearing crescent-shaped horns. Apollo and Luna both hold the whips they used to goad the horses pulling their chariots, solar or nocturnal. The paintings' position above the street's flurry made them visible, and their scale and color drew streetgoers' attention.[58] When streetgoers looked, how might they have "read" this display? They may have recognized the gods as four days of the week laid out in reverse order (Sunday, Thursday, Wednesday, and Monday).[59] But the paintings' commissioner probably had other intentions, too. Atop the façade, viewers could imagine a cosmological ensemble, framed by celestial bodies carrying the instruments of their movement and offering pride of place to the father of the heavens, Jupiter. Mercury, as we have seen, was oft revered along this commercial corridor, and he rightfully co-starred as financial guardian.[60]

A Procession of Cybele

On the right doorjamb the owner honored another deity and perhaps also celebrated a local ceremony that passed through Pompeii's streets (Plate IV). Here appeared a procession honoring the goddess Cybele, who was also known as *Mater De(or)um Magna Idaea* as the great mother of the gods from Mount Ida. Amid garlands, candelabra, and an altar, attention concentrates on the enthroned figure of Cybele. A turreted crown, representative of her role as a city protectress, tops her head. Next to her feet sits a pair of small lions symbolizing her place as a mistress of nature. The goddess bears a patera, a long golden sprig of vegetation, and a *tympanum*, or tambourine/drum. She is represented as a wooden statue, for she dwarfs the other figures and sits atop a *ferculum*, the litter borne in many Roman parades and festivals.[61] Those who ferry her through the streets stand alongside, their hands resting on canes.

Cybele was a relative newcomer to Italian soil, although she had long been revered in Phyrgia. When Romans were suffering at Hannibal's hands during the Second Punic War, the Sybilline books instructed them to bring Cybele's relic to Rome. In short order, a temple was built and games in the goddess's

---

[58] Viewers' attention would also have been drawn to the shop by the *gaze* of the deities, each angled slightly to turn toward the doorway's opening.

[59] Potts 2009, 61–63.

[60] Clarke 2003, 89, expresses a similar view. The following pages owe much to his interpretation.

[61] Abaecherli 1935–1936; Madigan 2012, esp. 39–42.

honor – the *ludi Megalenses* – joined Rome's festal calendar.[62] At Pompeii, our knowledge of the cult of Cybele beyond this painting is limited. Indications are that this was neither a mainstream cult nor a tiny sect. No temple has been found, and no surviving inscription mentions one.[63] A marble statue of Cybele's consort, Attis, near the forum, and three men's self-identification as *fanatici* provide hints of formalized worship.[64]

The cult of Cybele also aroused suspicion, particularly for the Roman elite. Literary sources fixate on priests of Cybele, the *galli*, who were reputed to imitate Cybele's consort, Attis, by castrating themselves in devotion to the goddess. The apprehension the *galli* engendered, according to Lucretius, sprung from the noise they aroused and the sight of the tools of their emasculation.[65] Dionysius of Halicarnassus, writing more than 150 years after the cult's introduction to Rome, still characterizes its rituals as foreign and describes the consequences:

> [The priests] carry the image in procession around the city, begging for alms (as is their custom), wearing medallions on their breasts and beating their tympana, while their followers play tunes on the flute in honor of the Mother of the Gods. But by a law and decree of the senate no native-born Roman walks through the city dressed in bright clothes, begging for alms or accompanied by flute players, nor worships the goddess with wild Phrygian ceremonies.[66]

Because of such misgivings, the ruling elite severely restricted the priests' movement around (and begging on) city streets, and Roman citizens were

---

[62] Arrival in Rome: Livy 29.11; 29.14; 36.36.3. The relic may have been a meteorite: Arnob. 6.11, 7.49. Temple dedication: Livy 36.36.4–5. Cic. *Har. resp.* 12.24 describes the games as particularly solemn and pious. Aristocratic families were especially active in the goddess's initial reception: Ov. *Fast.* 4.291–338, 4.347–348; Aur. Vict. *De viris illustribus* 46.1–3; Val Max. 1.8.11. See Vermaseren 1977a; Gruen 1990, esp. 5–33; Beard 1994.

[63] In Herculaneum in 76 CE, the emperor restored a temple of the mother of the gods that was damaged in an earthquake: *CIL* 10.1406.

[64] Vermaseren 1977b, 4.12, no. 24. *CIL* 4.2155. The discovery of nearly fifty artworks or graffiti identified with Cybele or Attis speak to the cult's diffusion through the city: Vermaseren 1977b, 4.12–28.

[65] Lucr. 2.618–623: "Taut drums thunder beneath their palms, and round about the curved cymbals crash; horns blast in a raucous strain, while the hollow pipe stirs the heart with its Phrygian tune. And they carry before them weapons, symbols of their mad frenzy, to strike awe into the ungrateful hearts and impious minds of the rabble with dread for the goddess's majesty." *Tympana tenta tonant palmis et cymbala circum / concava, raucisonoque minantur cornua cantu, / et Phrygio stimulat numero cava tibia mentis, / telaque praeportant, violenti signa furoris, / ingratos animos atque impia pectora volgi / conterrere metu quae possint numine divae.*

[66] Dion. Hal. *Ant. Rom.* 2.19.4–5: καὶ περιάγουσιν ἀνὰ τὴν πόλιν οὗτοι μητραγυρτοῦντες, ὥσπερ αὐτοῖς ἔθος, τύπους τε περικείμενοι τοῖς στήθεσι καὶ καταυλούμενοι πρὸς τῶν ἑπομένων τὰ μητρῷα μέλη καὶ τύμπανα κροτοῦντες· Ῥωμαίων δὲ τῶν αὐθιγενῶν οὔτε μητραγυρτῶν τις οὔτε καταυλούμενος πορεύεται διὰ τῆς πόλεως ποικίλην ἐνδεδυκὼς στολὴν οὔτε ὀργιάζει τὴν θεὸν τοῖς Φρυγίοις ὀργιασμοῖς κατὰ νόμον καὶ ψήφισμα βουλῆς. For a similar concentration on the group's sounds, see Juv. 6.511–516. Cf. Cat. 63.

apparently barred from joining the priestly order and from participating in self-mutilation.[67] By the time of this painting, reformation of the cult's practices had even drawn imperial attention.[68]

The fresco's commissioner and artist remained true to Cybele's worship but sought to quell any anxieties viewers felt about the goddess.[69] Streetgoers could discern a strict hierarchy and series of roles in the procession. At its front, the four identically dressed *ferculum*-bearers stand in position. Next come ten paraders whose leader, clothed in a white toga with red stripes, imitates Cybele's posture and attributes: his extended hands hold a green branch, a lamp-like object, and a gold patera. His two assistants in tunics complete the front row: one carrying the sacred *cista*, the other playing the pipes. Behind them, seven women wear colorful garments and hold items for the procession: a branch, a basket, tambourines, a vase, and cymbals. At the extreme left, two more musicians play the panpipes (*syrinx*) and cymbals. Separating them from the rest of the procession is an archaizing head of Dionysius. This deity had special relevance because he, too, was a once-rowdy god from Asia Minor who gained acceptance in Roman Italy and especially Campania.[70] On the whole, the depiction of Cybele's entourage is encyclopedic of the goddess's cult, representing all the technical aspects of the goddess's worship – music, drumming, *cistae*, sacrifice, and more. That said, the artist has taken pains to represent an organized affair that contrasts markedly with the frenzied scenes presented by textual sources. Nary a *gallus* can be identified, as the men wear mainstream garb, at least two have beards, and only the women and marginal musicians add a splash of color. Additionally, by showing the procession at rest, the fresco activates all the participants in their respective roles. So ordered is the representation that some scholars believe they can coordinate individual figures with cult offices known from inscriptions.[71] In other words, the fresco reassures Pompeians still wary of Cybele and her worshippers.

The painting may represent a procession that passed by this shop during celebrations of the goddess. We know of two possibilities from Rome. In late March, after several days of various activities (including carrying a recently cut tree, symbolic of the tree under which Attis, Cybele's consort, expired after castrating himself), worshippers processed Cybele's statue from her Palatine sanctuary to the river Almo for its ritual washing (*lavatio*). The other major cycle was the *ludi Megalenses* in early April, which culminated in the goddess's "birthday" (*dies natalis*). It featured a procession, theatrical

[67] Movement and begging limited: Diod. Sic. 36.13; Cic. *Leg.* 2.22.40. Prohibitions on Roman citizens: Val. Max. 7.6.

[68] *Dig.* 48.8.4.2; *Codex Iust.* 42.1; Vermaseren 1977a, 113.

[69] Here I largely follow the reading of Clarke 2003, 87–94.

[70] The archaic appearance of Dionysius, in fact, may have emphasized the god's long-standing stability in Pompeians' religious life – a place worshippers of Cybele hoped to attain.

[71] Spinazzola 1953, 233–237.

events, games at the Circus, and aristocratic banquets.[72] Ovid's description gives a sense of the parade:

> Let the heavens revolve three times on the eternal axis, let the sun hitch and unhitch his horses three times, and at once the curved Berecynthian flute will blow and the festival of the Great Mother of Ida will commence. The eunuchs will parade and strike their hollow tambourines, and the cymbal clashing on cymbal will jingle. Riding on the soft necks of her followers she will be carried through the city's streets amid their howling.[73]

The fresco certainly accords with this portrayal (though without the *galli*), while the branches carried by the retinue evoke the tree of the March cycle. They may have been a feature of the April cycle that go unmentioned, or the painting may have intentionally referenced multiple celebrations.[74]

Whichever celebration is shown, a procession like the one depicted would have made a powerful, if brief, impact at our corner.[75] Cymbals, drums, pipes, and ululations signaled the group's approach. As the parade neared, shoppers and vendors raised their voices, people squeezed onto the sidewalks, wine porters sought alternate routes, and kids scrambled atop the fountain for a better look. In sum, the street, its space, and its sensory environment were taken over by a restricted group of participants. Paraders, specially outfitted for the occasion, likely felt the spotlight. The *ferculum*'s weight lightened for its bearers, musicians played lustily, and the chief officiant reveled in appearing on an equal sartorial plane with civic officials. Similarly, the parade also forged a group identity. From their lining-up to the parade's conclusion, Cybele worshippers – like other groups that paraded through the streets (families, *collegia*, leading politicians and their supporters, etc.) – constituted a recognizable unit both to others and to themselves. The procession also extended Cybele's ritual space, momentarily rendering the route sacred to the goddess and avoiding the "symbolic atrophy" of immobile sculptures anchored in the forum or elsewhere.[76]

---

[72] On these March and April events, see Alvar 2008, 282–293.

[73] Ov. *Fasti* 4.179–187: *Ter sine perpetuo caelum versetur in axe, / ter iungat Titan terque resolvat equos, / protinus inflexo Berecyntia tibia cornu / flabit, et Idaeae festa parentis erunt. / ibunt semimares et inania tympana tundent, / aeraque tinnitus aere repulsa dabunt; / ipsa sedens molli comitum cervice feretur / urbis per medias exululata vias.*

[74] A strict reading of the painting suggests the procession's passage from left to right – that is, from west to east. But if events in Pompeii mimicked those in Rome, then the parade would thus be shown moving *away* from the theater district where the *ludi Megalenses* were supposed to unfold. To the east do lie both the amphitheater, which could have offered a suitable venue, and access points for the Sarno river, if the *lavatio* were performed at Pompeii.

[75] That the parade is depicted as halted in its course puts emphasis on specific points along the route, such as the shop, rather than upon the movement of the goddess and her retinue past them.

[76] Symbolic atrophy: Stewart 2003, 152.

The painting and real processions infused one another with meaning. When a parade made its way by, then the fresco, as a visual echo of an actual event, was legitimized. And procession participants who saw the painting could feel a special sense of reception, secure of a fellow worshipper's presence and devotion. Throughout the year, the image created anticipation for viewers, offering them a clue for what they would see and hear. Similarly, after the procession passed, the depiction shaped viewers' memories. If the procession had an impact on the scale our sources describe – with onlookers frightened and awestruck – then the painting helped to sustain reverence and wonder beyond the event.

Venus Pompeiana

On the doorway's left side and thus opposite Cybele's procession, the shop owner commissioned a fresco of an intensely local divinity, Venus Pompeiana (Plate IX). The patron goddess of the city stands about three times Cybele's size and is framed by flying cupids. Each extends emblems of triumph: one a vegetal crown, the other a palm. Venus's right hand grasps a branch while her left holds a scepter and rests on a rudder, both of gold. She is dripping with finery: a tiara bearing a diadem, pearl earrings, and numerous rings are visible, while gold edges her heavy purple tunic and mantle. Her barefoot son Eros stands on a platform at her right, wings extended and hands gripping a mirror.

In depicting Venus, the owner presented a goddess with persistence and increasingly important presence in Pompeii. Venus's Samnite-era cultic identity was strong enough that linguistic fossils from Oscan – especially the epithet *fisica* – continue to appear in Latin inscriptions honoring the goddess.[77] When Sulla established the Roman colony, Venus's name was written into the city's new moniker (*Colonia Cornelia Veneria Pompeianorum*), and, in a fitting location for a goddess overseeing maritime affairs, a huge temple to Venus soon loomed over the Bay of Naples in the city's southwestern corner.[78] As time went on, the goddess gained additional shades of meaning, particularly when Augustus claimed Venus Genetrix as both an ancestress and a national protectress.[79] In early imperial Pompeii, the city's most prominent public "priestesshood" was that of Venus.[80] After seismic activity shook the city in the 60s CE, Nero and his wife Poppaea Sabina apparently gave jewelry and gold to Venus.

---

[77] The goddess is referred to as Venus Fisica or Venus Fisica Pompeiana: Schilling 1954, 383–388; Carroll 2010, 96. The epithet *Fisica* may represent connections to Mefitis, a goddess worshipped in pre-Roman Southern Italy: Coarelli 1998; Coarelli, Forglia, and Foglia 2002, 88–89.

[78] Carroll 2010.

[79] Zanker 1988, 195–223.

[80] It is notable for the depth of her pre-Roman legacy that, even into the first century CE, women from the foremost noncolonist families held this position: Castrén 1975, 70–72, 96–98; Franklin 2001, 33–37.

Poppaea is said to have sent a beryl (a type of crystal), a drop-shaped pearl, and another large pearl, while Nero supposedly came with an amazing weight of gold, one piece of which – a lamp – may have been identified.[81] The connection between Pompeii and Venus was strong enough that Martial, mourning Campania after Vesuvius's eruption, could refer to the city by its divine shorthand, *Veneris sedes*, the "dwelling spot of Venus."[82]

In sum, the owner here portrayed a goddess with resonances simultaneously indigenous, local, and imperial. And our representation could have evoked those echoes: the rudder chimes with Venus's particular Pompeian location and function, viewers may have seen an Augustan element in her matronly proportions, and the pearls and abundant gold evoke imperial visits and donations. (The emblems of victory afforded by the cupids could even reference Venus Victrix, the aspect of the divinity favored by Sulla.) The commissioner displayed an image of the goddess that invited reverence on its own and also drew a favorable appraisal of the goddess's pendant, Cybele. Both hold branches and were celebrated in April festivals of fertility and renewal.[83] Through her mural crown, Magna Mater was recognized as a protective city goddess. If the appearance of Cybele continued to inspire trepidation, this figure of Venus offered viewers comfortable reassurance.

Venus Pompeiana's presentation is not always so richly ornamented, which raises questions about her appearance here.[84] There may be overlapping explanations. First, both Venus's purple garments and Eros's dark green mantle hang in heavy folds that may reflect a dense material. If this shop indeed housed felt-making, then the image (and also that of the beautifully adorned Cybele) could serve to advertise the goods produced (or on offer) here.[85] Second, Spinazzola argues on the basis of Venus's abundant jewelry that, as in the Cybele panel, streetgoers here saw representations of statues of Venus and Eros, which were ritually dressed and adorned by Pompeians and paraded through the streets on special occasions, not unlike processions the great excavator saw in Naples and Sorrento.[86] In his reading, the figures' elaborate clothing and ornament are gifts

---

[81] Temple disrepair: Carroll 2010, 87–89. The gifts of the imperial household are known from graffiti in the Casa di Julius Polybius: Giordano 1974, ns. 4–5. n. 4: *Munera Poppaea misit Veneri sanctissimae berullum helencumque; unio mixtus est.* n. 5: *Caesar ut ad Venerem venet sanctissimam ut tui te vexere pedes caelestes Auguste millia milliorum ponderis auri fuit.* Gold lamp: De Caro 1998.

[82] Mart 4.44.5.

[83] Potts 2009, 61–62.

[84] For instance, in the depiction of the twelve gods across the alley, she wears a veil and no discernible jewelry. A richly ornamented female bust in the Casa di Maius Castricius (VII.16.17) has been identified as Venus Pompeiana: Varriale 2006, 439–442.

[85] A view shared by Kellum 1999, 289.

[86] Spinazzola 1953, 216–217. He also contends that the base on which the "statue" of Venus is mounted is made of wood and could have been carried by worshippers. The green ground on which Venus stands, however, is drawn impressionistically with broad brush strokes and thus does not cohere with the careful execution on which Spinazzola's hypothesis depends.

presented by reverent worshippers. If Spinazzola is correct, then the shop owner's image conjures up another civically important activity on Pompeii's streets and along the Via dell'Abbondanza. Unfortunately, while groups calling themselves the *Venerii* and *Veneriosi* were present at Pompeii, Spinazzola's suggestion otherwise stretches the evidence.[87] The final possible explanation for the overwhelming finery blends spatial context, commercial activity, and religious allusion by looking to another painting of Venus Pompeiana that decorated the façade of a potential rival felt-maker just down the street. We continue westward toward that property.

STORY FOUR: A CONCATENATION OF CLOTH

Next door to the Cybele-Venus shop, as we noted, opened another broad shop-style doorway (IX.7.2). The little unearthed beyond its façade deepens our sense of this corner's character. Just inside its opening squats a heavy cylindrical furnace containing a deep leaden cauldron. An electoral poster on the adjacent doorjamb offers the support of the *infectores* (dye workers).[88] Dying wool or cloth could be a messy process that involved soaking material in large vats of softening agents before immersing it in cauldrons of dye. The sidewalk-side fire thus lends a sense of heat and possibly also smell to our street. Pedestrians approaching the shop may have spied wisps of smoke and crossed the street on the stepping stones just to the west, or the furnace's eye-catching decoration may have warned them off: on its front, a vertical phallus dwelled within a small temple (whose acroteria are also phalloi), while a horizontal phallus appeared on the side.

Beyond reminding us of sensory phenomena, the dye shop also speaks to the social dynamics among neighborhood workers. While the *quactiliarii*, the felt-makers, endorsed candidates next door, the *infectores* do the same here. Across the street and about 15 meters to the west stood one of Pompeii's largest fulleries (I.6.5–7). Once a house with an atrium at its core, the industrial *fullonica* dedicated its space to cleaning dirty cloth and preparing new cloth for sale.[89] (Since fulleries were renowned for their stench, we can probably add the odor of urine to the corner's sensory inventory.)[90] All the fullers (*universi fullones*) advocate for a candidate along the façade, thus joining their cloth-working neighbors.[91] Group endorsements are widely attested at Pompeii, and scholars usually mine them for lists of occupations. What comes across clearly here is how much individuals identified with their work and their fellow

---

[87] *Venerii: CIL* 4.1146; *Veneriosi: CIL* 4.7791.
[88] *CIL* 4.7812.
[89] The so-called Fullery of Stephanus: Flohr 2009.
[90] Smells of fulleries: Plaut. *Asin.* 907; Mart. 9.63; Suet. *Vesp.* 23.
[91] *CIL* 4.7164.

laborers and how that labor was both specialized and tightly packed because related but distinct segments of the cloth industry voiced their support separately on adjacent segments of wall.[92] But such proximity may also have fueled conflicts among those sharing the same business.

Verecundus, Cloth for Sale, and Dueling Goddesses

Immediately opposite the fullery was yet another establishment linked to cloth manufacture, processing, and sale. Streetgoers could recognize its three-doorway façade (IX.7.5–7; Fig. 88) as a single unit from indications below their feet to above their head.[93] A travertine threshold and a pair of eye-catching frescoes singled out the westernmost opening to form a fascinating and potentially combative ensemble.[94]

On the doorway's narrow left jamb appears a painting in two registers (Fig. 89). An electoral *programma* occupies most of the upper panel. It is Cuculla's endorsement of C. Julius Polybius that was whitewashed, just as Zmyrina's was at the bar.[95] Since the figural painting below occupies a relatively small space, the inscription was likely part of the painting's initial design, which raises more questions about why Cuculla's name was stricken. The panel's remainder shows Mercury standing on a temple pronaos, dressed in elegant winged shoes, wearing a cape, and holding his caduceus. The patron god of commerce also grasps a cloth sack full, presumably, of coins. In the lower register, the scene shifts to earthly concerns and a scene of exchange. A woman seated behind a counter exhibits merchandise to a customer seated at a high-backed bench. Holding shoes in her hands, the saleswoman looks out over a spread of objects including glass cups and additional shoes. A second table in the foreground carries multicolored bundles of cloth as well as still more shoes and glassware. The proliferation of goods suggests a successful transaction in idealized circumstances. A comfortable customer surveys a bevy of goods similar to those worn by Mercury in the register above.

The right jamb repeats the two-register configuration (Fig. 90). In the upper scene, Venus Pompeiana reappears — and she bears a striking resemblance to the image five doors to the east. Eros again holds a mirror at her side; the goddess

---

[92] Joshel 1992.

[93] Along the street, a coherent set of curbstones fronted the façade. They bordered a sidewalk distinguished from its neighbors by marble chips set into a black *cocciopesto*. Additionally, stones set flush into the walkway spanned its width to frame the sidewalk decoration. Similar blocks elsewhere are thought to have marked property lines: Saliou 1999, 169–171. The structure's eastern neighbor projects into the sidewalk, thus strengthening the argument. Finally, a roof projecting low over the frontage spanned the three doorways to tie them together.

[94] On the façade in general: Spinazzola 1953, 189–210; Angelone 1986; Fröhlich 1991, 172–174, 333–335; Clarke 2003, 105–112; Varone 2007, 126–128.

[95] *CIL* 4.7841.

88. At IX.7.5–7, another property apparently dedicated to cloth manufacture and sale opened three doorways to the street under a low-slung roof.
Photo: author. Courtesy: Soprintendenza Speciale per Pompei, Ercolano e Stabia.

cradles her rudder and scepter, and she is bedecked with jewelry. As down the street, palm- and crown-bearing cupids fly in from the sides. In this ensemble, however, the goddess's chiton and mantle are a bright bluish-green, and she wears a mural crown confirming (if there were any doubt) her protection of Pompeii. Moreover, a team of elephants pulls her atop a quadriga that takes the shape of a red-prowed boat, another symbol (like the rudder) of her maritime connections. Venus is joined by Fortuna, who stands atop a globe and herself holds a rudder, and by a *genius*, who pours a libation; both clutch cornucopias.

Below the divine realm, the commissioner placed a companion to the sales scene – a view of the "factory floor" that generates the final products on offer. At the center, four bare-torsoed workers roll animal fibers in coagulant to bind them into felt near a wood-fired furnace.[96] (Their work surface funnels excess binding agent back into the heater.) To the sides, three additional figures sit at low tables preparing wool for spinning by drawing it through combs fastened to columns running through the tables. One last personage occupies the panel's extreme right. A male figure holds up the finished product – a light brown garment with reddish-purple stripes – while wearing a hooded cloak and felt

[96] If a passerby were still confused, then an electoral poster running through the register might have offered clarification. In it, the *quactiliar(ii)*, or felt-makers, endorse Vettius Firmus for aedile: *CIL* 4.7838.

89. To the left of doorway IX.7.7, a two-register painting featured Mercury on a temple porch and a sales scene.
Photo: Soprintendenza Speciale per Pompei, Ercolano e Stabia, Archivio Fotografico degli Scavi, C499.

shoes (both of which might have been for sale here). A passerby likely concluded that this man was responsible for the product, first, because his standing position and dress distinguish him as the overseer of the workers and, second, because his name, Verecundus, "modest," was written in small letters below. If viewers, like modern scholars, understood the seated woman in the sales scene to be his wife, then both figures exhibit the merchandise as they bracket the lower scenes.

It is fascinating to take stock of Verecundus's self-presentation. Elite texts show disdain about close associations between "proper" Romans and the realms of trade, commerce, and production, but the evidence on the ground suggests that figures like Verecundus had few such qualms. In fact, the lower register emphasizes both his products' range and his operation's scale. Wool combers and felt pressers represent two initial steps in different industrial processes, and they invite viewers to reflect on the other stages (and workers) involved in producing the two materials, such as flattening, cutting, sewing, and fashioning the felt into its final product and forming yarn from the wool, weaving it into cloth, dispelling impurities, and then adding color. In other words, Verecundus might have represented additional felt- or wool-creation steps, but it would have been at the cost of showing fewer workers. A painted inscription at the property's east end mentions a linen tunic with threads of gold, *tunica lintea aur(ata)*, which could be another piece of merchandise on offer from Verecundus. It thus potentially expands the range and elevates the price of the shop's goods.[97] Additionally, a graffito inside a house four blocks away (V.2.16) seems to mention the proprietor again, now with his full *tria nomina* and a title: *M. Vecilius*

97 *CIL* 4.9083.

90. On the right jamb of IX.7.7 appears, in the upper register, a painting of a bejeweled Venus
Pompeiana drawn in a red-prowed ship by four elephants; she is accompanied by a cupid and
flanked by the goddess Fortune and a *genius* figure. In the lower register is a representation of
a shop floor, showing wool-carders, felt makers, and the proud owner, labeled "Verecundus,"
holding up the finished product.
Photo: Soprintendenza Speciale per Pompei, Ercolano e Stabia, Archivio Fotografico degli
Scavi, C501.

Verecundus vestiar(ius).[98] *Vestiarius* would suit Verecundus's self-presentation
well since it broadly encompasses dealings in cloth, both in manufacture and
sale.

[98] *CIL* 4.3130. Another graffito along a street (*CIL* IV.3103) seeks to denigrate some
Verecundus by saying that he performs a sexual act.

Although the lack of excavation limits our knowledge of what took place inside the building, it is probably no accident that the sales scene was painted in closest correspondence to the fanciest doorway, while the manufacture scene appears closer to doorways with simpler thresholds. If Verecundus took a spot on the sidewalk or hawked his goods and proclaimed their variety and crafts-manship, he did so against a backdrop dedicated primarily to divinities. Mercury's bag of coins and the cornucopias of Venus's flanking figures helped boast his wealth and, through their garments, probably also its source. There is no reason to doubt Verecundus's gratitude to them, but the presentation of Venus Pompeiana – the elevated centerpiece drawn on her elephant quadriga and decked out in sumptuous garments, precious metals, and gems – strikes a hyperbolic note. An attentive or repeat viewer of this frontage could hardly have missed its similarity to the Venus Pompeiana five doors down (Plate IX).

Because both spaces conceivably shared an involvement in felting, viewers did not merely see two depictions of Venus but dueling images of the city's patroness, with one responding to and attempting to outdo its neighborhood rival. Evidence for the relative dating of the two Venuses is inconclusive, but, whichever came first, the other may well offer a response to its rival.[99] On the one hand, the repetition of Venus Pompeiana certainly speaks to her image's power, both as the object of reverence and as a visual vehicle for self-aggrandizement. Cloth merchants, like the neighborhood officials who also depicted her, venerated the city's patroness and cultivated connections with her. Registers of life, from the divine heavens to the quotidian shop floor, become conflated and exist almost seamlessly on the same walls. On the other hand, as part of that process, we here witness a further strategy of streetward display, namely reusing a neighbor's powerful image and attempting to outstrip it. In a space where getting attention and outshining others was critical, even the city's gods were not above the iconographical fray.

STORY FIVE: DOMESTIC EXCLUSION AND PERSONAL CLAIMS AT THE CASA DI PAQUIUS PROCULUS

Across the Via dell'Abbondanza from the bar staffed by Asellina and her colleagues, a tall doorway loomed over those passing along the street (I.7.1; Fig. 91). Strong and severe cubic capitals carried an architrave, above which hung a roof spanning the house's frontage and towering 5 meters above the sidewalk. On a street where low-slung balconies and jetties loomed over pedestrians before nearly every building, and where people came and went

---

[99] *Contra* Fröhlich 1991, 333–335. An electoral endorsement of Paquius Proculus was apparently partially covered when the socle below the depiction of Venus Pompeiana at IX.7.1 was painted, but that act need not have been contemporary with the creation of the goddess above.

91. The façade of the Casa di Paquius Proculus (I.7.1) – with its taller elevation, paucity of doorways, and cubic capitals – stood in contrast to its neighbors along the Via dell'Abbondanza. Electoral posters once covered its façade, while an endorsement in verse was painted on the inside face of the western pilaster.
Photo: author. Courtesy: Soprintendenza Speciale per Pompei, Ercolano e Stabia.

through many closely packed doorways, this structure's lofty façade, pierced by one stately doorway, signaled that it was a different realm.[100]

Exterior Aspect and the Visibility of P. Paquius Proculus

Amid a wall crowded with electoral posters, streetgoers could read the name of this house's apparent owner in the city's last years – P. Paquius Proculus – in three different places. The largest and most beautifully drawn *dipinti* flanked the doorway and splashed Paquius's name across the façade. On the right, his *vicini* or neighbors endorsed him for duumvir, while a huge endorsement on the left broke from endorsements' conventional brevity to spell out his worthiness: *dignus est*, it declares.[101] Paquius is the only named endorser on the façade, and other posters hint at well-forged political ties. In particular, one declares the support of the *sanctus ordo*, presumably the sacred rank of the decurions, for M. Epidius Sabinus for duumvir and warmly greets T. Suedius Clemens,

[100] On this house: Ehrhardt 1998.
[101] CIL 4.7197, 4.7208. CIL 4.7819, discovered near the shop decorated with the procession in honor of Magna Mater, is another endorsement of P. Paquius Proculus by his *vicini*.

an agent of the emperor Vespasian, as *sanctus iudex*, sacred judge.[102] Paquius presumably enjoyed being publicly associated with heady company.

Paquius's epigraphic visibility along this street extended beyond his house. Whoever passed through our corner encountered Paquius's name, often at a large scale, in at least eight other spots. And these formed just a fraction of the nearly 100 times his name appeared in electoral posters citywide.[103] Two points can be made: first, that any streetgoer paying attention to the house façade could easily deduce that Paquius ran in Pompeii's highest circles. Indeed, although streetgoers could not see them, graffiti within the house suggest his contacts stretched still higher: Nero or his eponymous month is named at least five times, and a financial official from the imperial household named Cucuta (or Cicuta) is mentioned three times.[104] Second, if others in the neighborhood – like the altar's officials, the barmaids, or Verecundus – were pleased to have their names listed, Paquius's epigraphic presence both at his house and through the city reflected his greater position. While their impression was locally important, his impact was both profound at this corner and widespread throughout the city's streets.

Looking In: Domestic Display and Social Exclusion

Even when Paquius himself was not grabbing the spotlight by giving games or by parading to the forum amid a retinue of supporters, his house offered a striking stand-in. Whoever was enticed by its exterior to peer in soaked up a resplendent display (Fig. 92). The polychrome mosaics carpeting the atrium impressed with their sheer size, while bright painting and stuccowork pilasters contributed the house's stateliness. But streetgoers could also look deep into the house to the lush peristyle garden, which included an outdoor dining area underneath a pergola and two small pools, one with jetting water.[105] In other words, amid the hot, bright, and dirty street, people making an offering at the altar, grabbing a snack at the bar, or simply shuffling along gained a view into a splendid and potentially tempting setting.

I argued in Chapter 5 that those who looked into a house but were not invited to enter received a message of social exclusion. At Paquius's house, the

---

[102]   *CIL* 4.7203. See Franklin 2001, 156–163 for more on M. Epidius Rufus and T. Suedius Clemens. Only *rogator*: *CIL* 4.7210, which registers support for L. Popidius Ampliatus, a candidate for aedile who lived along with his civically active family in a monumental house (the Casa del Citarista, I.4.25) two blocks to the west. Two amphorae discovered within I.7.1 seem to reference Paquius's name: *CIL* 4.9333–9334. Mouritsen 1988, 182, n. 60.

[103]   Mouritsen 1988, 144–145. One inscription from the amphitheater claims that all the Pompeians (*universi Pompeiani*) brought him to office: *CIL* 4.1122.

[104]   Nero: *CIL* 4.8064, 4.8078a, 4.8092, and perhaps also 4.8095, 4.8119. Cucuta: *CIL* 4. 8065–8066, 4.8075. For more, see Magaldi 1939, 129–132; Franklin 2001, 106–109.

[105]   Jashemski 1979, 2.37.

92. A glance through the doorway of the Casa di Paquius Proculus (I.7.1) presented a view of distinct luxury and opulence.
Photo: Erich Lessing/Art Resource, New York.

mosaic paving of the *fauces* made this point still more clearly. The dwelling's double doors were recessed about 1 meter from the sidewalk and façade, thus requiring anyone wishing to enter to step into a liminal position between outside and inside. Here, a viewer confronted a tri-color mosaic of a dog chained in front of a set of double doors (Fig. 93). The immense canine spans the entire mosaic doorway and sits on his haunches, as though prepared to pounce. An open mouth reveals sharp teeth and a red tongue, but a chain linking his red collar to the door leaf restrains him.[106]

Viewers may have recoiled at the sight of the huge dog. When the narrator of Petronius's *Satyricon* first enters his host's house for a dinner, he suddenly lurches back and nearly breaks his leg when he mistakes a painting of a dog for the real ticket. Paquius's example lacks the *cave canem* inscription described in the novel and visible in the *fauces* of the Casa del Poeta Tragico (VI.8.5), which also depicts a menacing yet chained dog.[107] Though the novel plays the episode for laughs,

---

[106] Dating of the mosaic program varies considerably: Ehrhardt 1998, 141–142 (before 30 BCE); Clarke 2007, 54 (third style); Blake 1930, 122–123 (ca. 50 CE); Dexter 1975, 9 (perhaps fourth style). The right leaf stands open, but curiously opens outward, whereas almost all front doors at Pompeii open inward, including the real one here.

[107] Petr. 29. Clarke 1979, 7–14. Paintings of dogs: I.12.3; IX.2.26.

93. Immediately inside the threshold of the Casa di Paquius Proculus (I.7.1), viewers encountered a mosaic of a dog chained to double doors.
Photo: Alinari Archive, Florence.

neither the words nor the images suggest a playful reading. Moreover, visitors
might have heard barking as they encountered the mosaic, for the remains of an
actual canine were identified near Paquius's doorway.[108] The mosaic's setting
also upped the effect, for the artwork depicted the very space where it was
located: the area immediately in front of the house's double doors. The martial
implements depicted on the mosaic's door leaves – a shield and spear on the left,
a double axe on the right – could not have eased the trepidation of viewers who
gazed down. Although a colorful mosaic traversing the end of the *fauces* hinted at
a mythological realm of centaurs and wildlife deeper within the house, its canine
companion – in this dance of invitation and exclusion, attraction and repulsion –
presented anything but a welcome mat to those lured by the vista and thinking of
entering Paquius's stately realm.

---

[108] Varone 1987, 133–134 for this and other examples.

Modest?! I'll Show You Modest

One final feature of Paquius's house likely caught the eye of those moving west along the Via dell'Abbondanza. Situated high on the inside face of the doorway's right pilaster, an elegantly painted red dipinto stood out from the white background:

Gaium Cuspium aedilem	Gaius Cuspius for Aedile
Si qua verecunde viventi gloria danda est	If glory is to be given to someone who lives modestly,
huic iuveni debet gloria digna dari	To this young man ought the glory he deserves be given.[109]

The inscription is one of only several *programmata* written in verse – here, the last two lines form an elegiac couplet.[110] As such, it advertised to readers and those within earshot, if a reader pronounced it aloud, the "literary literacy" of the unnamed endorser.[111] The poster's position – elevated out of reach and embraced within the entryway – suggests that this was more than an anonymous endorsement and that Paquius had a hand in its creation.

Paquius stood to benefit by cultivating and advertising a connection to this *iuvenis* because Gaius Cuspius's *cognomen* was Pansa, and he was the scion of an ancient and preeminent Pompeian line.[112] A family monument in the amphitheater marked gifts to the city, and the candidate's grandfather had been duumvir four times, held an extraordinary office, and received, in connection with his son (our candidate's father, who himself served as *pontifex* and duumvir), the signal honor of a statue in the forum.[113] With his name painted all over the city, the Gaius Cuspius named here was well-known, particularly in this neighborhood since locals could watch his comings and goings from his house, which stood just west of Paquius's abode.[114] The larger letters of another endorsement of Cuspius on the opposite wall of the doorway caught the attention of those moving east.[115] It is not possible to know whether Cuspius needed Paquius's support, but playing to the street in this way signaled for neighbors Paquius's connections to a well-heeled family and, when Cuspius saw the ensemble, could only help cement that tie.

---

[109] *CIL* 4.7201.

[110] Milnor 2014, 104–118. See esp. *CIL* 4.6626 (to which this bears close similarities). Cf. *CIL* 4.7065.

[111] Phrase from Milnor 2009.

[112] The family could make claims to be leaders in the early years of Roman Pompeii because a Cuspius held the position of *quattorvir: CIL* 10.937–938.

[113] Careers of the elder C. Cuspii Pansae: Mouritsen 1988, 100–101; Franklin 2001, 149–152. The grandfather apparently held the title of *praefectus iure dicundo ex decreto decurionum lege Petronia.* Amphitheater shrine: *CIL* 10.858. Forum statues: *CIL* 10.790.

[114] Location of the ninety-plus posters for Cuspius' aedilician campaign: Mouritsen 1988, 133; Fig. 6. House location: Mouritsen 1988, 54.

[115] *CIL* 4.7200.

What messages may have been sent to streetgoers by the poetic endorsement? First, by breaking from posters' standard formulae, the inscription aided the house's architecture in distinguishing this stretch of property from its surroundings. Second, the content made clear, despite and in contrast to the rote repetition of stock phrases, that the stakes of political fortune are potentially high. Words like *gloria* are not thrown around willy-nilly.[116] Finally, the use of the adverb *verecunde*, "modestly," was striking for two potential reasons. On the one hand, Cuspius may have stood for aedile at the minimum age, which would explain endorsements where he is also referred to as a young man (*iuvens*) and where he and his running mate are jointly called *probos, dignos*, and *egregios* – adjectives whose manifold positive meanings cannot be captured adequately with one English term.[117] Among a citywide list of moral qualities for young Cuspius, the poetic description of his modesty fits in well.[118]

Yet, on the other hand, *verecunde* may well have had a special ring in this location because reader-viewers were looking westward and thus toward the structure apparently belonging to the cloth producer and purveyor of the same name, Verecundus. He had proudly shown his merchandise's production and sale, and he had pictured and named himself and his goods. For someone like Paquius, such a combination of name and behavior likely struck an ironic chord, since Verecundus hardly lived up to his modest moniker by showing restraint or by seeming to be guided by a sense of shame.[119] Who was he – someone may have questioned – to be calling himself by this name, which resonated so deeply with elite scruples about honor? Were not his painting, livelihood, and braggadocio – someone could have huffed – the antithesis of *verecunditas*? Was the wordplay of *verecunde* intended as a wicked jibe, a clever and friendly joke, something in between, or none of the above? Did someone reciting this poster mistakenly attract Verecundus's attention by pronouncing a homophone of his name in the vocative? Answers are elusive, but if the adverb is a neighborhood cross-reference, then it underscores a phenomenon we have seen time and again. This corner was a densely packed, thickly interwoven, and deeply competitive space, where neighborhood residents and those who passed through vied for attention and control, often through statements, sometimes through responses and retorts.

---

[116] A form of *gloria* appears only once in the index of the first *CIL* 4 volume: *CIL* 4.1237.

[117] *Iuvenis: CIL* 4.317. Cf. *CIL* 4.566, 4.702. *CIL* 4.709 (*probos, dignos*), 785a (*dignos*), 1022 (*egreg[ios]*). See *OLD*, s.v. for approximate meanings.

[118] Cuspius is not unique in being described as *verecundus*: e.g., *CIL* 4.309 (*verecundissimus*), 4.456 (*verecundissimus*), 4.968 (L. Popidius Secundus is a *verecundus adulescens*), 4.3009, 4.7542 (*verecundissimus*). Paquius, our houseowner and perhaps implied endorser, was himself apparently described in one poster as very modest, *verecundiss[imus]*.

[119] See *OLD*, s.v. "verecundus." Intriguingly, Paquius himself may have felt the sting of a verse endorsement because someone named as *Procula* is celebrated as aedile in *CIL* 4.7065. Della Corte (1926, 148) takes the inscription as a maligning of P. Paquius Proculus through ironic means.

CONCLUSION: THE VIA DELL'ABBONDANZA IN COMPARATIVE PERSPECTIVE

When we assess this stretch of the Via dell'Abbondanza in comparison to the segment of Herculaneum's *decumanus maximus* that was the subject of Chapter 7, we recognize several distinctive qualities. Far from Pompeii's monumental centers, our thoroughfare did not have the citywide importance of its counterpart, and fewer power players vied for control through direct intervention here. But they were hardly absent, since, beyond Paquius Proculus and his impressive house, we have also seen candidates' names painted big and bold across façades as well as images of key deities deployed for many goals. In other words, this second case study shows how much, on a street that was important for movement but lacked symbolic cachet, the impact and visibility of leading figures still permeated the urban fabric and offered reminders aplenty of the power structure.

Even if our corner's actors drew mostly from the lower ranks of society, the stakes of street presentations were no lower from their perspective. Indeed, a greater range of participants has come into focus in Pompeii, and we witness these nonelite actors feverishly making their claims in front of venues associated with commerce, production, food and drink, and religion. Just as importantly, we note the responses of others. If the Herculaneum case study largely showcased individuals laying claim to status and only hinted at further interactions, then the material remains of the Via dell'Abbondanza have revealed those exchanges and contestations: the updating of the altar's painting, the whitewashing of Zmyrina's name and its apparent reply, the dueling Venuses, the potentially cutting reference to Verecundus's immodest behavior. These material remains serve as physical artifacts of both the critical eye that Romans brought to the street and their reactions to slights or challenges. And, of course, their words and images are not merely reflective, but were also intended to be affective: Pompeians made their critiques visible and thereby aimed to shape others' perceptions. The street's contentious nature is rarely more visible than in these exchanges, which extended well beyond the highest ranks and most formal zones of urban life.

If the differences between the two case studies are notable, we might suggest several overlapping explanations. First is the nature of the evidence available along each street. Buildings and paintings survive to a similar degree at both locations – a function, as much as anything else, of their excavation in the first half of the twentieth century. Yet at Pompeii, the proliferation of political posters grants us a broad cast list for the street's dramas, and the frescoes suggest what occurred within shops where other evidence (or even excavation of any sort) is lacking. Meanwhile, at Herculaneum, the dossiers of wooden tablets permit deep dives into individuals' lives, and a spate of monumental building projects gives voice to shifting political fortunes. How our inquiry takes shape and what we can therefore know about a corner's life is deeply influenced by the evidence at hand.

Second, some differences in evidence and therefore focus result directly from the streets' vital characteristics. As we saw in Chapter 1, there was no such thing as "the" Roman street either in the Roman mindset or in the physical remains, and these two stretches, though both major avenues, underscore that point. Physically, of course, they differed: the *decumanus maximus* limited wheeled traffic, boasted a pair of drainage canals, and stood about 50 percent wider than our stretch of the Via dell'Abbondanza, which saw more carts and wagons jostle along its rutted pavers. But a side-by-side comparison also highlights the "charge" they had: the one dominated at each end by columnar or arched closures belonging to monumental civic complexes, the other about 200 meters from the closest public building. If two broad and important streets could contrast to this degree, the difference urges us to question what unfolded on side streets nearby, such as Cardo IV in Herculaneum or the segment of the Vicolo di Pacquio Proculo that heads into the unexcavated escarpment. And what happened farther afield, away from the pulse of traffic, on narrow and virtually unadorned pathways?

Third, such questions prompt us to recognize the distinctly localized flavor of urban life in Roman cities, which others have emphasized in recent years. Wallace-Hadrill, for instance, has noted Rome's fragmentary nature, which had "a cellular structure operating on a local level."[120] Fountains and compital altars offer obvious focal points of neighborhood interaction and identity, but the density of claims and counterclaims traced in this chapter speaks to the intensity of social processes that occurred among those living and working in close proximity. They saw and heard each other every day, brushed up against one another in the street, patronized each other's businesses, shared gossip over a bowl of food, kindled petty rivalries, needled nemeses, and responded in turn. When we look at neighborhood interaction, then, we must be aware that our own notions of "neighborliness" and "neighborhood" can be too romantic. With houses, shops, bars, and other buildings stuck cheek-by-jowl, urbanites were intimately tied up in one another's lives. We only need to consider the web of signatories on the wooden tablets in Herculaneum to recognize this. And, along the Via dell'Abbondanza, the people brought together in the street were not a "cozy circle of like-minded souls," but a contentious group who regularly sought to retort, one-up, or erase one another through their material claims.[121] If such struggles are decipherable at a distance, we can only imagine

[120] Wallace-Hadrill 2003, 195.
[121] Cohen and Cohen 2001–2002, 68.

what would be perceptible if we could witness these individuals in the flesh or had at our fingertips the rich documentary material of later periods.

Even as we acknowledge differences and limitations, we should not overlook a distinct commonality between the streets discussed in the previous two chapters – the qualitative breadth of what occurred along each short segment of street. First, we can note the forms of street-oriented communication, which stretched from concrete shapes of monuments, sidewalks, houses, paintings, and inscriptions to personal appearances, clothing, personal interactions, and laws. Second are the various ambits of Roman life in which statements were made. To name but some: law and urban administration, commerce and religion, pride and pleasure – all have been mixed and intermingled. Finally, remarkable groups of players and registers have emerged; divinities and the emperor's *genius* share space with foreign-born slaves and barmaids, felters and metalworkers, notices about *stercus* and political couplets. Such an admixture raises two points. First, it offers a reminder that if we expect to pigeonhole individual spheres of urban life on the street, then we are sorely mistaken. Second, building an investigation around an interstitial space allows this rich confluence of realms to emerge; in an inquiry based on one group, individual, building type, or ambit of life, it might have remained hidden.

At the beginning of Part III, I argued that one of the advantages of studying individual corners was the ability to witness a range of society in action. Zeroing in on particular streets was supposed to delimit our attention, but, perhaps ironically, these chapters have instead forced us to recognize that individual streets and street corners were in dialogue with a host of sizeable issues. Still other streets, of course, had their own dramas and their own contests, yet they would likely also prompt us to recognize the potential all streets have for not just juxtaposing different realms, players, registers, and scales of activity, but fusing them together within one space.

EPILOGUE

I WAS FIRST DRAWN TO STREETS BY THE CHANCE TO STUDY THE dialectical relationship between society and the built environment. And – because streets consisted of both "empty" spaces between buildings as well as those structures' façades, sidewalks, benches, and the like – a central goal of this book has been to set people and their physical environment in dialogue, to animate the buildings that we encounter on site and to watch people shape them, interact amidst them, and be impressed, frustrated, comforted, intimidated, or bruised by them. As a final example, I want to concentrate on one of the very few passages in Latin literature that offers a glimpse at wayfinding; that is, it depicts someone giving directions through city streets and therefore discussing what might stand out. Visiting this passage draws together threads from the preceding chapters and, in so doing, illustrates the new light this book sheds on familiar territory.

When theatergoers took their seats in the early Empire, they might have enjoyed a production of Terence's *Adelphoe*, a comedy penned in the middle of the second century BCE about strategies of child-rearing.[1] Much of what unfolded on stage would have seemed ridiculous – the oddball incidents and complications that were part and parcel of a complex plot. But other aspects of the play, even though it was a couple of centuries old, would have seemed more familiar because they closely paralleled the audience's daily life. One such

---

[1] On the reception and performance of Terence in antiquity, see Ferri 2014.

episode occurs when a character named Demea searches for his brother, Micio. Micio's smooth-operating slave Syrus knows his master's whereabouts and gives Demea directions (*Adel.* 572–583)[2]:

SYR: You know the portico down that way by the market?

DEM: Of course I know it.

SYR: Go past it straight up the street. When you get to the top, there's a downhill slope in front of you; run down there. Then there's a small shrine on this side and not far away there's an alley.

DEM: Which one?

SYR: The one by the large fig tree.

DEM: I know it.

SYR: Proceed down this.

DEM: But there's no through way.

SYR: Of course not. Rats! You must think I'm bonkers! My mistake. Go back to the portico. In fact this is a much shorter route and there's less chance of losing your way. You know the house of that wealthy guy Cratinus?

DEM: Yes.

SYR: When you've passed this, turn left, go straight down the street, and, when you get to Diana's temple, go right. Before you get to the city gate, right by the pond, there's a bakery, and facing that a workshop. That's where he is.

For the audience, the scene was hyperbolic and funny – the "mistake" of the dead-end street, for example – but not bizarre, since Syrus's explanation of urban navigation chimed with their own experience. For us, meanwhile, the episode highlights essential aspects of moving along streets as people navigate the built environment and those structures in turn shape behavior and perceptions.

Syrus's account is notably path-specific. He plots a course for Demea not by cardinal directions and in measured distances – head north 200 paces, then east 100 – but specifically according to what he will experience. Such a kinetic and embodied street-level perspective, dependent upon urban features and sensitive to topography – hills, boulevards, alleys, and a lack of signage – was, of course, the manner in which Romans encountered their cities everyday. Throughout this book, I have tried to imagine the streets of Roman Italy similarly: not from a detached, on-high perspective, but from the experience of

---

[2] Syr: *nostin porticum apud macellum hanc deorsum?* Dem: *quidni noverim?* Syr: *praeterito hanc recta platea sursum. ubi eo veneris, clivos derosum vorsumst: hac te praecipitato. postea est ad hanc manum sacellum: ibi angiportum propter est.* Dem: *quoddam?* Syr: *illi ubi etiam caprificus magnast.* Dem: *novi.* Syr: *hac pergito.* Dem: *id quidem angiportum non est pervium.* Syr: *verum hercle. vah! censen hominem me esse? erravi. in porticum rursum redi. sane hac multo propius ibis et minor est erratio. scin Cratini huius ditis aedis?* Dem: *scio.* Syr: *ubi eas praeterieris, ad sinistram hac recta platea, ubi ad Dianae veneris, ito ad dextram. prius quam ad portam venias, apud ipsum lacum est pistrilla et exadvorsum fabrica: ibist.*

a streetgoer who met all manner of people, obstacles, nuisances, sights, sounds, and even smells.

Similarly, in Syrus's directions a striking range of streetside features serve as landmarks. They belong to many spheres of city life: the sacred (the temple and shrine), the commercial (the workshop and bakery), the civic (the portico and city gates), the domestic (the house), and even the horticultural (the fig tree). In reality, as in Terence's literary creation, these ambits and others butted up against one another; they were connected by and drew people to the street. Their diversity offers a reminder that, as often as people simply used streets to get from one place to another, the urban population also found countless other uses for thoroughfares: worshipping, shopping, begging, parading, lingering and loitering, noshing and boozing, cruising for sex, hawking goods, eavesdropping, amassing for demonstrations, and settling scores. The street did not foster neat categories, but its unscripted and constantly shifting environment spanned and blurred diverse spheres of urban life.

Given this atmosphere, the picture of the street that emerges from Syrus and Demea's exchange is surprisingly depopulated. Many scholarly conceptions of the Roman street have likewise been devoid of people. In both views, destinations abound, but few persons move among them. We do not need to look far in the *Adelphoe*, however, to encounter a rich picture of street life. After all, a conceit of Roman comedy (and Greek comedy before it) was that the action took place in front of two or three house façades, in an area understood to be the street. Such an environment encouraged the encounters that fueled Terence's laughlines. Throughout the play, pimps, slaves, country bumpkins, coddled sons, music girls, and urban spendthrifts bump into one another on the street, often make inquiries, sometimes brawl, and regularly exchange news. Such interaction, even if dramatic, reflects a society in which much life was lived and much news was spread both outdoors and in informal spots well away from official places of business.

The street's spontaneous "human friction" across a broad swath of society enabled two different types of behavior. First, it rendered the street a stage on which to showcase one's aspirations, through adornment, mode of conveyance, entourage, and many other signs. Free from the "charge" and framing devices of the forum, theater, or home, the street allowed city dwellers to appear as they wished. Second, the same conspicuousness, openness, and commonality also made the street a space where many sought to critique posers, to reveal imposters, to lodge protests, and to attempt to outdo or humiliate rivals. Rarely in this book has such a dynamic been clearer than in the many give-and-take exchanges on the Pompeian street of Chapter 8. In that close space, neighborhood actors spanning slave to decurion put their best face forward through paintings of gods, electoral endorsements, personal actions, and other media, yet virtually no claim went unanswered. A braggart cloth merchant was chided, a barmaid fired back with a retort after her name was erased — we could go on. This was the double-edged sword of the street; it offered both an audience and a set of critics. Or, we might characterize the street slightly differently by reversing action and reaction: the street was prone to chaos and complexity on many fronts — not least socially and sensorily — yet many sought to tame the bedlam, assert a hierarchy, exercise control, and draw streetgoers' eyes and ears.

If the Terence passage and its mix of streetside landmarks describes the conditions for a chaotic scene, it also implies multiple attempts in the built environment to participate in and influence any unscripted action. Syrus's directions through the city notably include the house of a city dweller, the man described as *hic ditis Cratinus*, a name that tellingly Latinized the Greek word for "powerful," *kratinos*.[3] I want to make several points about Cratinus and his house. First, this type of encounter with a house — embedded within the city, jammed up close with other sundry structures, and viewed from outside — was the most common for Roman urbanites yet has rarely been considered by scholars who have largely focused on house interiors and often considered houses as isolated structures. A focus on the street has shed light on how Roman houses were not solely inward-looking but sought to impact their physical environment and those who passed through it.

Second, the bond between house and owner was fundamental for Romans, and Syrus's words both reconfirm this connection and draw in the owner's characteristics. That is, he mentions not just the house of Cratinus, but "this rich guy Cratinus" — a connection that raises the question of what visual cues were embedded within the house's external architecture to allow the characterization. Perhaps Terence imagined a house that occupied an entire city block, that boasted a towering doorway, or that mimicked temple fronts. Whatever its form, my consideration of house exteriors underscores the way that owners showcased their power and status, both to those about to enter and those not allowed in, with meaningful social effects.

Third, the inclusion of Cratinus's house among the cityscape's distinctive landmarks speaks to another architectural goal of houses along the street. Drawing the visual attention of streetgoers was a powerful means of self-presentation because it meant extending the owner's image into the city. Many Romans indeed wanted their houses to be points of reference for someone giving or getting directions, and they attracted the eyes and minds of streetgoers by creating ramped or decorated sidewalks, building benches that offered a shady resting spot or that dictated pedestrians' movement, hosting huddles of clients outside a prominent doorway, dominating pedestrians' views along a street, or presenting a coherent façade.

[3] Austin 1921, 438.

Finally, in Syrus's litany, Cratinus's house was not out of place amid public and religious architecture. Mentioned in the same breath as shrines, temples, porticos, and city gates, this house enjoyed a position to which many residences aspired, and we have seen how owners deployed the architectural and decorative idiom of civic buildings on their façades as a way of claiming a prominent status. The impulse for official recognition on the street extended to figures like the toga-clad sacrificing neighborhood officials, Ennychus the slave-turned-Augustalis, the rival shop owners, and the Augustales, all of whom employed symbols, monuments, and rituals of established civic and sacred authority. And even those already in power did not pass up the opportunity to celebrate their position. Alficius the aedile, for instance, crafted a decree that, by assigning punishments differentiated by the rank of offenders, acted in many ways like its counterparts in the built environment: it outright attempted to construct and assert social hierarchies on the street. Yet again, as in the personal realm, efforts at gaining distinction in the built environment were themselves undermined at times. Graffiti parodied façade images of Romulus and Aeneas, people amassed for nocturnal ruckuses outside house doors, or rumors spread about the guy who built a bench that blocked the sidewalk . . . and not even in a shady spot at that.

In the end, neither control nor complexity, neither showy display nor bottom-up protests, neither Demea and his desire for order nor Syrus and his humiliating antics ultimately triumphed in the street. Even if one did prevail occasionally and temporarily, that fact is ultimately less important and less interesting than watching the struggle. When we simultaneously observe people, buildings, paintings, and monuments in the street, tensions come to light along many axes, not least power, identity, and status. Moreover, by moving away from the clearly defined arenas of civic life and into improvised and interstitial spaces, we broaden the set of players and reveal different sides and strategies of the urban experience. Taking the street as a locus of inquiry opens a profound and underexploited view into the rich and complex social dynamics of Roman city life.

BIBLIOGRAPHY

Abaecherli, A. 1935–1936. "Fercula, Carpenta, and Tensae in the Roman procession." *BStM* 6: 1–28.

Abramenko, A. 1997. *Die munizipale Mittelschicht im kaiserzeitlichen Italien*. Frankfurt am Main: P. Lang.

Adamo Muscettola, S. 1982. "Nuove lettere borboniche: i Nonii Balbi ed il Foro di Ercolano." *Prospettiva* 28: 2–16.

Adams, J. 1982. *The Latin Sexual Vocabulary*. Baltimore: Johns Hopkins University Press.

Allison, P. 2004. *Pompeian Households: An Analysis of the Material Culture*. Los Angeles: Cotsen Institute of Archaeology, UCLA.

Allroggen-Bedel, A. 1974. "Das sogennante Forum von Herculaneum und die borbonische Grabungen von 1739." *CronErcol* 4: 97–109.

Allroggen-Bedel, A. 1983. "Dokumente des 18. Jahrhunderts zur Topographie von Herculaneum." *CronErcol* 13: 139–156.

Allroggen-Bedel, A. 1993. "Gli scavi di Ercolano nella politica culturale dei Borboni." In *Ercolano 1738–1988. 250 anni di ricerca archeologica*, edited by L. Franchi Dell'Orto, 35–40. Rome: L'Erma di Bretschneider.

Allroggen-Bedel, A. 1996. "Archäologie und Politik. Herculaneum und Pompeji im 18. Jh." *Hephaistos* 14: 217–252.

Allroggen-Bedel, A. 2008a. "L'Augusteum." In *Ercolano. Tre secoli di scoperte*, edited by M. Guidobaldi, 35–45. Milan: Electa.

Allroggen-Bedel, A. 2008b. "La Basilica Noniana," In *Ercolano. Tre secoli di scoperte*, edited by M. Guidobaldi, 47–53. Milan: Electa.

Alston, R. 1997. "Philo's *In Flaccum*: Ethnicity and social space in Roman Alexandria." *Greece & Rome* 44: 165–175.

Alvar, J. 2008. *Romanising Oriental Gods. Myth, Salvation and Ethics in the Cults of Cybele, Isis and Mithras*. Translated and edited by R. Gordon. Religions in the Graeco-Roman World 165. Leiden and Boston: Brill.

André, J. 1950. "Les noms latins du chemin et de la rue." *RÉL* 28: 104–134.

Andreau, J. 1974. *Les Affaires de Monsieur Jucundus*. Rome: École française de Rome.

Andrews, J. 2006. "The use and development of upper floors in houses at Herculaneum." Ph. D. diss., University of Reading.

Angelone, R. 1986. *L'officina coactiliaria di M. Vecilio Verecundo a Pompei*. Naples: Arte Tipografica.

Anguissola, A. 2010. *Intimità a Pompei: riservatezza, condivisione e prestigio negli ambienti ad alcova di Pompei*. Image & Context 8. Berlin and New York: Walter de Gruyter.

Anter, K. 2011. "Colour in the Pompeiian cityscape." Appendix to Weilguni, M. *Streets, Spaces and Places: Three Pompeiian Movement Axes Analysed*. Boreas. Uppsala Studies in Ancient Mediterranean and Near Eastern Civilizations 33, 243–313.

Appleyard, D. 1981. *Liveable Streets*. Berkeley: University of California Press.

Arangio-Ruiz, V. 1974. *Studi epigrafici e papirologiche*. Edited by L. Bove. Naples: Giannini.

Austin, J. 1921. "The significant name in Terence." Ph.D. diss., University of Illinois.

Bal, M., and N. Bryson. 1991. "Semiotics and art history." *ArtB* 73: 174–208.

Balasco, A., and M. Pagano. 2004. "Indicazioni preliminari per un progetto di documentazione del tempio 'delle quattro divinità' dell'area sacra di Ercolano." *RStPomp* 15: 194–198.

Ballet, P., N. Dieudonné-Glad, and C. Saliou, eds. 2008. *La rue dans l'antiquité: définition, aménagement et devenir de l'orient méditerranéen à la Gaule.* Rennes: Presses Universitaires de Rennes.

Barbet, A. 1985. *La peinture murale romaine: les styles décoratifs pompéiens.* Paris: Picard.

Beacham, R. 1999. *Spectacle Entertainments of Early Imperial Rome.* New Haven: Yale University Press.

Beard, M. 1994. "The Roman and the foreign: The cult of the 'Great Mother' in Imperial Rome." In *Shamanism, History, and the State*, edited by N. Thomas and C. Humphrey, 164–190. Ann Arbor: University of Michigan Press.

Beard, M. 2007. *The Roman Triumph.* Cambridge, MA and London: Harvard University Press.

Beard, M. 2008. *The Fires of Vesuvius: Pompeii Lost and Found.* Cambridge, MA: Harvard University Press.

Bejor, G. 2003. "L'apporto dell'edilizia privata al paessagio urbano." In *Amplissimae atque ornatissimae domus. L'edilizia residenziale nelle città della Tunisia romana*, edited by S. Bullo and F. Ghedini, 9–19. Rome: Quasar.

Bek, L. 1980. *Towards Paradise on Earth. AnalRom* Suppl. 9. Odense: Odense University Press.

Benefiel, R. 2008. "Amianth, a ball-game, and making one's mark." *ZPE* 167: 193–200.

Bernstein, F. 1988. "Pompeian women and the programmata." In *Studia Pompeiana et Classica in Honor of Wilhemina F. Jashemski*, edited by R. Curtis, 1–18. New York: Orpheus Publishing Inc.

Bernstein, F. 2007. "Pompeian women." In *The World of Pompeii*, edited by P. Foss and J. Dobbins, 526–537. London and New York: Routledge.

Berry, J. 1997. "Household artefacts: Towards a reinterpretation of Roman domestic space." In *Domestic Space in the Roman World: Pompeii and Beyond*, edited by R. Laurence and A. Wallace Hadrill. *JRA* Suppl. 22: 183–195.

Betts, E. 2011. "Towards a multisensory experience of movement in the city of Rome." In *Rome, Ostia, and Pompeii: Movement and Space*, edited by R. Laurence and D. Newsome, 118–132. Oxford and New York: Oxford University Press.

Biundo, R. 1996. "I rogatores nei programmata elettorali pompeiani." *Cahiers Gustave Glotz* 7: 179–188.

Biundo, R. 2003. "La propaganda elettorale a Pompei: La funzione e il valore dei programmata nell'organizzazione della campagna." *Athenaeum* 81: 53–116.

Blake, M. 1930. "The pavements of the Roman buildings of the Republic and early Empire." *MAAR* 8: 7–160.

Bodel, J. 1999. "Death on display: Looking at Roman funerals." In *The Art of Ancient Spectacle*, edited by B. Bergmann and C. Kondoleon, 259–281. Studies in the History of Art 56. Washington: National Gallery of Art.

Bodel, J. 2008. "Cicero's Minerva, Penates, and the Mother of the Lares. An outline of Roman domestic religion." In *Household and Family Religion in Antiquity: Contextual and Comparative Perspectives*, edited by J. Bodel and S. M. Olyan, 248–275. Malden, MA and Oxford: Wiley-Blackwell.

Bollmann, B. 1998. *Römische Vereinshäuser: Untersuchungen zu den Scholae der römischen Berufs-, Kult- und Augustalen-Kollegien in Italien.* Mainz: Philipp von Zabern.

Braund, S., ed. 1996. *Juvenal: Satires, Book I.* Cambridge: Cambridge University Press.

Braund, S., ed. 1989a. "Satire and society in Ancient Rome." *Exeter Studies in History* 23: v–150.

Braund, S. 1989b. "Juvenal and the East: Satire as an historical source." In *The Eastern Frontier of the Roman Empire*, edited by D. French and C. Lightfoot, 45–52. Oxford: BAR.

Brown, R. 1983. "The litter: A satirical symbol in Juvenal and others." In *Studies in Latin Literature and Roman History*. 3rd ed., edited by C. Deroux, 266–282. Brussels: Latomus.

Bruno, V. 1969. "Antecedents of the Pompeian first style." *AJA* 73: 305–317.

Budetta, T., and M. Pagano. 1988. *Legni e piccoli bronzi di Ercolano.* Soprintendenza Archeologica di Pompei, Le Mostre 3. Rome: CETSS.

Calthorpe, P., and W. Fulton. 2001. *The Regional City: Planning for the End of Sprawl*. Washington: Island Press.

Camardo, D. 2006. "Gli scavi ed i restauri di Amedeo Maiuri: Ercolano e l'esperimento di una città museo." *Ocnus* 14: 69–81.

Camardo, D. 2007. "Ercolano: la gestione delle acque in una città romana." *Oebalus* 2: 167–187.

Camardo, D., M. Castaldi, and J. Thompson. 2006. "Water supply and drainage at Herculaneum." In *Cura Aquarum in Ephesus: Proceedings of the Twelfth International Congress on the History of Water Management and Hydraulic Engineering in the Mediterranean Region*, edited by G. Wiplinger, 183–192. Dudley, MA: Peeters.

Camodeca, G. 2002. "Per una riedizione dell'archivio ercolanese di L. Venidius Ennychus. I." *CronErcol*: 32: 257–280.

Camodeca, G. 2006. "Per una riedizione dell'archivio ercolanese di L. Venidius Ennychus. II." *CronErcol* 36: 189–211.

Camodeca, G. 2008. "Le iscrizioni di dedica del Tempio di Venere e delle imagines Caesarum ad opera di Vibidia Saturnina e di A. Furius Saturninus." In *Ercolano. Tre secoli di scoperte*, edited by M. Guidobaldi, 59–61. Milan: Electa.

Camodeca, G. 2009. "Gli archivi privati di tabulae ceratae e di papiri documentari a Pompei ed Ercolano: case, ambienti e modalità di conservazione." *Vesuviana* 1: 17–42.

Capasso, L. 2001. *I fuggiaschi di Ercolano: paleobiologia delle vittime dell'eruzione vesuviana del 79 D. C.* Rome: "L'Erma" di Bretschneider.

Capelli, R., ed. 1991. *Viae Publicae Romanae*. Rome: Leonardo-DeLuca.

Cassanelli, R. 2002. "Images of Pompeii: From engravings to photography." In *Houses and Monuments of Pompeii: The Works of Fausto and Felice Niccolini*, edited by R. Cassanelli, S. De Caro, and T. Hartmann, 48–51. Los Angeles: J. Paul Getty Museum.

Castrén, P. 1975. *Ordo Populusque Pompeianus. Polity and Society in Roman Pompeii*. Rome: Bardi.

Carretoni, G. 1983. *Das Haus des Augustus auf dem Palatin*. Mainz am Rhein: P. von Zabern.

Carroll, M. 2010. "Exploring the sanctuary of Venus and its sacred grove: Politics, cult and identity in Roman Pompeii." *PBSR* 78: 63–106.

Catalano, V., L. García y García, and G. Panzera. 2002. *Case, abitanti, e culti di Ercolano. Nuova edizione*. Rome: Bardi Editore.

Cerulli Irelli, G. 1975. "Archaeological research in the area of Vesuvius." *The Maryland Historian* 6.2: 85–116.

Chevallier, R. 1997. *Les Voies Romaines*. 2nd ed. Paris: Picard.

Chiavia, C. 2002. *Programmata: Manifesti elettorali nella colonia romana di Pompei*. Turin: S. Zamorani.

Chiaramonte, C. 2007. "The walls and gates." In *The World of Pompeii*, edited by J. Dobbins and P. Foss, 140–149. London and New York: Routledge.

Ciarallo, A., E. De Carolis, and M. Auricchio. 2001. *La Casa di Giulio Polibio: Studi Interdisciplinari*. Tokyo: Edizione Centro studi arti figurative.

Clarke, J. 1979. *Roman Black-and-White Figural Mosaics*. New York: New York University Press for the College Art Association of America.

Clarke, J. 1991. *The Houses of Roman Italy, 100 B.C.-A.D. 250: Ritual, Space, and Decoration*. Berkeley: University of California Press.

Clarke, J. 2003. *Art in the Lives of Ordinary Romans: Visual Representation and Non-Elite Viewers in Italy, 100 B.C.-A.D. 315*. Berkeley and Los Angeles: University of California Press.

Clarke, J. 2007. *Looking at Laughter: Humor, Power, and Transgression in Roman Visual Culture, 100 B.C.-A.D. 250*. Berkeley: University of California Press.

Cline, L. 2012. "Imitation vs. reality: Zebra stripe paintings and imitation marble in the late fourth style at Oplontis." In *Actes du XIe Colloqie de l'Association Internationale pour la Peinture Murale Antique*, edited by Norbert Zimmerman. Vienna.

Coarelli, F. 1998. "Il Culto di Mefitis in Campania e a Roma." In *I Culti della Campania Antica. Atti del convegno internazionale di studi in ricordo di*

Nazarena Valenza Mele, 185–190. Rome: Bretschneider.

Coarelli, F., A. Foglia, and P. Foglia. 2002. *Pompeii*. New York: Riverside Book.

Cohen, E. 1992. "Honor and gender in the streets of early modern Rome." *Journal of Interdisciplinary History* 22: 597–625.

Cohen, E. 2008. "To pray, to work, to hear, to speak: Women in Roman streets c.1600." *Journal of Early Modern History* 12: 289–311.

Cohen, E., and T. Cohen. 2001–2002. "Open and shut: The social meanings of the Cinquecento Roman house." *Studies in the Decorative Arts* 9.1: 61–84.

Colleran, K. 2010. "Scampanata at the widows' windows: A case-study of sound and ritual insult in Cinquecento Florence." *Urban History* 36.3: 359–378.

Compostella, C. 1989. "Iconografia, ideologia e status a Brixia nel I secolo D.C.: la lastra sepolcrale del seviro Anteros Asiaticus." *RivIstArch* 13: 59–75.

Conticello De Spagnolis, M., and E. De Carolis. 1988. *Le lucerne di bronzo di Ercolano e Pompei*. Ministero per i beni culturali ed ambientali, Soprintendenza archeologica di Pompei, Cataloghi 2. Roma: L'Erma di Bretschneider.

Cooley, A., and M. Cooley. 2004. *Pompeii: A Sourcebook*. London and New York: Routledge.

Copley, F. 1939. "A paraclausithyron from Pompeii: A study of CIL, IV, Suppl. 5296." *AJP* 60: 333–349.

Copley, F. 1956. *Exclusus Amator: A Study in Latin Love Poetry*. Monographs of the American Philological Society 17. Madison, WI: American Philological Association.

Coralini, A. 2001. *Hercules domesticus: immagini di Ercole nelle case della regione vesuviana: I secolo A. C.-79. D.C.* Naples: Electa Napoli.

Corbeill, A. 2002. "Political movement: Walking and ideology in republican Rome." In *The Roman Gaze: Vision, Power, and the Body*, edited by D. Frederick, 182–215. Baltimore: Johns Hopkins University Press.

Corbeill, A. 2004. *Nature Embodied: Gesture in Ancient Rome*. Princeton: Princeton University Press.

Cracco Ruggini, L. 2003. "Rome in late antiquity: Clientship, urban topography, and prosopography." *CP* 98.4: 366–382.

Crawford, M., ed. 1996. *Roman Statutes*, 2 vols. London: Institute of Classical Studies, University of London.

Crook, J. 1967. *Law and Life of Rome, 90 BC–AD 212*. Ithaca: Cornell University Press.

Culham, P. 1982. "The *Lex Oppia*." *Latomus* 41: 786–793.

Curriero, F. 2001. "Analysis of the association between extreme precipitation and waterborne disease outbreaks in the US, 1948–1994." *American Journal of Public Health* 91: 1194–1199.

D'Ambrosio, A., P. Guzzo, and M. Mastroroberto. 2003. *Storie da un'eruzione: Pompei, Ercolano, Oplontis*. Milan: Mondatori Electa.

Daremberg, C., and E. Saglio, eds. 1877–1919. *Dictionnaire des antiquités grecques et romaines d'après les textes et les monuments*, 5 vols. Paris: Hachette.

D'Arms, J. 1970. *Romans on the Bay of Naples*. Cambridge: Harvard University Press.

D'Arms, J. 2000. "Memory, money, and status at Misenum." *JRS* 90: 126–44.

Daube, D. 1953. "'Ne quid infammandi causa fiat': The Roman law of defamation." *AttiCongVerona* 3: 411–450.

David, R. 1978. "Manila's street life: A visual ethnography." In *A Comparative Study of Street Life, Tokyo, Manila, New York*, edited by H. Kato, W. Whyte, and R. David, 19–44. Tokyo: Research Institute for Oriental Cultures, Gakushuin University.

Davis, N. 1975. *Society and Culture in Early Modern France: Eight Essays*. Stanford: Stanford University Press.

Davis, N. 2006. *Trickster Travels: A Sixteenth-century Muslim Between Worlds*. New York: Hill and Wang.

De Caro, S. 1998. "La lucerne d'oro di Pompei: un dono di Nerone a Venere Pompeiana." In *I culti della Campania antica. Atti del convegno internazionale di studi in ricordo di Nazarena Valenza Mele, Napoli 1995*, edited by N. Mele, 239–244. Rome: Giorgio Bretschneider.

De Certeau, M. 1984. *The Practice of Everyday Life*. Translated by S. Rendall. Berkeley: University of California Press.

De Crescenzo, L. 1979. *La Napoli di Bellavista: sono figlio di persone antiche*. Milano: A. Mondadori.

De Franciscis, A. 1991. *Il sacello degli Augustali a Miseno*. Naples: Arte Tipografica.

De Kind, R. 1998. *Houses in Herculaneum: A New View on the Town Planning and the Building of Insulae III and IV*. Amsterdam: Gieben.

de Ligt, L., and P. Garnsey. 2012. "The Album of Herculaneum and a model of the town's demography." *JRA* 25: 69–94.

Della Corte, M. 1911a. "Pompei—Scavi e scoperte di antichità avvenute durante il mese di novembre." *NSc* 8: 417–432.

Della Corte, M. 1911b. "Pompei—Scavi di antichità avvenute durante il mese di decembre." *NSc* 8: 455–460.

Della Corte, M. 1912a. "Pompei—Scavi e scoperte durante il mese di gennaio 1912." *NSc* 9: 27–32.

Della Corte, M. 1912b. "Pompei—Continuazzione dello scavo della Via dell'Abbondanza." *NSc* 9: 135–148.

Della Corte, M. 1912c. "Pompei—Continuazzione dello scavo della Via dell'Abbondanza." *NSc* 9: 174–192.

Della Corte, M. 1912d. "Pompei—Continuazzione dello scavo di Via dell'Abbondanza durante il mese di luglio 1912." *NSc* 9: 246–259.

Della Corte, M. 1926. "Publius Paquius Proculus." *JRS* 16: 145–154.

Della Corte, M. 1927. "Pompei—Relazione sui lavori di scavo dal marzo 1924 al marzo 1926." *NSc* 3: 3–116.

Della Corte, M. 1936. "Nuove scoperte epigrafiche." *NSc* 14: 299–352.

Della Corte, M. 1958. "Le iscrizioni di Ercolano." *RendNap* 33: 239–308.

Della Corte, M. 1965. *Case ed abitanti di Pompei*. Naples: Faustino Fiorentino.

Del Negro, G. P. 2004. *Passeggiata and Popular Culture in an Italian Town: Folklore and the Performance of Modernity*. Montreal: McGill-Queen's Press.

Delpino, F. 2001. "Vittorio Spinazzola. Tra Napoli e Pompei, fra scandali e scavi." In *Pompei: Scienza e Società*, edited by P. Guzzo, 51–62. Milan: Electa.

Dennis, F. 2008–2009. "Sound and domestic space in fifteenth- and sixteenth-century Italy." *Studies in the Decorative Arts* 16: 7–19.

De Simone, A. 1985. "Il complesso monumentale di San Lorenzo Maggiore." In *Napoli Antica*, edited by E. Pozzi, 185–195. Naples: G. Macchiaroli.

De Simone, A. 1986. "S. Lorenzo Maggiore in Napoli: il monument e l'area." In *Neapolis: Atti del venticinquesimo convegno di studi sulla Magna Grecia*, 233–253. Taranto: Istituto per la storia e l'archeologia della Magna Grecia.

Desrochers, B. 2003. "Giorgio Sommer's photographs of Pompeii." *History of Photography* 27.2: 111–129.

De Vos, A., and M. De Vos. 1982. *Pompei, Ercolano, Stabia*. Rome and Bari: Laterza.

Dexter, C. 1975. "The Casa di L. Cecilio Giocondo in Pompeii." Ph.D. diss., Duke University.

Dickmann, J. 1999. *Domus frequentata: anspruchs-volles Wohnen im pompejanischen Stadthaus*. Munich: Verlag Dr. Friedrich Pfeil.

Donahue, J. 2004. *The Roman Community at Table During the Principate*. Ann Arbor: University of Michigan Press.

Downey, G. 1961. *A History of Antioch in Syria: From Seleucus to the Arab Conquest*. Princeton: Princeton University Press.

Drerup, H. 1959. "Bildraum und Realraum in der römischen Architektur." *RM* 66: 147–174.

Duany, A., and E. Plater-Zyberk. 1992. *Towns and Town-Making Principles*. New York: Rizzoli.

Duany, A., E. Plater-Zyberk, and J. Speck. 2001. *Suburban Nation: The Rise of Sprawl and the Decline of the American Dream*. New York: North Point Press.

Dunbabin, K. 1999. *Mosaics of the Greek and Roman World*. Cambridge: Cambridge University Press.

Duneier, M. 1999. *Sidewalk*. New York: Farrar, Straus, and Giroux.

Dupré Raventós, X., and J. Vallverdù, eds. 1999. *Sordes urbis. L'eliminazione dei rifiuti nella città romana*. Rome: L'Erma di Bretschneider.

Duthoy, R. 1978. "Les *Augustales." *ANRW* 2: 1254–1309.

Dwyer, E. 1991. "The Pompeian atrium house in theory and practice." In *Roman Art in the Private Sphere: New Perspectives on the Architecture and Decor of the Domus, Villa, and Insula*, edited by E. Gazda, 25–48. Ann Arbor: University of Michigan Press.

Eck, W. 1987. "Die Wasserversorgung im römischen Reich: Sozio-politische Bedingungen, Recht und Administration." In *Die Wasserversorgung Antiker Städte*, 49–102. Mainz am Rhein: P. von Zabern.

Edensor, T. 1998. "The culture of the Indian street." In *Images of the Street: Planning, Identity and Control in Public Space*, edited by N. Fyfe, 205–221. London and New York: Routledge.

Edmonson, J. 1996. "Dynamic arenas: Gladiatorial presentations in the city of Rome and the construction of Roman society during the early empire." In *Roman Theater and Society*, edited by W. Slater, 69–112. Ann Arbor: University of Michigan Press.

Edmondson, J. 2008. "Public dress and social control in late republican and early imperial Rome." In *Roman Dress and the Fabrics of Roman Culture*, edited by J. Edmondson and A. Keith, 21–46. Toronto and Buffalo: University of Toronto Press.

Ehrhardt, W. 1998. *Casa di Paquius Proculus*. Häuser in Pompeji 9. Munich: Hirmer Verlag.

Elet, Y. 2002. "Seats of power: The outdoor benches of early modern Florence." *JSAH* 61: 444–469.

Ellis, S. 2004. "The distribution of bars at Pompeii: Archaeological, spatial and viewshed analyses." *JRA* 17: 371–384.

Ellis, S. 2005. "The Pompeian bar and the city: Defining food and drink outlets and identifying their place in an urban environment." Ph.D. diss., University of Sydney.

Ellis, S. 2008. "The use and misuse of 'legacy data' in identifying a typology of retail outlets at Pompeii." *Internet Archaeology* 24: intarch. ac.uk/journal/issue24.

Ellis, S. 2011. "*Pes Dexter*: Superstition and the state in the shaping of shopfronts and street

activity in the Roman world." In *Rome, Ostia, Pompeii: Movement and Space*, edited by D. Newsome and R. Laurence, 160–173. Oxford and New York: Oxford University Press.

Elsner, J. 1995. *Art and the Roman Viewer: The Transformation of Art from the Pagan World to Christianity*. Cambridge: Cambridge University Press.

Eschebach, H. 1975. "Erläuterungen zum Plan Pompejis." In *Neue Forschungen in Pompeji*, edited by B. Andreae and H. Kyrielis, 331–338. Recklinghausen: Bongers.

Eschebach, H. 1982. "Katalog der pompejanischen Laufbrunnen und ihrer Reliefs." *AW* 13: 21–26.

Eschebach, H., and T. Schäfer. 1983. "Die öffentlichen Laufbrunnen Pompejis: Katalog und Beschreibung." *Pompei-Ercolano-Stabia Bolletino di Associazione Internazionale Amici di Pompeji* 1: 11–40.

Etienne, R. 1993. "A propos du cosidetto édifice des Augustales d'Herculanum." In *Ercolano 1738–1988: 250 anni di ricerca archeologica*, edited by L. Franchi dell'Orto, 345–349. Rome: L'Erma di Bretschneider.

Fagan, G. 1999. *Bathing in Public in the Roman World*. Ann Arbor: University of Michigan Press.

Falcone L., F. Bloisi, V. Califano, M. Pagano, and L. Vicari. 2008. "An old notice board at ancient Herculaneum studied using near infrared reflectography." *JAS* 35: 1708–1716.

Fant, J., and D. Attanasio. 2009. "Bars with marble surfaces at Pompeii: Evidence for sub-elite marble use." *Fasti Online* 159: 1–10.

Favro, D. 1996. *The Urban Image of Augustan Rome*. Cambridge: Cambridge University Press.

Favro, D. 2011. "Construction traffic in imperial Rome: Building the Arch of Septimius Severus." In *Rome, Ostia, Pompeii: Movement and Space*, edited by D. Newsome and R. Laurence, 332–360. Oxford and New York: Oxford University Press.

Favro, D., and C. Johanson. 2010. "Death in motion: Funeral processions in the Roman forum." *JSAH* 69: 12–37.

Ferri, R. 2014. "The reception of Plautus in antiquity." In *The Oxford Handbook of Greek and Roman Comedy*, edited by M. Fontaine and A. Scafuro, 767–781. Oxford and New York: Oxford University Press.

Finley, M. 1973. *The Ancient Economy*. Berkeley: University of California Press.

Fitzgerald, W. 2007. *Martial: The World of the Epigram*. Chicago: University of Chicago Press.

Flohr, M. 2007. "*Nec quicquam ingenuum habere potest officina*? Spatial contexts of urban production at Pompeii, AD 79." *BABesch* 82: 129–148.

Flohr, M. 2009. "The social world of Roman fullonicae." In *TRAC 2008: Proceedings of the Eighteenth Annual Theoretical Roman Archaeology Conference*, edited by M. Driessen et al., 173–186. Oxford: Oxbow Books.

Flower, H. 1996. *Ancestor Masks and Aristocratic Power in Roman Culture*. Oxford: Clarendon Press.

Fraenkel, H. 1961. "Two poems of *Catullus*." *JRS* 51: 46–53.

Frakes, J. 2009. *Framing Public Life: The Portico in Roman Gaul*. Vienna: Phoibos.

Franklin, J. 1980. *Pompeii: The Electoral Programmata, Campaigns and Politics, AD 71–79*. *PAAR* Suppl. 28. Rome: American Academy in Rome.

Franklin, J. 1986. "Games and a Lupanar: Prosopography of a neighborhood in ancient Pompeii." *CJ* 81: 319–328.

Franklin, J. 2001. *Pompeis difficile est: Studies in the Political Life of Imperial Pompeii*. Ann Arbor: University of Michigan Press.

Friedländer, L. 1907. *Roman Life and Manners Under the Early Empire*, 4 vols. Translated by L. Magnus. New York: Barnes & Noble.

Fröhlich, T. 1991. *Lararien- und Fassadenbilder in den Vesuvstädten. Untersuchungen zur 'volkstümlichen' pompejanischen Malerei*. *RM-EH* Suppl. 32. Mainz: P. von Zabern.

Fuhrmann, C. 2012. *Policing the Roman Empire: Soldiers, Administration, and Public Order*. Oxford and New York: Oxford University Press.

Gambetti, S. 2009. *The Alexandrian Riots of 38 C. E. and the Persecution of the Jews: A Historical Reconstruction*. Supplements to the *Journal for the Study of Judaism* 135. Leiden and Boston: Brill.

Ganschow, T. 1989. *Untersuchungen zur Baugeschichte in Herculaneum*. Bonn: R. Habelt.

Garnsey, P. 1970. *Social Status and Legal Privilege in the Roman Empire*. Oxford: Clarendon Press.

Garrioch, D. 2003. "Sounds of the city: The soundscape of early modern European towns." *Urban History* 30: 5–25.

Gassner, V. 1986. "Die Kaufläden in Pompeji." Ph.D. diss., University of Vienna.

Gazda, E., ed. 1991. *Roman Art in the Private Sphere: New Perspectives of the Architecture and Décor of the Domus, Villa, and Insula*. Ann Arbor: University of Michigan Press.

George, M. 1998. "Elements of the peristyle in Campanian Atria." *JRA* 11: 82–100.

George, M. 2008. "The 'dark side' of the toga." In *Roman Dress and the Fabric of Roman Culture*, edited by J. Edmondson and A. Keith, 94–112. Toronto: University of Toronto Press.

Gering, A. 2004. "Plätze und Strassensperren an Promenaden. Zum Funktionswandel Ostias in der Spätantike." *RM* 111: 299–382.

Gesemann, B. 1996. *Die Strassen der antiken Stadt Pompeji: Entwicklung und Gestaltung*. Frankfurt am Main: Lang.

Giacobello, F. 2008. *Larari pompeiani: iconografia e culto dei Lari in ambito domestico*. Milano: LED.

Giordano, C. 1974. "Iscrizioni graffite e dipinte nella casa di C. Giulio Polibio." *RendNap* 49: 21–28.

Gleason, M. 1995. *Making Men: Sophists and Self-Presentation in Ancient Rome*. Princeton: Princeton University Press.

Gleason, M. 1999. "Elite male identity in the Roman Empire." In *Life, Death, and Entertainment in the Roman Empire*, edited by D. Potter and D. Mattingly, 67–84. Ann Arbor: University of Michigan Press.

González, J. 1986. "The Lex Irnitana: A new copy of the Flavian municipal law." *JRS* 76: 147–243.

Gordon, M. 1931. "The freedman's son in municipal life." *JRS* 21: 65–77.

Goulet, C. 2001–2002. "The 'zebra stripe' design: An investigation of Roman wall painting in the periphery." *RStPomp* 12–13: 53–94.

Gradel, I. 2002. *Emperor Worship and Roman Religion*. Oxford: Clarendon Press.

Graf, F. 2005. "Satire in a ritual context." In *The Cambridge Companion to Roman Satire*, edited by K. Freudenburg, 192–206. Cambridge and New York: Cambridge University Press.

Grahame, M. 2000. *Reading Space: Social Interaction and Identity in the Houses of Roman Pompeii: A Syntactical Approach to the Analysis and Interpretation of Built Space*. Oxford: Archeopress.

Gruen, E. 1990. *Studies in Greek Culture and Roman Policy*. Berkeley and Los Angeles: University of California Press.

Guadagno, G. 1977. "Frammenti inediti di albi degli augustali." *CronErcol* 7: 114–123.

Guadagno, G. 1978. "Supplemento epigrafico ercolanese." *CronErcol* 8: 132–155.

Guadagno, G. 1983. "Herculanensium Augustalium Aedes." *CronErcol* 13: 159–173.

Guadagno, G. 1988. "I graffiti della aedes Augustalium. Documenti sull'accesso all'Augustalità." *CronErcol* 18: 199–203.

Guadagno, G. 1993. "Eredità di cultura e nuovi dati." In *Ercolano 1738–1988: 250 anni di ricerca archeologica*, edited by L. Franchi dell'Orto, 73–98. Rome: L'Erma di Bretschneider.

Guadagno, G. 1995. "Documenti epigrafici ercolanesi relativi ad un terremoto." In *Archäologie und Seismologie. La Regione Vesuviana dal 62 al 79 D.C. Problemi archeologici e sismologici*, edited by T. Fröhlich and L. Jacobelli, 119–128. Munich: Biering and Brinkmann.

Guidobaldi, M. 2003. "La bottega di un *gemmarius* (*ins. or.* II, 10) e l'ingannevole 'stanza della ricamatrice.'" In *Storie da un'eruzione: Pompei, Ercolano, Oplontis*, edited by A. D'Ambrosio, 102–111. Milan: Mondadori Electa.

Guidobaldi, M. 2006. "Casa del Salone Nero." In *Gli ozi di Ercole: residenze di lusso a Pompei ed Ercolano*, edited by P. Fabrizio and M. Guidobaldi, 190–199. Rome: L'Erma di Bretschneider.

Guidobaldi, M. 2008a. "L'area sacra suburbana." In *Ercolano. Tre secoli di scoperte*, edited by M. Guidobaldi, 55–58. Milan: Electa.

Guidobaldi, M. 2008b. "La terrazza di M. Nonio Balbo" and "Le Terme Suburbane." In *Ercolano. Tre secoli di scoperte*, edited by M. Guidobaldi, 63–69. Milan: Electa.

Haarløv, B. 1977. *The Half-open Door: A Common Symbolic Motif within Roman Sepulchral Sculpture*. Odense: Odense University Press.

Hackworth Petersen, L. 2006. *The Freedman in Roman Art and Art History*. New York and Cambridge: Cambridge University Press.

Hales, S. 2003. *The Roman House and Social Identity*. Cambridge: Cambridge University Press.

Hallett, J. 1980. "*Ianua Iucunda*: The characterization of the door in Catullus 67." In *Studies in Latin Literature*, edited by C. Deroux, 106–122. Brussels: Latomus.

Harmon, D. 1978. "The family festivals of Rome." *ANRW* 2: 1557–1603.

Harsh, F. 1937. "'Angiportum,' 'Platea,' and 'Vicus.'" *CP* 32: 44–58.

Hartnett, J. 2008a. "*Si quis hic sederit*: Streetside benches and urban society in Pompeii." *AJA* 112: 91–119.

Hartnett, J. 2008b. "Fountains at Herculaneum: Sacred history, topography, and civic identity." *RStPomp* 19: 77–89.

Hartnett, J. 2011a. "Excavation photographs and the imagining of Pompeii's streets: Vittorio Spinazzola and the Via dell'Abbondanza." In *Pompeii in the Public Imagination from Its Rediscovery to Today*, edited by S. Hales and J. Paul, 246–269. Oxford: Oxford University Press.

Hartnett, J. 2011b. "The power of nuisances on the Roman street." In *Rome, Ostia, and Pompeii: Movement and Space*, edited by R. Laurence and D. Newsome, 135–159. Oxford and New York: Oxford University Press.

Hasenohr, C. 2003. "Les Compitalia à Délos." *BCH* 127: 167–249.

Havelock, C. 1995. *The Aphrodite of Knidos and Her Successors: A Historical Review of the Female Nude in Greek Art*. Ann Arbor: University of Michigan Press.

Helg, R. 2009a. "La forma e lo sviluppo dei prospetti nell'architettura e nell'urbanistica di Pompei e di Ercolano." Ph.D. diss., Università di Padova.

Helg, R. 2009b. "Architettura della facciata nella casa romana: Pompei ed Ercolano." In *Vesuviana. Archeologie a Confronto: Atti del Convegno Internazionale (Bologna, 14–16 Gennaio 2008)*, edited by A. Coralini, 497–508. Bologna: Ante Quem.

Helg, R. 2012. "Transformation of domestic space in the Vesuvian cities: From the development of the upper floors and façades to a new dimension of intimacy." In *Privata Luxuria – Towards an Archaeology of Intimacy: Pompeii and Beyond*, edited by A. Anguissola, 143–160. Munich: Herbert Utz Verlag.

Hemelrijk, E. 1987. "Women's demonstrations in republican Rome." In *Sexual Asymmetry*, edited by J. Blok and P. Mason, 217–240. Amsterdam: Gieben.

Henderson, J. 1999. *Writing Down Rome. Satire, Comedy and Other Offences in Latin Poetry*. Oxford: Clarendon Press.

Hersch, K. 2010. *The Roman Wedding: Ritual and Meaning in Antiquity*. Cambridge and New York: Cambridge University Press.

Hermansen, G. 1982. *Ostia: Aspects of Roman City Life*. Edmonton: University of Alberta Press.

Hoffman, A. 1990. "Elemente bürgerliche Repräsentation: Eine späthellenistische Hausfassade in Pompeji." In *Akten des XII. Internationalen Kongresses für Klassische Archäeologie in Berlin 1988*, 490–495. Mainz: P. von Zabern.

Hoffman, A. 1996. "Die Casa del Fauno in Pompeji. Ein Haus wie ein Palast. Kurzfassung," In *Basileia. Die Paläste der hellenistischen Könige: internationales symposion in Berlin vom 16.12.1992 bis 20.12.1992*, edited by W. Hoepner and G. Brands, 258–259. Mainz: P. von Zabern.

Hoffman, A., and A. Faber. 2009. *Die Casa del Fauno in Pompeji (VI 12)*. Wiesbaden: Reichert.

Holleran, C. 2011a. "The street life of ancient Rome." In *Rome, Ostia, and Pompeii.*

Movement and Space, edited by R. Laurence and D. Newsome, 245–261. Oxford and New York: Oxford University Press.

Holleran, C. 2011b. "Migration and the urban economy of Rome." In *Demography and the Greco-Roman World: New Insights and Approaches*, edited by C. Holleran and A. Pudsey, 155–180. Cambridge: Cambridge University Press.

Holleran, C. 2012. *Shopping in Ancient Rome: The Retail Trade in the Late Republic and the Principate*. Oxford: Oxford University Press.

Hopkins, K. 1993. "Novel evidence for Roman slavery." *PastPres* 138: 3–27.

Howell, P. 1995. *Martial: The Epigrams Book V*. Warminster: Aris & Phillips.

Jacobs, J. 1961. *The Death and Life of Great American Cities*. New York: Random House.

Jacobs, A. 1995. *Great Streets*. Cambridge, MA: MIT Press.

Jacobs, A., and D. Appleyard. 1987. "Towards an urban design manifesto." *Journal of the American Planning Association* 53: 112–120.

Jansen, G. 1991. "Water systems and sanitation in the houses of Herculaneum." *Meded* 50: 145–166.

Jansen G. 2002. *Water in de Romeinse stad. Pompeji – Herculaneum – Ostia*. Leuven: Peeters.

Jashemski, W. 1979. *The Gardens of Pompeii, Herculaneum, and the Villas Destroyed by Vesuvius*. New Rochelle, NY: Caratzas Bros.

Jashemski, W. 1993. *The Gardens of Pompeii, Herculaneum, and the Villas Destroyed by Vesuvius*, Vol. 2: *The Appendices*. New Rochelle, NY: Caratzas Bros.

Jones, R., and D. Robinson. 2004. "Water, wealth, and social status at Pompeii: The House of the Vestals in the first century AD." *AJA* 109: 695–710.

Jongmann, W. 1988. *The Economy and Society of Pompeii*. Amsterdam: Gieben.

Joshel, S. 1992. *Work, Identity, and Legal Status at Rome: A Study of the Occupational Inscriptions*. Norman: University of Oklahoma Press.

Joshel, S., and L. Hackworth Petersen. 2014. *The Material Lives of Roman Slaves*. New York: Cambridge University Press.

Joyner, C. 1999. *Shared Traditions: Southern History and Folk Culture*. Urbana: University of Illinois Press.

Jung, F. 1984. "Gebaute Bilder." *AntK* 27: 71–122.

Kaiser, A. 2011a. *Roman Urban Street Networks: Streets and the Organization of Space in Four Cities*. New York: Routledge.

Kaiser, A. 2011b. "Cart traffic flow in Pompeii and Rome." In *Rome, Ostia, Pompeii: Movement and Space*, edited by R. Laurence and D. Newsome, 174–193. Oxford and New York: Oxford University Press.

Kaiser, A. 2011c. "What was a *via*?: An integrated archaeological and textual approach." In *Pompeii: Industry, Art, and Infrastructure*, edited by E. Poehler, K. Cole, and M. Flohr, 106–121. Oxford: Oxbow Books.

Kampen, N. 1981. *Image and Status: Roman Working Women in Ostia*. Berlin: Mann.

Kapossy, B. 1969. *Brunnenfiguren der hellenistischen und römischen Zeit*. Zurich: Juris-Verlag.

Kato, H., W. Whyte, and R. David. 1978. *A Comparative Study of Street Life: Tokyo, Manila, New York*. Tokyo: Research Institute for Oriental Cultures, Gakushuin University.

Katz, P. 1994. *The New Urbanism: Towards an Architecture of Community*. New York: McGraw Hill.

Kellum, B. 1999. "The spectacle of the street." In *The Art of Ancient Spectacle*, edited by B. Bergmann and C. Kondoleon, 283–299. Studies in the History of Art 56. Washington: National Gallery of Art.

Kelly, B. 2007. "Riot control and imperial ideology in the Roman Empire." *Phoenix* 61: 150–176.

Kelly, J. 1966. *Roman Litigation*. Oxford: Clarendon Press.

Kleberg, T. 1957. *Hôtels, restaurants et cabarets dans l'antiquité romaine: études historiques et philologiques*. Uppsala: Almqvist & Wiksells boktr.

Kockel, V. 1983. *Die Grabbauten vor dem Herkulaner Tor in Pompeji*. Mainz: P. von Zabern.

Kockel, V. 1986. "Archäologische Funde und Forschungen in den Vesuvstädten, II." *AA* 101: 443–569.

Koloski-Ostrow, A. 1990. *The Sarno Bath Complex*. Rome: L'Erma di Bretschneider.

Kostof, S. 1985. *A History of Architecture: Settings and Rituals*. New York: Oxford University Press.

Laes, C. 2011. *Children in the Roman Empire: Outsiders Within*. Cambridge: Cambridge University Press.

Lafon, X. 1997. "Dehors ou dedans? Le *vestibulum* dans les *domus* aristocratiques à la fin de la République et au début de l'empire." *Klio* 77: 405–423.

Laidlaw, A. 1985. *The First Style in Pompeii: Painting and Architecture*. Rome: G. Bretschneider.

Laird, M. 2002. "Evidence in context: The public and funerary monuments of the Seviri Augustales at Ostia." Ph.D. diss., Princeton University.

Laird, M. 2006. "Private memory and public interest: Municipal identity in imperial Italy." In *The Art of Citizens, Soldiers and Freedmen in the Roman World. An Illustrated Anthology*, edited by E. D'Ambra and G. P. R. Métraux, 31–43. London: Archeopress.

Laitinen, R., and T. Cohen, eds. 2008. "Cultural history of early modern streets: An introduction." *Journal of Early Modern History* 12.3–4: 1–10.

Larmour, D. 2007. "Holes in the body: Sites of abjection in Juvenal's Rome." In *The Sites of Rome: Time, Space, and Memory*, edited by D. Larmour and D. Spencer, 168–210. Oxford: Oxford University Press.

Larmour, D., and D. Spencer. 2007. "Introduction—*Roma, recepta*: A topography of the imagination." In *The Sites of Rome: Time, Space, and Memory*, edited by D. Larmour and D. Spencer, 1–60. Oxford: Oxford University Press.

La Torre, G. 1988. "Gli impianti commerciali ed artigiani nel tessato urbano di Pompei." In *Pompei, L'informatica al servizio di una città antica*, edited by C. Neapolis and F. Dell'Orto, 75–102. Rome: L'Erma di Bretschneider.

Laurence, R. 1997. "Writing the Roman metropolis." In *Roman Urbanism: Beyond the*

Consumer City, edited by H. Parkin, 1–20. London: Routledge.

Laurence, R. 2007. *Roman Pompeii: Space and Society*. 2nd ed. London: Routledge.

Laurence, R. 2008. "City traffic and the archaeology of Roman streets from Pompeii to Rome: The nature of traffic in the ancient city." In *Stadtverkehr in der Antiken Welt/ Traffico Urbano nel Mondo Antico*, edited by D. Mertens, 87–106. Wiesbaden: Reichert.

Laurence, R., and D. Newsome, eds. 2011. *Rome, Ostia, and Pompeii: Movement and Space*. Oxford and New York: Oxford University Press.

Laurence, R., and A. Wallace-Hadrill, eds. 1997. *Domestic Space in the Roman World: Pompeii and Beyond*. JRA Suppl. 22. Portsmouth, RI: Journal of Roman Archaeology.

Lauritsen, T. 2011. "Doors in domestic space at Pompeii and Herculaneum: A preliminary study." In *TRAC 2010: Proceedings of the Twentieth Annual Theoretical Roman Archaeology Conference*, edited by B. Russell and D. Mladenovic, 59–75. Oxford: Oxbow Books.

Lauritsen, T. 2013. "The form and function of boundaries in the Campanian house." In *Privata Luxuria: Towards an Archaeology of Intimacy: Pompeii and Beyond*, edited by A. Anguissola, 95–114. Munich: Herbert Utz Verlag.

Lauter, H. 1972. "Fassadenmotive und Fassadenstrukturen der hellenistischen und spätrepublikanischer Zeit. Ausgehend von der Fassade des Hauses IX 1,20 in Pompeji." Habilitationsschrift Erlangen: unpublished.

Lauter, H. 2009. *Die Fassade des Hauses IX 1,20 in Pompeji: Gestalt und Bedeutung*. Mainz: Philipp von Zabern.

Lavan, L. 2008. "The monumental streets of Sagalassos in late antiquity: An interpretative study." In *La rue dans l'Antiquité: définition, aménagement et devenir de l'orient méditerranéen à la Gaule*, edited by P. Ballet, N. Dieudonné-Glad, and C. Saliou, 201–214. Rennes: Presses Universitaires de Rennes.

Le Corbusier. 1929. *The City of Tomorrow and Its Planning*. Translated by F. Etchells. London: Rodker.

Leach, E. 1993. "The entrance room in the House of Julius Polybius and the nature of the Roman vestibulum." In *Functional and Spatial Analysis of Wall Painting: Proceedings of the Fifth International Congress on Ancient Wall Painting*, edited by E. Moormann, 23–28. *BABesch* Supplement 3. Leiden: Stichting Babesch.

Leach, E. 1997. "Oecus on Ibycus: Investigating the vocabulary of the Roman house." In *Sequence and Space in Pompeii*, edited by S. Bon and R. Jones, 50–72. Oxbow Monograph 77. Oxford: Oxbow Books.

Leach, E. 2004. *The Social Life of Painting in Ancient Rome and on the Bay of Naples*. Cambridge: Cambridge University Press.

Lehnen, J. 1997. *Adventus principis: Untersuchungen zu Sinngehalt und Zeremoniell der Kaiserankunft in den Städten des Imperium Romanum*. Frankfurt am Main: P. Lang.

Levi, D. 1947. *Antioch Mosaic Pavements*. Princeton: Princeton University Press.

Levitas, G. 1986. "Anthropology and sociology of streets." In *On Streets*, edited by S. Anderson, 225–239. Cambridge, MA; London: MIT Press.

Lewis, H., P. Johnson, and R. Payne. 2002. *The Architecture of Philip Johnson*. Boston: Bulfinch Press.

Ling, R. 1990a. "A stranger in town: Finding the way in an ancient city." *GaR* 37: 204–214.

Ling, R. 1990b. "Street plaques at Pompeii." In *Architecture and Architectural Sculpture in the Roman Empire*, edited by M. Henig, 51–66. Oxford: Oxbow Books.

Ling, R. 1991. *Roman Painting*. Cambridge and New York: Cambridge University Press.

Ling, R. 1997. *The Insula of the Menander at Pompeii*. Oxford: Clarendon Press.

Lintott, A. 1968. *Violence in Republican Rome*. Oxford: Oxford University Press.

Lintott, A. 2002. "Freedmen and slaves in the light of legal documents from first-century AD Campania." *CQ* 52: 555–565.

Liu, J. 2009. *Collegia Centonariorum: The Guilds of Textile Dealers in the Roman West*. Leiden and Boston: Brill.

Lolos, Y. 2003. "Greek roads: A commentary on the ancient terms." *Glotta* 79: 137–174.

Long-Solis, J. 2007. "A survey of street foods in Mexico City." *Food & Foodways* 15: 213–236.

Lopez Barja de Quiroga, P. 1998. "Junian Latins: Status and numbers." *Athenaeum* 86: 133–163.

Lott, J. 2004. *The Neighborhoods of Augustan Rome*. Cambridge and New York: Cambridge University Press.

Lyons, C. 2005. *Antiquity & Photography: Early Views of Ancient Mediterranean Sites*. Los Angeles: J. Paul Getty Museum.

Macauley-Lewis, E. 2008. "The city in motion: Movement and space in Roman architecture and gardens from 100 BC to AD 150." Ph. D. diss., University of Oxford.

Macauley-Lewis, E. 2011. "The city in motion: Walking for transport and leisure in the city of Rome." In *Rome, Ostia, Pompeii: Movement and Space*, edited by R. Laurence and D. Newsome, 262–289. Oxford and New York: Oxford University Press.

MacCormack, S. 1981. *Art and Ceremony in Late Antiquity*. Berkeley: University of California Press.

MacMahon, A. 2003. "The realm of Janus: Doorways in the Roman world." In *TRAC 2002: Proceedings of the Twelfth Annual Theoretical Roman Archaeology Conference, Kent 2002*, edited by G. Carr, E. Swift, and J. Weekes, 58–73. Oxford: Oxbow Books.

Madigan, B. 2012. *The Ceremonial Sculptures of the Roman Gods*. Leiden and Boston: Brill.

Maddison, A. 2007. *Contours of the World Economy 1–2030 AD: Essays in Macro-Economic History*. Oxford: Oxford University Press.

Maffioli, M., ed. 1990. *Fotografi a Pompeii nell'800: dalle collezioni del Museo Alinari*. Florence: Alinari.

Magaldi, E. 1939. "Echi di Roma a Pompei III." *RSP* 3: 21–60.

Magazine, R. 2003. "Action, personhood and the gift economy among so-called street children in Mexico City." *Social Anthropology* 11: 303–318.

Maiuri, A. 1942. "Un decreto onorario di M. Nonio Balbo scoperto recentemente ad Ercolano." *RendLinc* 8: 253–278.

Maiuri, A. 1958. *Ercolano: i nuovi scavi (1927–1958)*. Rome: Libreria dello Stato.

Maiuri, A. 2000. *La casa pompeiana. Struttura, ambienti, storia nella magistrale descrizione d'un grande archeologo*. Edited by A. Ragozzino. Naples: Generoso Procaccini.

Maiuri, B. 1947. "Rilievo gladiatorio di Pompei." *MemLinc* 8: 491–510.

Manfredini, A. 1979. *La diffamazione verbale nel diritto romano*. Milan: Giuffrè.

Manganaro, G. 1989. "Inscrizioni latine nuove e vecchie della Sicilia." *Epigraphica* 51: 161–196.

Marquadt, J. 1886. *Das Privatleben der Römer*. Leipzig: S. Hirzel.

Mastroroberto, M. 2001. "Il quartiere sul Sarno e i recenti rinvenimenti a Moregine." *MÉFRA* 113: 953–966.

Matthews, J. 2006. *The Journey of Theophanes: Travel, Costs, and Diet in the Later Roman East*. New Haven: Yale University Press.

Mattingly, D. 1990. "Paintings, presses, and perfume production at Pompeii." *OJA* 9: 71–90.

Mau, A. 1882. *Geschichte der decorativen Wandmalerei in Pompeji*. Berlin: G. Reimer.

Mayeske, B. 1972. "Bakeries, bakers and bread at Pompeii." Ph.D. diss., University of Maryland.

McGinn, T. 1997–1998. "*Feminae Probrosae* and the litter." *CJ* 93: 241–250.

McGinn, T. 2004. *The Economy of Prostitution in the Roman World: A Study of Social History and the Brothel*. Ann Arbor: University of Michigan Press.

Mertens, D. ed. 2008. *Stadtverkehr in der Antiken Welt/Traffico Urbano nel Mondo Antico. Palilia 13*. Wiesbaden: Reichert.

Meyer, E. 2004. *Legitimacy and Law in the Roman World*. Cambridge: Cambridge University Press.

Michel, D. 1990. *Casa dei Cei: (I 6, 15)*. Häuser in Pompeji Vol. 3. Munich: Hirmer Verlag.

Miller, P. 2007. "'I get around': Sadism, desire, and metonymy on the streets of Rome with Horace, Ovid, and Juvenal." In *Sites of Rome*, edited by D. Larmour and D. Spencer, 138–167. Oxford: Oxford University Press.

Milnor, K. 2005. *Gender, Domesticity, and the Age of Augustus: Inventing Private Life*. Oxford and New York: Oxford University Press.

Milnor, K. 2009. "Literary literacy in Roman Pompeii: The case of Virgil's *Aeneid*." In *Ancient Literacies: The Culture of Reading in Greece and Rome*. Edited by W. Johnson and H. Parker, 288–319. Oxford and New York: Oxford University Press.

Milnor, K. 2014. *Graffiti and the Literary Landscape in Roman Pompeii*. Oxford: Oxford University Press.

Moeller, W. 1976. *The Wool Trade of Ancient Pompeii*. Leiden: Brill.

Mols, S. 1999. *Wooden Furniture in Herculaneum: Form, Technique, and Function*. Translated by R. Bland. Amsterdam: Gieben.

Mommsen, T. 1887. *Römisches Staatsrecht*. Leipzig: S. Herzel.

Monteix, N. 2003. "Reprise de la fouille de la boutique VI, 15 à Herculanum." *RStPomp* XIV: 333–341.

Monteix, N. 2005. "Fouilles de l'atelier de métallurgie du plomb (VI, 12) et de la boutique VI, 15 en façade de la Casa del Salone Nero à Herculanum." *RStPomp* 16: 262–274.

Monteix, N. 2006. "Les boutiques et les ateliers de l'insula VI à Herculanum." In *Contributi di Archeologia Vesuviana*, 1, 7–76. Rome: L'Erma di Bretschneider.

Monteix, N. 2007a. "*Cauponae, popinae* et 'thermopolia,' de la norme littéraire à la réalité pompéienne." In *Contributi di Archeologia Vesuviana*, 3, 115–126. Rome: L'Erma di Bretschneider.

Monteix, N. 2007b. "Fouilles des boutiques en façade de la Casa del Salone Nero à Herculanum (VI, 12, VI, 14 et VI, 15)." *RStPomp* 18: 168–184.

Monteix, N. 2010. *Les lieux de métier: boutiques et ateliers d'Herculanum*. Rome: École française de Rome.

Moormann, E. 1983. "Sulle pitture della Herculanensium Augustalium Aedes." *CronErcol* 13: 175–177.

Moormann, E. 2011. *Divine Interiors: Mural Paintings in Greek and Roman Sanctuaries*. Amsterdam: Amsterdam University Press.

Motto, A., and J. Clark. 1965. "*Per iter tenebricosum*: The Mythos of Juvenal 3." *TAPA* 96: 267–276.

Mouritsen, H. 1988. *Elections, Magistrates and Municipal Elite: Studies in Pompeian Epigraphy*. *AnalRom* Suppl. 15. Rome: L'Erma di Bretschneider.

Mouritsen, H. 1999. "Electoral Campaigning in Pompeii: A Reconsideration." *Athenaeum* 87: 515–522.

Mouritsen, H. 2011. *The Freedman in the Roman World*. Cambridge: Cambridge University Press.

Najbjerg, T. 1997. "Public painted and sculptural programs of the early Roman Empire: A case-study of the so-called basilica in Herculaneum." Ph.D. diss., Princeton University.

Najbjerg, T. 2002. "A reconstruction and reconsideration of the so-called basilica in Herculaneum." *JRA* Suppl. 47: 122–165.

Nappo, S. 1991. "Fregio dipinto del 'praedium' di Giulia Felice con rappresentazione del foro di Pompei." *RStPomp* 5: 79–96.

Nevett, L. 2009. "Domestic façades: A 'feature' of the urban landscape of Greek poleis?" In *Inside the City in the Greek World*, edited by S. Owen and L. Preston, 118–130. Oxford: Oxbow.

Newbold, R. 2000. "Non-verbal communication in Suetonius and the *Historia Augusta*: power, posture and proxemics." *Acta Classica* 43: 101–118.

Newsome, D. 2009. "Traffic, space and legal change around the Casa del Marinaio at Pompeii (VII.15.1–2)." *BABesch* 84: 121–142.

Newsome, D. 2011. "Introduction: Making movement meaningful." In *Rome, Ostia, Pompeii. Movement and Space*, edited by R. Laurence and D. Newsome, 1–54. Oxford and New York: Oxford University Press.

Nicolet, C. 1987. "La Table d'Héraclée et les origines du cadastre romain." In *L'Urbs: Espace urbain et histoire*, 1–25. *CÉFR* Suppl. 98. Rome: École française de Rome.

Nielsen, I. 1993. *Thermae et Balnea: The Architecture and Cultural History of Roman Public Baths*. 2nd ed. 2 vols. Aarhus: Aarhus University Press.

Nieuwenhuizen, P. 2006. *Street Children in Bangalore (India): Their Dreams and Their Future*. Antwerpen: Het Spinhuis.

Nippel, W. 1984. "Policing Rome." *JRS* 74: 20–29.

Nippel, W. 1995. *Public Order in Ancient Rome.* Cambridge: Cambridge University Press.

Nutton, V. 2000. "Medical thoughts on urban pollution." In *Death and Disease in the Ancient City.* Edited by V. Hope and E. Marshall, 65–73. London and New York: Routledge.

O'Neill, P. 2003. "Going round in circles: Popular speech in ancient Rome." *ClAnt* 22: 135–176.

O'Sullivan, T. 2011. *Walking in Roman Culture.* Cambridge: Cambridge University Press.

Ogle, B. 1911. "House-door in religion and folklore." *AJP* 32: 251–271.

Ohr, K. 1991. *Die Basilika in Pompeji.* Berlin and New York: Walter de Gruyter.

Olson, K. 2008. *Dress and the Roman Woman: Self-Presentation and Society.* London; New York: Routledge.

Onorato, G. O. 1951. "La sistemazione stradale del quartiere del Foro Triangolare di Pompei." *RendLinc* (8th series) 6: 250–264.

Orr, D. 1973. "Roman domestic religion: A study of the Roman household deities and their shrines at Pompeii and Herculaneum." Ph.D. diss., University of Maryland.

Ostrow, S. 1985. "*Augustales* on the Bay of Naples: A case study for their early growth." *Historia* 34: 64–101.

Owens, E. 1991. *The City in the Greek and Roman World.* London: Routledge.

Pagano, M. 1987. "Una iscrizione elettorale da Ercolano." *CronErcol* 17: 141–152.

Pagano, M. 1988. "Semo Sancus in una insegna di bottega a Ercolano." *CronErcol* 18: 209–214.

Pagano, M. 1990. "Un ciclo di imprese di Ercole con inscrizioni greche ad Ercolano." *RM* 97: 153–161.

Pagano, M. 1991. "La villa romana di contrada Sora a Torre del Greco." *CronErcol* 21: 149–186.

Pagano, M. 1992. "Nuovi frammenti di albi da Ercolano." *CronErcol* 22: 189–195.

Pagano, M. 1993. "Ricerche sull'impianto urbano di Ercolano." In *Ercolano 1738–1988: 250 anni di ricerca archeologica,* edited by L. Franchi dell'Orto, 595–608. Rome: L'Erma di Bretschneider.

Pagano, M. 1996. "La nuova pianta della città e di alcuni edifici pubblici di Ercolano." *CronErcol* 26: 229–262.

Pagano, M. 2001. "Rappresentazioni di imprese di Ercole ad Ercolano: alcune novità." *MÉFRA* 113: 913–923.

Pannuti, U. 1983. "Il 'giornale degli scavi' di Ercolano (1738–1756)." *MemLinc* 26: 163–410.

Parkin, A. 2006. "'You do him no service': An exploration of pagan almsgiving." In *Poverty in the Roman World,* edited by M. Atkins and R. Osborne, 60–82. Cambridge: Cambridge University Press.

Parkins, H., ed. 1997. *Roman Urbanism: Beyond the Consumer City.* London and New York: Routledge.

Parslow, C. 1989. "The *Praedia Iuliae Felicis* in Pompeii." Ph.D. diss., Duke University.

Parslow, C. 1995. *Rediscovering Antiquity: Karl Weber and the Excavation of Herculaneum, Pompeii, and Stabiae.* Cambridge: Cambridge University Press.

Patterson, J. 2006. *Landscapes and Cities: Rural Settlement and Civic Transformation in Early Imperial Italy.* Oxford and New York: Oxford University Press.

Peralta, F. 2009. "Street children in Mexico." In *The World of Child Labor: An Historical and Regional Survey,* edited by H. Hindman, 404–405. Armonk, NY: M. E. Sharpe.

Perry, E. 2005. *The Aesthetics of Emulation in the Visual Arts of Ancient Rome.* Cambridge: Cambridge University Press.

Pesando, F. 1996. "Autocelebrazione aristocratica e propaganda politica in ambiente privato: la casa del Fauno a Pompei." *Cahiers du Centre Gustave-Glotz* 7: 189–228.

Pirson, F. 1997. "Rented accommodation at Pompeii: The evidence of the Insula Arriana Polliana VI 6." In *Domestic Space in the Roman World: Pompeii and Beyond,* edited by R. Laurence and A. Wallace Hadrill, 165–181. *JRA* Suppl. 22. Portsmouth, RI: Journal of Roman Archaeology.

Pirson, F. 1999. *Mietwohnungen in Pompeji und Herculaneum.* Munich: Freidrich Pfeil.

Poehler, E. 2006. "The circulation of traffic in Pompeii's *Regio* VI." *JRA* 19: 53–74.

Poehler, E. 2009. "The organization of Pompeii's system of traffic: An analysis of the evidence and its impact on the infrastructure, economy and urbanism of the ancient city." Ph.D. diss., University of Virginia.

Poehler, E. 2012. "The drainage system at Pompeii: Mechanisms, operation, and design." *JRA* 25: 95–120.

Pólay, E. 1986. *Iniuria Types in Roman Law*. Translated by J. Szabó. Budapest: Akademiai Kiadó.

Potenza, U. 1996. "Gli acquedotti romani di Serino." In *Cura Aquarum in Campania*, edited by N. De Haan and G. Jansen, 93–100. *BABesch* Suppl. 4. Leiden: Stichting Babesch.

Potter, D. 1999. "Odor and power in the Roman world." In *Constructions of the Classical Body*, edited by J. Porter, 169–189. Ann Arbor: University of Michigan Press.

Potts, C. 2009. "The art of piety and profit at Pompeii: A new interpretation of the painted shop façade at ix.7.1–2." *GaR* 56: 55–70.

Pozzi, E. 1960. "Exedra funeraria fuori la Porta di Stabia." *RendNap* 35: 175–186.

Proudfoot, E. 2013. "Secondary doors in entranceways at Pompeii: Reconsidering access and the 'view from the street'." In TRAC *2012: Proceedings of the Twenty-Second Annual Theoretical Roman Archaeology Conference*, edited by A. Bokern, M. Bolder-Boos, S. Krmnicek, D. Maschek, and S. Page, 91–115. Oxford: Oxbow Books.

Purcell, N. 1987. "Town in country and country in town." In *Ancient Roman Villa Gardens*, edited by E. MacDougall, 187–203. Washington: Dumbarton Oaks.

Quilici, L. 1990. *Le strade: viabilità tra Roma e Lazio*. Roma: Quasar.

Raban, J. 1974. *Soft City: A Documentary Exploration of Metropolitan Life*. London: Collins Harvill.

Raper, R. 1977. "The analysis of the urban structure of Pompeii: A sociological study of land use." In *Spatial Archaeology*, edited by D. Clarke, 189–221. London and New York: Academic Press.

Rawson, E. 1987. "Discrimina Ordinum: The Lex Julia Theatralis." *PBSR* 55: 83–114.

Rawson, E. 1990. "The antiquarian tradition: Spoils and representations of foreign armour." In *Staat und Staatlichkeit in der frühen römischen Republik*. Edited by W. Eder, 157–173. Stuttgart: Steiner.

Richardson, L. 1988. *Pompeii: An Architectural History*. Baltimore: Johns Hopkins University Press.

Richlin, A. 1992. *The Garden of Priapus: Sexuality and Aggression in Roman Humor*. New York: Oxford University Press.

Robinson, D. 1997. "The social texture of Pompeii." In *Sequence and Space in Pompeii*, edited by S. Bon and R. Jones, 135–144. Oxbow Monograph 77. Oxford: Oxbow Books.

Robinson, O. 1992. *Ancient Rome: City Planning and Administration*. London and New York: Routledge.

Rodríguez-Almeida, E. 1988. "Un frammento di una nuova pianta marmorea di Roma." *JRA* 1: 120–131.

Rogers, G. 1991. *The Sacred Identity of Ephesus: Foundation Myths of a Roman City*. London and New York: Routledge.

Roller, M. 2006. *Dining Posture in Ancient Rome: Bodies, Values, and Status*. Princeton: Princeton University Press.

Roman, L. 2010. "Martial and the city of Rome." *JRS* 100: 88–117.

Rose, P. 2005. "Spectators and spectator comfort in Roman entertainment buildings: A study in functional design." *PBSR* 73: 99–130.

Ruggiero, M. 1885. *Storia degli scavi di Ercolano ricomposta su' documenti superstiti*. Naples: Tipografia dell'Accademia reale delle scienze.

Ryberg, I. 1955. *Rites of the State Religion in Roman Art*. MAAR Suppl. 22. Rome: American Academy in Rome.

Saliou, C. 1999. "Les trottoirs de Pompéi: une première approche." *BABesch* 74: 161–218.

Saller, R. 1984. "*Familia*, domus, and the Roman conception of the family." *Phoenix* 38: 336–355.

Saller, R. 1989. "Patronage and friendship in early imperial Rome: Drawing the distinction." In *Patronage in Ancient Society*, edited by A. Wallace-Hadrill, 49–62. London: Routledge.

Savunen, L. 1995. "Women and elections in Pompeii." In *Women in Antiquity: New Assessments*, edited by R. Hawley and B. Levick, 194–206. London: Routledge.

Savunen, L. 1997. "Women in the Urban Texture of Pompeii." Ph.D. diss., University of Helsinki.

Sbriglio, J. 2007. *Le Corbusier: The Villa Savoye.* Basel: Birkhäuser.

Scagliarini, D. 1974–1976. "Spazio e decorazione nella pittura pompeiana." *Palladio* 23–25: 3–44.

Scagliarini Corlàita, D. 2007. "De Pompéi à Ostie: naissance de la façade." In *Vivre en Europe romaine*, edited by J.-P. Petit and S. Santoro, 95–101. Paris: Éd. Errance.

Scatozza Höricht, L. 1985. "Ville nel territorio ercolanese." *CronErcol* 15: 131–165.

Scatozza Höricht, L. 1986. *I vetri romani di Ercolano.* Rome: L'Erma di Bretschneider.

Scatozza Höricht, L. 1989. *I monili di Ercolano.* Roma: L'Erma di Bretschneider.

Scheidel, W. 2003. "Germs for Rome." In *Rome the Cosmopolis*, edited by C. Edwards and G. Woolf, 158–176. Cambridge: Cambridge University Press.

Schilling, J. 1954. *La Religion romaine de Vénus, depuis les origines jusqu'au temps d'Auguste.* Paris: E. de Boccard.

Schindler, R. 1998. "The archaeology of Aphrodite in the Greek West, ca. 650–480 BC." Ph.D. diss., University of Michigan.

Schoonhoven, A. 2006. *Metrology and Meaning in Pompeii: The Urban Arrangement of Regio VI.* Roma: L'Erma di Bretschneider.

Schumacher, L. 1976. "Das Ehrendekret für M. Nonius Balbus aus Herculaneum." *Chiron* 6: 165–184.

Scobie, A. 1986. "Slums, sanitation, and mortality in the Roman world." *Klio* 68: 399–433.

Settimo, G. 1989. *Un caffè per favore. L'espresso al bar in Italia: Una straordinaria ricerca su tutto il territorio nazionale.* Milano: Pubblistampa.

Sgobbo, I. 1938. "L'acquedotto romano della Campania 'Fontis Augustei Aquaeductus.'" *NSc* 14: 75–97.

Shaw, B. 1984. "Water and society in the ancient Maghrib: Technology, property, and development." *AntAfr* 20: 121–173.

Shaw, B. 1991. "The noblest monuments and the smallest things: Wells, walls, and aqueducts in the making of Roman Africa." In *Future Currents in Aqueduct Studies*, edited by A. Hodge, 63–91. Leeds: F. Cairns.

Shoemaker, R. B. 2000. "The decline of public insult in London." *PastPres* 169: 97–131.

Skinner, W., ed. 1977. *The City in Late Imperial China.* Stanford: Stanford University Press.

Smith, B. R. 1999. *The Acoustic World of Early Modern England: Attending to the O-factor.* Chicago: University of Chicago Press.

Smith, M. 2007. "Form and meaning in the earliest cities: A new approach to ancient urban planning." *Journal of Planning History* 6: 3–47.

Spano, G. 1912. "Pompei—Scavi e scoperte di antichità avvenute durante il mese di marzo." *NSc* 9: 102–120.

Spinazzola, V. 1953. *Pompei alla luce degli scavi nuovi di Via dell'Abbondanza (anni 1910–1923).* 2 vols. Rome: Libreria dello Stato.

Staccioli, R. 2003. *Roads of the Romans.* Los Angeles: J. Paul Getty Museum.

Staley, G. 2000. "Juvenal's third satire: Umbricius' Rome, Vergil's Troy." *MAAR* 45: 85–98.

Stamper, J. 2005. *The Architecture of Roman Temples: The Republic to the Middle Empire.* Cambridge and New York: Cambridge University Press.

Stek, T. 2008. "A Roman cult in the Italian countryside? The Compitalia and the shrines of the lares compitales." *BABesch* 83: 111–132.

Stewart, P. 2003. *Statues in Roman Society: Representation and Response.* Oxford and New York: Oxford University Press.

Stöger, H. 2011. "The spatial organization of the movement economy: The analysis of Ostia's *scholae*." In *Rome, Ostia, and Pompeii: Movement and Space*, edited by R. Laurence and D. Newsome, 215–242. Oxford and New York: Oxford University Press.

Stone, S. 1994. "The toga: From national to ceremonial costume." In *The World of Roman Costume*, edited by J. Sebesta and L. Bonfante, 13–45. Madison: University of Wisconsin Press.

Sumi, G. 2002. "Impersonating the dead: Mimes at Roman funerals." *AJP* 123: 559–585.

Suttles, G. 1968. *The Social Order of the Slum: Ethnicity and Territory in the Inner City.* Chicago: University of Chicago Press.

Tantner, A. 2009. "Addressing the houses: The introduction of house numbering in Europe." *Histoire & Mesure* 24.2: 7–30.

Thébert, Y. 1987. "Private life and domestic architecture in Roman Africa." In *A History of Private Life: From Pagan Rome to Byzantium*, edited by P. Veyne, 313–409. Cambridge, MA and London: Harvard University Press.

Tinker, I. 1997. *Street Foods: Urban Food and Employment in Developing Countries.* Oxford and New York: Oxford University Press.

Toner, J. 1995. *Leisure and Ancient Rome.* Cambridge: Polity Press.

Toner, J. 2009. *Popular Culture in Ancient Rome.* Cambridge, UK and Malden, MA: Polity Press.

Torelli, M. 2004. "La Basilica di Ercolano. Una proposta di lettura." *Eidola* 1: 117–149.

Treggiari, S. 2002. *Roman Social History.* London and New York: Routledge.

Trifilò, F. 2008. "Power, architecture and community in the distribution of honorary statues in Roman public space." In *TRAC 2007: Proceedings of the Seventeenth Annual Theoretical Roman Archaeology Conference*, edited by C. Fenwick, M. Wiggins, and D. Wythe, 109–120. Oxford: Oxbow Books.

Tsujimura, S. 1991. "Ruts in Pompeii. The traffic system in the Roman city." *Opuscula Pompeiana* 2: 58–86.

Van Andringa, W. 2000. "Autels de carrefour, organisation vicinale et rapports de voisinage à Pompéi." *RStPomp* 11: 47–86.

Van Andringa, W. 2009. *Quotidien des dieux et des hommes: la vie religieuse dans les cités du Vésuve à l'époque romaine.* Rome: École française de Rome.

van Binnebeke, M. 2007. "Law and loca publica in Roman times." *Fragmenta* 1: 1–23.

van der Horst, P. 2003. *Philo's Flaccus: The First Pogrom: Introduction, Translation and Commentary.* Leiden: Brill.

Van der Poel, H. 1986. *Corpus Topographicum Pompeianum: The Insulae of Regions I–V.* Rome: The University of Texas at Austin.

van Tilburg, C. 2007. *Traffic and Congestion in the Roman Empire.* London and New York: Routledge.

Varone, A. 1987. "Pompei. Attività dell'Ufficio Scavi: 1985–1986." *RStPomp* 1: 131–135.

Varone, A. 2007. "Iscrizioni e dipinti lungo via dell'Abbondanza: uno spaccato di vita reale nella Pompei del I sec. D.C." In *Pompei, Via dell'Abbondanza: Ricerche, restauri e nuove technologie*, edited by S. Curuni and N. Santopuoli, 123–141. Milan: Skira.

Varriale, I. 2006. "VII 16 Insula Occidentalis 17. Casa di Maius Castricius." In *Pompei (Regiones VI–VII). Insula Occidentalis* I, edited by M. Aoyagi and U. Pappalardo, 419–504. Naples: Valtrend Editore.

Vermaseren, M. 1977a. *Cybele and Attis: The Myth and the Cult.* London: Thames and Hudson.

Vermaseren, M. 1977b. *Corpus cultus Cybelae Attidisque (CCCA).* Leiden: Brill.

Viitanen, E., L. Nissinen, and K. Korhonen. 2013. "Street activity, dwellings and wall inscriptions in ancient Pompeii: A holistic study of neighbourhood relations." In *TRAC 2012: Proceedings of the Twenty-Second Annual Theoretical Roman Archaeology Conference*, edited by A. Bokurn, M. Bolder-Boos, S. Krmnicek, D. Maschek, and S. Page, 61–80. Oxford: Oxbow Books.

Vout, C. 1996. "The myth of the toga. Understanding the history of Roman dress." *GaR* 43: 204–220.

Wallace-Hadrill, A. 1988. "The social structure of the Roman house." *PBSR* 56: 43–97.

Wallace-Hadrill, A. 1989. "Patronage in Roman society: From republic to empire." In *Patronage in Ancient Society*, edited by A. Wallace-Hadrill, 63–88. London: Routledge.

Wallace-Hadrill, A. 1994. *Houses and Society in Pompeii and Herculaneum.* Princeton: Princeton University Press.

Wallace-Hadrill, A. 1995. "Public honour and private shame: The urban texture of Pompeii." In *Urban Society in Roman Italy*, edited by T. Cornell and K. Lomas, 39–62. London: UCL Press.

Wallace-Hadrill, A. 2003. "The streets of Rome as a representation of imperial power." In *The Representation and Perception of Imperial Power*. Edited by L. de Blois, 189–206. Amsterdam: Gieben.

Wallace-Hadrill, A. 2011a. *Herculaneum: Past and Future*. London: Frances Lincoln Limited Publishers.

Wallace-Hadrill, A. 2011b. "The monumental centre of Herculaneum: In search of the identities of the public buildings." *JRA* 24: 121–160.

Ward-Perkins, J. 1974. *Cities of Ancient Greece and Italy: Planning in Antiquity*. London: George Braziller.

Watts, C. 1987. "A pattern language for houses at Pompeii, Herculaneum and Ostia." Ph. D. diss., University of Texas at Austin.

Weaver, P. 1990. "Where have all the Junian Latins gone? Nomenclature and status in the early empire." *Chiron* 20: 275–305.

Weaver, P. 1991. "Children of freedmen (and freedwomen)." In *Marriage, Divorce, and Children in Ancient Rome*, edited by B. Rawson, 166–190. Oxford: Clarendon Press.

Weaver, P. 1997. "Children of Junian Latins." In *The Roman Family in Italy: Status, Sentiment, Space*, edited by B. Rawson and P. Weaver, 55–72. Oxford: Clarendon Press.

Weber, M. 1958. *The City*. Translated and edited by D. Martindale and G. Neuwirth. Glencoe, IL: Free Press.

Weiss, C. 2010. "Determining function of Pompeian sidewalk features through GIS analysis." In *Making History Interactive. Computer Applications and Quantitative Methods in Archaeology (CAA). Proceedings of the 37th International Conference, Williamsburg, Virginia, United States of America, March 22–26, 2009*, edited by B. Frischer, J. Crawford, and D. Koller, 363–372. Oxford: Archeopress.

Wheatley, P. 1971. *Pivot of the Four Quarters*. Chicago: Aldine Publishing Co.

Whyte, W. 1943. *Street Corner Society: The Social Structure of an Italian Slum*. Chicago: University of Chicago Press.

Whyte, W. 1988. *City: Rediscovering the Center*. New York: Doubleday.

Wilpert, P., and S. Zenker. 1950. "Auge." *Reallexicon für Antike und Christentum* 1: 957–963.

Wilson, A. 2011. "City sizes and urbanization in the Roman Empire." In *Settlement, Urbanization, and Population: Oxford Studies on the Roman Economy*, edited by A. Bowman and A. Wilson, 161–195. Oxford and New York: Oxford University Press.

Winkler, M. 1983. *The Persona in Three Satires of Juvenal*. Hildesheim and New York: Olms.

Wiseman, T. 1982. "*Pete nobiles amicos*: Poets and patrons in late republican Rome." In *Literary and Artistic Patronage in Ancient Rome*, edited by B. Gold, 28–49. Austin: University of Texas Press.

Wiseman, T. 1987. "*Conspicui postes tectaque digna deo*: The public image of aristocratic and imperial houses in the late republic and early empire." In *L'Urbs: Espace urbain et histoire*, 393–413. *CÉFR* Suppl. 98. Rome: École française de Rome.

Wojcik, M. 1986. *La Villa dei Papiri ad Ercolano*. Rome: L'Erma di Bretschneider.

Woods, A. 1991. "The funerary monuments of the Augustales in Italy." Ph.D. diss., UCLA.

Wright, F. 1935. "Broadacre City. A new community plan." *Architectural Record* 77: 243–254.

Yardley, J. C. 1978. "The elegiac paraclausithyron." *Eranos* 76: 19–34.

Yegül, F. 1992. *Baths and Bathing in Classical Antiquity*. New York: Architectural History Foundation.

Yegül, F. 1993. "The Palestra at Herculaneum as a new architectural type." In *Eius Virtutis Studiosi: Classical and Postclassical Studies in Memory of Frank Brown*, edited by R. Scott, 369–393. Washington: National Gallery of Art.

Yegül, F. 2010. *Bathing in the Roman World*. New York: Cambridge University Press.

Zaccaria Ruggiu, A. 1994. "Rapporto tra vie urbane e abitazioni nella città romana." In *Mélanges Raymond Chevallier, II, Histoire et archéologie, 1*, edited by R. Bedon and P. Martin, 223–265. Limoges: Presses universitaires de Limoges.

Zaccaria Ruggiu, A. 1995. *Spazio privato e spazio pubblico nella città romana.* *CÉFR* Suppl. 210. Rome: École française de Rome.

Zanker, P. 1988. *The Power of Images in the Age of Augustus.* Translated by A. Shapiro. Ann Arbor: University of Michigan Press.

Zanker, P. 1998. *Pompeii: Public and Private Life.* Translated by D. Schneider. Cambridge, MA: Harvard University Press.

Zevi, F. 1998. "Die Casa del Fauno in Pompeji und das Alexandermosaik." *RM* 105: 21–65.

INDEX

Printed in Great Britain
by Amazon